HOPE OVER FEAR

HOPE OVER FEAR

Bridges Toward a Better World

History of Dallas Chapter United Nations Association
of the United States of America 1953–2015

On the occasion of the 70th Anniversary
of the United Nations 1945–2015

Norma Tevis Matthews
Bill (John W.) Matthews

Library of Congress Control Number: 2017914226
ISBN: Hardcover   978-1-5434-5145-0
               Softcover   978-1-5434-5146-7
               eBook   978-1-5434-5147-4

Print information available on the last page.

Rev. date: 10/06/2017

To order additional copies of this book, contact:
Xlibris
1-888-795-4274
www.Xlibris.com
Orders@Xlibris.com
742918

CONTENTS

FOREWORD

Vivian Castleberry, founder of Peacemakers, Inc., sponsor of
International Women's Peace Conferences with DUNA

For those of us who lived through the Cold War years in Dallas, this book
is a sometimes-painful journey through a past we would most like to forget.

At the same time, it is a reminder of the integrity, tenacity, and courage
of the few brave souls who kept faith in the sure knowledge that right will
win out and whose leadership has led us to a new day in our city—warts
and all!

This is the story of the Dallas Chapter United Nations Association, long overdue.

Norma and Bill Matthews, both of whom are past presidents of DUNA, have done a masterful job of probing the past, ferreting out nuggets of history tucked into boxes and stashed away in family attics, backroom nooks, and office storerooms. For much of the time since its founding in 1953, DUNA has had no permanent home or office; and its records have been at the mercy of whoever was its leader, always with the possibility that succeeding generations of its founders would not recognize the merits of those sealed boxes and would destroy them.

Using endless newspaper files, mostly from the *Dallas Morning News* and some from the late *Dallas Times Herald* and *Fort Worth Star Telegram*, the Matthews writing team has been able to follow the founding, development, and leadership of DUNA and is vastly enriched by personal stories of individuals who kept the flame alive in good times and bad.

Early organizers of DUNA, not long after the national organization was created, sought a prominent man to lead it. In those days, the bank presidents ran Dallas, but not a single banker would accept the role. They found their savior in a feisty fifty-seven-year-old federal judge named Sarah T. Hughes. They could not have had a better leader.

Judge Hughes invited former first lady Eleanor Roosevelt to Dallas to help her rally the troops. Mrs. Roosevelt made her first appearance in Dallas on January 11, 1955, and would return several more times to support and promote the organization. Judge Hughes was also recruiting local leaders and spokespersons, among them Louise and Grier Raggio, who for the first three years of DUNA's existence made countless appearances, both in person and on the radio, to spread the word about the United Nations.

Through those early years, many prominent men and women assumed leadership roles, among them Jack Goren, Johnnie-Marie Grimes, Stanley Marcus, Maura McNiel, Rabbi Levi Olan, Ray Nasher, Ed Winn, and a tiny dynamo named Cordye Hall, who may hold the record for writing letters to the editor.

None of this was easy. Leaders of DUNA were castigated and sometimes threatened. A small, but vocal and mostly wealthy group of individuals opposed the organization, claiming that it was subversive and would lead to a communistic nation. Among the detractors were H. L. Hunt; Gen. Edwin A. Walker; Bruce Alger; and members of the John

Birch Society. Hundreds of cars moving on Dallas streets each bore the sticker on its back bumper, "Get the UN out of the US."

Most, if not all, of those early detractors are gone now, and the United Nations prevails.

It's all here in this carefully researched story. Read on . . .

Dallas, Texas   Vivian Castleberry
May 2017   Founder, Peacemakers, Inc.

Visionary Woman and Mentor for Peace April 8, 1922 - October 4, 2017

Advisory Comittee	Description
Charlotte Karam	Proofread many articles, sent articles
Beth Weems Pirtle	Sent material, provided guidance
Harbans Lal	Sent article
Patty Jantho	Sent original play
Linda Evans	Provided refugee information, oral assistance
Nadine Bell	Wrote about events of her administration
David Reid	Ex-officio, sent articles
Nelda Reid	Ex-officio, sent articles
Vivian Castleberry	Advisory, wrote foreword for book, provided pictures, edited first draft
Karen Blessen	Advisory, info on printing and encouragement
Norma Matthews	Project manager
Bill Matthews	Assistant manager, wrote articles, organized photos, coauthor
Tatiana Androsov	Wrote story of her UN journey

Acknowledgments

Marshall Doke, attorney	Had interview in his office, provided files from 1980s
Adlene Harrison	Former mayor of Dallas, EPA, Dallas housing, phone interview
David Winn	Son of Ed Winn, searched for Dad's papers
Allen Winn	Son of Ed Winn, searched for Dad's papers

Charles Hosch, attorney	Provided help and information on permissions
Jan Sanders	Gave info on Sarah T. Hughes flag, on Winn family, loaned book
Noeli Biggs	Sent information from her presidential period
Connie Rensink	Sent articles on CTAUN, chair UN seventieth anniversary, Dallas
Marzuq Jaami	Sent article on why he supports Dallas UNA
Kambiz Rafraf	Sent information on Women's Conference
Don Adams	Judge, loaned me *Dallas 1963*
John Goren	Son of Jack Goren, gave me advice and information
Chandler R. Lindsley	Granddaughter of ER, loaned me books from ER library
Guy Gooding	Former UNA president, wrote article, had interview
Stanley Ukeni	Former UNA president, sent article
William Simon	Author, gave advice/information
Dallas Public Library, downtown	Texas/Dallas History & Archives Section, provided help, links, information, resource books
Darwin Payne	Historian, sent advice, granted permission to quote from books
Dallas Historical Society	Attended Legacies 17th Annual Conference, Jan. 30, 2016
Ray Nasher's Archives office/ family	Provided pictures, information, Karen Roden graciously connected us with DUNA related files
The Delta Kappa Gamma Society International	Eta Zeta Chapter provided author with scholarships to attend UNA and CTAUN conferences

Melvin Weinberg	Provided information on Rabbi Levi Olan
Dr. Nancy Matthews	Assisted in rewriting chapter 4 media reports
Garrison Reid	Graphic designer, book cover
Shabnam Modgil	Sent article on UN radio, produced daily from FunAsia Radio, provided storage for UNA, provided meals for UNA meetings
Dr. Andrew Graybill	Professor/chair SMU History Department, advice
Dr. John R. Chavez	SMU, director of graduate studies, recommendation
Christy Carry	Editorial consultant, SMU alumna, grateful for assistance
Bill Kelly	Gratitude for his many donations to Dallas UNA
Juliette Fowler Communities	Grateful for temporary extra storage space for UNA material
Thomas Guerin	Made contacts for us at *Dallas Morning News*
Bob Mong, president University of North Texas at Dallas	Worked for permissions for us at *Dallas Morning News*
Jim Moroney, CEO *Dallas Morning News*	Advised that the *Dallas Morning News* granted Bill & Norma Matthews a limited license for various references in *Hope Over Fear*, the history of the Dallas UNA
Robyn Short, publisher, Good Media Press	Met with us, gave advice
Daniel Shrader	Advised us while we were "trying on" titles for the book
Ronald Chrisman, Director, University of North Texas Press	Read samples of the Dallas UNA history book, gave advice

Bernard Fulton family	Sent obituary of Bernard Fulton, second president of Dallas UNA
Bradley Sue Howell	Advised on style, content, and index
Elizabeth N. Thurmond	Proofreading, grateful for the help
Debra M. Shrader	Proofreading and suggestions, thanks for long distance help
Jo Wharton	Donated U.N Stamps, First Day Issues, Peace Bell
Ejay Moore	Donated "Be At Peace," 3-2009 painting to Dallas Chapter UNA 4-2009
Debra, Nancy, Rebecca, Mary Beth	Grateful for our daughters' support and love
Peacemakers, Inc.	Norma and Bill honored with Peace Patron Award 2017

Past Presidents of Dallas Chapter United Nations Association

Year	Name
1953	Judge Sarah T. Hughes
1954	Bernard Fulton, elected 5-18-54; worked with Eleanor Roosevelt; founder of Greenhill School (d. 6-19-2009, in his 100th year, information from Fulton family)
1956	Mrs. George Abbott (*DMN* 3-28-56)
1958	Donald Lewis (*DMN* 2-16-58)
1958	Raymond Nasher (*DMN* 3-17-58)
1959	Dr. Merrimon Cuninggim (*DMN* 3-20-59, 9-17-59*)*
1960	Rabbi Levi Olan (*DMN* 6-10-60 and 10-23-60)
1961	Robert Storey Jr. (*DMN* 10-23-61, d. 4-19-62, 40 years old)
1962	Judge Sarah T. Hughes (*DMN* 10-12-62, 10-25-62)

1963	Judge Sarah T. Hughes, president, February 1963 (Payne, 2004, p.236)
1963	Jack Goren, VP Neiman-Marcus (*DMN* 3-24-63 will succeed Judge Sarah T. Hughes to become president Dallas Chapter UNA)
1965	Henry Lanz (*DMN* 6-18-65, Letters from Readers)
1966	Edward B. Winn (*DMN* 4-17-66)
1969	Fred Bryson
1970	Edward B. Winn
1971	Rev. Thomas Fry, Pastor First Presbyterian Church, Dallas, (*DMN* 10- 5-71) (Dr. Fry left in 1972 to take a position in Memphis, TN.)
1972	Otto Mullinax, President (*DMN* article on UN week, 10-21-72)
1973	Annette Strauss, second woman elected president of Dallas UNA, *DMN* 4-05-73
1973	Mrs. Clyde (Lorinne) Emery (*DMN* 4-1-74)
1974	Ambassador Richard Rubottom
1976	Thomas Rhodes
1978	Edward B. Winn (d. 3-11-07)
1980	George DeWald
1982	Dr. Neill McFarland (d. 7-14-2017)
1984	Dick Sloos (d. 5-5-15)
1986	Marvin Sadovsky
1988	Annemarie Brown
1990	Guy Gooding
1992	Beth Huddleston
1993	Nadine Bell
1996	Stanley Ukeni
1998	Beth Weems Pirtle
2000	Kambiz Rafraf
2002	Rev. Bill Matthews
2004	Tina Patterson

2006	Beth Weems Pirtle
2007	Latha Nehru
2008	Dagmar Fleming
2008	Noeli Piccoli Biggs
2009	Sundiata Xian Tellum
2010	Latha Nehru, Rev. Bill Matthews, interim presidents
2011	David & Nelda Reid, copresidents
2013	Norma Matthews
2015	David Reid
2017	Shabnam Modgil

AUTHOR'S NOTE

This list of past presidents has been put together by the authors to the best of our ability, using the files and archives that have been available to us.

In a letter dated August 1, 1989, from President Beth Huddleston to Raymond Nasher, the names of **Ambassador Robert W. Dean**, **Marshall Doke** and **Edward Richards** appear on the letterhead as past presidents. The same names appear on an August 1998 list of past presidents of Dallas UNA mailed out by President Beth W. Pirtle. In a 2001 list, the same names appear again. The author has not been able to confirm these persons as being president or the dates when they served.

In the UNA personal files of Marshall Doke, given to Norma Matthews in March 2016, Marshall Doke is referred to as a past president several times, but in an oral interview on January 26, 2015, he claims he was never a president. He was active in the Dallas UNA as an international lawyer. In the minutes of the Dallas UNA board meeting on June 11, 1983, Dr. Neill McFarland, president, suggested that Mr. Marshall J. Doke Jr., a Dallas attorney active in international law, be the speaker at the UN Day to highlight the Metroplex area as an emerging international entity. Mr. Doke also served as chairman of the International Committee of the Dallas Chamber of Commerce.

NM

Sources:

Dallas Morning News Archives. Dallas, Texas.
Payne, Darwin. *Indomitable Sarah*. Dallas: Southern Methodist University Press, 2004.
Dallas Chapter UNA-USA file papers, minutes, and oral history.
Personal files of Marshall Doke presented to Chapter March 2016.
Personal files of Raymond Nasher from Nasher Archives.

Introduction to the Dallas UNA History Project

It was late in 2014. I was completing my two-year term as president of the Dallas Chapter United Nations Association (DUNA). The chapter had already named its nominations for new officers, the election had been held, and David and Nelda Reid had accepted the Dallas UNA offices respectively as president and regional representative to the South Central Region of the United Nations Association USA's steering committee.

Bill & Norma Matthews, at UNA-USA 2014

In January 2015, I began toying with the idea that something should be done about a history of the Dallas chapter UNA. I first began my serious contemplation of this subject after I talked with my mentor and good friend, Vivian Castleberry. I began asking her questions about her book, *Daughters of Dallas*. I owned a copy of this book and was very much awed by the amount of work that had gone into producing this book. As Vivian and I talked one time, I asked her about the Dallas United Nations chapter. She told me that she could find no written history about the chapter when she wrote her book. She had done extensive research, but found very little. I was particularly interested in her research on Judge Sarah T. Hughes because I knew that Sarah T. Hughes had been a founder of the Dallas chapter, and Vivian had written about Sarah T. Hughes in her book. She was one of the famous Dallas women in *Daughters*.

Vivian and I talked some more and discussed various authors who might be willing to write something on the subject. I discussed possibilities with Darwin Payne, historian and professor emeritus of communications at Southern Methodist University; Dr. Andrew Graybill, professor of history, SMU; Charles Hosch, attorney in the field of intellectual property with Strasburger & Price LLP and SMU Law School; and Nadine Bell, consultant and past president Dallas chapter UNA 1993.

I also decided to form an advisory committee. I contacted several knowledgeable people in the field, including relatives of deceased past presidents, trusted friends, family members who had done professional writing, and other acquaintances. Through the magic of e-mail, I was able to get ten people to agree to serve in an advisory capacity by February 2015. As the project progressed, I was able to add others to that list who were willing to make other contributions or give advice. That core group has continued to function all through the project. I've been very appreciative of their giving of their time and their willingness to make suggestions and offers of help.

Several authors were contacted who were not able to take on the project. I met with one professional author who was quite helpful in explaining the three processes of getting a book published: hiring the writer for the manuscript; choosing a graphic artist that would do photos, layout, and design; and finally, the production and printing. I decided I needed to apply for a grant to get this work accomplished. I did that, making two applications very shortly. I also attended seminars on grant applications and talked to many people whom I thought would be knowledgeable.

As time passed, nothing was happening with the grants. In the meantime, I had begun to gather all the material we had in our house related to the Dallas UNA. I knew we had a lot because our house has been the storage place for all the files for several years. I finally said to my family and anyone else who would listen, "I can do this! I'm a college graduate with a master's degree and a lot of experience in writing (not fictional writing), and my husband, Bill, is a college graduate with a master's in communication and is a superb writer! We can do this together—at least get the manuscript started!"

Here's what I wrote in my update to the advisory committee on April 23, 2015:

> After much discussion with several different people this past month, I have decided to go forward with collecting interviews and information about the history of the Dallas Chapter UNA. If we hire a writer, it's going to be costly—several thousand dollars. And guess who will have to find all the information and go through all the files and provide a lot of the answers??? Yes, Bill and I and some others of you who know the history. Therefore, right now I'm thinking that we can just do it with the help of several of you providing articles and information. At least we can hopefully get a first draft done.

So that's when we decided to "go for it" and we began to put some ideas down on paper. Production, printing, and other decisions could be made later.

As of the writing of this piece on March 12, 2016, many people have contributed to the book, for which I am grateful. We still have no budget; Bill and I are contributing our time and talents. Our chapter work is all voluntary; we have no local dues that are paid, only national membership dues. I will continue to search for funds for publication.

We have done research at the Dallas Public Library, have read numerous books, and collected information from various leaders in the organization. We have been somewhat limited in obtaining information from the years 1974 through 2003. Bill took five boxes of UNA material to the Dallas Public Library in 2003 to be archived. The material was archived, but that section of the downtown Dallas Public Library has been under renovation for the past year, and we have been unable to look at the material. Recently, we found a list of the contents, but few details.

Bill and I hope that the information contained in the various chapters of these archives will provide meaningful glimpses into the history of the Dallas Chapter of the United Nations Association of the United States of America. We hold in high esteem and wish to honor all the former leaders and presidents of this organization. Many have worked diligently, often at great odds, enduring harsh criticism of the United Nations while embroiled in an environment of anti–United Nations sentiments. May their steadfast, persistent commitment to the principles and purposes of the international UN charter continue to inform and inspire succeeding generations to peaceful resolutions for a better world.

Norma Matthews
History Project Manager
Dallas Chapter United Nations Association
March 12, 2016

CHAPTER 1

The United Nations Officially Comes into Existence

World War II had been raging during the 1940s. "The name 'United Nations,' coined by United States President Franklin D. Roosevelt, was first used in the 'Declaration by United Nations' on January 1, 1942, during the Second World War, when representatives of 26 nations pledged their governments to continue fighting together against the Axis Powers."[1]

Before this time, international organizations to cooperate on specific matters related to peace were established in the 1800s and 1900s:

- The International Telecommunication Union was founded in 1865 as the International Telegraph Union.
- The Universal Postal Union was established in 1874. Both have been United Nations specialized agencies.
- The first International Peace Conference was held in The Hague in 1899 to elaborate instruments for settling crises peacefully, preventing wars and codifying rules of warfare.
- It adopted the Convention for the Pacific Settlement of International Disputes and established the Permanent Court of Arbitration, which began work in 1902.

---

[1]   *Basic Facts about the United Nations* (New York: News and Media Division, United Nations Department of Public Information, 2003), 3–5.

———

1

The forerunner of the United Nations was the League of Nations, conceived during the First World War and established in 1919 under the Treaty of Versailles "to promote international cooperation and to achieve peace and security."[2]

President Harry S. Truman (USA) being greeted at the airport in San Francisco by members of the United States Delegation: Edward R. Stettinius, Jr. to the right and Senator Tom Connally to the left, 1945

In 1945, representatives of fifty countries met in San Francisco at the United Nations Conference on International Organization to draw up the United Nations Charter. Those delegates deliberated on the basis of proposals worked out by the representatives of China, the Soviet Union, the United Kingdom, and the United States at Dumbarton Oaks, United States, in August–October 1944. The charter was signed on June 26, 1945, by the representatives of the fifty countries. Poland, which was not represented at the conference, signed it later and became one of the original fifty-one member states.[3]

---

[2]   Ibid.

[3]   Ibid.

United States representatives in the meeting hall in 1945, before the first session of the United Nations General Assembly: from left to right: Senator Warren R. Austin, Delegation chairman; Senator Tom Connally; Mrs. Franklin D. Roosevelt, and Senator Arthur Vandenberg

United Nations Charter

The charter is the constituting instrument of the organization, setting out the rights and obligations of member states and establishing the United Nations organs and procedures. An international treaty, the charter codifies the major principles of international relations—from the sovereign equality of states to prohibition of the use of force in international relations in any manner inconsistent with the purposes of the United Nations.[4]

---

[4]   Ibid.

Preamble to the Charter

The Preamble to the Charter expresses the ideals and common aims of all the peoples whose governments joined together to form the United Nations:

WE THE PEOPLES OF THE UNITED NATIONS DETERMINED to save succeeding generations from the scourge of war, which twice in our lifetime has brought untold sorrow to mankind, and to reaffirm faith in fundamental human rights, in the dignity and worth of the human person, in the equal rights of men and women and of nations large and small, and to establish conditions under which justice and respect for the obligations arising from treaties and other sources of international law can be maintained, and to promote social progress and better standards of life in larger freedom,

AND FOR THESE ENDS to practice tolerance and live together in peace with one another as good neighbours, and to unite our strength to maintain international peace and security, and to ensure, by the acceptance of principles and the institution of methods, that armed force shall not be used, save in the common interest, and to employ international machinery for the promotion of the economic and social advancement of all peoples,

HAVE RESOLVED TO COMBINE OUR EFFORTS TO ACCOMPLISH THESE AIMS. Accordingly, our respective Governments, through representatives assembled in the city of San Francisco, who have exhibited their full powers found to be in good and due form, have agreed to the present Charter of the United Nations and do hereby establish an international organization to be known as the United Nations.[5]

---

[5]   Ibid.

United Nations Association of the USA—About Us

The United Nations Association of the United States of America (UNA-USA) is a membership organization dedicated to inform, inspire, and mobilize the American people to support the ideals and vital work of the United Nations. For 70 years UNA-USA has worked to accomplish its mission through its national network of Chapters, youth engagement, advocacy efforts, education programs, and public events. UNA-USA is a program of the United Nations Foundation. UNA-USA and its sister organization, the Better World Campaign, represent the single largest network of advocates and supporters of the United Nations in the world. Learn more about UNA-USA's programs and initiatives at www.unausa.org.

Our Mission

We are dedicated to educating, inspiring and mobilizing Americans to support the principles and vital work of the United Nations, strengthening the United Nations system, promoting constructive United States leadership in that system and achieving the goals of the United Nations Charter.

UNA-USA's History

UNA-USA works closely with the United Nations Foundation and its sister organization, the Better World Campaign, to strengthen the U.S.-UN relationship. These current partnerships continue a long history of UNA-USA helping bolster American support for the UN.

The American Association for the United Nations, UNA-USA's predecessor organization, grew from the League of Nations Association in 1943. A group of prominent citizens, including the first executive director, Clark M. Eichelberger, activated the association to promote acceptance of the Dumbarton Oaks proposals in the late years of World War II. Among the association's early actions was a national tour by a number of US representatives to spread the word and gain support for American adherence to the Dumbarton proposals, which led to the creation of the UN.

E.R. Stettinius Jr. (United States), Chairman of the delegation of the United States, and Nelson Rockefeller, Assistant Secretary of States of the United States, attending the Fifth Plenary Session of the Conference, 1945

When First Lady Eleanor Roosevelt, a member of the association's board of directors, completed her term as a US representative to the UN General Assembly in late 1951, she walked into the association's offices and asked for something to do. Her offer was gratefully accepted, and in early 1953, she established an office at the association's headquarters.

This was the quiet beginning of a major campaign in which Mrs. Roosevelt carried the message of the American Association for the United Nations across the country through personal appearances, recruitment speeches and fund-raising efforts that continued until her death in November 1962. She was elected chairwoman of the board in 1961.

In 1964, the Association merged with the US Committee for the United Nations, a group of 138 national organizations supporting the work of the UN, thereby creating the United Nations Association of the United States of America. Since then, several distinguished Americans have served in positions of leadership at UNA-USA. These include Arthur J. Goldberg, former Justice of the US Supreme Court and US permanent representative to the United Nations; James S. McDonnell, former chairman of the McDonnell-Douglas Corporation; Elliot L. Richardson, former US attorney general and US representative to the Law of the Sea Conference; William Scranton, former governor of Pennsylvania and US permanent representative to the United Nations; Cyrus Vance, former secretary of state; and John C. Whitehead, former deputy secretary of state.[6]

From the 1970s through the 1990s the UNA-USA's annual revenues and expenditures fluctuated. The deficits caused a problem for the UNA-USA to meet the needs of the humanitarian programs that the organization was committed to carry out. There were high-level, important people in the administrative offices constantly searching for more funding for the grass-roots advocacy program. Soon it became apparent that the "very viability and existence of UNA-USA was threatened, unless a savior appeared quickly. And fortunately, the United Nations Foundation was a possibility.[7]

---

[6]   Ross Feldman, "About Us," *United Nations Association of the USA*, accessed January 22, 2017, http://unausa.org/about-us.

[7]   James Wurst, *The UN Association-USA: A Little Known History of Advocacy and Action* (Boulder, CO: Lynne Rienner Publishers, Inc., 2016), 322.

The UNA-USA Alliance with the UN Foundation

It was well-known that Ted Turner was a popular public figure, the founder of CNN, owner of other TV networks, and a former owner of the Atlanta Braves baseball team, with involvement in several other enterprises. And it was public knowledge that Turner was a billionaire. But no one had a clue of what was about to happen that evening at the gala even though the public knew of his support and interest in the UN.[8]

Ted Turner was the invited speaker. The surprise event took place on September 19, 1997, at the UNA's Global Leadership Award gala at the Marriott Marquis Hotel in New York. Turner announced that he was making a gift to the UN of one billion dollars. At first the guests were only mildly excited. They thought that he said he was making a gift of one million dollars. Then suddenly it was repeated and the crowd heard "one billion dollars." It was the largest single charitable donation in history. "The gift became legendary."[9]

Soon Turner learned that he wasn't permitted to give the gift to the UN. There was a law that the UN could only accept large donations from member countries. From this event came the need for a charitable foundation. Ted Turner's donation initiated the UN Foundation.

> In 2010, UNA-USA formed a strategic alliance with the UN Foundation. Under the new alliance UNA-USA continued as a robust membership program of the Foundation. Together, UNA-USA and the UN Foundation are pooling their talents to increase public education and advocacy on the work of the UN.[10]

Within this context, the paramount importance of continuing advocacy work by DUNA, the Dallas Chapter of UNA-USA, working through the grassroots constituents, is clear. As history moves from the historic base to the future, past national president Ed Elmendorf's observations on the role of chapters is prophetic:

---

8   Ibid.
9   Ibid., 323.
10   Feldman, "About Us."

The UNA-USA was able to bring . . . a nationwide presence on the ground, a hundred-plus chapters across the country, individual members, and a capacity through that network to speak publicly and to engage in advocacy with our elected representatives on UN issues.[11]

The Millennium Development Goals (MDGs) 2000–2015[12]

At the beginning of the 21st century, United Nations Member States unanimously agreed to forge a commitment, through the Millennium Declaration, to help the poorest to achieve better life by the year 2015. The framework was outlined in a set of time-bound common goals and targets embodied in the Millennium Development Goals (MDGs).

Progress toward the MDGs was monitored through a set of 21 measurable and time-bound targets and 60 indicators, which addressed extreme poverty and hunger, education, women's empowerment and gender equality, health, environmental sustainability and global partnership.

---

[11] Wurst, *The UN Association-USA: A Little Known History of Advocacy and Action*, 329.

[12] Ban Ki-moon, "At General Assembly Debate, Secretary-General Says Regional Organizations Critical to Shaping Post-2015 Agenda, Reaching Sustainable Development Goals | Meetings Coverage and Press Releases," *United Nations Meeting Coverages and Press Releases*, May 4, 2015, http://www. un.org/press/en/2015/sgsm16729.doc.htm. For more current information on the work and organization of the United Nations go to www.un.org or www. unfoundation.org.

Mothers and children awaiting medical care through UNICEF, one
Millennium Development Goal addressed in the 2000-2015 program

GOAL 1   Eradicate extreme poverty and hunger

GOAL 2   Achieve universal primary education

GOAL 3   Promote gender equality and empower women

GOAL 4   Reduce child mortality

GOAL 5   Improve maternal health

GOAL 6   Combat HIV/AIDS, malaria and other diseases

GOAL 7   Ensure environmental sustainability

GOAL 8   Develop a global partnership for development

The MDGs helped to lift more than one billion people
out of extreme poverty, to make inroads against hunger,
to enable more girls to attend school than ever before
and to protect our planet. By putting people and their
immediate needs at the forefront, the MDGs reshaped
decision-making in developed and developing countries
alike.

African Kids in a Unity Circle

The emerging post-2015 development agenda, including the set of Sustainable Development Goals, strives to reflect these lessons, build on our successes and put all countries, together, firmly ontrack towards a more prosperous, sustainable and equitable world.

2015 is a milestone year. We will complete the Millennium Development Goals.

We are forging a bold vision for sustainable development, including a set of sustainable development goals. And we are aiming for a new, universal climate agreement. (Ban Ki-moon, secretary general, United Nations)

Health Goals Met, More Yet to Do[13]

GENEVA—May 13, 2015

The World Health Organization reports the world is less poor and healthier now than it was 15 years ago when the United Nations launched the Millennium Development Goals.

The Millennium Development Goal to cut poverty in half by 2015 was met five years ago. Globally, 700 million fewer people lived in extreme poverty in 2010 than in 1990.

WHO Health Statistics and Information Systems Director Ties Boerma says he expects the global targets for increasing safe drinking water and turning around the epidemics of HIV, malaria, and tuberculosis will be met by the end of the year. He says great progress has been made in child survival, though mortality remains high.

Changing national and world political developments intensify the advocacy functions of all citizens to preserve "Hope Over Fear" for ensuing generations. The United Nations continues its foundational influence and action to fulfill universal fulfillment of its essential ideals.

---

[13] Lisa Schlein, "WHO: Progress in Millennium Development Goals Still Not Sufficient," *VOA*, May 13, 2015, http://www.voanews.com/a/progress-in-millennium-development-goals-still-not-sufficient/2765936.html.

CHAPTER 2

The Early Days

The Birth of Dallas Chapter United Nations Association

Texas' first female judge, first president of DUNA

Sarah Tilghman Hughes is the "birth mother" of the Dallas United Nations Association. When "World War II was over, the United Nations Charter had been signed in San Francisco, the boys were coming home, and it was a time of joy for America: 1946, 1947. But, there prevailed in the United States a feeling of uneasiness due to groups which had sprung into being, creating fear and dissension where none need exist—creating enemies from former allies." These words were written by Cordye Hall, a young Texas activist living in Dallas during these times.[1]

Hate groups were growing, and people were saying that there might be another world war. Cordye Hall was totally perplexed and alarmed that even though Russia had fought on the side of the United States and had lost 20 million people to the war, Americans were so suspicious of anyone working for World Peace that they were labeled communists. The anticommunist movement grew, and Cordye asked a friend, Robert St. John, a war correspondent, "What can one person do?"[2]

Out of this encounter grew the Dallas Chapter of United World Federalists: "The United World Federalists point out that all nations, so far as their relationships with other nations are concerned, must be governed by world law." They "were just getting a Dallas Chapter of UWF formed when the United Nations came under such attack that the group met and decided to form a local chapter of the United Nations—one that could not be accused of having Communists in its membership because we could track down any such accusation immediately and expose it as a lie."[3] The membership was made up of intellectuals, mostly concerned about the way the country was developing. This was the period when Senator "Joseph McCarthy was accusing every organization working for peace, particularly the United Nations, of being infested with Communists. He saw any country that did not have a government similar to the United States government as a threat to our country. It was a frightening time because families whose sons had just returned (if they did return) were being faced with threats of another war right on the heels of World War II."[4] Thus, the Dallas Chapter of United World Federalists was a precursor to the Dallas Chapter UNA.

The United Nations Association Dallas Chapter was formed to defend the UN in Dallas where such false and vicious attacks were being made against it. Cordye Hall reports the names of some in that early group: Cordye Hall; Judge Sarah T. Hughes; Mrs. John Kilgore; Paul Lay; Mrs.

---

[1] Cordye Hall, "What Can One Person Do?" (International Women's Global Peace Conference, Dallas, TX: Ken Gjemre, 1988), 1.
[2] Ibid., 2.
[3] Ibid., 3.
[4] Ibid., 2.

Rudy Biesele; Canon Ferguson of the Episcopal Farmers Foundation; Bill and Caroline Cage; Carol Weaverling; Carl and Laura Brannin; Ned Fritz; Mrs. J. W. Day; and Louise and Grier Raggio.[5]

Cordye Hall wrote that she was on the nominating committee to identify leaders for the new Dallas Chapter UNA. In late 1952, the group began seeking a prominent local person to take the chair position. A prominent local as chair decreased the likelihood that UN opponents would accuse him/her of being a communist. Despite little evidence of communist sympathies, the milieu at the time was one such that any effort toward international unity was a ripe target for witch-hunting accusers. After several meetings, the group of supporters for the United Nations met in January 1953 to organize officially. The founding members prevailed upon Judge Sarah T. Hughes to become the first president of the chapter.[6]

Four months later, the new organization received notice of its accreditation as an official unit of the American Association for the United Nations. Thus, the Dallas chapter of the United Nations Association of the USA was born on May 12, 1953, with Judge Sarah Tilghman Hughes as its leader.

These quotes are taken from activist Cordye Hall in *What Can One Person Do?*, a private manuscript published by Ken Gjemre in Dallas, Texas, 1988, for the International Women's Global Peace Conference, held the week of August 8, 1988, assisted by Sandy Hall-Chiles, granddaughter, and from Ruthe Winegarten's oral history of Cordye Hall in the 1970s.

Sarah T. Hughes (1896–1985)
First President of Dallas United Nations Association, 1953
First Recipient of Arnold Goodman UNA-USA
Lifetime Achievement Award 1981

Sarah Tilghman was born in Baltimore in 1896. Sarah received a scholarship to attend Goucher College, and she graduated three years later with a biology degree, with honors. She taught school in Winston-Salem, North Carolina, for two years, but she soon decided that teaching was not

---

[5]   Ibid., 4.

[6]   Ibid.

her interest. When she was twenty years old, she went back to Baltimore to manage her ailing mother's boardinghouse.

That fall, Sarah enrolled in George Washington University School of Law. To support herself, she got a job with the Metropolitan Police Department of Washington, DC, as one of the first female police officers. She worked on cases involving children, and at night, she patrolled the streets and dance halls. In 1922, Sarah was licensed to practice law in the District of Columbia and in Texas. Sarah loved to debate politics and social issues with her classmates.

Sarah met George Hughes, an older man, whose personality was the opposite of hers. He was quiet and disliked politics. He preferred solitude; she loved being out with people. They were married in 1922, and "despite amazing and ever-increasing differences in their personalities and interests, it was a marriage that would endure for 42 years until George's death in 1964."[7]

The Hughes family soon moved to Dallas. George got a job with the Veterans Administration; Sarah applied for many jobs, but she was not hired, learning much later that it was because she was a woman. In the 1930s, Sarah ran for state representative and won three terms. In 1935, Gov. James V. Allred named Sarah judge of the Fourteenth District Court of Texas. Sen. Claude Westerfield of Dallas opposed the appointment, announcing that "Sarah Hughes is a woman, and women should be home washing dishes." Many women were outraged. She was confirmed and was the state's first female district judge. By 1960, she was reelected to her seventh term. "Politics, she said, was in her blood."[8]

During the 1950s and 1960s, "Sarah became involved in the women's liberation movement long before it had a name. As such, she was leader and mentor to many women who longed to be free of the obstructions that society imposed upon them. She gave presence and her effort to the advancement of women in public life . . . She was president of the National Federation of Business and Professional Women's Clubs after serving as the head of the Dallas Business and Professional Women. She was first vice president of the International Federation of Business and Professional

---

7   Vivian Castleberry, *Daughters of Dallas* (Dallas: Odenwald Press, 1994), 281.
8   Ibid., 282.

Women. She was also president of the Zonta Club." She later became one of the organizers of the Women's Center of Dallas.[9]

Sarah Hughes believed that it was her duty to advocate for prison reform and "an enlightened view toward crime and punishment at a time when these subjects were considered political suicide." She exclaimed that it was her responsibility to take sides on community issues that matter.[10]

In the late 1940s, there was another issue that rose to prominence in the public's mind: the Cold War. "A general fear existed that an outbreak of hostilities in this nuclear age would mean the end of civilization. Avoiding this awful possibility occupied the minds of many. It seemed apparent that something stronger than the new United Nations would be needed to end conflicts between nations and alliances." The United Nations Charter had been signed in San Francisco in 1945, and now there was interest in a movement that would create "a world federal government in which a single international authority would supersede national sovereignties."

By April 1947, the Dallas chapter of the United World Federalists was reported to have seven hundred members, among them liberal-minded people of Dallas including Sarah and George Hughes. Sarah Hughes spoke on these viewpoints in a panel discussion at SMU in March 1948: "In her opinion, the United Nations, although certainly a step in the right direction, was inadequate to the task. For it to succeed, the organization would need a police force and the ability to make decisions on a majority basis." The UN would need to be strengthened.[11]

Even though Judge Hughes continued her support for a world government, she soon realized that the United Nations was assuming an active role in the Korean conflict and that the World Federalist movement was losing its momentum. The World Federalists was a precursor to the United Nations. Hughes began switching her primary allegiances to the United Nations. She became an ardent supporter of the United Nations, and her interest in a world federation began to wane.

The political climate in Dallas had become increasingly conservative by the 1950s. In 1953, in the midst of the McCarthy hearings, the rise of the John Birch Society, and several other anticommunist movements that

---

[9]   Ibid., 283.

[10]   Ibid.

[11]   Darwin Payne, *Indomitable Sarah: The Life of Judge Sarah T. Hughes* (Dallas, TX: Southern Methodist University Press, 2004), 150–51.

---

dominated the US landscape (particularly in Dallas), Sarah Hughes agreed to be the organizing president of a Dallas United Nations Association even when colleagues warned her against it. This was the seed of the beginning of the Dallas Chapter United Nations Association.[12]

Judge Sarah T. Hughes, first DUNA president, 1954

In 1954, a national magazine described Sarah T. Hughes as being "well known throughout Texas for her work in promoting understanding of the United Nations and for her efforts to obtain service on juries for women."[13] In 1958, when she was campaigning for a seat on the Texas Supreme Court, she spoke at a Rotary Club meeting in Sulphur Springs. The "question of the United Nations came up, and she reaffirmed her belief that it was the world's best hope for peace."[14] In the spring of 1960, Judge Sarah attended a conference in Buenos Aires in her capacity as UN chairman for the

---

12   Castleberry, *Daughters of Dallas*, 283.
13   Payne, *Indomitable Sarah: The Life of Judge Sarah T. Hughes*, 182.
14   Ibid., 190.

International Federation of Business & Professional Women (B&PW). At that meeting, the fourteenth session of the UN Commission on the Status of Women, Hughes spoke on behalf of the B&PW on her favorite topic, political rights for women, before delegates from countries around the world.

In 1961 President John F. Kennedy appointed her US District Judge for the Northern District of Texas. Every woman's organization, the bar associations, and all of the elected officials—Johnson, Rayburn, Yarborough and many others—in whose campaigns she had been a tireless worker supported her appointment. When she was sworn into the judgeship on October 16, 1961, Lyndon Johnson said he "trusted that each of her gray hairs would represent wisdom for a troubled and critical period."[15]

Little did he know that it would be Sarah T. Hughes who would swear him in as president of the United States in November 1963 after President John F. Kennedy was assassinated.

Judge Sarah T. Hughes, swore in LBJ as President, 1963.

---

[15]   Castleberry, *Daughters of Dallas*, 283.

In October 1962, Hughes returned to the presidency of the Dallas Chapter UNA. Many liberal-minded Dallasites such as the Hugheses found an outlet for their idealism in the UNA. The harsh anti-UN sentiment in the area had grown stronger since her first term nearly a decade earlier, as evidenced by a legislative controversy over whether the United Nations flag could be flown on property owned by the state, or city, or political subdivision of the state. Judge Hughes wrote to Gov. John B. Connally in 1963 urging him to veto this bill that would make flying the UN flag illegal. She announced that this "bill is intended to be an attack on the United Nations and disapproval of its accomplishments . . . To prohibit the flying of this flag would be a poor advertisement for our state." One representative who spoke in favor of the UN reported that his position had generated letters from people who were "dangerously extreme" and "emotionally disturbed." The bill failed to gain the two-thirds vote needed for immediate consideration and did not reemerge before the legislative session ended. Hughes stated that there was a need for a higher profile of the UN and its goals so that the public could better understand its benefits. Opponents of the UN seemed to have no problem in attracting attention.[16]

Hughes organized her UNA Dallas chapter. As reported in the 1962 annual report, UNA members made seventy-eight speeches in support of the United Nations in front of ten thousand people.

Judge Hughes' successor as president of the Dallas UNA in March 1963 was Jack Goren, a vice president at Neiman-Marcus, a prominent Dallas department store. Goren soon realized that some customers might view his new visibility as a liability. However, he reminded "those who complained that his work with the United Nations Association had nothing at all to do with his position at Neiman-Marcus." He had plenty of other prominent Dallas leaders to keep him company who were supporters of Dallas UNA: "Raymond Nasher who was planning to build NorthPark; the Reverend Baxton Bryant, a liberal Baptist [sic] [Methodist] minister; Edward B. Winn, an attorney; and Gerald C. Mann, former Texas attorney general, a football hero of Southern Methodist University in the 1930s, and a friend of Hughes since her days in the Texas Legislature."[17]

Sarah T. Hughes continued her work in support of the United Nations and women's rights into the 1970s and 1980s. By the 1970s, the issue

---

16   Payne, *Indomitable Sarah: The Life of Judge Sarah T. Hughes*, 237.
17   Ibid., 238.

of women's rights had become one of the liveliest topics in the national dialogue. Now, more women with strident voices and a flair for publicity dominated the public discussions. Hughes continued to mentor women who would take up the cause. She enjoyed near-legendary status in her later life. She was famous for her tough-mindedness and uniqueness. She never retired; she took senior status in her job, meaning she could select the cases she would hear.

George Ernest Hughes, her husband of forty-two years, died on June 1, 1964, at the age of seventy-two. After his death, Hughes began to travel, something that gave her much satisfaction. She attended many conferences on subjects that interested her, and she began taking personal cruises with friends. She thoroughly enjoyed foreign travel.[18]

Sarah T. Hughes died quietly and peacefully on April 24, 1985. The *Dallas Times Herald* described her as a "women's movement pioneer."[19] The headline for the editorial in the *Dallas Morning News* was "Indomitable Sarah" from "the newspaper whose conservative philosophy had run counter to Hughes for so many years . . .one of the things that made Judge Hughes distinctive, and, yes, admirable, was that you always knew where she stood . . .She leaves a tall legacy in consequence of a remarkable career."[20]

(Two primary resources for this section are from Vivian Castleberry, *Daughters of Dallas*, Dallas: Odenwald Press, 1994, 280–283, and Darwin Payne, *Indomitable Sarah: The Life of Judge Sarah T. Hughes*, Dallas: Southern Methodist University Press, 2004, 150–395.)

---

[18]   Ibid., 385.

[19]   Ibid., 395.

[20]   Ibid., 394–95.

Postscript

UNA-USA Lifetime Achievement Award plaque
shows Sarah T. Hughes first recipient

When Bill and Norma Matthews attended the 2016 UNA-USA Leadership Summit in Washington, DC, they were awarded the 2016 Arnold Goodman Lifetime Achievement Award. When the large plaque that hangs in the UNA offices in Washington, DC, was presented to them with all the names of those recipients of that award, they were surprised to see that Sarah T. Hughes was the first recipient of that award in 1981. That was the first knowledge they had that she had received the award. Nothing has been found in the archives noting that occasion. The picture of her name on the plaque is included in this history.

Regina Montoya, Peacemakers, Inc. friend and supporter.

In another ironic twist, we later learned that Regina Montoya, our long-time supporter in Peacemakers, Inc., had clerked for Judge Hughes in 1979. She carries on the tradition of peacemaker by volunteering to serve the causes of peace and justice into the twenty-first century.

(June 2016, NTM)

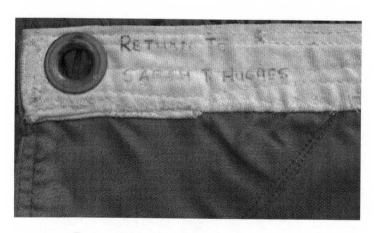

Personal UN Flag, Judge Sarah T. Hughes.

The United Nations flag of Sarah T. Hughes was found in her belongings at the time of her death. The executor of her estate made contact with Judge Barefoot Sanders, US district judge for the

1953—Founder, Dallas Chapter UNA

1963—Swore in LBJ as president, after JFK's death

1985—Her own personal symbolic flag, DUNA archives

Northern District of Texas, and his wife Jan Sanders, knowing that the Sanderses had been DUNA members since its inception in the early fifties.

Judge Sarah T. Hughes had told Jan Sanders many years ago that if she had had a son, she would have liked him to be like Barefoot Sanders. The Hughes never had any children.

The executor of Sarah Hughes estate determined that the flag should go to the Sanderses. The flag was archived with the Dallas Chapter United Nations Association in 1985. As of 2017, it is archived with the Dallas Chapter UNA records at the Dallas Public Library downtown. On the binding of the flag is written "Return to Sarah T. Hughes."

The flag is a symbol of the great work that Sarah T. Hughes did in establishing the Dallas Chapter UNA. It was probably used in many UNA meetings. The flag measures five feet by nine and a half feet.[21]

These are NTM author's notes from a conversation with Jan Sanders, widow of Judge Barefoot Sanders, in spring 2015, at Northaven United Methodist Church, Dallas, Texas.

Dallas Chapter UNA: The Early Days
A Readers Theater Presentation
Dallas UNA Celebration of United Nations Day
October 24, 2013, FunAsia Restaurant
by Patty N. Jantho

Readers: Beth Weems Pirtle (BWP), Anya Cooper (AC)
Narrators: Patty Jantho (PJ: Judge Sarah T. Hughes), Anya Cooper (AC: Eleanor Roosevelt), members of Dallas United Nations Association

---

21 Jan Sanders, Conversation with Jan Sanders, Widow of Judge Barefoot Sanders. Northaven United Methodist Church, Dallas, Texas, Spring 2015.

DUNA Readers Theater 60th Anniversary

First Speaker (BWP): The United Nations was founded in 1945 after the Second World War. Fifty-one member countries committed themselves to peace and to make the world a better place for all people—what a challenge!

Second Speaker (AC): Not everyone was happy with joining an organization that some believed would cause the United States to give up some of its "quote unquote" rights.

First Speaker (BWP): That's why the United Nations Association was formed.

Second Speaker (AC): What about Dallas? When was our organization formed?

First Speaker (BWP): It was formed in 1953—60 years ago. Interestingly enough, it centers on the story of one woman—a groundbreaking leader on many fronts—Sarah Tilghman Hughes.

Sarah T. Hughes (PJ): "That's me. I was born in Baltimore, Maryland in 1896. I always had 'spirit.' I was only a bit over 5 feet tall but my classmates described me as 'small but terrible.'"

Second Speaker (AC): She graduated from Goucher, moved to Washington D.C., attended law school at night, and worked during the day as a police officer.

Hughes (PJ): "I didn't carry a gun or wear a uniform because I was working to prevent crimes among women and girls—patrolling areas where female prostitutes and runaways were normally found—this was the start of my commitment to women and girls."

First Speaker (BWP): She married, and then moved to Dallas. She became active in local women's organizations—Zonta, Business & Professional Women, the Dallas Women's Political League, the League of Women Voters, the YWCA and the American Association of University Women.

Hughes (PJ): "After practicing law for eight years in Dallas, I was elected to the Texas House of Representatives in 1930."

Second Speaker (AC): In 1935, she was appointed as a state judge for the 14th District Court in Dallas, becoming the State's first female district judge. In 1961, President Kennedy appointed Hughes to the United States District Court for the Northern District of Texas.

Hughes (PJ): "You may remember me from 1963, when I administered the oath to Lyndon Johnson—our 36th president—on that sad day after President Kennedy's assassination."

First Speaker (BWP): Hughes served on the three-judge panel that first heard the Texas case, Roe v. Wade, resulting in a decision later upheld by the Supreme Court in 1973. It granted women the right to choose abortion.

Second Speaker (AC): Now, back to our story of the founding of UNA Dallas.

Hughes (PJ): "In 1952, I was sent by our government with a group of US women leaders to meet with women's groups in Germany. I saw how interacting with people from other countries could be a means of establishing world peace. Back home, I was appointed to the US National Commission for the United Nations Educational, Scientific and Cultural Organization (UNESCO). It was our role to advise the US State Department on its participation in UNESCO."

First Speaker (BWP): Then in 1953, she convened a group of like-minded friends to organize the Dallas United Nations Association.

Hughes (PJ): "I was convinced that the UN was the best vehicle for obtaining peace."

Second Speaker (AC): A board was elected and accreditation was granted in May, 1953, by the American Association for the United Nations—the name was formally changed to the United Nations Association in 1964. The stated purpose was to promote understanding of the United Nations and to win support for its objectives. Special committees included: UN Week, Radio, Membership, Study Groups, Publicity, Evaluation, Research, and Legislation Program.

Hughes (PJ): "We had our work cut out for us. There was a thriving anti-UN sentiment that attacked the UN on a regular basis. We countered those attacks promptly at every opportunity. I think our Speakers Bureau was our most important tool. We sent letters to some 500 civic, religious and educational groups announcing the availability of individuals who could give factual talks about the UN and its work."

First Speaker (BWP): Hughes was herself the most frequently called-upon speaker. She would outline the goals of the various UN agencies and the benefits the US received from UN membership.

Hughes (PJ): "It seemed to me that the only alternative to the United Nations was war. It will be a 'long and tough road,' but peace could be achieved."

Second Speaker (AC): So persistent was public criticism in Dallas that one of the members prepared a chronological account of attacks and the organization's response to each.

Hughes (PJ): "During our first year, we were regularly on the defensive, but there were successes as well. We had 175 people at our first luncheon; we obtained a mayoral proclamation for our first UN Week with participation by 65 organizations. There were speeches, flag raisings, information booths, and news coverage by radio and TV."

First Speaker (BWP): A first visit by Eleanor Roosevelt in 1955 was a special success with luncheon attendance by several hundred. An otherwise favorable *Dallas Morning News* editorial stated that Mrs. Roosevelt's problem was "her blanket defense of the special agencies of the UN, some of which have spread socialized programs over the world at our expense." The newspaper suggested that while well intended, some of the special agencies had "fallen into the hands of crackpots." In defense of the United Nations Mrs. Roosevelt said:

Mrs. Roosevelt (AC): "There was a time when people disillusioned by the League of Nations could scoff at the idea of another world organization designed to work for the peaceful settlement of international disputes . . .Today we are seeing more and more clearly that it *can* work, that it *does* work, and it will be increasingly effective if we back it with all our strength."

Hughes (PJ): "During the red scare of the 1950s, someone reported that I had attended a subversive meeting at a Highland Park church. I was called 'socialistic' and that the meeting was held either by the Communist Party or by persons leaning that way . . . The FBI learned that the 'subversive meeting' was actually a public affairs discussion at the Unitarian Church and quickly dropped the matter."

First Speaker (BWP): The power of the "far right" came to the fore in November 1954, when Bruce Alger was elected as the only Republican Congressman from Texas at the time. Alger consistently urged Congress to withdraw from the United Nations. That was the beginning of the exodus of conservative Democrats into the Republican Party.

Second Speaker (AC): In the 60 years since the founding of UNA Dallas, much has changed. There are now 193 member states within the United Nations. Within the US Congress, there are still continuing efforts to block US financial support to the UN.

First Speaker (BWP): Today the challenge continues. As Dallas UNA, we continue to be advocates, to arm ourselves with facts to counter erroneous statements and myths about the UN. Indeed, there is still much to be done. Thank you.

This presentation was developed, written, and performed with Patty N. Jantho, member of the Dallas Chapter United Nations Association.

Bernard L. Fulton (1910–2009)
Second President of Dallas United Nations Association, 1954

Bernard Fulton, second president of DUNA

Dr. Bernard L. Fulton, founder of Greenhill School in 1950, worked in 1954–1955 with Mrs. Eleanor Roosevelt to further establish the United Nations Association of the USA in Dallas and North Texas. Fulton was the second president of the Dallas UNA, following Judge Sarah T. Hughes.

A member of Rotary International, Fulton was also a regional commissioner for the Boy Scouts of America. He was a member of the North Dallas Chamber of Commerce and board president of the Addison Independent School District from 1940–1950.

Fulton rose from humble beginnings, first working in the coal mines of West Virginia and becoming principal of a two-room schoolhouse in the Appalachian Mountains. His football prowess brought him to Dallas, where he played for Peacock Military Academy and Troop E of the 112th US Cavalry.

Fulton attended Southern Methodist University (SMU) and earned a bachelor of science and a master of arts in education, administration, and history. He was recognized as an SMU Distinguished Alumnus in 1976.

Mary Hardin Baylor University conferred an honorary doctorate degree in 1973.

Known and respected as a visionary pioneer in education and civic affairs, he encouraged every individual to fulfill his or her aspirations. Fulton was headmaster at the Texas Country Day School, now St. Mark's School of Texas, for thirteen years beginning in the 1930s. He founded the Greenhill School with his wife Helen and several of their friends and fellow educators, and he served as headmaster from 1950 to 1976. Fulton then led Lakehill Preparatory School for two years and became a site visitor for the Exemplary School Program of the US Department of Education from 1979 to 1985, through which he found and acknowledged the best schools in the nation.

In addition to the Greenhill School, he was on the board of the Fulton School, named for him, in Heath, Texas, as well as the boards of the Dallas Creative Learning Center, Southwest Academy, Canterbury School, Shelton School, and Winston School in Dallas and the Clear Spring School in Eureka Springs, Arkansas.

Charter members of the University Park United Methodist Church, he and Helen Smith Fulton were married for seventy-three years until her death in 2007. They had four children, seven grandchildren, and four great-grandchildren along with numerous nieces and nephews, friends, and fellow educators. Bernard Fulton was a friend and supporter of the United Nations Association until his death in 2009.[22]

This material was based on information provided by daughter, Molly Fulton Seeligson, director of the Eugene McDermott Scholars Program, University of Texas at Dallas.

Eleanor Roosevelt, a Strong National Influence for the United Nations and Human Rights

Eleanor Roosevelt was one of the most strong, influential women of the 1950s. After her husband's death on April 12, 1945, Eleanor Roosevelt began a long period of self-discovery and building her own persona. She was not bound by the demands of being the first lady and wife of FDR and

---

[22] Molly Fulton Seeligson, Conversation with Molly Fulton Seeligson, Daughter of Bernard Fulton, Second President of the Dallas United Nations Association, 1954, Unknown.

could pursue her own goals. She became more self-confident and began questioning what she could do on her own. She realized that she could be herself.[23]

Eleanor Roosevelt now became aware that she had always lived in someone else's shadow. Her mother, Anna Hall Roosevelt, was one of New York Society's most beautiful women; her teacher, Marie Souvestre, continually prodded her to develop her own opinions; and her uncle, Theodore Roosevelt, the president, had "transformed the presidency into a national bully pulpit."[24]

Eleanor struggled in marriage, too. She lived with family members with divergent aims: her mother-in-law, Sara Delano Roosevelt, always sided with her grandchildren against their mother; her husband, Franklin Delano Roosevelt, "charmed his way through New York politics and Washington social circles; and her friend and social secretary, the stylish Lucy Mercer, became one of the great loves of FDR's life."[25]

Eleanor Roosevelt was dealing with a widow's change of status: "Within a week of FDR's death, Eleanor Roosevelt coordinated his funeral, responded to friends' condolences, oversaw the boxing of possessions acquired and documents generated during her twelve years in Washington, said goodbye to colleagues and staff, and pondered her future."[26]

The public speculated on what actions Eleanor should or would do. It was at this time that Speaker of the House Sam Rayburn and New Jersey congresswoman Mary Norton urged Eleanor to join the American delegation charged with planning the United Nations. It is very important that your voice be heard, they told her. Her friends urged her to consider carefully what she might do. They reminded her that she was going to be her own agent now and free to make her own decisions. They said that Eleanor must be prepared for the very active and important place that was awaiting her. Henry Morgenthau Jr. told her that FDR's estate must be settled as quickly as possible so that she could speak out to the world as Eleanor Roosevelt.[27]

---

23 Allida M. Black, *Casting Her Own Shadow* (New York: Columbia University Press, 1996), 7.

24 Ibid.

25 Ibid.

26 Ibid., 52.

27 Ibid.

In 1945, Eleanor Roosevelt found herself impatient with slow-paced domestic reform and uncomfortable with her undefined future. "Of one thing I am sure," she wrote in May 1945, "in order to be useful we must stand for the things we feel are right, and we must work for those things wherever we find ourselves. It does very little good to believe something unless you tell your friends and associates of your beliefs."[28] She vowed that she would define the parameters of a new life in politics. She intended to work to promote the goals and ideals of the New Deal.[29]

President Harry Truman appointed Eleanor Roosevelt to the United States delegation to the United Nations in 1946 during a particularly difficult time for labor relations in the United States. She believed that the world could not be understood from a single point of view. She thought this was one of the blind spots of Americans. She linked American economic policies to international perceptions of democracy in general and the United States in particular. She said that facing the needs of human beings, the dispute over rights and wrongs between American management and labor suddenly falls into perspective. She stated that the world was watching America to see if democracy was a viable alternative to the trend toward socialism. She stated that labor, management, and the government needed to look at their actions from the world point of view and provide economic leadership that would expand faith in democratic capitalism. She always stood for an expanded view of the world. The issue of full and fair employment at just wages continued to be a goal for her while supporting both labor and the administration.[30]

The world cannot be understood from a single point of view. I keep repeating this because this is one of our blind spots as Americans.[31]

The next issue for Eleanor Roosevelt was championing civil rights. She became involved in the NAACP's "appeal for redress." She was a member of the UN's Human Rights Commission and was also a member of the NAACP national board. She was the logical choice to champion the cause for minorities and discrimination.[32]

---

[28]   Ibid., 53.
[29]   Ibid.
[30]   Ibid., 74.
[31]   Eleanor Roosevelt, *Tomorrow Is Now* (New York: Harper & Row, 1963), 87.
[32]   Black, *Casting Her Own Shadow*, 100.

Eleanor Roosevelt was one of the leaders in drafting *The Declaration of Human Rights*. The Declaration was commissioned in 1946 and was drafted over two years by the Commission on Human Rights. The commission consisted of eighteen members from various nationalities and political backgrounds. Eleanor Roosevelt, who was known for her human rights advocacy, chaired the Universal Declaration of Human Rights Drafting Committee.

> We stand today at the threshold of a great event both in the life of the United Nations and in the life of mankind, that is the approval by the General Assembly of the Universal Declaration of Human Rights recommended by the Third Committee.[33]

On December 10, 1948, the Universal Declaration was adopted by the General Assembly of the United Nations by a vote of forty-eight nations in favor, zero against, and eight abstentions. Six abstaining nations were communist, and the Union of South Africa abstained to protect their system of apartheid. The Kingdom of Saudi Arabia abstained due to opposition to Article 18 (stating that all have the right to change religion or belief) and Article 16 (protecting equal marriage rights). Roosevelt attributed the abstention of the Soviet bloc nations to opposition to Article 13, which provided the right of citizens to leave their countries. Honduras and Yemen—both contemporary UN members—failed to vote or abstain.[34]

> The United Nations is not a club of congenial people; it is, as it should be, a reflection of the whole world, with its turmoil, its conflicting interests, its diverse viewpoints.[35]

[33] Eleanor Roosevelt, "Statement to the United Nations' General Assembly on the Universal Declaration of Human Rights, 9 December 1948," accessed February 15, 2017, http://www2.gwu.edu/~erpapers/documents/displaydoc.cfm?_t=speeches&_docid=spc057137.

[34] "The Universal Declaration of Human Rights" (United Nations General Assembly (General Assembly Resolution 217A), December 10, 1948), http://www.un.org/en/universal-declaration-human-rights/index.html.

[35] Roosevelt, *Tomorrow Is Now*, 113.

One of the great stumbling blocks in the acceptance of our institution, of course, was the jealous clashes and distrust between state and federal groups. Everyone was afraid of having to give up a little.[36]

The adoption of the Universal Declaration is a significant international commemoration marked each year on December 10, now known as Human Rights Day or International Human Rights Day. Individuals, community and religious groups, human rights organizations, parliaments, governments, and the United Nations observe the commemoration. The year 2008 marked the sixtieth anniversary of the declaration, and it was accompanied by yearlong activities around the theme "Dignity and justice for all of us."[37]

One great strength of the United Nations is often not recognized; indeed, it is often regarded as a weakness. That is the amount of talk that goes on. Now the value of a public forum where people can protest their wrongs is enormous.[38]

In the 1950s, writings and media reports indicate that Eleanor Roosevelt had great influence in Dallas, Texas. She had become friends with Judge Sarah T. Hughes, and Judge Hughes had entertained Eleanor Roosevelt in her home several times. Also, in attendance were Grier and Louise Raggio and other persons interested in the new Dallas United Nations organization. Dallas attorney Louise Raggio reported in her book that Eleanor Roosevelt was a strong supporter of the new Dallas UNA chapter and that Roosevelt came several times to Dallas to encourage the chapter. ER had been a United States UN delegate.[39]

Judge Sarah Hughes had been appointed to the US National Commission for the United Nations Educational, Scientific, and Cultural

---

36 Ibid., 104.
37 "Human Rights Day, 10 December 2008," accessed February 15, 2017, http://www.un.org/en/events/humanrightsday/2008/.
38 Roosevelt, *Tomorrow Is Now*, 114–115.
39 Louise Ballerstedt Raggio and Vivian Castleberry, *Texas Tornado* (New York: Citadel Press, 2003), 137.

Organization (UNESCO), a body established by the US Congress to advise the State Department.

> In January 1953, soon after her UNESCO appointment, Hughes and a handful of like-minded friends met in a downtown bank auditorium to organize a United Nations support group—the Dallas United Nations Association. The idea to form a local organization had been discussed among this small group in the late Fall 1952 in three separate meetings because of an increasing number of bitter attacks in Dallas against the UN and particularly against UNESCO.

Several right-wing groups organized by H. L. Hunt were responsible for many of the attacks. Hughes appointment to the UNESCO commission likely was what inspired her and her friends to immediate action.[40]

> The effort to bring understanding and appreciation for the United Nations received a boost when the Dallas organization entered its third year and Eleanor Roosevelt spoke at a January 1955 meeting. The former first lady was chairman of the board of governors of the American Association for the United Nations, the national organization. Hughes introduced Mrs. Roosevelt at a news conference at the Press Club of Dallas, and a picture of the two of them together appeared in the *Dallas Morning News*. After the press conference, the Hugheses entertained Mrs. Roosevelt and several friends and associates at their home. It was the first of several occasions in coming years in which Sarah Hughes would entertain Eleanor Roosevelt at her home.[41]

> People constantly ask how we can help to strengthen the United Nations. The way to do this is to strengthen our support here at home and to show by example that we are trying to live up to the ideals established by the organization.[42]

---

[40] Payne, *Indomitable Sarah: The Life of Judge Sarah T. Hughes*, 172–73.
[41] Ibid., 176.
[42] Roosevelt, *Tomorrow Is Now*, 118.

Eleanor Roosevelt grew into a strong leader gradually. It took her many years to develop the skills necessary to promote her agenda effectively. She became a practical politician and learned early in her career that the media should be her friend. She was an active supporter of integration and a champion of integrated schools, housing projects, labor unions, and neighborhoods. Her stature in the civil rights movement enhanced her stature within the Democratic Party: "She was a passionate reformer who walked the delicate line between a wavering faith in public character and an unyielding commitment to democratic politics."[43]

We are the government. The basic power still lies in the hands of the citizens. But we must use it. That means that in every small unit of government, each individual citizen must feel his individual responsibility to do the best with his citizenship that he possibly can achieve.[44]

Eleanor Roosevelt was a woman, not a saint. She was a power broker, not an elected official. Nevertheless she cast a long shadow across the nation. As Martin Luther King, Jr., wrote, "the impact of her personality and its unwavering dedication to high principle and purpose cannot be contained in a single day or era." She set standards by which all future first ladies will be judged and played a key role in defining American liberalism and Democratic idealism.[45]

One thing there is no denying. Any change and raising of the standards of civilization can come only from the people within the country itself. Civilization cannot be imposed from without on reluctant people.[46]

Eleanor Roosevelt lived a long life of dedication and commitment to noble causes. She returned from Europe in February 1962. After taping three interviews for her television program, she gradually became weak and tired and died of tuberculosis on November 7, 1962, in her New York City apartment.[47]

---

[43]   Black, *Casting Her Own Shadow*, 200.
[44]   Roosevelt, *Tomorrow Is Now*, 124.
[45]   Black, *Casting Her Own Shadow*, 203.
[46]   Roosevelt, *Tomorrow Is Now*, 126.
[47]   Black, *Casting Her Own Shadow*, 194,197.

CHAPTER 3

Political Climate in Dallas in 1950s and 1960s

Part A: Hopes for Peace Arouse Dallas

Conflict arose between United Nations activists and antagonists. The activists believed that the United Nations was the best hope for world peace. The antagonists, fueled by paranoia over the perceived threat of communism to the United States, opposed the organization of the institution.

A.A. Gromyko (left) of the USSR conversing with Senator Tom Connally (United States) at a meeting of Commission II, Security Council, Committee 1, Structure and Procedures, held on 14 June 1945

With universal membership, the United Nations was a forum for airing differences and bringing disagreements before that body to be settled by law.[1]

Illustrating the conflict, the next sentence reported, "United States Senator Tom Connally of Texas, with little knowledge of world affairs, had hastened from the signing of the UN Charter in San Francisco to the U. S. Senate, where he was successful in getting passed the Connally Amendment, absolving the United States of an obligation to abide by International Law."[2]

President Harry S. Truman (USA) being greeted at the airport in San Francisco by members of the United States Delegation: Edward R. Stettinius, Jr. to the right and Senator Tom Connally to the left, 1945

---

[1] Cordye Hall, "What Can One Person Do?" (International Women's Global Peace Conference, Dallas, TX: Ken Gjemre, 1988), 2–3.
[2] Ibid.

This chapter juxtaposes the standpoints of leading activists and antagonists as they occurred during the first decades of DUNA—the fledgling Dallas Chapter of the United Nations Association-USA.

Cordye McLaurine Hall, 1899–1994

Vivian Castleberry wrote in *Daughters of Dallas*, "Cordye McLaurine Hall is the conscience of Dallas."[3] Hall was orphaned at age thirteen. She came to Dallas and lived with family friends, eventually enrolling at Ursuline Academy. She loved school, and the nuns were kind to her. When the United States entered World War I, all three of her brothers went overseas. Hall graduated from school and began working at various jobs. As she entered the workforce, she noticed that men were paid more than she was for the same work. She married and had two sons, but the marriage did not last. Both of her sons participated in World War II. One of her sons in the air force flew 182 missions over the Himalaya Mountains. The other son joined the Navy V-2 program. Both men returned safely.

But Hall realized that there was uneasiness in the world. It was as if the United States had gotten rid of one enemy and that they could not survive unless they found another to hate. Communism became that enemy. The nation seemed to lose all sanity as individual after individual, many in positions of great responsibility, reacted against the "threat" of communism. The Russians became the principal target with many signs "Better dead than red!" A national madness reached its peak when Sen. Joseph McCarthy led national hearings accusing many leading citizens of being communists or communist sympathizers.

> All organizations and groups that were openly working for peace became targets of the anti-Communist crusade, especially the fledgling United Nations. The UN, an organization of nations for maintenance of world peace, was structured at a conference in San Francisco in 1945.[4]

Fifty-one nations signed the new charter. The fear of communism became so great that Congress passed a law freeing the United States from

---

3   Vivian Castleberry, *Daughters of Dallas* (Dallas: Odenwald Press, 1994), 424.
4   Ibid., 428.

complying with the international laws that they had just recently passed. Cordye Hall read and studied what people were saying and insisted on working for peace and understanding. Hall then helped organize the Dallas United Nations Association. She served on the nominating committee to select its officers and helped persuade Sarah Hughes to become its first president.

By the end of World War II, many nations were in ruins, and the world yearned for peace.

Cordye Hall organized an informal committee that promoted the work of the new UN by writing Letters to the Editor in newspapers. Around the same time, attorneys Louise and Grier Raggio began speaking publicly in support of the UN. All of these people—Cordye Hall, the Raggios, and Sarah Hughes—were attacked.

Hall also took issue with the Facts Forum organization founded in 1951 by the immensely wealthy H. L. Hunt. Upon visiting his library, she found literature attacking her favorite organizations—the World Federalists and the United Nations. She confronted him, but he did not agree with her. She challenged the *Dallas Morning News* on May 11, 1953, when she read the first of three columns by H. L. Hunt promoting his anti-UN and scare tactics agenda. Eleanor Roosevelt cancelled her scheduled appearance in Dallas to appear on a Facts Forum program as a result of Hall sending her material about the organization.[5]

Hall supported the United World Federalists, the UN, and the United Nations Educational, Scientific and Cultural Organization (UNESCO). During the Vietnam War, she formed "a Dallas group of Another Mother for Peace, the principal protest group that women waged against the Vietnam War."[6] The nonprofit, nonpartisan association's "goal was to eliminate war as a means of settling disputes between nations, people and ideologies." She had one simple slogan: "War is not healthy for children and other living things."[7]

Cordye Hall never stopped working for world peace. She was always searching for a "solution other than war." She stated that women are a mighty force and that the "world had a way to settle disputes: The International Court of Justice, a court of law and a function of the United Nations." She said that the women of the world could change the direction

---

[5]   Ibid., 429.
[6]   Ibid., 431.
[7]   Ibid., 432.

and find a better way to solve the problems that created those deadly wars. If we "name the foul deed . . . and try to stop it, world peace will emanate from our homes with each of us teaching, living and respecting life."[8]

Cordye Hall had a part in helping to organize the 1988 International Women's Peace Conference, which Vivian Castleberry envisioned. The Peacemakers Steering Committee presided over the conference held at Southern Methodist University and included many leading peace activists in Dallas. Approximately two thousand women attended this event from twenty different countries.

Adlene Nathanson Harrison, 1923–

Another strong woman, Adlene Harrison, emerged as a leader in the late 1950s. Adlene was born to Russian parents who migrated to the United States and married in Dallas. Adlene stated that her mother never raised her voice and her father always spoke very quietly. But Harrison got the reputation of being outspoken early in life. She saw political events in the city of Dallas that she found extremely disturbing. She was determined not to let those who were powerful take advantage of those without power.

First Jewish woman Mayor of Dallas, 1976, still going strong

[8]   Ibid.

In 1957, "the city was teetering on the brink of great change—politically, economically and ethnically. Harrison became more and more involved in volunteer work in the community."[9] In 1963, Harrison was named to the City Plan Commission, a post she held for eight years. When she arrived at her first meeting of the commission, she was "told that the last woman who served on the commission always brought home-baked cookies." She said, "Gentleman, you have the wrong woman. I do not bake cookies. I'm here to help you take care of our city."[10] She wanted to be sensitive to the needs of children and women in Dallas and cared about family neighborhoods. She was proud of her legacy with the City Plan Commission. She felt that she had helped to create a climate conducive for neighborhood groups to organize.

Harrison was a Dallas City councilwoman from 1973–1977. She helped to implement the court ruling on schools (March 10, 1976) and also sponsored the first historic ordinance in Dallas for Swiss Avenue. She led the rezoning ordinance for Bryan Place that brought the first major living accommodations back to near the downtown. She also helped to create West End, the "mecca for upscale restaurants and favorite meeting places for young professionals."[11]

Harrison fought the longest for day care, stating that unless a city takes care of its children, it will eventually lose the struggle to upgrade all of its other resources. She continued to work for housing for the poor and limited income population. She spoke to the Dallas Chapter United Nations Association on this topic, and though she was never a member, she always supported it. She was present at the Dallas Memorial Auditorium Theater on the night of October 24, 1963, when right-wing socialite Cora Lacy Frederickson assaulted US ambassador to the United Nations Adlai Stevenson after his speech. Frederickson hit Stevenson on the head with a placard denouncing the UN and was arrested despite Stevenson failing to press charges.

In 1976, Harrison became the first female mayor of Dallas when Wes Wise resigned to run for Congress. As mayor pro tem of the Dallas City Council, she became mayor when Wise resigned. She served only until the end of the year when a new election was held for mayor.

Harrison unsuccessfully fought against the Comanche Peak Plant project, thinking it too expensive and unsafe. In 1977, she resigned from

---

[9]   Ibid., 436.
[10]   Ibid.
[11]   Ibid., 440.

city council when Jimmy Carter appointed her regional administrator of the US Environmental Protection Agency. She traveled to Arkansas many times in this capacity to work with young Bill Clinton, whom she admired as an intellectual.

Adlene Harrison earned many awards during her years of public service: the Zonta Award, the National Brotherhood and Humanitarian Award from the National Conference of Christians and Jews, the Dallas Historical Society Award for Excellence in Public Service, the Women's Center Women Helping Women Award, and honors from the Dallas Press Club, the Black Chamber of Commerce, and the American Jewish Committee.[12]

There were many crises, she says. The school desegregation case had the most potential for being volatile. But she had Jack Lowe Sr. to help her, and together they created the Magnet School System in the Dallas Independent School District. Harrison continued to work for more women in public office. She said she would always care about her city and would raise her voice to discipline it when she disapproves of the direction it is taking.[13]

Maura McNiel 1921–

Another Dallas woman, Maura McNiel, was involved in many human rights issues as they surfaced in the 1960s—equal opportunities for Native Americans, blacks and Hispanics, environmental issues, assistance to children and youth, voting rights, political campaigns, and numerous other groundbreaking activities. When the civil rights movement began, she devoted her time to desegregation of schools and worked through numerous organizations for issues that concerned her. She was on the board of both the Dallas Council on World Affairs and Pan American Round Table in the 1950s. She was a founder of Save Open Spaces and Block Partnership, and she served on the boards of Dallas United Nations Association, Domestic Violence Intervention Association, National Conference of Christians and Jews, Common Cause, and KERA-TV.

McNiel became her own person in 1968 when she signed up for a course at Northaven United Methodist Church called Explore: "The course involved helping a woman look seriously at her life and take control of it." McNiel was also deeply involved in her church, Midway Hills

---

12   Ibid.
13   Ibid., 441.

Christian, serving as a senior high Sunday school teacher, then as youth education director, and also as an elder on the church's board.

Maura McNiel became known as the mother of the women's liberation movement in Dallas.[14] As a result of all this involvement, McNiel helped organize a group called Women for Change in 1971. Judge Sarah T. Hughes was a part of this plan, along with Johnnie-Marie Grimes, a women's-issues advocate from First United Methodist Church. The organization grew rapidly, and at the second meeting, feminist Gloria Steinem spoke at Southern Methodist University. Women for Change eventually grew into the Women's Center of Dallas. Other groups grew out of this effort—the Family Place (a shelter for battered women and their children), the Dallas Women's Coalition, Women's Issues Network, the Dallas Women's Foundation, and the Summit. McNiel worked in more than fifty political campaigns. The mayor of Dallas named her to the first Dallas Commission on the Status of Women. In 1973, Maura McNiel was honored with the first Women Helping Women Award. In 1988, that award was renamed the Maura Award.[15]

Maura McNiel, DUNA Board and community organizer for women's and human rights, 1960s and 70s

<hr>

[14] Ibid., 352.
[15] Ibid., 357.

Oral interview with Maura McNiel at the *Tea and Conversations with Icons* reception at the home of Dr. Harryette Ehrhardt, Dallas, Texas, on March 13, 2016, celebrating National Women's History Month:

When I arrived at the tea, I was delighted to see that Maura McNiel had come from California as one of the honorees. This was my opportunity to ask her about her involvement in the Dallas Chapter United Nations Association. I knew that she was a member of the board of the UNA, along with being involved in other organizations, but it wasn't clear just how much she had worked in the Dallas UNA. She told me that she had been a member since the Dallas chapter began and that she had worked closely with Sarah T. Hughes and Louise Raggio to help start the chapter.

There was a strong group of involved women who were working during that time on women's issues—racial equality, child care opportunities for working women, creating a shelter for battered wives, and the desegregation of the schools. They were all members in such organizations as Women for Change, Save Open Spaces, and the United Nations Association.

Maura said that in 1975, about eight to ten women from the Dallas UNA attended the International Women's Year Conference in Mexico City, joining eight thousand women there from every country. The Dallas women were inspired by the feminists who were at the conference and the work that they were doing. They learned that there was much work to be done in the area of women's issues. We are grateful to Maura McNiel and all the women who gave so much time and energy to issues that have resulted in more freedom and better lives for women.[16]

The first world conference on the status of women was convened in Mexico City to coincide with the 1975 International Women's Year, observed to remind the international community that discrimination against women continued to be a persistent problem in much of the world.[17]

---

[16]   Norma Matthews, Oral Interview Maura McNiel at the Tea and Conversations with Icons Reception, March 13, 2016.

[17]   "1975 World Conference on Women, Mexico City, June 19–July 2, 1975," *5ᵗʰ Women's World Conference*, 2006, http://www.5wwc.org/conference_background/1975_WCW.html.

The Mexico City Conference was called for by the United Nations General Assembly to focus international attention on the need to develop future oriented goals, effective strategies and plans of action for the advancement of women. To this end, the General Assembly identified three key objectives that would become the basis for the work of the United Nations on behalf of women:

- Full gender equality and the elimination of gender discrimination;
- The integration and full participation of women in development;
- An increased contribution by women in the strengthening of world peace.

The Conference, along with the United Nations Decade for Women (1976–1985) proclaimed by the General Assembly five months later at the urging of the Conference, launched a new era in global efforts to promote the advancement of women by opening a worldwide dialogue on gender equality.[18]

Louise Raggio, 1919–2011

Louise and Grier Raggio moved to Dallas from South Texas in 1945 when Grier left the army. Grier, a handsome man of Italian descent, was a graduate of George Washington University School of Law. The couple had two children when Grier urged Louise to go to law school. Louise began night classes at SMU, but she was soon pregnant again with their third child. She rode her bicycle to class with the baby in a basket. Louise enrolled as a full-time student and graduated from SMU Law School in 1952. At that time, no jobs for female attorneys existed. During 1952 and 1953, she spent her time being active in her children's activities, taking part in the League of Women Voters, the Women's Alliance of the Unitarian Church, and "in giving birth to a Dallas Chapter of the United Nations Association." She met Judge Sarah T. Hughes during this period. Louise

---

[18] "First World Conference on Women (1975)," *United Nations System: Chief Executives Board for Coordination*, 2016, http://www.unsceb.org/content/first-world-conference-women-1975-0.

soon realized that Judge Hughes was the area's strongest advocate for women's rights. She became a "fellow traveler" with Sarah and often saw herself as Sarah's sidekick, at times even her errand girl.

Louise Raggio (center) is shown with friend and fellow women's rights pioneer Vivian Castleberry (left) and the late Texas Governor Ann Richards, at an SMU Raggio Lecture in 2003. Hillsman Davis, SMU photo.

Soon Louise and Grier became well-known as Dallas' "fringey liberals." They joined the Unitarian Church, and Louise found companionship among the intellectuals in the women's group. They were charter members of the Dallas United Nations Association. They joined the Young Democrats club where they met Sarah Hughes. In 1954, Sarah Hughes told Louise to apply for a job in District Attorney Henry Wade's office. Wade hired her to oversee the Juvenile Delinquency Department. She handled all domestic relations and soon gained a reputation as a family lawyer. In 1956, they opened their own law practice, Raggio & Raggio.[19]

Louise Raggio was a late participant in getting the ERA, Equal Rights Amendment, passed. Her early objections centered around delaying voting on the ERA until other statutes passed. Once those statutes were enacted, the ERA passed in 1971. Louise, along with Hermine Tobolowsky and

---

[19] Castleberry, *Daughters of Dallas*, 377.

Sarah T. Hughes, was one of the strong supporters. It became a part of the Texas constitution in 1972.[20]

In the 1970s, the governor of Texas created a Texas Commission on the Status of Women and named Sarah Hughes, Mary Kay Ash, Vivian Castleberry, and Louise Raggio as Dallas members. Even though a lot of the work was superficial, Louise said the group worked hard, and the Commission served as another opening wedge for women's rights.[21]

Louise chaired the Family Law Section of the State Bar Association that rewrote the marital property laws for Texas and, eventually, completely revised the Family Law Code.[22]

She became president of the Summit, which was established in 1989 "as a force in Dallas so that women become full participants in all decision-making processes to create a whole, just and abundant community."[23] She was a charter member of the Dallas Forum, an elite group of corporate executive women. She was elected a director of the State Bar Association and was the first woman to be a trustee of the Texas Bar Foundation. In 1983, she was named one of the twenty-two best family lawyers in America. Louise Raggio said she would do anything within the integrity of her profession to keep children from being harmed in divorce and custody battles. Louise Raggio was named the "Mother of Family Law in Texas."[24]

In 1988, friends and family established the Louise Ballerstedt Raggio Endowed Lecture Series in Women's Studies at Southern Methodist University. Her three sons and a grandson carry on the family law firm. Louise Raggio died on January 23, 2011. (SMU 2011 Archives Law School)

Johnnie Marie Grimes, 1905–1997

Not only was Johnnie Marie Grimes a prominent figure at SMU at mid-century, but also she volunteered tirelessly for women's rights and education. Born in Bellville, Texas, she believed in the value of a strong

---

[20]   Darwin Payne, *Indomitable Sarah: The Life of Judge Sarah T. Hughes* (Dallas, TX: Southern Methodist University Press, 2004), 403.

[21]   Louise Ballerstedt Raggio and Vivian Castleberry, *Texas Tornado* (New York: Citadel Press, 2003), TT.

[22]   Castleberry, *Daughters of Dallas*, 377.

[23]   Ibid.

[24]   Ibid.

educational foundation and received degrees from Southwestern University, Columbia University Teacher's College, and Union Theological Seminary in New York.

For twenty-two years, Johnnie Marie served as assistant to the president of Southern Methodist University, a position that gave her significant access to the developments of the growing university. She used her knowledge of the field of education to broaden the scope of her impact by serving on the Texas State Board of Education from the Fifth Congressional District. She also showed support for women's causes by serving for over two decades of duty in the local YWCA and on its board for most of those years. (SMU Archives online)

Johnnie Marie Grimes was an ardent supporter of the newly formed Dallas Chapter of the United Nations Association in 1953 and the years following. During those early years, there was a thriving anti-UN sentiment prevalent in the city. The organizers of the new Dallas UNA Chapter realized there was much work to be done.

> Bitter criticisms were being aired on a regular basis, and the new chapter now began countering them promptly at every opportunity. A committee headed by Cordye Hall sought to respond to each letter critical of the UN that appeared in the two daily newspapers.[25]

> The speakers bureau, headed by Johnnie Marie Grimes, secretary to the president of Southern Methodist University, sent letters to some five hundred civic, religious, and educational groups announcing the availability of individuals who could give factual talks about the UN and its work. This activity, Hughes (STH) believed, was the new organization's most important endeavor.[26]

---

[25] Payne, *Indomitable Sarah: The Life of Judge Sarah T. Hughes*, 173.
[26] Ibid.

Part B: Strong Dallas Community Advocates for UN
Raymond D. Nasher 1921–2007

- Vice president, Dallas UNA, 1957
- President, Dallas UNA, 1958
- Texas chair, American Association of United Nations, 1959
- Delegate to UN General Assembly, New York, during the LBJ administration
- President Texas Division UNA, 1963–1965
- Executive Director of White House Conference on International Cooperation Year, October 1964
- Member US Commission for UNESCO, 1962–1965
- Ambassador of Cultural Affairs, City of Dallas—appointed by Mayor Annette Strauss, 1988

Raymond Nasher was born October 26, 1921, and died on March 16, 2007. He was a native of Boston, an alumnus of Boston Latin School, and graduated from Duke University Phi Beta Kappa in 1943. After graduation, he worked for his father's apparel firm, opening new stores while attending night-school classes to complete a master's degree in economics from Boston University. He also did graduate study at Harvard's business school.[27]

When Nasher came to Texas, he was originally planning to work in the oil business, but soon he changed his mind in favor of real estate. He married a Dallas girl, Patsy Rabinowitz, and became interested in neighborhood and urban planning.

In the early 1960s, Nasher was responsible for founding NorthPark Center, the mall that began as the largest in Texas. At the time of its founding, it was the largest climate-controlled, indoor building in the world.[28]

Raymond Nasher became interested in the new United Nations Association Chapter in Dallas that had been organized in 1953. He became president of the Dallas Chapter UNA in 1958. He had served on the Board of Directors of the Dallas United Nations Association Chapter, along with

---

[27] "Raymond Nasher," *Wikipedia*, September 12, 2016, https://en.wikipedia. org/w/index.php?title=Raymond_Nasher&oldid=739067610.

[28] Ibid.

---

other Dallas leaders: Stanley Marcus, the head of Neiman Marcus; Jack Goren, vice president of Neiman Marcus who was later president of the Dallas Chapter UNA in 1963; and Edward B. Winn, a Dallas attorney who became president of the Dallas UNA in 1970. These leaders were among those who were attempting to educate the public about the aims, objectives, and organization of the United Nations. Anti-UN sentiment was growing in Dallas.[29]

During the LBJ administration, Raymond Nasher was appointed as a delegate to the General Assembly of the United Nations in New York. President Johnson soon asked him to serve as executive director of the White House Conference on International Cooperation Year in October 1964, a thinktank for urban development, a free exchange of ideas. Nasher also served as a member of the US Commission for UNESCO, a one-hundred-member group appointed by the secretary of state. (Nasher Archives)

Mr. Raymond Nasher, pivotal leader of DUNA and with national UNA-USA

---

[29]   Payne, *Indomitable Sarah: The Life of Judge Sarah T. Hughes*, 238.

Raymond Nasher was a dedicated United Nations supporter. Besides serving on the local board of the Dallas chapter, he was a Texas Division leader and served for several years on the national executive board of the UNA of the USA, a nongovernmental group whose purpose is to support the UN and educate Americans about its activities.

Raymond Nasher and his wife Patsy also had another passion. They were avid art collectors and became interested in sculpture. They built the Nasher Sculpture Center in downtown Dallas next door to the Dallas Museum of Art. It is one of the leading sculpture museums in the world, exchanging art pieces frequently with other important museums.[30]

Raymond Nasher was truly a citizen interested in city planning, urban development, art, and the world, serving society in so many capacities, and especially the work of the United Nations.

Judge Barefoot Sanders, 1925–2008

Harold Barefoot Sanders Jr. (February 5, 1925–September 21, 2008) was a longtime United States district judge and counsel to President Lyndon B. Johnson. He was best known for overseeing the lawsuit to desegregate the Dallas Independent School District. Judge Sanders was married to the former Jan Scurlock. They had four children and nine grandchildren.[31]

Sanders graduated from North Dallas High School in 1942. He served in the United States Navy during World War II between 1943 and 1946. While attending the University of Texas, Sanders was elected student body president in 1947. He received an AB degree from the University of Texas in 1949 and a JD in 1950 from the University of Texas School of Law.[32]

Sanders was a crucial behind-the-scenes facilitator for Judge Sarah T. Hughes, making hasty but capable arrangements for her to administer the presidential oath of office to Vice President Lyndon B. Johnson on Air Force One, less than three hours after the assassination of President John F. Kennedy on November 23, 1963.[33]

---

[30]   "Nasher Sculpture Center," *Wikipedia*, February 27, 2017, https://en.wikipedia. org/w/index.php?title=Nasher_Sculpture_Center&oldid=767703319.

[31]   "Barefoot Sanders," *Wikipedia*, November 14, 2016, https://en.wikipedia. org/w/index.php?title=Barefoot_Sanders&oldid=749559950.

[32]   Ibid.

[33]   Payne, *Indomitable Sarah: The Life of Judge Sarah T. Hughes*, 254.

On February 6, 1979, Sanders was nominated by President Jimmy Carter to the United States District Court for the Northern District of Texas and confirmed by the United States Senate on April 24, 1979. He served as chief judge of the Northern District of Texas from 1989 until 1995.[34]

Though Sanders handled thousands of civil and criminal cases during his tenure as a federal judge, he is best known in Texas for his role as judge in the Tasby litigation brought against the Dallas Independent School District in the 1970s, in which plaintiff Sam Tasby charged that the Dallas ISD was still a segregated school district.[35]

Sanders became a federal judge and took over the case until its conclusion in 2003, having oversight of many Dallas ISD activities related to racial balance until that time. Decades of oversight finally came to an end in June 2003, when he ruled that Dallas ISD was no longer subject to his oversight and was desegregated.[36]

During the summer of 2009, Sanders was honored by the Dallas ISD when the board of trustees renamed the Law Magnet at the Yvonne A. Ewell Townview Center to the Judge Barefoot Sanders Magnet Center for Public Service: Government, Law and Law Enforcement. His wife, Jan, a peace activist volunteer in the Dallas Peace Center and the Dallas United Nations Association, among other community interests, graciously accepted the accolades for her late husband.[37]

Judge Hughes entrusted her historic United Nations flag to Jan Sanders, who donated it to the archives of the Dallas UNA Chapter.

The Reverend Luther Holcomb, 1911–2015

The Reverend Luther Holcomb was among the small group that worked with Judge Sarah T. Hughes to form the Dallas Chapter of United Nations Association in 1953. Holcomb's public and behind-the-scenes work in Dallas during the 1950s and early 1960s helped Dallas achieve peaceful racial integration of its public schools, restaurants, and hotels and remove barriers to employment opportunities. He was a Southern Baptist

---

[34]   Ibid., 381.
[35]   "Barefoot Sanders."
[36]   Ibid.
[37]   Ibid.

minister who served several terms as executive secretary of the Greater Dallas Community of Churches.

Holcomb met Pres. John F. Kennedy at the Dallas Love Field Airport on Nov. 22, 1963, and later announced to the crowd waiting to hear him speak that Kennedy had been shot. Holcomb led the stunned audience in the Dallas Trade Mart in a moving prayer, opening with a verse from Psalms in the Bible, "Lord lead us to a rock."

Citing his work in Dallas, President Kennedy had appointed Holcomb to represent Texas on the US Civil Rights Commission in 1961. In 1965, President Lyndon B. Johnson named Holcomb vice chairman of the US Equal Employment Commission, then a new regulatory agency created to enforce the employment opportunity provisions of the Civil Rights Act of 1964. In 1970, President Richard M. Nixon reappointed him to a second term.

Luther Holcomb died on Oct. 1, 2015, at the age of seventy.[38]

Rabbi Levi A. Olan, 1903–1984, President of Dallas UNA 1960

Rabbi Levi Olan of Temple Emanu-El was elected the new president of the Dallas United Nations Association in June 1960. Other officers included Mrs. Johnnie Marie Grimes; Douglas Jackson; Mrs. Taylor Robinson; Mrs. Marion B. Richmond; and Norman Freeman.[39]

Levi Arthur Olan was born Lemel Olanovsky on March 22, 1903, in a small village near Kiev, Ukraine. He, along with his father and mother, left Russia for the United States to escape the impending revolution sparked by the persecutions of Czar Nicholas II. As was the custom of the time, the Olanovsky name was changed to Olan at the suggestion of immigration officials. The family settled in Rochester, New York.[40]

Levi graduated from Rochester High School in New York and eventually went to the University of Cincinnati and simultaneously attended classes at the Hebrew Union College to pursue rabbinic studies.

---

38 Hyfler/Rosner, "The Rev. Luther Holcomb; Met JFK at Dallas Airport," Google Groups, *Alt.obituaries*, (November 20, 2003), https://groups.google.com/forum/#!topic/alt.obituaries/pTlVMDuVAFM.

39 *Dallas Morning News*, 6/10/1960, Dallas Morning News Historical Archives.

40 Melvin H. Weinberg, "Rabbi Levi A. Olan (An Untired Liberal)" (Spertus Institute for Jewish Learning and Leadership, 2015).

It was during this period that he was influenced to make a commitment to social justice and to his responsibilities as a Jew and to the Reform Movement. Olan graduated from the University of Cincinnati in 1925 and was ordained by the Hebrew Union College in 1929.

Rabbi Olan served two congregations during his lifetime—the first in Worcester, Massachusetts, from 1929–1949, and the second at Temple Emanu-El in Dallas, Texas, 1949–1970. Levi Olan was married to Sarita Messer in 1931. Many scholars recognized Rabbi Olan's great intellect and his ability as a public speaker. Olan continually preached "on the relationship of religion to key societal issues—poverty, segregation and race relations, ignorance, unemployment, education, housing, the elderly, disease, and such global issues as the potential for nuclear holocaust." He opposed McCarthyism, anti-Semitism, and racism "as he championed federal public housing and the integration of public schools. In his depiction of America as the land of plenty, he continually spoke out against the want and desperation of societies' less-privileged classes."[41]

As an outspoken preacher and public speaker, Olan's presence was continually in demand in both religious and civic functions. He was a visiting professor at Perkins School of Theology of Southern Methodist University in Dallas, the University of Texas at Arlington, the University of Texas at Austin, Emory University in Atlanta, and Leo Baeck College in London, and a visiting lecturer at Texas Christian University in Fort Worth. He was also president of the Central Conference of American Rabbis. The respected rabbi had a secluded area in Bridwell Library at SMU's Perkins School of Theology, his "hideaway" for study, where he participated in a regular gathering of religious thinkers. Olan became known as the "conscience of clergy in Dallas" and also "the conscience of the city" during the time "when liberal voices were depressingly scarce."[42]

It was during the period in the early 1960s when Rabbi Olan was chosen to lead the Dallas United Nations Association. In June 1960, he spoke to the UN Association meeting in Selecman Hall at SMU and declared that American foreign policy was "behind the times." He outlined a three-point program to improve foreign policy: what we do domestically is part of foreign policy, use US wealth to build a free economic community, and pursue a multilateral rather than a unilateral policy. He added that

41   Ibid.
42   Ibid.

with NATO, we have "the most successful of operations from a military standpoint."[43] It was reported that Rabbi Olan spoke at a meeting at SMU in 1963 on the topic "Universal Declaration of Human Rights by the United Nations," obviously referring to the well-known document that Eleanor Roosevelt helped create and adopted by the United Nations in 1948[44] *(DMN* 11-14-63).

At the time of Rabbi Olan's death, Dr. Albert C. Outler, professor emeritus at SMU, stated,

> Rabbi Olan was one of the most remarkable combinations of a genuine intellect and a deeply spiritual man. He had a wonderful way of keeping things in perspective, uplifting the downtrodden and redressing the balances of people who got out of line . . . Olan was an outspoken advocate of equality and humanity who struggled to correct the ills he felt society had inflicted upon those least able to fight back.[45] *(DMN,* 10-18-84)

Rabbi Olan died at age eighty-one, after having served Temple Emanu-El for twenty years. He continued to be a staunch supporter of the Dallas United Nations Association through his entire life.

Stanley Marcus, 1905–2002
Dallas Internationalist and UNA Activist

Stanley Marcus was one of the most respected citizens of Dallas during his business years in Dallas as an early president and later chairman of the board of the luxury retail store, Neiman Marcus, in Dallas, Texas. He was a published author and also wrote a regular column in the *Dallas Morning News.* In the 1960s, Marcus was an early supporter of the United Nations and the Dallas UNA Chapter. "In his 1953 work *Neiman-Marcus, Texas,* Frank

---

[43] *The Dallas Morning News,* 6/10/1960, The Dallas Morning News Historical Archives.

[44] Ibid.*The Dallas Morning News,* 11/14/1963, The Dallas Morning News Historical Archives.

[45] Ibid.,*The Dallas Morning News,* 10/18/1984, The Dallas Morning News Historical Archives.

X. Tolbert called Marcus Dallas' most internationally famous citizen and worthy of being called 'the Southwest's No. 1 businessman-intellectual.'"[46]

Every time Stanley Marcus flew into Dallas' Love Field, he felt like he was an ambassador returning home. He saw the tall downtown buildings spread out on the prairie. He knew that his famous store, Neiman Marcus, was the most visible symbol of globalism in the city. He was proud of the fact that he felt that he had a large part in bringing the United Nations' "culture" to Dallas. He funded major art exhibitions and brought the finest things from Europe and Asia to his store.[47]

At Neiman Marcus, he also created an extravagant October festival devoted to the world's cultures. Known as the "Fortnight," the two-week exposition highlighted a particular country or region chosen specifically by Marcus. He was convinced that this business of the "Fortnight" was "nourishing Dallas' soul, making the city realize that the things from the outside, from the other worlds, are not so threatening. It is enlightened self-interest—it is good for Marcus and it is good for Dallas."[48]

> It was profitable, and the city, in turn, is made more hospitable, more open, and more tolerant. In the end, if it helps to tamp down the wicked extremism—the swastikas, the cross burnings, the almost knee-jerk hatred of Dr. King and President Kennedy and the United Nations—it is all good for the city.[49]

> It is no coincidence that he plans this year's (1963) extravaganza to overlap with the annual commemoration of United Nations Day. October 24 recognizes the founding of the international body in 1948 [sic]. Despite the anti-United Nations resistance emanating from the *Dallas Morning News*, Alger, Walker, Criswell, and Hunt (Bruce Alger, General Edwin Walker, Dr. W. A. Criswell, and H. L. Hunt), many people in Dallas have

---

[46] "Stanley Marcus," *Wikipedia*, February 18, 2017, https://en.wikipedia.org/w/index.php?title=Stanley_Marcus&oldid=766135689.

[47] Bill Minutaglio and Steven L. Davis, *Dallas 1963* (New York: Twelve Hachette Book Group, 2013), 229.

[48] Ibid.

[49] Ibid.

been early and enthusiastic adopters of UN Day—and for years several civic organizations have tried to highlight UN contributions to world peace.[50]

Marcus often told people to remember World War II and to think of the United Nations as a bulwark for peace. He would proclaim that "the best tool that I know of to prevent an outbreak of World War III" is the United Nations.[51]

Marcus was a member of the Dallas Council on World Affairs, and through this connection brought hundreds of foreign dignitaries to Dallas over the last ten years. Many would agree that Stanley Marcus was Dallas' most prominent internationalist. And yet, he was the "one high-profile figure in the city who fears his home is too often consumed by xenophobia."[52]

On the morning of October 24, 1963, Stanley Marcus met Adlai Stevenson, the US ambassador to the United Nations, at Love Field. Stevenson had been invited by Stanley Marcus and the other Jewish leaders at his store to be the speaker at the annual United Nations Day event at the Dallas Memorial Auditorium that night.[53]

Adlai Stevenson attended a luncheon in his honor at the Sheraton and toured Neiman Marcus and the Dallas Press Club. As he stepped out of an elevator, he heard a derisive voice calling after him: "What the hell's the United Nations for, anyway?" He looked to the sky and saw a large banner trailing behind a plane, proclaiming *"Get U.S. Out of UN."* Marcus's people sent a security man back to the police chief to ask for more protection.[54]

As the evening began at the auditorium, anxious groups of UN supporters mixed uneasily with anti-UN supporters of Larrie Schmidt and General Edwin Walker. People jostled through the lobby, and suddenly a man yelled out, "Nazis!" This is precisely what Larrie Schmidt was hoping for. He planned the political theater to make his groups look like martyrs. "He wants news to emerge that pro-United Nations goons are bullying his peaceful, reasonable picketers in Dallas."[55]

---

[50]   Ibid.

[51]   Ibid.

[52]   Ibid., 228.

[53]   Ibid., 233.

[54]   Ibid., 242–43.

[55]   Ibid., 244.

Stanley Marcus's role was to introduce Stevenson in the midst of a cacophony of boos and catcalls from the picketers. Frank McGehee, organizer of the National Indignation Convention, kept rising from his seat and screaming out questions to Stevenson asking why Stevenson insisted on negotiating with communist dictators. McGehee was ushered out of the auditorium by the police. It was an ugly evening. Stevenson issued a parting shot to McGehee: "For my part, I believe in the forgiveness of sin and the redemption of ignorance." At the end of the event, one of the protesters hit Adlai Stevenson on the head with a large sign she was carrying: "Adlai, Who Elected You?"[56]

Adlai Stevenson departed early the next day from Dallas. After he landed in Los Angeles, Stevenson spoke about the Dallas incident: "I'm glad to be here at all, especially alive, indeed not even wounded." He stated that there were far more supporters in Dallas than the crowd that assaulted him. Stevenson remained gracious and complimentary toward his hosts in Dallas even though the "problem was the violent behavior of a few."[57]

Marcus was a world traveler, and he served on a prominent national committee in support of the United Nations. He was the state chair for the United Nations Day Committee in Texas in 1963. One of his highest-ranking employees was president of the Dallas United Nations Association, Jack Goren. Marcus was a fierce admirer of Adlai Stevenson, the US ambassador to the United Nations.[58] He remained a fervent supporter of the United Nations even though it was an unpopular position in Dallas in the 1950s and 1960s.[59]

---

[56]   Ibid., 243–44, 247.

[57]   Ibid., 250.

[58]   Ibid., 228.

[59]   "Stanley Marcus."

Jack Goren, President Dallas UNA 1963
President Texas Division UNA 1965

Vision: UN for World Peace

DUNA president Jack Goren, 1963

The composed Main Street executive listened politely while an irate matron in a large purple hat slammed him with a barrage of words and gestures criticizing the United Nations. With a subtle professional air toned to Neiman Marcus luster, Jack Goren thrust home his one reply: "And what, ma'am, is the alternative?" That is his probing query of anyone who wished to abolish the United Nations. Until someone found a working alternative to the United Nations, Jack Goren pledged to work relentlessly for it. "The United Nations is one of the major instruments for peace in this world," he said. "It gives the United States a vehicle for world leadership. We cannot abdicate from our role as guide to the small independent countries. The United Nations must survive."[60]

Concise dedication like that moved Goren to the helm of the Dallas United Nations Association. He succeeded federal judge Sarah T. Hughes to the presidency of the Dallas UNA in March 1963.

Goren's concern for world affairs stemmed from a childhood in San Angelo, Texas. As a youth, he was active in all-boy-type pursuits, but he soon became increasingly more interested in public speaking, debating, and then politics. An enterprising spirit arose, and during the Depression, he had a series of part-time jobs. He worked his way through the University of Texas pursuing a dream of becoming a political science professor.

Later on, he realized that his dream was impractical. Goren left his university life for work in public relations in New York, next in Sakowitz in Houston, and for the next thirteen years with Neiman Marcus, where he became a vice president. Meanwhile, he blended his mercantile work with his political and international interests.

Goren was southwest regional president of the Institute of Human Relations. Through this organization and its famous humanities library in New York, Goren was able to reach world leaders and educators, making documents of democratic processes and the American way available to many more than a classroom.

Through the American Jewish Committee (of which he was also southwest regional president), he added more work in the field of human relations. The Dallas Council on World Affairs, the Dallas Symphony, Dallas Museum of Fine Arts, Dallas Museum of Contemporary Arts, the Dallas Civic Ballet were all outlets he utilized for educating people and simultaneously raising a city's standards.[61]

---

[60]   Ann Adams Melvin, "Headliner Portrait: Jack Goren," *Dallas Morning News*, March 24, 1963, Dallas Morning News Archives.

[61]   Ibid.

Leadership through DUNA

As president of the Dallas United Nations Association, Goren believed he had found an immediate vehicle with which to educate an entire city on the full scope of world affairs. In Dallas, that was quite a job, and he was the first to admit it.

When Goren was elected, he stated,

> There is a very adverse climate of understanding toward the United Nations in Dallas and throughout the United States. We must improve it. I am concerned that while there is constructive criticism of the United Nations, Dallas seems to be the lair of destructive criticism aimed at the UN. This city is completely out of tune with the rest of the United States. It is almost as if ardent partisans did not realize the United Nations is a bi-partisan product, begun and supported by both the Republicans and Democratic parties. Why people will tell you the United Nations should be done away with! What do they offer to put in its place?[62]

Host during Critical Times

Jack Goren was president of the Dallas Chapter UNA at the time of the Adlai Stevenson incident in 1963. John Goren, Jack's son, stated that his father was the host of Adlai Stevenson at the UN Day event in Dallas Memorial Auditorium on October 24, 1963. John reported that there were a lot of John Birch members and Gen. Edwin Walker followers in attendance that night. The crowd became boisterous, and John said at one time at one of these meetings while Adlai was here, his father grabbed him and put him behind him to protect the son.

John also told me that during that week, police were stationed in front of the Goren home. There was great fear of violence. John told me that his dad made Adlai Stevenson promise to tell Pres. John F. Kennedy not to come to Dallas. "This was never reported," he said, but he knew it was

---

[62]   Ibid.

true. As we all know now, President Kennedy came to Dallas the next month and was assassinated.

The evening of October 24, 1963, Adlai Stevenson gave the young Goren boy a special gift, a PT109 tie clip. The tie clip was named for the ship that Kennedy commanded in World War II. The souvenir became a famous item and was much in demand.[63]

Goren believed a more mature sophistication was needed to cope with the problems that were shown in extreme Dallas sentiment. He responded,

> I agree . . . it is a shame we cannot wish away Red China, Russia. But that is the crux of the matter. They are here. We will never wish away this great ideological conflict. What we must do then is stay in the fight for democracy.[64]

> Goren was concerned that opponents of the UN attack it as being un-national.

> Who would be left to lead the independent countries to our democratic ways if we abdicate? The history of the United Nations is proof overwhelming that on a majority of matters other nations have been impressed with our methods, our democracy—for on the majority of basic conflicts they have voted with the West, with us. And it is there, where other nations can see us work, in the United Nations, that the world will be won.[65]

---

63 John Goren, Oral Interview with John Goren, Dallas, Texas, May 8, 2015.

64 Melvin, "Headliner Portrait: Jack Goren."

65 Melvin, "Headliner Portrait: Jack Goren."

Edward B. Winn, 1920–2007
President of Dallas Chapter UNA 1966, 1970, 1978

Attorney Edward B. Winn, DUNA Board president

Edward B. Winn was born September 23, 1920, and died on March 11, 2007, at the age of eighty-six. He was a lifelong resident of Dallas and graduated from Woodrow Wilson High School, the University of Texas, and Yale University's School of Law. After graduating from the University of Texas in 1942, Ed went off to the war and became a lieutenant and LST commander in the navy, participating in all the major seaborne landing assaults in the European theater. He was commended for bravery.[66]

Ed married Conchita Hassell in 1945. He was enrolled in Yale Law School, and Conchita was completing her PhD in Hispanic literature from Columbia University. After graduation, they moved to Dallas and eventually had five sons, including two sets of twins.[67] After WWII, Ed remained in the US Naval Reserve for many years and served on the staff of Lyndon Johnson's US Senate Armed Forces Preparedness Subcommittee.[68]

Jan Sanders, the wife of Judge Barefoot Sanders, was a friend of the family during the growing-up period of the five boys. Jan said she observed

---

[66] "Obituary," *Dallas Morning News*, March 14, 2007.

[67] Ibid.

[68] "Edward Winn Obituary - Dallas, TX | Dallas Morning News," accessed June 18, 2017, http://www.legacy.com/obituaries/dallasmorningnews/obituary.aspx?pid=86788108.

a good parenting model and was always impressed with how the Winn family provided many enrichment activities for their sons—activities that led to their being "world citizens" at a young age.[69]

Ed Winn was an "ebullient, optimistic man who cared for justice and earned the love and respect of all who knew him."[70] He served as president and director of the Dallas United Nations Association and also on the board of governors of the United Nations Association of America (UNAA). He was a lifelong Kennedy Democrat and served the Democratic Party in several capacities. Beginning in 1948, he was actively involved in the practice of law in Dallas and became a leader in the legal profession. He served the State Bar of Texas, Texas Young Lawyers Association, Dallas Bar Association, and as president of the Dallas Junior Bar Association.

> He served the Southwestern Legal foundation in Dallas, now known as The Center for American and International Law . . . He was a partner in the law firm of Winn, Beaudry & Winn LLP until his retirement . . . He enjoyed life, people, his work, his family, public service, travel, good conversation, Democratic politics and SMU football.[71]

Darwin Payne, the Dallas historian, lists Ed Winn as one of the prominent Dallasites who actively supported the work of the Dallas United Nations Association, along with the national United Nations. Others listed were Stanley Marcus, retailer; Raymond Nasher, developer; Reverend Baxton Bryant, a liberal Methodist minister; and Gerald C. Mann, former Texas attorney general, a football hero of SMU in the 1930s and a friend of Sarah T. Hughes since her days in the Texas legislature.[72]

Attorney Winn was elected president of the Dallas United Nations Association for the first time in April 1966. Other officers were Robert L. Lichten; Mrs. Herbert Wincorn; Philip Vogel; and Mrs. H.Y. Benedict. New board members as reported by the *Dallas Morning News* were Malcolm

---

[69]   Jan Sanders, Conversation with Jan Sanders, Widow of Judge Barefoot Sanders. Northaven United Methodist Church, Dallas, Texas, Spring 2015.

[70]   "Edward Winn Obituary - Dallas, TX | Dallas Morning News."

[71]   Ibid.

[72]   Payne, *Indomitable Sarah: The Life of Judge Sarah T. Hughes*, 238. Payne identifies Bryant as Baptist, but Methodist official papers correctly identify him as Methodist.

J. Brachman; Mrs. Sam Corfman Jr.; Richard Galland; the Reverend Zan W. Holmes Jr.; William A. Jenkins Jr.; George T. Lee Jr.; Mrs. Colin T. MacDonald; and Jack P. Pierce.[73]

Reverend Baxton Bryant

Interview with DUNA Activist Reverend Baxton Bryant 1919–1996 Eyewitness Account about JFK Assassination, Dallas, Nov. 22, 1963[74]

My Interview w/Rev. Baxton Bryant & Family
alt.conspiracy.jfk – no...@webtv.net
1/5/04 – 1 post by 1 author identified only as "Bob."

Dallas activist, Rev. Baxton Bryant, greeted the Kennedys,
arriving at Love Field on Nov 3, 1963

I will write some of the highlights of my interview with Rev. Baxton Bryant and his family beginning September 12, 1989. I spent several days and hours with them. It would be very difficult and time consuming to print the interviews in their entirety.

---

[73]   n.d., no. 4/17/1966.
[74]   n***@webtv.net, "My Interview W/Rev. Baxton Bryant & Family," *NARKIVE: Newsgroup Archive*, January 6, 2004, http://alt.assassination.jfk. narkive.com/cMGKabE0/my-interview-w-rev-baxton-bryant-family#post1.

Rev. Bryant did shake hands with JFK at Love Field. The family gave me the picture of that moment. The family has no interest in the Kennedy case. Baxton Bryant died January 21, 1996, and is buried near his 400-acre farm in Western N.C.

He was quite a character. He wore a long, gray beard and a sweat stained straw hat and did use some language I have never heard before from a minister. He was pretty cool.

Bob—Mr. Bryant, can you tell me about some of your background?

Baxton Bryant—Well, first of all let me show you some things. Just follow me. We entered his huge cabin and he pointed to several pictures hanging on his wall. Most all of the pictures were autographed. One was President Harry Truman and Bryant, one was JFK and Bryant, one was LBJ and Bryant. Several others included Sam Rayburn and other U.S. dignitaries. Bryant then handed me a small yellow book. He told me that Penn Jones had given it to him several years ago. It was an original copy of "Forgive My Grief," Volume I.

Baxton Bryant—Ok, let's go back out on the porch. Getting back to that question. I'm now 70 years old. I was born July 10, 1919, in Texarkana, Arkansas. My father was a dairy farmer and logger. In the early 40's I attended Southern Methodist University and earned my degree in theology. I was in my ministry for almost 5 years when the war began so I enlisted in the Navy as a radar operator and served aboard the USS Dennis J. Buckley.

After my time in the Navy, I attended Henderson State Teachers College and majored in History. Two weeks after graduation from Henderson I took a job as a Minister in Bonham, Texas. I lived close to Sam Rayburn, and we would sit on his porch and talk for hours at a time.

On one occasion Rayburn invited President Harry Truman to Bonham. Truman accepted and met with the Bonham political group. I attended, and after meeting Truman, I was sold.

In 1957 we pulled up our roots and moved to Dallas, Texas. I took a full-time minister position at the Elmwood Methodist Church. It was located at 1315 Beckley Ave, there in Oak Cliff. That first year in Dallas, I helped form a coalition group called the Loyal Liberal Labor Minority of Dallas Democrats. I was elected Chairman and held that office for several years.

In 1960 I acquired a 20-minute spot on a local TV station KXIL and gave a speech called "A Plea For American Fair Play." Baxton's family later gave me the original copy of the speech that he had written and read. That same year I was asked by Sam Rayburn, to come to Washington as guest Chaplain in the Senate. My office was part of Speaker Sam Rayburn's office. My first time as Chaplain, I was introduced by Richard Nixon. I also met JFK the same day. When I would talk to Kennedy, he would look you straight in the eyes as to absorb every single word that was spoken to him.

In 1962 I ran for Congress and took a one-year sabbatical. Out of 100,000 votes cast, I lost by 367 votes. I had my campaign headquarters set up in the Adolphus Hotel. Jack Ruby came in several times for coffee.

Zoe Bryant—(Baxton's daughter) Guess who his secretary was? Ann Richards. (Zoe then showed me a picture of Bryant standing in front of his campaign headquarters)

Zoe Bryant—I went with my father, along with my sister Phala, to Love Field to see President Kennedy. We arrived at about 8:30 that morning. I was 16. We took some lady with us who was in a wheelchair.

Baxton Bryant—When I was shaking hands with Kennedy he asked me if I was going to the Trade Mart. I told him yes, that Senator Yarborough had given us tickets (The family still has the tickets which are framed.).

Lacrisha Bryant—(Baxton's daughter) I went ahead of the family and was at the Trade Mart. I worked at the Court House and rode with a Judge to the Trade Mart. They announced that Kennedy had been shot, on a loudspeaker.

Bob—Mr. Bryant. Can you tell me about where you were on November 22, 1963?

Bryant—Kennedy came to Dallas to raise money from the fat cats. I sent a telegram to the White House warning him of the dangers and requested a meeting with him while in Dallas. I finally called Kennedy at the White House and talked with him. He guaranteed that he would meet us at the airport, Love Field. I stayed up all night making the signs for the young grassroots Democrats. I hauled them to the airport in the back of my car.

Zoe Bryant—I had already got into our car ready to go to the Trade Mart when people started talking about Kennedy being shot. I could hear people screaming and it sounded like someone dropping dishes in the airport snack shop. My father got into the car and turned on the radio where they announced that Kennedy had been shot. My father started crying. The last thing I remember about that was my father was being yelled at by a Dallas motorcycle police officer for driving in circles in the parking lot.

Bob—What did you think about the Warren Commission conclusion and do you agree that Oswald acted alone?

Baxton Bryant—I think a lot of things were not followed up. I think it's a poor job for the caliber of men doing it. There are plenty of people in Dallas that would have had to do it, whether they did or not, I don't know.

Bob—Do you believe that Lyndon Johnson had anything to do with JFK's death?

Baxton Bryant—I have no idea.

Beatrice Bryant—(Baxton's wife) I was on Main St. in front of the Sanger Harris store watching the motorcade. I heard only two shots.

Annette (Mrs. Ted) Strauss, 1924–1998
President, Dallas UNA 1973

Mayor Annette Strauss, second woman elected DUNA president, 1973

Annette Strauss served in 1973 for one year as president of the Dallas Chapter of United Nations Association USA, only the second woman to be elected to this post after Judge Sarah T. Hughes had served almost twenty years before.

Strauss immersed herself in volunteer work in the Dallas community, serving on the boards of countless educational, arts, healthcare, and social services organizations. Her efforts at fund-raising in the midsixties made her known as the only alternative at that time for what one article refers to as "driven Dallas women."[75]

> In her first of two, two-year terms as the first elected woman mayor of Dallas, which began in 1987, a Congressional committee held hearings on police shootings of civilians,

[75] "The Annette Strauss Legacy," *Moody College of Communication*, accessed March 12, 2017, http://moody.utexas.edu/strauss/annette-strauss-legacy.

five police officers were killed, the Federal Bureau of Investigation released unsettling figures about Dallas crime and a community group strongly criticized the city on race relations. Mrs. Strauss also presided over the turbulent and racially divisive realignment of the City Council into single-member districts. "I'm not so sure that without her grace and compassion that Dallas would've survived that period of time," Mayor Ron Kirk said. Mrs. Strauss might be best remembered for her interest in the arts, including helping to get the Morton H. Meyerson Symphony Center built.[76]

Born and reared in Houston, she was the daughter of an insurance executive who lost a fortune in the Depression. Mrs. Strauss received Phi Beta Kappa honors at the University of Texas at Austin, where she was also a Ping-Pong champion. She received a master's degree in sociology at Columbia University. While in New York she met Ted Strauss and, after marrying, they moved to Dallas in the 1940's.[77]

Mrs. Strauss quickly became adept at raising money for institutions like the Dallas Symphony Orchestra, Southern Methodist University, the United Way, the United Jewish Appeal and others. She estimated that she raised more than $9 million for various groups.[78]

In the 1970's, Mrs. Strauss served on city boards dealing with parks, libraries, recreation and movie ratings, then won a seat on the City Council in 1983, where she acquired a reputation for working both with business leaders and community groups. In 1987, Mrs. Strauss scored a major upset by winning the mayor's office over a heavily favored opponent who had the support of four former mayors and

---

[76] The Associated Press, "Annette Strauss, 74, Former Mayor of Dallas," *The New York Times*, December 21, 1998, http://www.nytimes.com/1998/12/21/us/annette-strauss-74-former-mayor-of-dallas.html.

[77] Ibid.

[78] Ibid.

many in the city's business establishment. She continued to be active on state and local boards until 1998 (sic).[79]

Just this month, the City Council renamed Artist Square, an outdoor performance venue in the downtown arts district, as the Annette Strauss Artist Square. Annette Strauss, who as the only woman to be elected Mayor of Dallas oversaw one of the rockiest periods in the city's recent history, died at her home in Dallas on Dec. 14, 1998 (sic). She was 74.[80]

Mrs. Strauss died five months after surgery for a malignant brain tumor. In addition to her husband, Mrs. Strauss is survived by two daughters, Nancy Halbreich and Janie McGarr, both of Dallas.[81]

Pearl L. Wincorn, DUNA Volunteer, 1981–1986

Pearl Wincorn appeared in DUNA records many times, the first in 1981, with her election to the board as vice president of program and hosting the meeting at her home. Several outstanding programs were reported in the chapter minutes in following months. She was named to the nominating committee in 1982.

Pearl's DUNA service was highlighted publicly "on the Board of the U. N. Association of Dallas . . . where for many years she directed a youth workshop." Evidently, she was also a frequent speaker to community groups on topics of environmental and foreign policy issues. Her service had earlier centered on her ongoing fight for human rights, taking active part in the civil rights movement in the 1960s.

She hosted a *Great Decisions* group, a DUNA feature for several years, for six months in 1983 and a reception for the UN Day speaker, the Honorable Robert Ratner, in April 1983. Her name also appears in board minutes in 1984, 1985, and 1986.

Born in New York City on May 5, 1908, Pearl Wincorn graduated from New York University with a bachelor's degree in economics. As a reporter

---

[79]   Ibid.

[80]   Ibid.

[81]   Ibid.

for the *New York Journal of Commerce* during World War II, she covered the Office of Price Administration and the War Production Board, among other things.

She and her family moved to Dallas in 1946, where they were active members of the First Unitarian Church of Dallas. She was the first female member of the Dallas Transit Board from 1974–77 and also served on the board of the Visiting Nurse Association and as president of the League of Women Voters of Dallas, 1977–79. The memorial celebration of her life was held at her church on August 12, 2002.[82]

Robert Muller 1923–2010, International Civil Servant

Robert G. Muller, UN Assistant Secretary General, 1971

---

[82] "Pearl Lichtenberg Wincorn's Obituary on Dallas Morning News," *Dallas Morning News*, accessed March 13, 2017, http://www.legacy.com/obituaries/dallasmorningnews/obituary.aspx?n=pearl-lichtenberg-wincorn&pid=425875.

Robert Muller was born in Belgium in 1923 and raised in the Alsace-Lorraine region in France; he experienced constant political and cultural turmoil during his youth.

Dr. Muller devoted years of his life behind the scenes at the United Nations focusing his energies on world peace. He rose through the ranks at the UN to the official position of assistant secretary general.

Robert Muller was a deeply spiritual person. From his vantage point of a top-level global statesperson, he saw a strong connection between spirituality and the political/cultural scene. He created a "World Core Curriculum" and is known throughout the world as the "father of global education." More than thirty Robert Muller schools were founded throughout the world, including the Dallas Fort Worth area, the first organizer and sponsor of GEMUN, the Global Elementary Model United Nations events.

He received the UNESCO Peace Education Prize in 1989. He was a candidate as a global citizen in 1996 for the post of secretary general of the United Nations.

In active "retirement," Dr. Muller was chancellor of the University for Peace created by the United Nations in demilitarized Costa Rica. He was the recipient of the Albert Schweitzer International Prize for the Humanities and the Eleanor Roosevelt Man of Vision Award. He had published his Testament to the UN as well as his plans and dreams for a peaceful, happy world.

Robert Muller died September 20, 2010.[83]

Barack Obama Inspired, US Senator (D-IL) 2006

Reading his book *The Audacity of Hope*, written before his two terms as president of the United States, one resonates with his inspiring tribute to the spirit of the American people at their best, in face of daunting multifaceted challenges within the expanding ethos of the so-called "global village," vividly represented by the United Nations.

In the epilogue, he reflects on the audacity to believe despite all the evidence to the contrary that we could

---

[83]   "Robert Muller," *Wikipedia*, December 17, 2016, https://en.wikipedia.org/w/index.php?title=Robert_Muller&oldid=755403177.

---

restore a sense of community to a nation torn by conflict; the gall to believe that despite personal setbacks . . . we had some control—and therefore responsibility—over our own fate.[84]

He closes with a stirring citation:

like Lincoln and King, who ultimately laid down their lives in the service of perfecting an imperfect union . . . and all the faceless, nameless men and women, slaves and soldiers and tailors and butchers, constructing lives for themselves and their children and grandchildren, brick by brick, rail by rail, calloused hand by calloused hand, to fill in the landscape of our collective dreams.[85]

President Obama supported the UN during his presidency, 2008-2016, despite frequent adversarial resistance. He was awarded the Nobel Peace Prize in 2009.[86]

Clearly it was that same positive resolve that had emboldened DUNA, the Dallas Chapter of the United Nations Association, to be formed and which sustained its development over a long and enduring history. Powerfully, this had also been furthered by the vision of the 1948 Universal Declaration of Human Rights, extended to all the peoples of the world with no exceptions.

Part C: Antagonists to the UN in Dallas Area

From Authors' Note (Minutaglio & Davis):
Our book begins in early 1960 and ends in late 1963 . . . *Dallas 1963* is an exploration of how fear and unease can take root, how suspicions can emerge in a seemingly orderly universe. How, as Flannery O'Connor wrote,

[84] Barack Obama, *The Audacity of Hope* (Vintage Books, Random House, Inc., 2006), 421.
[85] Ibid., 427.
[86] "Barack Obama," *Biography*, accessed March 13, 2017, http://www.biography.com/people/barack-obama-12782369.

Everything That Rises Must Converge. How no one—
including a doomed president—could have understood
the full measure of the swirling forces at work in a place
called Dallas.

—Bill Minutaglio & Steven L. Davis, Texas, 2013
Used by Permission (in front matter)

In the late 1950s there was a great feeling of unease in Dallas. Citizens
were worried about the U.S. losing Cuba to the communists, atomic
weapons, Soviet rockets to the moon, civil rights protesters, Red China,
the Supreme Court ordering Dallas to integrate its schools, and the general
threat of communism to the United States.

In key corners of the city, an urgent confederacy of
persuasive, often powerful men is forming. Ministers,
publishers, congressmen, generals, and oilmen are
meeting—at first informally, and then by clear design—
and coming to the same conclusions: Dallas and America
are in danger.[87]

There is agreement that the "East Coast liberals, the big-city Catholics,
and the government-loving socialists are sapping the faith and eroding the
bedrock of the Republic." This group began to believe that this was real
and that too many people were not paying attention.[88]

The names listed below were some of the leaders in the 1950s and
1960s that bombarded Dallas with extremist views and scare tactics on the
threat of communism and anti-Kennedy and anti–United Nations views.
It was said by many that this fervent movement in Dallas and Texas led to
the climate in which the JFK assassination could take place.

Bruce Alger. In 1954, Bruce Alger was the first Republican to win
a congressional seat from Texas. He won again in 1958, 1960, and 1962.

In five terms in office he gained a reputation as one of
the most conservative Congressmen in the nation. He
spoke ardently against creeping socialism, communistic

---

[87] Minutaglio and Davis, *Dallas 1963*, Front Matter, Prelude, 3-4.
[88] Ibid.

tendencies, and communism. He sponsored bills to withdraw from the United Nations and to break diplomatic relations with the Soviet Union.[89]

After the Kennedy assassination, the Dallas establishment

realized that something must be done to counter the city's widespread reputation for extremism. An obvious target was Congressman Bruce Alger, whose unmitigated conservatism had been highlighted for a decade as representative of Dallas' political mood.[90]

Earle Cabell, a conservative Democrat, finally beat Alger in the 1964 fall election. Dallas felt a new "cloak of moderation." Sarah T. Hughes reluctantly acknowledged some improvement in the political climate as early as January 1964, but she stated, "I am not at all sure that the condition has improved to any apparent degree; however, I do see some slight changes."[91]

Rev. W. A. Criswell. Reverend W.A. Criswell, pastor of First Baptist Church, Dallas, was active with extremists and was successor to George W. Truett, who was a reserved, intellectual preacher. Criswell was "a bundle of nervous energy, moving incessantly around the pulpit, and stomping his feet . . . arms flailing." He bellowed across the church and pounded his fists, constantly attacking what he saw as the interrelated evils of communism, socialism, and liberalism. Criswell said that the Bible taught that there were existing social and racial hierarchies, denouncing biological evolution.[92]

E. M. "Ted" Dealey. E. M. "Ted" Dealy was publisher and chairman of the board of the *Dallas Morning News* in 1964 and was a supporter of conservative activities. "Ted Dealey was a rabid anti-Communist who loathed welfare, federal aid, and the United Nations. . . . The *News* under Ted Dealey provided right-wing organizations with a prominent and sympathetic medium to express their viewpoints."[93]

---

[89] Darwin Payne, *Big D* (Dallas, TX: Three Forks Press, 1994), 282.

[90] Payne, *Indomitable Sarah: The Life of Judge Sarah T. Hughes*, 277.

[91] Ibid., 278.

[92] Edward H. Miller, *Nut Country: Right Wing Dallas and the Birth of the Southern Strategy* (Chicago, IL: The University of Chicago Press, 2015), 26–27.

[93] Ibid., 22.

Cora Lacy Frederickson. Cora Lacy Frederickson was the wife of a Dallas insurance executive and an activist in extremist activities. She was a staunch supporter of Gen. Edwin Walker and was a protester at the 1963 UN Day rally at Dallas Memorial Auditorium when UN Ambassador Adlai Stevenson was the guest speaker.[94]

H. L. Hunt. H.L. Hunt was a Dallas conservative oilman, and he was active in the John Birch Society.[95]"The United Nations is a favorite target of Hunt's *Life Line* program . . . Most Americans . . . have reached the reasoned conclusion that the United Nations has turned into a monstrous threat to the interests of the United States."[96]

Frank McGehee. Frank McGehee was organizer of the National Indignation Convention (later Conference).[97] He was an activist in anti-UN and anti-communist efforts, and he was a financial supporter of Gen. Edwin Walker.[98]

Dr. Robert B. Morris. Dr. Robert B. Morris was the far-right president of the University of Dallas, a new Catholic university. Some questioned just what the purpose of this new university was because of Morris' activities.[99]

Lee Harvey Oswald. Lee Harvey Oswald was a young Marxist who lived in Dallas and other cities. He was accused of attempting to assassinate Gen. Edwin Walker, but his shot missed. He later became infamous as the assassin of Pres. John F. Kennedy.[100]

Larrie Schmidt. Larrie Schmidt was an insurance man from Nebraska active with extremists. He did two tours in the army, and while he was in Germany, he devoted himself to reading about the communist menace. He read the same John Birch material that General Walker had given to his soldiers. After his discharge, he went to Dallas "which seemed to be the most promising right-wing citadel in America."[101]

Dan Smoot. Dan Smoot was an ex-FBI agent, former employee of H. L. Hunt and a conservative radio broadcaster. "Dan Smoot . . . writes and broadcasts some of the most virulent anti-Kennedy attacks in the

---

94   Minutaglio and Davis, *Dallas 1963*, 247.
95   Payne, *Big D*, 308.
96   Minutaglio and Davis, *Dallas 1963*, 231.
97   Payne, *Big D*, 308.
98   Minutaglio and Davis, *Dallas 1963*, 335.
99   Payne, *Big D*, 308.
100 Ibid.
101 Minutaglio and Davis, *Dallas 1963*, 335.

nation, warns that the UN and communism have the exact same objective: 'Creation of a world socialist system.'"[102] After Medgar Evers' murder in June 1963, Smoot wondered why Evers had been turned into a "national hero." Smoot continued in the summer of 1963 broadcasting his attacks. Finally, Smoot openly blamed John F. Kennedy, stating that Dallas and the nation "will soon be drenched in blood because of the president and his . . . embrace of those 'negro racial agitation groups' . . . John F. Kennedy, catering to this crowd, is sowing the seeds of hate and violence: the nation will reap a bloody harvest."[103]

Robert Surrey. Robert Surrey was an aide to General Walker who printed the WANTED FOR TREASON pamphlet spread during Kennedy's visit to Dallas.[104]

Gen. Edwin A. Walker. Maj. Gen. Edwin A. Walker was "the tough-talking leader of the Twenty-Fourth Infantry Division of the U.S. Army, at the very front lines of the Cold War Army" in Augsburg, West Germany. There, in 1960, General Walker issued a warning at the Parent Teachers Association that the United States was being taken over by communists and that the leading journalists were all communists. The wary families were stunned and wondered what was really happening back home in the United States.[105]

General Walker resigned his commission in 1961 after being accused of indoctrinating his troops with John Birch Society propaganda. He found his place in Dallas among the fanatical right-wing extremists. He suspected "that Lee Harvey Oswald had been the mystery man who'd attempted to kill him, a fact confirmed by Marina Oswald and the evidence found among Oswald's belongings."[106]

Robert Welch. The brainchild of the John Birch Society was Robert Welch. Welch was "a highly skilled organizer" and in the mid-1950s "amassed a small army of friends, colleagues, and employees to distribute his two widely read political tracts, *May God Forgive Us* and *John Birch* . . . Welch had a reputation as a thoughtful figure among conservative intellectuals."[107]

---

[102] Ibid., 231.

[103] Ibid., 221–22.

[104] Ibid., 269–70.

[105] Ibid., 20–21.

[106] Ibid., 215–16, 336.

[107] Miller, *Nut Country: Right Wing Dallas and the Birth of the Southern Strategy*, 88.

William F. Buckley, a leading journalist, "declared that he had produced "two of the finest pamphlets this country has read in a decade."[108]

"The John Birch Society was born and set out to convince others of the 'gigantic conspiracy to enslave mankind'. . . communism, which included Social Security checks, civil rights laws, mental health laws, and even fluoride in the water supply." In 1961, it was reported that there were approximately seven hundred members of the group in Dallas in thirty-five chapters.[109]

Dallas 1963 book, Citations from Chapter "October 1963"

Author's note. The following quotes are related to the extremists' views of JFK and the United Nations indicative of the political climate during October 1963 in Dallas. Comments from this particular date occurred on UN Day in Dallas when Adlai Stevenson, the United Nations Ambassador, had been invited to be the speaker. Stanley Marcus was embarrassed by the events. On page 253 of the *Dallas 1963* book, the authors quote from a letter that Stanley Marcus wrote to Joe Dealey, son of Ted, at the *Dallas Morning News* condemning the development of a hard core of unreasonable people intolerant of any views opposed to their own: "For many years . . . your paper has been preaching a doctrine of criticism of the Government and of the United Nations while at the same time giving solace to the extreme rightists like General Walker and his ilk . . . I think that the constant sowing of seeds of intolerance has made it possible for the extreme rightist groups to grow in the city of Dallas with some aura of respectability."[110]

Marcus wrote to Joe Dealey who had become president of the *Dallas Morning News*. It was reported that Joe had a reputation of being more reasonable than his father, Ted. Stanley Marcus never received a reply to his letter.[111]

NTM

---

[108] Ibid.
[109] Ibid., 89–90.
[110] Minutaglio and Davis, *Dallas 1963*, 253.
[111] Ibid., 253–54.

THE QUOTES

In many ways, Bruce Alger's political career remains defined by the searing moment out on the streets of Dallas in November 1960—when the world saw startling images of petite Lady Bird Johnson, her face twisted in fear and then anger, as the mink coat mob swirled around her, some spitting and pushing and screaming. Alger might have believed that the circumspect elders always resented him for it—that, even as much as they wanted LBJ, Lady Bird, and Kennedy assailed, it was never going to help the city's image. And now (October 1963) reporters are asking questions: *"What is waiting for John F. Kennedy, this time, in Dallas? What will Alger do when President Kennedy's motorcade passes through the downtown streets?"*[112]

General Edwin Walker is scanning the front-page stories touting Adlai Stevenson's upcoming visit. He is irritated. The communists are receiving free publicity, but his own U.S. Day rally (night before UN Day) is all but ignored.[113]

The local CBS television affiliate announces that Stevenson's speech will be broadcast live. No such provision is made for Walker. The general's aides have been whispering that they might not fill the auditorium. An extensive word-of-mouth campaign is launched. Walker's aide Robert Surrey has designed and printed hundreds of flyers and yard signs: U.S. OR UN IN 1964. Advertisements appear in the *Dallas Morning News:* U.S. DAY RALLY! . . . YOU CAN'T STRADDLE THIS![114]

Rumors are spreading across Dallas that hundreds of picket signs are stashed at Walker's headquarters. Neiman

[112]   Ibid., 236.
[113]   Ibid., 237.
[114]   Ibid., 238.

Marcus executives are worried, and they call Dallas Police Chief Jesse Curry to inquire about protection for Stevenson. The chief assures them there will be no danger.[115]

The Memorial Auditorium is filling up for Walker's rally. It's Oct. 23, 1963, the day before the UN Day rally in the same auditorium. Inside the auditorium are John Birchers, Minutemen, Young Americans for Freedom, (and) the National States Rights Party. Also in attendance is the former chairman of the now defunct National Indignation Convention, Frank McGehee, as well as Larrie Schmidt, along with his brother, who is still working as Walker's chauffeur. And still another man is present—he has come by himself.[116]

After being fired from his job, after failing to murder General Walker at his home, Lee Harvey Oswald decided to move to New Orleans, hoping that city would be more receptive to his pro-Cuba, pro-Castro politics. Marina joined him for a while but eventually returned to Dallas without him. Things in New Orleans spiraled quickly downward for Oswald. There were run-ins with the police-and he found virtually no support for his cause. New Orleans was, in many ways, a miserable experience punctuated with moments of paranoia, loneliness, and a simmering anger at the lack of support for his pro-Cuba agenda. Now he is back in Dallas.[117]

"Walker is still alive. He wouldn't be holding this rally, giving this speech, if Oswald had altered his shot by just a fraction of an inch-if his bullet hadn't hit the wood on the windowpane . . . Oswald . . . blends in perfectly."[118]

---

[115] Ibid.
[116] Ibid., 240.
[117] Ibid.
[118] Ibid.

General Walker is fidgeting nervously, chain-smoking . . . the event begins with the reading of supportive telegrams from patriots in Dallas-Bruce Alger, Hunt's former employee, the ex-FBI agent Dan Smoot, and former University of Dallas President Robert Morris, a close friend of Ted Dealey. Walker steps to the microphone. Oswald listens to the man he tried to kill five months ago: 'The main battleground in the world today is right here in America, and it involves the United States versus the United Nations.'[119]

Adlai's going to sell his hogwash, and here's who is sponsoring him in Dallas. Walker reads a long blacklist, stopping after each name to allow the audience to scream condemnations: The Boy Scouts of America, the YMCA, the League of Women Voters, the Kiwanis Clubs, the Optimists Clubs, and the Rotary Clubs, churches, temples . . . Southern Methodist University . . . indicting what he says are sixty-one anti-US organizations in Dallas.[120]

Then he turns his attention to national figures—Kennedy, Eisenhower, Roosevelt, Truman, the CIA, Nixon, the State Department…But most of his ire is saved for the United Nations: "I'll tell you who started the UN," he shouts into his microphone. "It was the communists . . ."[121]

"Tonight we stand on a battleground . . . the symbol of our sovereignty," Walker roars . . . Before he steps away from the microphone, Walker asks the crowd: *"Which side will Dallas choose?"*[122]

Larrie Schmidt is among the very first to arrive at the Dallas Memorial Auditorium, and he has brought

---

[119] Ibid., 240–41.
[120] Ibid., 241.
[121] Ibid.
[122] Ibid., 242.

company . . . a small platoon of sign-wielding college students-and now they are striding into the auditorium and setting up a picket line in the lobby.[123]

Marching together, they wave signs: ADLAI, WHO ELECTED YOU? They chant, "GET THE U.S. OUT OF THE UN"[124]

Anxious contingents of UN supporters mix uneasily with Schmidt and pro-Walker supporters. More protest signs are bobbing overhead, and some people are carrying Confederate flags, rattling Halloween noisemakers and shouting as they pour inside.[125]

It is precisely what Larrie Schmidt is hoping for...He wants news to emerge that pro-United Nations goons are bullying his peaceful, reasonable picketers in Dallas. Finally . . . cops begin arriving. They . . . take up stations around the arena, looking on grimly. There are now almost two thousand people inside the auditorium.[126]

. . . Stanley Marcus is beginning to realize that the confrontation Stevenson has been avoiding all day is finally arriving . . . and Marcus is stunned by its scope . . . Marcus' role is to introduce Stevenson, but as he walks to the podium a cacophony of boos and catcalls rains down on him. Positioned directly behind him is the official flag of the United Nations. Marcus, who has set the style for Dallas for so long, feels waves of hatred washing over him.[127]

He has not prepared any formal remarks. As he stands under the hot spotlight, sweating and facing an angry crowd, words suddenly flee. He is usually able to spin

---

[123] Ibid., 243.
[124] Ibid.
[125] Ibid.
[126] Ibid., 244.
[127] Ibid., 244–45.

a gossamer speech at any given moment, but now he is adrift. Visibly rattled, he limps through an abbreviated, halting introduction-punctuated by jeers. He takes a seat on stage, pulls out a handkerchief, and wipes sweat from his brow.[128]

Suddenly a large, bulky man near the front row rises from his seat. Frank McGehee is the Dallas founder of the National Indignation Convention . . . McGehee keeps shouting, raising his voice in defiance . . . cops move toward him . . . grab him by the arms as he tries to twist away . . . Stevenson says loudly, "I don't have to come here from Illinois to teach Texas manners, do I?" . . . Stevenson issues a parting shot: "For my part, I believe in the forgiveness of sin and the redemption of ignorance."[129]

. . . One of the protesters is Cora Lacy Frederickson, the wife of a Dallas insurance executive and a staunch supporter of General Walker. She attended Walker's U.S. Day rally last night. She is carrying a large sign nailed to a piece of wood. It is one of those used by Schmidt's group, and it reads: "ADLAI, WHO ELECTED YOU?"[130]

The cops quickly set up a rope line for Stevenson and Marcus to help them reach the waiting limousine . . . Frederickson suddenly flies toward Stevenson, her sign raised high. Flashbulbs are popping as her placard slams down on Stevenson's forehead, just missing his eye. The ambassador steps back under the blow. . . . Frederickson is seized by the police . . . Stevenson gathers his composure and yells to make himself heard over the crowd. He tells the police not to arrest the woman. He attempts to talk to her, even as the crowd pushes and heaves . . . "It's all right to have your own views . . . but don't hit anyone."[131]

---

[128] Ibid., 245.
[129] Ibid.
[130] Ibid., 247.
[131] Ibid.

... Cora Frederickson ... is explaining to reporters why her picket sign struck the U.S. ambassador to the United Nations on his head. "It was never my intention to hit him . . . Someone must have pushed the sign down on him . . . I felt someone take hold of the sign and push down on it . . . There were a bunch of colored people standing around in back of me . . . I was pushed from behind by a Negro."[132]

... Photographers are racing to darkrooms, and frantic newsmen are phoning their offices ... Audible gasps are heard in the studio as the film ... appears on the monitor ... There are no black citizens anywhere in the frame.[133]

Millions of Americans are opening their morning newspapers to find shocking photos from Dallas. Breathless reports describe a city that seems to have gone insane: Anti-United Nations demonstrators shoved, booed, beat, and spat in the face of Adlai E. Stevenson.[134]

Reporters summon references to 1960 when . . . a mob held vice-presidential candidate Lyndon Johnson and his wife at bay in a hotel lobby for almost an hour . . . Walter Cronkite seems to frown in disapproval as the footage from Dallas airs . . .[135]

Having been in Dallas less than twenty-four hours, Stevenson departs early Friday morning . . . Later in the day . . . in Los Angeles . . . He remains gracious and complimentary toward his hosts in Dallas (Stanley Marcus): "I've never had a more enthusiastic reception than in Dallas,' he says. 'The problem was the violent behavior of a few."[136]

[132] Ibid., 248.
[133] Ibid., 249.
[134] Ibid.
[135] Ibid., 250.
[136] Ibid.

Quotes and Comments from *Nut Country: Right-Wing Dallas and the Birth of the Southern Strategy* Citing the United Nations and Its Agencies (Published 2015)

> Convinced that the mainstream media was dominated by liberalism and collectivism, conservative moderates turned to sympathetic bookstores and a growing array of conservative publications for their news and information. Many erstwhile Democrats became staunch Republicans after concluding that leftists were concealing the truth and conservative authors were the only reliable sources.[137]

> By the 1960's conservatives in Dallas County had gained two additional weekly newspapers owned by local Giles Miller . . . Miller purchased *Park Cities News* . . . and changed its name to the *North Dallas-Park Cities News* . . . Miller's own column censured the supposed liberalism at Southern Methodist University, vilifying the school's Perkins School of Theology as harboring dangerous ideas . . . [138]

> The American Bookstore, located in . . . University Park, sold . . . pamphlets and books by conservative authors . . . Patrons [could] pick up Congressman James Utt's attack on UNESCO, *"Communism's Trap for our Youth"* . . .[139]

Ultraconservative Republicans often expressed themselves in apocalyptic terms. J. Evetts Haley, a historian in the 1960s, concluded that the 1964 Civil Rights Act would "end the American Republic": "Rev. W. A. Criswell, pastor of the First Baptist Church, claimed that communism, Soviet occupation, and the election of a Catholic president would all cause the 'end of religious freedom in America,' illustrating "just how deeply religion molded the worldview of the ultraconservatives."[140]

---

[137]   Miller, *Nut Country: Right Wing Dallas and the Birth of the Southern Strategy*, 45–46.
[138]   Ibid.
[139]   Ibid.
[140]   Ibid., 54.

All the characteristics of their secular doomsday—the grandiloquent and provocative announcements of finality, the anticipation of imminent and inevitable ruin, the specific date for the end, and the antipathy toward the United Nations and the Soviet Union—were carried over from their belief in a divinely inspired date of reckoning . . . to scenarios that Adolf Hitler, Benito Mussolini, or Franklin Delano Roosevelt-or eventually JFK-was the Antichrist . . . Dallas was an important location for this sort of biblical prophecy . . . Therefore, they vehemently opposed global alliances and supranational organizations like the United Nations and, indeed, identified them with the Antichrist . . . Accounting for ultraconservative antipathy for the United Nations, the Antichrist would then destroy Russia, and according to Pentecost, "rule over all the earth." There will be one world government, one world religion, one world dictator.[141]

Ultraconservatives (H. L. Hunt, Dan Smoot, and Ida Darden) wanted to repeal the Sixteenth Amendment, do away with income taxes, impeach John F. Kennedy for his foreign policy errors, abolish all disarmament treaties, end foreign aid, and remove the United States from the United Nations. According to one activist, Darden, the United States could defeat communism by pulling out of the United Nations, withdrawing recognition of Russia, and sending a company of marines "to take care of the Cuban beatnik."[142]

H. L. Hunt referred to anybody who disagreed with his positions as "the Mistaken."

Having observed, for instance, that '9 out of 10 Americans think we should not leave the UN . . . Hunt responded that 'the public apparently failed to recognize that Khrushchev . . . can control the UN at will . . . the head of the UN Military Staff is always a Communist . . . and

---

[141]   Ibid., 55–57.
[142]   Ibid.

the existence of the UN supplants the sovereignty of the US . . .[143]

Ultraconservatives stockpiled "evidence" of treason through a process of examining decisions made by American policymakers and presupposing that errors in judgment were conscious, intentional, and sinister . . . For instance, *The Politician,* by John Birch Society founder Robert Welch, backed up its claim that President Eisenhower was a Communist with more than a hundred pages of footnotes.[144]

Ida Darden charged that teachers had been subverted by the United Nations Educational, Scientific, and Cultural Organization (UNESCO) and the National Education Association . . . In the early 1950s, after hearing the protests of the Minute Women, an anti-Communist women's group that successfully elected some members to the Houston school board, the city censored high school textbooks that contained favorable references to the United Nations . . .[145]

After launching an unsuccessful attack in 1960 on Southern Methodist University, which he called a haven for left-wingers, Haley turned his attention to the Texas textbook market, which annually grossed from six to ten million dollars. Urging that high school students "should be taught only the American side," Haley argued, "the stressing of both sides of a controversy only confuses the young and encourages them to make snap decisions based on insufficient evidence." The State Textbook Committee acquiesced to censors like Haley, removing or expurgating schoolbooks that included favorable references to integration, the United Nations, and activist musician Pete Seeger.[146]

---

[143] Ibid., 60–61.

[144] Ibid.

[145] Ibid., 66–67.

[146] Ibid.

A twelve-year-old junior high student shared Haley's concern that current textbooks were undermining Texans' faith in free enterprise and Christianity . . . The student stated that "we'll never get peace until the second coming of Christ. They talk about world peace in there and I'm not in favor of that."[147]

Dallasites absorbed segregationist teachings and repeatedly invoked God's will throughout 1955 to defend segregation. "God hates the sin of mongrelization," observed a Dallas citizen. "At the Tower of Babel they were all of one mind and language, integrated, an ancient 'United Nations.' And God scattered and confounded them."[148]

If Robert Welch was the best-known figure in the John Birch Society, General Edwin Walker was its most controversial. Like Welch, the Dallas-based Walker challenged, molded, and solidified the identity of Dallas Conservatives.[149]

General Walker had resigned from the army in the fall of 1961 after being charged with distributing John Birch Society pamphlets to his troops and advising them to vote exclusively for conservative candidates. He also "prescribed a reading program for his troops that included Robert Welch's *Life of John Birch* and literature from the militant Christian anti-Communists Edgar Bundy, Billy James Hargis, and George Benson."

Walker then settled in Dallas and set up headquarters on Turtle Creek Boulevard. Walker's zealotry and obsession with conspiracy theories were so great that at times they crossed the line into paranoia . . . At a press conference at the Baker Hotel . . . he held up what he termed a State Department 'blueprint' that supposedly placed American military personnel and weapons under the control of the United Nations.[150]

---

[147] Ibid.
[148] Ibid., 73.
[149] Minutaglio and Davis, *Dallas 1963*, 95.
[150] Ibid., 95–99.

He stated that the plan now was to "UN-ize" the American soldier and to place all armed forces and weapons under the United Nations.[151]

Another individual who joined the ultraconservatives during the 1960s was Robert Morris. He had served as the chief counsel for Sen. Pat McCarran's Internal Security Subcommittee and gained a reputation as an indefatigable fighter of communism. Yet he was no ultraconservative Republican in 1961 when he moved to Dallas and accepted the position of president of the fledgling University of Dallas.[152]

> [The] Walker case nudged Robert Morris into the ultraconservative camp . . . He began embracing conspiracy theories, and soon adopted the belief that Kennedy was planning a "merger" with the Soviet Union and ceding national sovereignty to a world government controlled by the United Nations. He announced that . . . "merger with the Soviet Union under the direction of the United Nations is our new national policy."[153]

Robert Morris began protesting against the need for mental health programs. Dan Smoot agreed with Morris. Smoot said,

> The new mental health laws being written by state legislatures . . . make it easier for bureaucrats, and political enemies, and selfish relatives to get someone committed as a "mentally ill" person and thus get them out of the way. "The Fountainhead" for the propaganda about the need for mental health programs has been the UN.[154]

Rita Bass was a moderate Republican who began her political career by working with and organizing Republican women. Her "politics changed when she encountered the ideas of Robert Morris . . . Morris' radicalization had an effect on Bass, particularly on the issue of nuclear

---

[151] Ibid.

[152] Miller, *Nut Country: Right Wing Dallas and the Birth of the Southern Strategy*, 106.

[153] Ibid.

[154] Ibid., 107.

disarmament . . . Morris moved in the same circles as Bass."[155] When Bass read Morris's *Disarmanent Weapon of Conquest*, she became an activist and joined "80 Women from Dallas," an organization opposed to disarmament. Morris had made "the assertion that the Kennedy administration's disarmament program entailed dismantling the nation's armed forces and substituting 'rule of the world and ourselves by a UN Peace Force.'"[156]

> Bass and the "80 Women" soon became fastidious fact collectors . . . In late October 1962—in the immediate aftermath of Cuban Missile Crisis—"80 Women" heard Morris make his case that disarmament was a furtive plan to surrender political sovereignty to a United Nations peace force. Bass took copious notes.[157]

Here's a quote from the end of the book:

> Today's far right embraces absolutism and opposes any efforts to find middle ground . . . As of 2014, many far-right Republicans whose ideology would likely receive the approbation of H. L. Hunt and Dan Smoot remain prominent leaders in Congress and call for ever greater deficit reductions . . . Few contemporary leaders of either party today dare to repudiate such domestic extremism. President Kennedy had intended to forcefully denounce Dallas ultraconservatism on November 22, 1963. Had his motorcade safely made it to the Trade Mart, he would have told the citizens of Dallas that there will "always be dissident voices heard in the land . . . But today other voices are heard in the land-voices preaching doctrines wholly unrelated to reality, wholly unsuited to the Sixties, doctrines which apparently assume that words will suffice without weapons, that vituperation is as good as victory and that peace is a sign of weakness.

---

[155] Ibid., 109.
[156] Ibid.
[157] Ibid.

"We can hope," Kennedy would have said, "that fewer people will listen to nonsense." Today the American people could certainly use a strong dose of the same advice.[158]

---

[158] Ibid., 151–52.

CHAPTER 4

Media Reports

History of DUNA: Dallas UNA-USA
Through the Eyes of the Media, 1952–2015[1]

From the perspective of sixty years on, it is easy to forget how controversial the United Nations was and how crucial prominent business leaders were to promote US involvement in the UN. This was true in Dallas, where many gatherings and events involving national figures were focused on educating the public about the United Nations. We can observe these controversies taking place through spirited media debates that appear in the local press starting in the early 1950s.

---

[1] Newspaper citations for this chapter were accessed for research through the Dallas Public Library Archives or directly from the paper. Each is credited to the Dallas Morning News (DMN with date), Letters to the Editors (DMN/ LTE with date), Fort Worth Star Telegram (FWST with date), and White Rock Lake Weekly (WRLW with date). All references are included on the basis of fair use for educational nonprofit purposes.

Texas Senator Thomas Connally Signed the UN Charter, 1945.
He returned to Texas, filed a Senate Bill to affirm the "sovereignty
of the United States of America." Texas Senator Thomas Connally
Signed the UN Charter, 1945. He returned to Texas, filed a Senate
Bill to affirm the "sovereignty of the United States of America."

The Dallas United Nations Association (DUNA) and its precursor, the American Association for the United Nations, were successful in participating in the local and national debates through steady and lively public programs and by getting media attention for the issues.

This chapter tracks the media coverage of the Dallas UNA and the enmity it encountered from the 1950s to 2015. Dallas UNA was especially successful in coverage by media from 1952 through the 1960s. By the early 1970s, coverage dropped off, which represented shifts in the bigger picture of community influence. By "media" we mean the press, particularly the *Dallas Morning News* and the *Fort Worth Star Telegram*. Radio and television news are beyond the scope of this history. Of course, these events occurred long before the advent of our current media platforms, such as twenty-four-hour cable news, the internet, and social media! By the 2000s, newspaper coverage of the UNA became less frequent, but still revealed the dynamics that swirled around the United Nations in this important American city.

"Prefiguring the Super State" versus "Hope of the World"

Two items from late 1952 and early 1953 represent the simmering debate over the value of the UN. Prominent *DMN* columnist Lynn Landrum proclaimed that the "United Nations is another prefiguring of the super state—in the minds of some. But we must ask ourselves always for whose benefit the super state is to be . . . UNESCO is under fire now, and rightly so, because it is attempting to proceed by destroying patriotism" (*DMN* 12-30-1952).

Criticizing UNESCO as "busybodies," Landrum linked its purported destruction of patriotism to the "Communistic world policy is simply the expansion of Russian domination over the world."

Eleanor Roosevelt listens in at the UN, 1947

On the other hand, a few weeks later, a news item in the *Fort Worth Star Telegram* reported on a speech by Eleanor Roosevelt as she stepped down from being a US delegate to the UN.

> Mrs. Franklin D. Roosevelt, for six years the UN's star diplomatic attraction, declared Sunday the UN remains 'the hope of the world' despite its shortcomings and Soviet obstructionism. (*FWST* 01-19-1953)

The article continued, reporting Roosevelt's response to the growing Red Scare of the period, which was increasing in intensity.

A.A. Gromyko (left) of the USSR conversing with Senator Tom Connally (United States) at a meeting of Commission II, Security Council, Committee 1, Structure and Procedures, held on 14 June 1945

Mrs. Roosevelt had sharp words of warning against what she called "fear" and "hysteria" in the United States as a result of indiscriminate attacks on public figures for alleged communist ties or subversive activities. She asserted that such attacks undermine public confidence and added that "it is not healthy for us as a nation" to lend credence to "all" accusations concerning communism. Mrs. Roosevelt said that it was a "total misunderstanding" about the accusations of disloyal Americans at the UN (*FWST* 01-19-1953).

Eleanor Roosevelt listens beside Henri Laugier,
Human Rights Commission 1948

Less than ten years after the founding of the United Nations, the organization remained controversial and was a hot-button issue in the Cold War. Mrs. Roosevelt committed herself to stepping down from her official UN role to engage in "promoting goodwill and understanding about the United Nations through the American Association for the United Nations, a private cultural organization" (*FWST* 01-19-1953). Indeed, Mrs. Roosevelt's influence continued to be felt as she worked to build chapters across the country, including Dallas. Over the following decade, Mrs. Roosevelt appeared in Dallas several times as a guest of the Dallas United Nations Association.

Mrs. Eleanor Roosevelt, US leader in framing the Universal
Declaration of Human Rights, adopted in 1948

Despite Mrs. Roosevelt's stature, Dallas news articles from this
period of the mid-1950s demonstrate the concerns of conservatives that
the UN would threaten United States' sovereignty, security, and power.
In January of 1953, an article was headlined "US Internal Threat Seen
in Power of UN" (*DMN* 01-30-53). It focused on divisions within the
Eisenhower administration, that "a recent anti-American decision in
the UN's economic and financial committee jeopardized present and
prospective US's investments abroad." Routine news about the UN, such as
the election of Dag Hammarskjold of Sweden as the new secretary general,
were covered as well in short news items. However, extended coverage was
given to events that highlighted the fears of communist infiltration.

First Press Attention to DUNA Began as an Attack

Indeed, the first mention of the Dallas United Nations Association (DUNA) appears in an April, 1953 article, reporting on statements by the leader of the National Association of Pro-America, who sounded "a blunt call to arms against Communist infiltration before some seventy members and guests of the association's Dallas chapter" (*DMN* 04-09-53). The article continues, "Mrs. Enid Griswold of Montclair, N.J., stated that 'I can assure you that this infiltration exists in every walk of life—in our schools, churches, women's groups and men's groups.'" She later "named several Dallas organizations whose members she believes are unwittingly following the Communist-Socialist line." Among those was the United Nations Association. She condemned the "sincere" people who thought the UN was doing good, but were being duped into supporting "the aspirations of millions of Socialists and Communists" (*DMN* 04-09-53).

Interestingly, the *DMN* gave substantial coverage a few months later to the visit of Dr. Sudjarwo Tjondronegoro, Republic of Indonesia representative to the United Nations, who passed through the city on his way to Sudan in Lamb County, Texas, to speak at the second annual Sudan United Nations Festival. Indonesia at this time was only a few years old as an independent country, and it is surprising that a small town in Texas held such an event during this period. As the news coverage states,

> The UN festival in the small Texas town received world-wide publicity last year and is expected to draw thousands of people again this year. Residents will dress in traditional costumes of the United Nations. A parade through the Sudan business district will include a visiting sheriff's posse with each carrying United Nations flags. Climax of the festival, whose theme is "United Nations and World Peace," is a twilight pageant in the city park. (*DMN* 09-26-53)

In 1954, the Dallas UNA Appeared Regularly in the Local Press

Members of the public were often vocal about the United Nations in Letters to the Editor. Some of these represent religious extremism of the time, which equated the Soviet Union with evil.

> Does . . . really believe that the UN will stop Russia from attacking us when she has the evil thought mentioned in the thirty-eighth chapter of Ezekiel? . . . The Anglo-Saxon-Celtic-Scandinavian people form the Kingdom of God on earth—established at Sinai. It is all outlined in the Bible and there is no other solution . . . (*DMN*/LTE 01-29-53)

Another example in February 1953 quoted Proverbs: "Whoso is partner with a thief hateth his own soul" (Proverbs 28:24) (*DMN*/LTE 02-15-53).

However, others expressed more political skepticism about the potential for worldwide democracy:

> A well-known Dallas jurist [perhaps Judge Sarah Hughes] recently speaking for "One World," admitted that two thirds of the people of the world were unable to govern themselves. "One World," of course, means democracy, where every man's vote is as good as another's. That means that two thirds of the people who cannot govern themselves will tell the other one third what to do. Majority rules in a democracy. (*DMN*/LTE 01-29-53)

Judge Sarah T. Hughes, first DUNA president, elected 1953.

The Dallas chapter of the UNA really got organized to publicize its work in 1954. The *Dallas Morning News* published numerous announcements of DUNA events that were likely based on press releases by the organization. This success demonstrates the interest in the topics and the influence the organization held. Coverage of the organization included announcements of its annual meetings, election of leadership, and projects the DUNA was working on. These newspaper items give a sense of who was involved and what they were doing. Judge Sarah T. Hughes was elected president of the Dallas UNA, followed by the election of Bernard Fulton, director of the Greenhill School, elected in May 1954.

Bernard Fulton, second president of DUNA

The annual report of the group cited as the top project of the year the cooperation of activities for the observance of UN week, which had sixty-five organizations participating. Plans for the celebration of UN Week this year in 'Dallas and Texas were discussed. Other officers elected were Mrs. E. R. Brownscombs, the Rev. Edward B. Ferguson, the Rev. Luther Holcomb and Mrs. George Abbott, vice-presidents; Mrs. H. J. Barnes, secretary, and Dr. R. I. Slobod, treasurer. (*DMN* 05-18-54)

Three additional published press releases in 1954 announce UNA speakers, which demonstrates the active work of the organization, particularly promoting its UN Week in October.

Bernard Fulton, president of the Dallas UNA, will appear as Carolyn Cole's guest on Ladies First (WFAA-570). (*DMN* 10-11-54)

Mrs. Louise B. Raggio, Dallas attorney and member of the UNA Dallas, will speak on UN activities at a meeting of the Exchange Club of Oak Cliff. (*DMN* 10-20-54)

Even after Their Big UN Week Event, the Dallas UNA Did Not Rest

1953 UNESCO commitment to Literacy in Korea

In January 1955, DUNA brought Luther Evans, the director general of UNESCO, to speak at a dinner on Monday at First Methodist Church, Dallas. Evans, a native Texan, is stationed in Paris, France, and is a graduate of University of Texas. The dean of Perkins School of Theology at SMU, Merrimon Cuninggim, presided, showing the early involvement of academic and religious leaders in this movement. The *Dallas Morning News* covered the event with a substantial article titled "Kind Word for UNESCO."

The UN Educational, Scientific and Cultural Organization has never enjoyed the popularity in Texas which many UN enthusiasts have wished for it. Opposition, in fact, to this UN satellite has been pronounced and even bitter here. UNESCO remains the most "controversial" of all the international activities spawned at the pivotal San Francisco Assembly in 1945. (*DMN* 01-08-55)

Certainly, the work of this agency has never been presented in a more favorable light in Dallas than it was on Monday night by Dr. Luther Evans, the Texan from Bastrop, who now heads UNESCO as its director general.

The writer notes that suspicions of UNESCO were dispelled somewhat by this Texan speaker: "Dr. Evans speaks the plain language of everyday Texans. He impresses as one who has his feet firmly on the ground, fully able to keep his world-wide enterprise true to its purely educational aim" (*DMN* 01-08-55).

Just days after the event above, DUNA brought Eleanor Roosevelt to speak about her decade of work with the UN and her role in the national organization, the American Association for the UN (*DMN* 01-09-55). The *Dallas Morning News* reported on January 11, 1955, that several hundred people had packed the luncheon where the former first lady recounted being appointed by President Truman to the "Provisional Assembly of the UN when it began in London 10 years ago, to set up the permanent UN organization" and her work with the committee on cultural, human, and educational relations:

> That proved a happy choice, because in 1947 she was made chairman of the committee on human rights of the UN Economic and Social Council. Until 1952 she represented this country in the UN General Assemblies. Now as Board Chairman of the American Association for the UN, she is touring the country to inform citizens about the work of the UN. (*DMN* 01-11-55)

> Mrs. Roosevelt stated that our great good fortune in the US brings great responsibility. She pointed out how specialized UN agencies in agriculture, health and technical assistance work as teams in far corners of the world to raise living standards. (*DMN* 01-11-55)

While in Dallas, Mrs. Roosevelt also appeared on a panel discussion of "Three Continents View the United Nations" on WFAA-820 (*DMN* 01-16-55).

The remainder of 1955 saw several more DUNA-related events getting press coverage. Judge Sarah Hughes, the previous president of the Dallas UNA and then member of the national committee of UNESCO, spoke at the local B'nai B'rith luncheon. The press release was used as a continuing tool to inform the public about the UN and the UNA and its future events: "She will help impress upon the group what the UN means to individual and family living. B'nai B'rith is one of the non-governing agencies (NGOs) to have representation with the UN, and is one of the 60 sponsoring organizations helping Dallas County to celebrate UN Week Oct. 17–24" (*DMN* 10-16-55). A member of the DUNA board, Dr. William E. Barnett, spoke at the Dallas chapter of the National Secretaries Association meeting as part of UN Week (*DMN* 10-19-55).

The paper reported a few months later on the DUNA meeting at which Dr. Robert Smith, a government professor at SMU, reviewed UN work of the past decade. In the remarks quoted, we can see the controversies of that period in which the basic mission of the UN still needed explaining and defending: "The sole purpose of the UN is to preserve world peace and security," Dr. Smith said. "Its goal is not to develop a world state or destroy nations; instead, the UN works to preserve the independence and sovereignty of every nation," he asserted (*DMN* 03-28-56).

He pointed to UN efforts in the Middle East. He stressed the role of the UN in refugee work, dispute mediation, disarmament, and the discussion of peaceful uses of atomic energy. That UN-sponsored meeting in Geneva was "one of the most important scientific meetings of all time." (*DMN* 03-28-56)

Further news items from this period announced fund-raising efforts, to be used to promote better understanding of the UN. Prominent names from the Dallas community appear in the press releases, including Mrs. George H. Abbott (president of the organization, in a time in which married women were known by their husbands' names!), Elsie Vandermiller, and Raymond Nasher (*DMN* 07-08-56). The paper also covered the United Nations Week in Dallas in October 1956 and reported on a donation designed to spread the word.

Raymond Nasher, DUNA president, 1956

Eight sets of books, *"The UN Bookshelf,"* were given to the city and county library systems by Raymond D. Nasher, Dallas industrialist, on behalf of the DUNA, of which he is vice president. Miss Dorothy Kittel, head of the community living department of the Dallas Public Library, accepted for the city library. Mrs. Bess Ann Motley, Dallas County librarian, accepted for the county library.

Mr. Nasher said there is no more fitting place to make such a presentation than a library. "I hope the books will further the cause of peace," he added. Five sets of books went to the city library, and three will circulate among the county's 15-branch libraries. (*DMN* 10-21-56)

DUNA also promoted World Peace Sunday to area churches to encourage participation in UN Week (*DMN* 10-21-56). An event at the

Dallas Zoo as part of UN Week even honored Miss United Nations (a true anachronism today!), a young woman (Donna Sue Hill) born in Dallas on the same day the UN was formed (*DMN* 10-21-56).

As these reports show that during the period of the mid-1950s, DUNA's outreach to diverse local organizations was impressive—from the business community to SMU, from B'nai B'rith to secretaries! The organization increasingly collaborated with other mainstream civic organizations, such as the Dallas Junior Chamber of Commerce (*DMN* 10-20-57), United Church Women of Dallas, the League of Women Voters (*DMN* 10-31-58), the Dallas Council on World Affairs, and SMU (*DMN* 09-17-59), to promote knowledge about the UN's role in the world.

Dallas UNA Events in the Late 1950s

During the remainder of the 1950s, the Dallas UNA continued to appear regularly in the local press, which published information about its events and leadership. The following are some examples of events the group held:

International military briefing by Admiral Jerauld Wright, US Navy, the supreme Allied commander, and the Atlantic and foreign naval officers of the NATO staff to observe the twelfth anniversary of the founding of the United Nations. Chair of UN Week was Raymond Nasher, introducing the speaker, Mrs. Leon S. Price (*DMN* 10-20-57).

Representatives Chester E. Merrow (R-NH) and A. S. J. Carnahan (D-MO) of the House Foreign Affairs Committee on a tour of twenty-eight cities in an effort to inform the public about national and United Nations foreign aid and technical assistance (*DMN* 02-16-58). Three exchange students from Ecuador, Iran, and India spoke about what the UN has done in their countries at Perkins School of Theology, SMU (*DMN* 03-17-58).

Extensive plans for the UN Week Program in October 1958 were announced in an unpublished letter from DUNA president Raymond D. Nasher, beginning with a downtown Kiwanis luncheon (*DMN* 09-19-58).

UN Day—Sir Leslie Munro, Pres. Ex-officio of the UN General Assembly was to speak at McFarlin Auditorium, SMU in an evening meeting. (*DMN* 10-24-58)

Model UN Public Assembly cooperating with SMU. (*DMN* 10-24-25-58)

UN Booth at the State Fair of Texas, General Exhibits Building, featuring a film, "The Children's Fountain." (*DMN* 10-19-58)[2]

David Wade, TV gourmet, spoke on United Nations Food at a meeting of the B'nai B'rith Women of Dallas (*DMN* 10-12-58). A. Harris & Co. (department store) had a UNICEF greeting card booth to sell the famous international Christmas cards and a window display to celebrate UN Week. UNA members staffed the booth (*DMN* 10-23-58).Madam Rajkumari Amrit Kaur, former secretary to Gandhi and member of the Parliament of India, spoke at a tea at SMU, sponsored by the United Church Women of Dallas and the League of Women Voters (*DMN* 10-31-58).

And the series of DUNA activities continued in the community during the following year.

Mr. Charles Malik, president of the UN General Assembly, was to speak in Dallas, cosponsored by DUNA and the Dallas Council of World Affairs (*DMN* 01-08-59). Mrs. Eleanor Roosevelt spoke on "The United Nations and You" at SMU, presented by Judge Sarah T. Hughes, DUNA president Raymond Nasher (*DMN* 01-13-59). Raymond D. Nasher, president of the Dallas United Nations Association, was named to the board of directors of the American Association for United Nations Inc. (*DMN* 03-04-59).

Dr. Frank P. Graham, India and Pakistan representative to the United Nations, spoke at the sixth annual meeting of the Dallas UNA at Highland Park United Methodist Church (*DMN* 03-20-59). Dr. Paul Geren opened the Dallas college lecture course on current international issues, an eight-lecture series on world politics, speaking on "Communist Theory and Soviet Practice." Dr. Merrimon Cuninggim, dean of Perkins School of Theology and newly elected president of DUNA, closed the series with "The Role of the United Nations." "The fee is $10 for an individual or $15 for a married couple," sponsored by SMU Perkins School of Theology and Dallas Council on World Affairs (*DMN* 09-17-59).

Mrs. Eleanor Roosevelt, former US representative to the UN, was announced as the principal speaker during Dallas' observance of UN

---

[2]   Nasher Family Archives provided free access for helpful historical information, used by permission. Other family archives are respectfully noted and acknowledged by the authors.

Week, October 18–24. UN Week was to be sponsored by seventy-two organizations (*DMN* 10-07-59).

UN Week had become an important project of the organization, and closing out the 1950s, in 1959, the Dallas UNA hosted Eleanor Roosevelt again as the keynote speaker. The *Dallas Morning News* coverage of the event's opening had an optimistic tone and cited President Eisenhower's blessing of the event:

> As United Nations Week (October 18–24) heaves in today with a presidential blessing, noteworthy is the changed view of many in regard to an organization born in 1945. The shift has been from both sides, old pros gone anti, old cons gone for.
>
> For one thing, of course, experience has shaped the UN, 1959, so that it is not exactly what everyone saw it as in 1945. Some will think that good, others bad. Yet only one major change has been made in the operation of the organization, occurring by accident when Russia boycotted the UN and thereby opened the road to giving the General Assembly authority to get around some of the veto strength.
>
> Nothing so far has enabled UN realistically to assure peace. Nothing in the foreseeable future can do that. But it has been an agency for peace. It has some accomplishments to its credit in the way of forestalling or ending wars, some dismal failures.
>
> Dallas United Nations Association has arranged an impressive program in the way of making the week educational here. The list of 72 local sponsoring organizations testifies to the general recognition that, regardless of its faults, UN is a necessity. Paraphrasing a familiar epigram, if UN did not exist, you would have to invent it. The useful service of the detailed program here is that it offers an opportunity to everybody in Dallas to learn both what UN is and what it is not. (*DMN* 10-18-59)

Dallas UNA Events in the Early 1960s

As the decade of the 1960s opened, the Dallas UNA was well established and entered one of its most active decades with substantial media coverage achieved through effective press relations and the stature of the leadership in the wider Dallas community.

Edward B. Marks, former chief of the International Refugee Commission in Greece and executive director of the US Committee for Refugees, spoke on refugee camps in Central and Southern Europe at SMU (*DMN* 02-03-60). Students in six Dallas high schools had entered the national UN contest; local winners would receive prizes from the Dallas UNA (*DMN* 03-10-60). Rabbi Levi Olan of Temple Emanu-El is the new president of the Dallas United Nations Association. Other officers were Mrs. Howard Grimes, Douglas Jackson and Mrs. Taylor Robinson, vice presidents; Mrs. Marion B. Richmond, secretary; and Norman Freeman, treasurer (*DMN* 06-10-60). Dr. Levi Olan, rabbi of Temple Emanu-El, examined American foreign policy and diagnosed it as being behind the times (*DMN* 06-10-60).

UN Week Events

Dallas Symphony Orchestra presented a concert. The featured speaker was Robert H. Thayer, assistant secretary of state in charge of cultural and educational activities. Dr. Levi Olan, Rabbi of Temple Emanu-El and president of the DUNA, spoke on the book, *Bread and Wine* (*DMN* 10-23-60).

In the next month, Dallas attorneys Robert G. Storey Jr.; L.D.N. Wells; and Charles O. Shields led a discussion entitled "No Peace with Law" on the debate about the Connally Amendment related to World Court jurisdiction at SMU (*DMN* 11-30-60).

The year 1961 carried fewer reports.

Mrs. Howard Grimes, vice president of the Dallas United Nations Association, spoke on "The Security Council and the Veto" at First Unitarian Church (*DMN* 03-15-61).

> **UN Week**—Chester Bowles, the New Frontier's undersecretary of state, was announced to head a 6-man State Department delegation to Dallas, Oct. 27 and 28,

to explain "in depth" the nation's foreign policy; 2,600 invitations were sent, ranging from small town newspaper editors to public librarians. (*DMN* 10-12-61)

Panel debated "red infiltration" in the West with SMU law professors Dr. A. J. Thomas Jr. and Borris Kozolchyk at SMU (*DMN* 10-21-61). Mrs. George Baker, a director of United Nations Association of Dallas, was speaker on "Foreign Relations" at the Richardson Kiwanis Club (*DMN* 10-23-61). State Department representatives were in Dallas for the Regional Foreign Policy Briefing Conference, which highlighted United Nations Week. They were entertained at dinner parties, sponsored by the State Department and UNA (*DMN* 10-23-61).

UN Week in 1961 occurred in a fraught context of US-Soviet tensions. The Dallas UNA cosponsored with the US State Department a Regional Foreign Policy Briefing Conference, with six hundred people attending. The main speakers were US State Department undersecretary Chester Bowles and Russian specialist Charles E. Bohlen.

As the *DMN* reported, they "refused to comment on newest US-Russian clash that Soviet tanks had pulled up to the principal crossing on the East Berlin-West Berlin crossing. Bowles also turned away questions on Berlin. Bowles also stated that the question of Yugoslavia is tremendously complicated" (*DMN* 10-27-61).

Several Reports continued Coverage of the Dallas Chapter in 1962

Three study courses were offered by Oak Cliff League of Women Voters, Bishop College, and the Negro Business and Professional Women's Club (*DMN* 02-15-62). Mrs. Howard Grimes, vice president of the Dallas UNA, discussed the financial obligations of countries belonging to the world peace organization (*DMN* 02-25-62).

Preparations for UN Week in 1962 as covered in the press indicate an ambitious program. The timing was significant, occurring during the Cuban Missile Crisis. An intriguing news item hinted at dissension among those in the community interested in international politics: First, it was reported that the "internationally-minded Dallas Council on World Affairs can't make up its mind whether to help sponsor the internationally-minded

Dallas United Nations Association in the annual observance of United Nations Week here" (*DMN* 09-09-62).

Two weeks later, the column reported that they would participate "after all" (*DMN* 09-23-62).

Plans for UN Week included a major show at the 1962 Texas State Fair, for which the paper reported that the Dallas UNA was "assembling performers and international beauties from here and elsewhere, all to appear in costume" (*DMN* 09-30-62). A film festival at the public library and Roy Neal, NBC aerospace expert, speaking on "The United Nations in Space," along with forty other programs organized through a Dallas UNA speaker's bureau, were scheduled (*DMN* 10-12-62). The newspaper reported on the keynote speaker, ambassador and head of the US Information Agency, George Venable Allen, who addressed President Kennedy's actions in relation to Cuba: "The vigorous reaction of the US to the arming of Cuba by Russia is actually the reaction of much more—the US reaction to the accumulation of Red acts since 1948, said Allen" (*DMN* 10-25-62).

Controversies Heated Up in 1963

DUNA president Jack Goren, 1963

In 1963, the *DMN* reported on Dallas becoming the home to a regional office of the American Association for the UN, to be headquartered in the Dallas UNA office (*DMN* 02-04-63). This led to increased visibility and involvement of prominent Dallas leaders in both organizations, which was covered by the press (*DMN* 03-09-63). Jack Goren, vice president of Neiman Marcus, assumed leadership in the Dallas UNA this year and was featured in a lengthy profile by the *Dallas Morning News*, which gave a platform for his views on the UN:

> There is a very adverse climate of understanding toward the United Nations in Dallas and throughout the United States. We must improve it.
>
> I am concerned that while there is constructive criticism of the United Nations, Dallas seems to be the lair of destructive criticism aimed at the UN. This city is completely out of tune with the rest of the United States.
>
> It is almost as if ardent partisans did not realize the United Nations is a bi-partisan product, begun and supported by both the Republican and Democratic parties. Why people will tell you the United Nations should be done away with! What do they offer to put in its place? (*DMN* 03-24-63, Headliner Portrait: Jack Goren by Ann Adams Melvin)

Jack Goren's assumption of Dallas UNA leadership with Raymond Nasher leading the Texas UNA placed two very prominent business leaders in public view promoting the UN. Along with Judge Sarah T. Hughes, and many other leaders from various communities, their community awareness reached a peak of interest.

DUNA president Jack Goren applauds US Representative
to the UN Adlai Stevenson, UN Day 1963.

The UN Week in 1963 featured another prominent public figure, US
ambassador to the UN Adlai Stevenson. His "major foreign policy address
in Dallas" set off quite a Dallas firestorm, however, as he was assaulted at
his appearance (*DMN* 10-09-63).

> A right-wing woman, an insurance executive's wife and
> a prominent figure in downtown lunch clubs, assaulted
> US Ambassador to the United Nations Adlai Stevenson
> at Dallas' Memorial Auditorium Theater at the UN Day
> event on Oct. 24.

> Stevenson first approached a screaming Mrs. Cora Lacy
> Frederickson merely to ask her about the source of her
> anger. In response, she struck the ambassador over the
> head with her "Down with UN" picket sign. She was
> arrested, but Stevenson didn't press charges. (*DMN*
> 10-24-63)

Program

Music
531st Air Force Texas Air National Guard
Band and Color Guard, under the
direction of Lieutenant John M. Brown

Presentation of Colors

Introduction . . . . . . JACK GOREN, President,
Dallas United Nations Association

Preamble to the Universal Declaration
of Human Rights . . . . JUDGE SARAH T. HUGHES

Presentation of the Speaker . . STANLEY MARCUS

Address
His Excellency, MR. ADLAI STEVENSON
Ambassador Extraordinary and Plenipotentiary
of the United States to the United Nations

*   *   *

This public meeting is sponsored by the Dallas
United Nations Association, Jack Goren, Presi-
dent, and by the Dallas League of Women
Voters, Mrs. Edward C. Fritz, President.

Adlai Stevenson autographed UN Day program

Despite being assaulted and then heckled by a leader of the National Indignation Convention, Stephenson's speech was attended by an audience of 2000 (*DMN* 10-25-63). These events embarrassed many in the state of Texas, prompting numerous letters to the editors (*DMN* 10-30-63). The John Birch Society first appears to be an instigating force in these letters.

The Dallas UNA and its partners, such as the Dallas League of Women Voters, organized extraordinary events during these very tense times. Keep in mind that this was a mere month before the assassination of Pres. John F. Kennedy in Dallas, November 22, 1963.

Media Coverage Diminished in 1964

In 1964, news coverage of the Dallas UNA activities resumes with infrequent publication of announcements of their many events. Concerns addressed in their programs include the UN and Outer Space (*DMN* 01-27-64), the need for qualified leaders in Africa (*DMN* 03-04-64), and reducing conflict and the "nuclear trigger" (*DMN* 06-30-64). In addition, there are regular talks sponsored by the UNA, educating people about the UN, with many organizations cooperating in sponsorships (*DMN* 10-11-64).

Cooperating Organizations
United Nations Week

OCTOBER 18-24, 1964

American Association of University Women
American Institute of Architects, Dallas
  Chapter
American Jewish Committee
American Medical Center at Denver, Dallas
  Chapter
American Red Cross, Dallas County Chapter
Bahai Community of Dallas
Bahai Community, University Park
Bishop College
B'nai B'rith District Grand Lodge #7
B'nai B'rith Women's Council of Dallas
CARE, Inc.
Council and Federation of Negro Garden
  Clubs
Dallas AFL-CIO Council
Dallas Association of Directors of Christian
  Education
Dallas Bar Association
Dallas City Federation of Colored Women's
  Clubs
Dallas Council on World Affairs
Dallas County Camp Fire Girls, Inc.
Dallas County Democratic Executive
  Committee
Dallas District 3 Democrats
Dallas Health & Science Museum
Dallas Museum of Fine Arts
Dallas Negro Chamber of Commerce
Democratic Women of Dallas County
Democratic Women's Political Association
Federation of Mexican Societies
Friends of the Dallas Public Library
Greater Dallas Council of Churches
Greater White Rock District Two Democrats
Greenhill School
Hadassah, Dallas Chapter
Hockaday School
Holland-American Club
Hospitality House of Senior Citizens
  Foundation
Interdenominational Ministers Alliance

Jewish Welfare Federation
Jr. Bar Association of Dallas
League of Women Voters of Dallas
League of Women Voters of Irving, Texas
Links, Inc., Dallas Chapter
Methodist Church, Dallas North-East
  District
Mexican Cultural Society
National Association for the Advancement
  of Colored People
National Association of Social Workers,
  Dallas Chapter
National Conference of Christians and Jews
National Council of Jewish Women,
  Dallas Section
National Women's Committee of Brandeis
  University, Dallas Chapter
North Dallas Democrats
Patricia Stevens College
Pilot Club of Dallas
Pioneer Women, Rishona Chapter
St. Mark's School of Texas
Salvation Army
South and East Dallas Chamber of
  Commerce
Southern Methodist University
Study Action Club
Tejas Girl Scout Council
Temple Emanu-El Sisterhood
Unitarian Laymen's League
United Church Women
University of Dallas
Women's Alliance, First Unitarian Church
  of Dallas
Women's Council of Dallas County,
  Texas, Inc.
Women's Overseas Service League
Young Democratic Club of Dallas County
Young Men's Christian Association —
  Moreland Branch
Young Women's Christian Association of
  Dallas and Dallas County

However, there is scant attention in this year to UN Week compared to the previous two years, perhaps in the wake of the trauma of the assassination of the president in the city. DUNA did host, with the League of Women Voters again, a UN Day talk by Harlan Cleveland, assistant secretary of state for international organizations, at the Statler Hilton

Hotel. The paper noted that Mayor Erik Jonsson declared October 18–24 UN Week (*DMN* 10-15-64).

The press coverage of the Dallas UNA in 1965 through 1967 continued to be extensive, with a mixture of announcements of events and news coverage of both the Dallas and the statewide Texas UNA.

Prominent business leader Raymond Nasher, who had been president of the Dallas chapter, was by then leading the statewide organization, which led to additional attention for their programs.

In February 1965, the Texas Division of UNA held a daylong conference with Joseph J. Sisco, deputy assistant secretary of state for international organization affairs, as the keynote speaker. The *Dallas News* gave extended coverage to Estelle Linzer, a top national staffer with the UNA-USA and "something of an expert on extremists" (*DMN* 02-27-65) under the headline "Stop World: I Want to Get Off." The article focuses on Linzer's warnings about the problem of apathy and quoted her extensively:

She said, "The greatest problem we've got is not extremists, necessarily. We can combat that with calm reason and facts. The greatest problem is apathy and indifference. The danger of apathy is particularly strong among Americans 21 to 35 years old—the age group most concerned with marriage, careers, and young families." Miss Linzer feels that the UNA members must make these young adults feel that they have a stake in the UN, especially as a force for peace. "They want their children to grow up. It's just as callous as that . . . It's a tough world, and as President Eisenhower said, the UN is a mirror of the world . . . It should be criticized, but constructively." (*DMN* 02-27-65)

Mr. Jack Goren, 1963 president of DUNA

The local paper further covered the election of Jack Goren, executive vice president of Neiman Marcus, as the next president of the Texas UNA. Raymond Buck, the past president of the Fort Worth Chamber of Commerce, was elected vice president. These leaders further illustrate the involvement of the prominent business leaders in the movement to promote the UN.

Several news items in 1965 reported the premiere of the movie *The Greatest Story Ever Told*, occurring first in New York and later in Dallas, including a benefit showing for DUNA. In light of today's emphasis on interfaith dialogue and multiculturalism, it is striking how this unabashedly Christian cultural event was covered and the fact that it was cosponsored by the Dallas Council on World Affairs and the DUNA (*DMN* 03-05-65, 03-15-65, and 03-18-65). This was clearly an exciting event, featuring a reception to honor the movie stars, including a "typical klieg light opening" (*DMN* 03-15-65).

Other programs of DUNA that appeared in the press included a talk to social science teachers by Donald C. Dunham of New York City, director of public services for the United States United Nations delegation, on "The UN and US National Interests" (*DMN* 03-06-65) and a talk on "The Exploration of Space" by Dr. Francis S. Johnson, director of the earth and planetary sciences laboratory of the Southwest Center for Advance Studies of the Graduate Research Center of the Southwest (*DMN* 03-14-65). There was a talk by a DUNA member and Dallas attorney Mrs. Edith DeBusk to the National Association of Parliamentarians (*DMN* 03-19-65). The organization also brought Mrs. Marietta Tree, permanent US ambassador to the UN Mission, as the speaker for the twelfth annual dinner meeting (*DMN* 04-17-65).

Attitudes in North Texas were clearly still mixed about the UN, as shown by several letters to the editor, which praised a *Dallas Morning News* editorial that claimed that "so many of our people have been duped into believing that the UN is our best hope for peace, while in truth that organization is the greatest threat to our national security" (*DMN*/LTE 06-18-65).

But the DUNA also responded forthrightly to the editorial, with the president, Henry Lanz, clarifying the positive aspects of the UN in a Letter to the Editor:

I would like to point out in behalf of the 800-member Dallas United Nations Association that the hopes of mankind are still founded on the UN. That the UN is an "imperfect tool" because it "includes the defects of mankind" is no reason for despair. If we are to despair, then we must abandon all hope, for peace and progress can only be sought through human institutions. You speak of bringing the UN back to reality—the reality is that the mirror still reflects accurately and none of us likes what he sees. Either destroy the mirror or face the facts, but destroying the mirror will not change the facts . . .

The fact that an organization such as the UN is not perfect is no reason to abandon it unless the means of improvement are not available. A responsible editorial policy would suggest means of achieving this improvement or, if you feel that this is not possible, should suggest alternatives. Certainly a flippant approach to such a serious problem is unlikely to contribute to constructive thought. (*DMN*/LTE 06-18-65)

Broad community support was evidenced by participation of the honorary board as well as the League of Women Voters and the DUNA board leadership.

Honorary Committee
UNITED NATIONS DAY IN DALLAS
OCTOBER 24, 1964

Hon. Erik Jonsson
Mayor of Dallas
Chairman

James W. Aston	Jack Goren	Rabbi Levi Olan
Ed Barker	Ed Gossett	W. W. Overton
Charles E. Beard	A. C. Greene	Bishop Kenneth Pope
James H. Bond	Pat Haggerty	Troy V. Post
Roland S. Bond	Jake Hamon	Clyde Rembert
Maurice I. Carlson	Rev. Luther Holcomb	Hamilton Richardson
Paul Carrington	Judge Sarah T. Hughes	Julius Schepps
E. O. Cartwright	Dr. Henry Lanz	Mrs. L. Storey Stemmons
James F. Chambers, Jr.	Jack G. Lawrence	John M. Stemmons
William H. Clark, III	W. L. Lindholm	W. Dawson Sterling
Mrs. S. Constance Condos	Rev. I. B. Loud	Robert H. Stewart, III
Dr. Donald Cowan	Allen Maley	Robert S. Strauss
Robert B. Cullum	Neil Mallon	Dr. Willis M. Tate
Dr. M. K. Curry	Stanley Marcus	Robert L. Thornton, Jr.
Joe Dealey	Charles A. Meyer	Tom C. Unis
Rev. William H. Dickinson	Henry S. Miller, Jr.	Dan C. Williams
Mrs. E. C. (Ned) Fritz	Raymond Nasher	Edward B. Winn
Irving Goldberg	Msgr. William F. O'Brien	Ben H. Wooten

OFFICERS OF LEAGUE OF WOMEN VOTERS OF DALLAS

President................Mrs. Edward C. Feitz

Vice-President...............Mrs. Sam Faris

Vice-President...............Mrs. Ralph Bubis

Vice-President...........Mrs. Donald Sander

Secretary...............Mrs. Arthur Schneider

Treasurer................Mrs. Arnold Gaynor

OFFICERS OF DALLAS UNITED NATIONS ASSOCIATION OF THE U.S.A.

Chairman of the
Board....................Judge Sarah T. Hughes
President ....Jack Goren
First Vice-President.........Gerald C. Mann
Second Vice-
President ....Mrs. Frederick Smith
Third Vice-President....Mrs. Taylor Robinson
Fourth Vice-
President.....Mrs. John A. Whitcroft, Jr.
Fifth Vice-
President.........Mrs. George C. Baker, Jr.
Associate................Mrs. Herbert Wincorn
Sixth Vice-President....Mrs. Jack Reynolds
Seventh Vice-
President......Mrs. Raymond Holbrook
Secretary................Mrs. John E. George
Treasurer................Dr. Henry C. Lanz

As in 1964, coverage of the 1965 UN Week was modest, but yielded two short articles, one noting the attendance of Dean Rusk and "Mrs. Dean Rusk" as a highlight of the week (*DMN* 10-27-65). The other report in the *Fort Worth Star Telegram* covered a tree-planting ceremony.

> "The United Nations was likened here Friday to 'a tree that has to grow against a hostile climate.'" The Rev. William D. Hall of Brite Divinity School, Texas Christian University, spoke during ceremonies dedicating a tree planted eight years ago on the lawn next to City Hall by the Fort Worth Chapter of the UNA . . . "We are too inclined to look on the UN as a machine to be fixed to run as we want," he added. "The whole thing is a living, growing process." (*FWST* 10-30-65)

Leadership Develops Wider Worldview

In early 1966, the *DMN* featured a profile of real estate developer Raymond Nasher and included a description of his extensive involvement in foreign affairs, including his being a member of the one-hundred-member US Commission for UNESCO and his long involvement in the UNA-USA, "a non-governmental group whose purpose is to support the UN and educate Americans about its activities" (*DMN*/Headliner Portrait: Nasher: His Is a Broad View 03-13-66).

Upheaval in the wider world, especially the many revolutionary movements for independence from colonial powers, was a focus of programs in this period. An April panel discussion on "The Role of the UN in a World of Revolution" was covered under a headline of "UN Inadequate" (*DMN* 04-15-66). SMU law professor Dr. Howard J. Taubenfeld was cited as saying that the UN's "processes for dealing with this revolution-filled world are not adequate to handle the problem because the UN was formed with a more stable world in mind." Interestingly, this is the first time that Vietnam is mentioned.

A. C. Greene, book editor for the *Dallas Times Herald*, explored the area of world press opinion toward the organization. "The world press expects more from the UN than the US," Greene said, calling the expectations unrealistic. "The US is more introspective of the UN than most other countries." He said, "Vietnam has put the organization on the spot as far as being a peacekeeping body. Judge [Sarah T] Hughes said the principal objective of the UN is to save coming generations from war." (*DMN* 04-15-66)

This perspective was echoed a month later in an article reporting on another DUNA and Dallas Council on World Affairs meeting, with assistant secretary of state Joseph J. Sisco as the speaker. "The United Nations is in serious financial difficulty," he said. "It has neither the financial wherewithal nor the political consensus to act in Vietnam" (*DMN* 05-12-66). It is interesting to realize that the DUNA audience was contemplating the situation in Vietnam very early on during that conflict.

Significant Support by Business and Community Leaders

Business leaders continued to be prominent in DUNA work, supported by President Johnson's encouragement, as shown in the article quoted below. Announcing the October 1966 UN Day far in advance, in July, the *Dallas Morning News* published an extended announcement that describes the players the UNA had recruited to participate and the commitment of these business leaders to UN-US cooperation:

Five Dallas business executives are among a group of the nation's business leaders who will participate in UN Day activities Oct. 24. They are Stanley Marcus, president of Neiman-Marcus; Harding L. Lawrence, president of Braniff International; Fladger F. Tannery, president of Frito-Lay, Inc.; Raymond D. Nasher, head of Nasher Properties; and Pat E. Haggerty, president of Texas Instruments, Inc.

Edgar F. Kaiser, recently appointed national UN Day chairman by President Johnson, asked business leaders to open an extended dialogue with the United Nations and to lend their experience to its programs. Kaiser asked that the country's leading corporate executives help open a 2-day exchange of ideas with the UN through the medium of the UNA-USA.

The business men also will be asked to join a mass information campaign designed to focus public attention on UN and US participation in its projects, Kaiser said. Kaiser is president of Kaiser Industries Corp. and chairman of the board of a group of companies that operates in 47 UN countries. The UNA is engaged in research, he said, to define programs and policies most likely to improve living standards and raise average incomes. (*DMN* 07-11-66)

Dallas UNA Events in 1966 reported in the Press

The *Dallas Morning News* carried a string of program reports, dated during the year 1966:

1. Panel discussion on "The Role of the UN in a World of Revolution" by Dr. Howard J. Taubenfeld; Judge Sarah T. Hughes; and A. C. Greene (*DMN* 04-15-66).
2. Speech by assistant secretary of state Joseph J. Sisco, sponsored with the Dallas Council on World Affairs at SMU (*DMN* 05-12-66).
3. Appointment of Raymond Nasher to US National Commission for UNESCO (*DMN* 08-11-66).
4. Benefit performances of the film *John F. Kennedy: Years of Lightning, Day of Drums*, sponsored with the Greater Dallas Democrats (*DMN* 08-13-66).
5. "Insights into International Affairs," an informal adult course sponsored by SMU, the Dallas Council on World Affairs and the Dallas UNA Lecture series. "Cost was $10 or $15 per married couple" (*DMN* 09-11-66). Dr. August Spain, chair of department of government at TCU, spoke as part of the lecture series. (*DMN* 09-28-66).

Raymond D. Nasher, Dallas builder and developer, spoke at the Hockaday School on the topic of "The UN Nobody Knows" (*DMN* 10-16-66). L.N.D. Wells Jr., attorney, Dallas United Nations Association, spoke at Starlight Chapter of B'nai B'rith Women (*DMN* 10-23-66). Mayor Waggoner presented a United Nations Association distinguished service award to Ed Phelps Jr., who served as United Nations Day chairman for Grand Prairie (*DMN* 11-06-66). Dr. Arthur S. Lall, former senior career ambassador of India to the UN and Austria, spoke on India/Pakistan issues, sponsored jointly by the DUNA, the SMU Forum, the Dallas chapter of the American Association of University Women, and the League of Women Voters of Dallas (*DMN* 12-08-66).

As the summary shows, 1966 was a busy year in which major national conversations about the role of the UN in American and international politics were held in Dallas. However, it is interesting to note that no identified program about a 1966 UN Day was found to be reported in the press within the customary time frame around October 24.

Press Exposure Showed Diversity

The peak years for press coverage of Dallas UNA were 1966 and 1967. In 1967, the major UNA-related news coverage included a fracas over the DUNA being allowed a booth at the Texas State Fair in September while the John Birch Society was denied one and about Ambassador Henry Cabot Lodge, the US UN ambassador, who was the keynote speaker for 1967 UN Week. In addition to these highlights of the year, the DUNA continued to receive press coverage of its many other programs.

DUNA continued to host prominent world figures, including visits by the former prime minister of Hungary, Dr. Ferenc Nagy, and Lord Caradon, the British minister of state for foreign affairs and United Kingdom representative to the UN, in addition to many local speakers from the business, civic, and academic communities. The *Dallas Morning News* reported DUNA events with a generally positive tone, as exhibited in references through the year.

Former Hungarian prime minister Dr. Ferenc Nagy spoke on "the Sino-Soviet conflict—its impact on the communist camp and world politics" as part of the SMU Dallas College lectures on international events, sponsored with the Dallas Council on World Affairs and Dallas College (*DMN* 01-06-67). Mrs. Leon S. Price, DUNA member, was nominated as first vice president at the National Congress of Parents and Teachers convention in Minneapolis, Minnesota (*DMN* 01-13-67). Mrs. C. Wesley Goyer Jr., a DUNA member, was among ten women to be honored by the YWCA (*DMN* 01-20-67). William J. Green of the DUNA, spoke on "The United Nations Nobody Knows" to the Retired Employees Association (*DMN* 02-07-67).

Mrs. Ogden Baine, UNA activist and SMU dean of women, was selected as the 1967 recipient of the Mature Woman Award by the Altrusa

Club of Dallas (*DMN* 02-19-67). Dr. Robert Dale Judy, assistant professor of government at North Texas State University, spoke on the problems of underdeveloped nations (*DMN* 02-22-67). Dallas UNA honored three high school essay writers with awards (*DMN* 03-28-67). Ms. Ann Crisp, Dallas attorney and a member of the speakers' bureau of the DUNA, spoke on "A Look at the Changing Status of Women Worldwide," the first mention of women's issues (*DMN* 04-18-67).

Lord Caradon, British minister of state for foreign affairs and permanent United Kingdom representative to the United Nations, lectured on "A Start in Freedom: The Aftermath of Colonialism," cosponsored with Dallas Council on World Affairs, Dallas United Nations Association, Dallas Chapter of English-Speaking Unions, and SMU (*DMN* 05-09-67). David Williamson, a student at North Dallas High School, was cited for outstanding achievement in the UNA-USA essay contest on worldwide current events (*DMN* 05-30-67). US district judge Sarah T. Hughes was the featured commencement speaker and received an honorary doctor of laws degree at Indiana State University (*DMN* 06-05-67).

Dallas investments executive Garry A. Weber, DUNA member, served as general chairman of the 1968 March of Dimes appeal for the Metropolitan Dallas (*DMN* 09-03-67). The Honorable Yaacov Hess, consul of Israel in Texas, Oklahoma, and Louisiana, was questioned on "Voter's Digest" on KTVT, Channel 11, by Dr. Howard Taubenfeld, SMU law professor and a member of the DUNA (*DMN* 09-23-67). Otto Mullinax, attorney, spoke at the Western Heights Christian Church of Garland on "A Better Understanding of the UN and the Specialized Agencies" (*DMN* 09-26-67).

US ambassador at large Henry Cabot Lodge spoke at a UN Day address for DUNA, cosponsored with the Dallas Council on World Affairs, SMU, and the University of Texas at Arlington (*DMN* 10-24-67). Mrs. Katie Louchheim, deputy assistant secretary of state for educational and cultural affairs, spoke at a UNA meeting in Fort Worth at Arlington Heights Methodist Church (*FWST* 10-26-67)."Trick or Treat for UNICEF"— Texas governor John Connally designated October 31 as UNICEF Day in Texas (*DMN* 10-30-67).

Dr. Louis Kestenberg, a University of Houston history professor, spoke on the work of the United Nations Educational, Scientific and Cultural Organization (UNESCO) (*DMN* 11-16-67). A citizens' panel spoke against the US building an antiballistic missile defense system against Soviet rockets, sponsored by UNA-USA (*DMN* 11-26-67). UNICEF card sale was held at the DUNA office in Preston Center (*DMN* 11-28-67). The United Nations Association, Dallas, received $5,000 in funds from the Fund Solicitation Board (probably predecessor to United Way) (*DMN* 12-31-67).

State Fair of Texas Dispute

Perhaps the most telling press coverage revolving around the controversies of the times was the dispute over booths at the Texas State Fair, which prompted several articles and letters to the editor. The right-wing John Birch Society, denied a booth at the fair, explicitly complained about the United Nations Association having a booth. The western director of public relations for the society publicly complained, saying that "the Dallas United Nations Assoc. has participated in the Fair for years and asserted that he does not know of a more controversial group than the Dallas UN Association." He also claimed that "the fair has invited Communist countries to participate in the fair, and that it was disturbing that Communist countries are invited and groups such as the John Birch Society are excluded" (*DMN*/LTE 09-06-67).

The general manager of the Texas State Fair, on the other hand, "said it has been a long-standing policy to deny participation to organizations judged to be 'political or controversial.'" (*DMN* 09-06-67).

However, an opinion column on the same day defended the Birch Society's complaint:

If the John Birch Society is banned . . . members ask why the Dallas UNA has been given permission to set up a booth. They have a point . . . "It has become a convenient whipping boy for nearly every liberal polemicist around. It is regularly trotted out as a frightening example, repeatedly used to illustrate lectures by liberals who would like the nation to believe there is a diabolically clever right-wing conspiracy." . . . It is difficult to see why the fair has any more reason to bar it than to bar any other organization with a political complexion." (*DMN* 09-06-67)

This controversy stayed alive, as a letter to the editor nearly a month later also cites the "discriminatory and biased" decision to allow the UNA, but not the John Birch Society (*DMN*/LTE 10-04-67). This entire situation suggests that the United Nations Association had been very successful in positioning itself as a nonpolitical, noncontroversial organization that was completely in the mainstream of the times.

The political upheavals of the late 1960s appear in the remaining press coverage of 1967. A national column by William F. Buckley snidely critiqued the "childish" faith in the UN after the "UNA-USA had released a report by a 'panel of American businessmen and scholars' urging the recognition of Red China" (*DMN* 10-08-67). Buckley treats this UNA-USA recommendation as absurd, citing that congressman Dr. Walter Judd attended the newly formed World Anti-Communist League as a contrasting effort.

Ironically, US ambassador at large Henry Cabot Lodge, speaking for UN Day at SMU two weeks later, acknowledged the problem of "sentimentality and wishful thinking" in relation to the UN.

"It is inevitable that a world peace-making organization will either be contemptible or annoying," he said at a UN Day address before a capacity gathering in McFarlin Auditorium at SMU. "It has no choice. If it has no influence and it accomplishes nothing, it's contemptible. If the UN stops a country from doing something it wants to do, then it becomes very annoying. But when it is annoying, then it shows at least that it is doing something."

The ambassador said, "We should stay in the United Nations and build it up. There is going to be much work to do. But we ought not to flinch from work because, after all is said and done, the UN is one of humanity's best hopes for peace with freedom and for evolution toward its orderly world." (*DMN* 10-24-67)

The UN at twenty years old has become an institution that has disappointed many.

Lodge said the UN "has not worked out as its founders intended" because it was founded in 1948 under the assumption that the great powers of WWII would continue and that we and the Russians would go on working together. The very next year, that assumption broke down, and it's somewhat of a miracle that the UN went on at all" (*DMN* 10-24-67).

However, despite the frustrations that erupted in both the mainstream (William Buckley) and on the fringe (John Birch Society), most leaders continued to defend the necessity and the promise of the United Nations:

> Mrs. Katie Louchheim, deputy assistant secretary of state for educational and cultural affairs, speaking at a UNA meeting in Fort Worth at Arlington Heights Methodist Church . . . cited the UN's work in refugee assistance, economic development, human rights, family planning and economic sanctions . . . She also cited its work in preventing the spread and misuse of atomic weapons. "Some people," she said, "fail to see the UN as a most ingenious design for the peaceful evolution of modern society. It functions both as a safety valve for the tension and a sounding board for the ideas of man." (*FWST* 10-26-67)

After 1967, coverage of UNA in the Dallas press slows. In 1969, there is extensive coverage of Raymond Nasher, who has gone from being a local figure in UNA work to a national figure as well. The *Dallas Morning News* covered his talk to the UNA in March 1969. See the individual article on Mr. Nasher in chapter 3.

Reports in the 1970s Include Women's Rights

The US ambassador to the UN, Arthur J. Goldberg, pondered the problem of equal rights for women from his twenty-fourth-floor law office window in his beloved glass-walled UN Building.

> Women constitute the biggest bloc, they should stand for office more, and get more involved. But . . . she should be informed. An excellent way to get started is to join the local chapter of the United Nations Association. Discussion groups and other programs conducted by these grassroots chapters will help her better understand American foreign policy. (*DMN* 01-15-70)

1970 UN Japanese Peace Bell First Issue stamp

Illustrating the international character of the United Nations to the American public, the United Nations released two stamps on March 13. A reproduction of the Peace Bell, which had been presented to the UN in 1964 by the UNA of Japan as the fourth in its art series and a commemorative of the Lower Mekong Basin Development that honored flood control work in Southeast Asia. The postage value of each was six cents (*DMN* 02-23-70).[3]

Ms. Angie Brooks, a UN delegate from Liberia since 1964, spoke on the "Impact of Youth Upon International Affairs" on March 14, 1970. Her appearance was sponsored by the Youth Foundation of Emmanuel Chapel United Methodist Church and cosponsored by the DUNA, Dallas League of Women Voters, and the American Association of University Women, and Business and Professional Women of Dallas (*DMN* 03-01-70).

Her Excellency Ms. Brooks served as president of the UN General Assembly twenty-fourth session. As a poor black woman, she overcame many obstacles to achieve the highest eminence. One of nine children of an African Methodist Episcopal minister, she was reared in another home by a seamstress and always wanted to become a lawyer. A friend who later became prime minister of Liberia taught her law from a book; she is now an astute, plain-talking lady lawyer from Africa's oldest republic (*DMN* 03-14-70).

---

[3]   See pictures of additional first-day-issue stamps in the appendix.

A traveling exhibit of tapestries made in Poland from the original designs of children five to nine years old will be shown at a Wednesday cocktail party sponsored by the Dallas United Nations Association. The fund-raising event will be at One Main Place. Tickets are $7.50 each. Brief lectures on the more than 20 tapestries will be given by Miss Ann McGee and Mrs. Henry X. Salzberger. The Rev. Tomas A. Fry Jr. is honorary chairman, and Mrs. C. Wesley Goyer Jr. and Mrs. Donald Lewis are co-chairmen. (*DMN* 09-09-70)

Walt Rostow, former top presidential adviser to LBJ, will be the featured speaker when the Dallas United Nations Association marks its 25th anniversary at noon Thursday at the Sheraton-Dallas Hotel. He will address the Association again at 6:30 p.m. at SMU. Tickets are available to the public through the Dallas UNA. (*DMN* 10-18-70)

Expanding Consciousness of International Concerns Were Aired Later in the 1970s

Ecologist J. Ross Vincent will address the annual UNA meeting. Vincent is vice-president and director of research of the Ecology Center of Louisiana. He will attend the UN Conference on the Human Environment at Stockholm Sweden in June.

The UNA members will elect and install their new officers, according to Dr. Tom A Fry, Jr., DUNA president. Vincent also will be the key speaker at the annual student UN workshop at SMU with students from 19 Dallas County high schools in attendance. (*DMN* 04-09-71)

Wallace Irwin, the man in charge of ecology for the US delegation to the UN arrived in Dallas for appearances at the UTA, Weatherford College, North Texas State Univ., the Dallas UNA, and Dallas school students and faculty.

Irwin has been speech-writer for eight US ambassadors to the UN since he was hired by Henry Cabot Lodge in 1954. He said that the UN has "had its ups and downs" in importance, but is still the only place where most nations of the world can relate to each other. It has helped the US and Russia slowly inch toward each other in resolving difficulties. (*DMN* 04-28-71)

Irwin, special assistant to the US permanent representative to the UN, currently is setting up US participation in a Stockholm, Sweden, conference later this year on International Ecology. Irwin, who is concerned chiefly with UN activities in the field of human environment, has been with the US mission since 1954 when he was appointed director of the Office of Public Affairs. He serves under Ambassador George H. W. Bush. (*FWST* 04-28-71)

Debate over the goals of UNICEF aid was reported by Lea Donosky in the *DMN*:

> The President of the Dallas UNA and the coordinator of the local John Birch Society agree upon one aspect of the annual Halloween UN Children's Fund (UNICEF). Both say they want to get accurate information to the public and let them decide the merits of the program.

Dr. Thomas Fry, president of the Dallas UNA and pastor of the First Presbyterian Church of Dallas, said that he welcomed a letter to the *DMN* written by Larry Waters, coordinator for the local John Birch Society, outlining charges of "immoral" use of the funds collected for UNICEF.

Dr. Fry countered the charge with US State Dept. bulletins which "make it clear UNICEF funds have never been used for any other purpose than to bring better medical care, nutrition and education to millions of deprived children without regard for their race, religion or the political system of their countries." . . . Right now it (UNICEF) is feeding and sheltering millions of Pakistani refugees in India, he said. (*DMN* 10-05-71)

Dallas United Nations Association board members, Mrs. Theodore Strauss (Annette), Dr. Thomas Fry, and Mrs. Hal Watson, celebrated the 25th birthday of UNICEF, the UN Children's Fund (*DMN* 10-17-71).

"The problems of the world are greater now than ever before in the history of the world, but their solution will be much nearer if the United States does not turn its back on the United Nations," said Lord Caradon of England at the Dallas UNA annual meeting. Lord Caradon, chief of his country's delegation to the UN from 1964 through 1970, spoke to a crowd of approximately four hundred at the banquet at SMU (*DMN* 10-30-71).

DUNA continued its educational mission at the Dallas Federation of Women's Clubs meeting: "Maurice Carlson, who is serving on the board of directors of the Dallas UNA and is currently a professor of English and Greek at the University of Texas at Arlington, will speak on 'The UN's Newest Member—China'" (*DMN* 12-06-71).

A UNA National Policy Panel reflected the difficult mediating role of UN in dealing with regional conflicts.

> The warfare between India and Pakistan grows hotter, the language becomes more belligerent, national prides become more hopelessly involved. A pitiful situation seems certain to deteriorate into a calamitous war . . . Even when the matter is brought before the Security Council, as it must be, the question arises as to the UN's capability for effective action . . . Who is the culprit? (*DMN* 12-07-71)

Canada is building an atomic reactor on Taiwan for the Taiwanese Institute for Nuclear Energy Research. The device opens a chilling possibility. In 12 months of operation, the reactor can produce about 22 pounds of plutonium—which is roughly one and one-half times enough to produce a nuclear bomb.

A report of the "United Nations Association of the US, a private organization, emphasizes that Taiwan is not the first or the only country to acquire that potential. Israel and India already are operating similar reactors. The UNA asserts that Israel has manufactured about 88 pounds of plutonium and India some 209 pounds . . . Surely the world leaders, including our nation and Soviets, should seek in every way to bring all countries under the non-proliferation pact. (*FWST* 09-12-72)

Dr. Hyman Judah Schachtel, chief rabbi of the Congregation Beth Israel of Houston, will open United Nations Week observance in Dallas with a speech before the local UNA on Oct. 24 at SMU's Storey Hall. The public is invited to hear Dr. Schachtel discuss 'The United Nations-United States in This Critical Election Year,' according to Otto Mullinax, president of the Dallas UNA. (*DMN* 10-21-72)

Early in 1973, reports continued with some ambivalence. A report from the National UNA follows:

"Yes, there is frustration and disappointment that the UN is not doing an effective job," says UNA President Porter McKeever, emphasizing that he is speaking for himself rather than the organization . . . Three years ago UNA had 25,000 members: this year (1973) it expects membership to hit 100,000. The fee of $10 a year covers only part of the organization's budget; the rest comes from business, industry, foundation and civic contributions.

"UNA feels it is growing because the public still has faith in the UN approach despite frustration over results . . . Disillusion with the UN stems from 'public disenchantment over the whole range of foreign relationships, beginning with disillusion over the war in Vietnam," McKeever said. (*DMN* 01-08-73)

A 3-man panel will discuss world events with the Town North Business and Professional Women's Club on Feb. 27 at El Chico, Inwood Village. Panelists are Dr. David Reagan, US Dept. of Commerce, Walter V. Edwards, Dallas Office of US Immigration, and Otto C. Mullinax, president of the Dallas UNA. (*DMN* 02-18-73)

Jack Goren, well known Dallas civic leader, died Saturday at his home. A native of Dallas, Goren was graduated Phi Beta Kappa from the Univ. of Texas, Austin, with a degree in political science. He was vice president of Neiman-Marcus. He was a former president of the Dallas and Texas Associations of the United Nations and a member of the (national) UNA-USA. Goren was also a member of the Dallas Council of World Affairs and Community Relations Council and was on the national board of governors of the American Jewish Committee. (*DMN* 03-11-73)

Mayor Annette Strauss, second woman elected DUNA president, 1973

The election of new officers for the DUNA was announced in April. Mrs. Theodore (Annette) Strauss has become the second woman to be president of the Dallas United Nations Association. She succeeds out-going president Otto Mullinax. The first woman president elected by the group was Judge Sarah T. Hughes in 1953.

The speaker at the meeting was US representative to the UN Security Council W. Tapley Bennett, Jr. (*DMN* 04-05-73).

In a related story, Jeanne Singer, United Nations backer and UNA-USA vice-president, came to Dallas to attend a board meeting of the Dallas UNA in the home of the new president, Mrs. Theodore H. Strauss. Mrs. Singer [*sic*] stated that today's problems simply won't wait at a border while someone decides some issue. Boundaries are not respected by disease, pollution or ideas. That's the reason for the UN's existence.

Mrs. Singer travels twice a year visiting some of the national association's 175 or so local units which have a total of around 80,000 members. Mrs. Singer recalls that the first day she ever attended a UN session was the day Israel became a member. She has watched many other historic moments, "and I've seen many ups and downs at the UN in the public eye."

The polls consistently show Americans as pretty firm supporters of the UN, though they may disapprove of its performance in a given field or at a given moment. One example: the smallpox elimination program of the World Health Organization, a UN agency. That program has saved the federal government millions which used to be spent in annual inoculation drives . . . Mrs. Singer believes that many problems can be solved with patience and UN help. (*DMN* 04-13-73)

The 1973 UN Week program was the next media report:

US Sen. Gale McGee, D-Wyo., current chairman of the Senate Post Office and Civil Service Committee, will speak during the Dallas UNA's annual UN Week Banquet, scheduled Oct. 22 in SMU's Student Center. Judge Sarah T. Hughes, honorary chairman of activities here, will preside at the banquet sponsored by DUNA. (*DMN* 10-23-73)

Senator McGee, who is also the US Senate delegate to the United Nations, stated that the ceasefire has the best chance of any possible cease-fire because it was agreed on by the two great powers—the US and the Soviet Union. He said that no recent event has illustrated so dramatically that the UN is working than the peace resolution arranged by the US and Soviet Union and accepted by the UN Security Council.

"The problem is that we over-expect from the UN. It has no peace-keeping powers, adding that it merely provides a forum for communication away from the heat of battle. It's a role now often being jeopardized by the new isolationist sentiment in our country, including in Congress," he said, noting that the sentiment has arisen in part over dissatisfactions with the Vietnam War. (*DMN* 10-23-73)

There were no news reports published in 1974 until the annual meeting of DUNA in the spring.

Ambassador Barbara White was the speaker at a joint luncheon of SMU's Management Seminar for Women Executives and the Dallas UNA on March 27. Ambassador White is the top woman in this country's mission to the UN, where she serves as alternate representative for special political affairs and holds the rank of ambassador. Ms. White is on loan to the State Department from her permanent post as career minister for information with the US Information Service.

The audience was composed of Dallas UNA members and participants in the Management Seminar for Women Executives, sponsored by SMU's School of Continuing Education.

Ms. White cited five points for specific consideration by those who would assess US participation in the United Nations realistically as well as idealistically:

1. Whether we like it or not, many of the problems whose solutions are in our national interest can only be solved in an international forum.

2. Realism means recognition that because of the size, the power, the weight, the influence, the aspirations, the traditions of the US, we must play a leadership role. She says there can be no alternative.

3. Realism demands recognition that the form of international cooperation will vary according to the issue or the circumstances.

4. Realists must recognize that though the need for common action is great, the gulf separating outlooks and goals is also very great. The Common Goal for all of us is not to have the world blow up in our faces . . . and we all want prosperity.

5. Finally, realism demands recognition that our international institutions are still very primitive, except in certain technological fields where value judgments don't get in the way . . . the fact that the institutions are now in their infancy shouldn't discourage us; it should encourage us to tackle problems more vigorously . . . Narrow national attitudes that the United States can go it alone fly in the face of reality. (*DMN* 03-28-74)

Mrs. Lorinne Emery, active with International Visitors programs and other civic programs, was elected president for 1973-1974

"Mrs. Lorinne (Clyde) Emery will serve the Dallas United Nations Association as 1973–1974 president" (*DMN* 04-01-74).

> Once you knew the year was ripe and ready for the harvest by the frost on the pumpkin; now it's UNICEF on the move. Dallas volunteers for the United Nations Children's Fund are busy again at their regular autumn tasks, selling holiday greeting cards and gifts, planning for Halloween and United Nations Day, Oct. 24. Mrs. Clyde Emery heads the Dallas UNA, which will observe UN Day with a dinner on Oct. 24 in the Hilton Inn. (*DMN* 10-04-74)

"The Dallas UNA has designated Oct. 24 as United Nations Day, during UN Week, Oct. 20-27. Dr. Abram Sachar will speak at the dinner on UN Day at the Hilton Inn at 6 p.m. Tickets are $7.50 per person or $60 for a table for eight" (*DMN* 10-08-74).

The next news item appeared in 1975.

> Mrs. Clyde Emery, who formulated the concept of the Dallas Committee on Foreign Visitors in 1954 and continues to be active in it, and is also president of the Dallas UNA and secretary of the Association of Directors of Volunteers, has been nominated for the Zonta Award. (*DMN* 02-16-75)

Several Reports Were Published in 1976

> An international trade discussion dinner meeting will be held on Jan. 20, 1976, at the World Trade Club. Trade with Japan and North and South Korea will be discussed. Speakers include the South Korean ambassador to the UN and the vice-president of the Republic of Korea National Red Cross. The dinner is sponsored jointly by the Dallas UNA, Dallas Council on World Affairs, and the International Trade Association. (*DMN* 01-12-76)

Among the Letters to Readers to the *Dallas News*, a national board member responded to an earlier column:

Dick West's Jan. 25 column, "Distorted Views of Editorials, claims the UN has become "worse than a joke" and implies that the US is financially overburdened in its contributions to the UN.

"The US is the world's wealthiest nation; our gross national product is almost 40 per cent of the world's total. Each American pays just about 30 cents per year for the regular UN budget . . . Fourteen other countries pay a greater per capita amount than we do . . . While the antics of some representatives in the General Assembly receive all the publicity, 90 per cent of the total UN budget is being spent on a wide range of social, economic and humanitarian programs that benefit all mankind, including us. UN organizations that benefit Americans are WHO, World Health Organization; FAO, Food and Agriculture Organization; and the UN's World Weather Watch . . .

In our indignation over the actions of the General Assembly, only one body of the UN, we must not forget the essential place the world organization occupies in US relations and in our own daily lives" (signed) Joseph M. Segel, Member, Board of Governors, UNA, New York, NY. (*DMN/LTE* 02-14-76).

United Nations Undersecretary-General, William Buffum, spoke to the Dallas United Nations Association on Wednesday. Buffum deals directly with human rights issues in the world body. "The degree of application and priorities of human rights is bound to differ widely in various countries in the developing world," Buffum said. "He cited the need for basic necessities such as sufficient food supplies, education, and industrial development in developing countries, as among those areas considered to have higher priority in some nations." (*DMN* 03-31-76)

The highest ranking woman in the UN Secretariat will speak in Dallas Oct. 25 for United Nations Day. Helvi Sipila, assistant secretary-general for social development and humanitarian affairs, will speak at 6:30, Oct. 25, at the SMU Student Center. Mrs. Sipila was secretary-general for International Women's Year. She is from Finland and is an attorney and served as an official in various courts in Finland prior to her UN duties. (*DMN* 10-09-76)

The 1980s to the Present

During the 1970s, press coverage of the Dallas UNA had become less frequent, and this trend continued through the 1980s and 1990s. This may have been because the organization was less active during this time or because other forms of communication with the public took the place of the print media.

Definitely since the turn of the millennium, other forms of media and communication have replaced the local newspaper as the primary source of information. Brief meeting announcements on event calendars made up the substance of most entries, with occasional expansion in opinion columns or letters. The timeline capsules in chapter 5 draw from DUNA archives to offer wider perspective.

> Human Rights Day workshop, led by Willis Harman, NorthPark Inn, sponsored by Dallas United Nations Association. Contact: Marvin Sadovsky, 521-6860. (*DMN* 12-06-83)

> The United Nations Association will meet in the Grand Ballroom, SMU Student Center. Contact: George DeWald, 238-6008. (*DMN* 04-03-84)

Later in 1984, Dallas and DUNA lost a longtime human rights leader and advocate. His obituary stated the following:

> Levi A. Olan's journey through life took him from a land ruled by czars which was rife with anti-Semitism, to honor and prestige as the rabbi of Temple Emanu-El in Dallas ... Olan served as president of the Dallas United Nations Association in 1960 and the president of the Central Conference of American Rabbis. (*DMN* 10-18-84)

See more information on Rabbi Olan in chapter 3 of this history.

> Hurst—"The Bedford Baha'i community and the United Nations Association of Dallas will sponsor a panel discussion on human rights at 7:30, Friday, at the Hurst

Public Library . . . The public is invited to hear guest speakers Dick Sloos, President of the area UNA; Monirch Kazemzadeh, representative to the UN for the National Spiritual Assembly of the Baha'is of the US; and Allen Saxe, professor of political science at the University of Texas at Arlington." (*DMN* 12-05-84)

An ad in the *DMN* noted the information: "December 10— Traditionally recognized throughout the world as Human Rights Day— Quotes from Universal Declaration of Human Rights." (*DMN* 12-10-84)

The sparse coverage continued, with the next entry in digital archives from the *Fort Worth Star Telegram*: "A program about human rights issues in Dallas, sponsored by the Dallas UNA and SMU, is scheduled from 7 to 9 p.m. Thursday in Karcher Auditorium in Storey Hall at SMU" (*FWST* 12-11-86).

Next Media Entry Appeared in 2001

In the Gather Around column of the *DMN*:

An article in the *DMN* reports that Beth Pirtle reads to students at Stark Elementary of Carrollton-Farmers Branch school district. Beth is with the Dallas chapter of the UNA, which gave books to C-FB schools. Beth is a past president of the Dallas UNA. (*DMN* 05-25-01)

Robert Miller cited a milestone celebration in the Business Day column:

It's been a half-century since the Dallas chapter of the United Nations Association of the United States was founded. The group will celebrate that milestone on Tuesday at Maggiano's Little Italy Restaurant at NorthPark Center . . . the public is invited. Dr. Jeff Dumas, professor of political economy at UT-Dallas, will deliver the keynote address. The Rev. Bill Matthews, the current president, said several of the chapter's past presidents are expected to attend. The nonprofit, nonpartisan organization works to educate people about the United Nations and its agencies. (*DMN* 02-26-02)

Ever wished you could have met Eleanor Roosevelt? The Dallas Public Library brings you the next best thing when Boston Actress Elena Dodd brings the one-woman play 'Meet Eleanor Roosevelt' to the auditorium of the J. Erik Jonsson Central Library Saturday afternoon. The show is sponsored by the Dallas chapter of the UNA and by the library's government documents division.

The play highlights Mrs. Roosevelt's years as a widow, when she chaired the UN Commission on Human Rights and directed the drafting of the organization's unprecedented Universal Declaration of Human Rights. The text is based on her own writings . . .

The performance will be repeated Monday night at the University Park United Methodist Church with an additional sponsor, the Genesis Class of UPUMC. (*DMN* 03-05-03)

In the *DMN* Community Clipboard calendar, "The UNA of Dallas will host a panel discussion about human trafficking Thursday night at the Center for Community Cooperation. Panel participants will discuss efforts to deal with human trafficking" (*DMN* 04-09-03).

Robert Miller announced the Spotlight on Rights:

The Dallas Chapter of the UNA will discuss human rights next week at its second Business Connection luncheon on transnational business issues. The event will be Wednesday at the Park City Club, 5956 Sherry Lane, 17th floor. Chapter spokesman Paul Pederson said the speakers will be:

Joe W. "Chip" Pitts III, a director of Amnesty International USA and former chief legal officer of Nokia Inc. Mr. Pitts is also a delegate to the UN Commission on Human Rights and a frequent writer and speaker on corporate social responsibility.

Oscar Gonzalez, an attorney with Gonzalez Rolon Valdespino & Rodriquez LLC who writes and speaks on ethics in transnational trade, the Foreign Corrupt Practices Act and export and customs compliance.

Sponsors are American Airlines, Nexen Petroleum USA Inc. and PricewaterhouseCoopers. Tickets are $35. Business attire. (*DMN* 06-03-04)

In the 2000s, one of the few, but quite notable instances of press coverage of the Dallas UNA appeared in 2004. In the first is a column by Terrence Stutz:

Perry disagreed with proclamation signed by Bush, and the [*sic*] Dallas mayor.

Gov. Rick Perry rejected a request to issue a proclamation recognizing last Sunday as United Nations Day while President Bush and Dallas Mayor Laura Miller, a Democrat, each signed UN Day proclamations. President Bush also urged governors of the 50 states to "honor the observance of UN Day" in his proclamation.

The president of the Texas division of the UNA on Wednesday called the governor's decision an embarrassment to the state and a slap at an organization that is focused on eliminating unequal treatment of women around the world. "We're very disappointed and embarrassed that the governor would do something like this," said Beth Weems Pirtle of Dallas, state president of the UNA. "Rick Perry is trying to make the UN a political football, and it's not a political football. It is a nonpartisan organization that helps people all over the world."

While the UN enjoys strong support in many places in the world, the Republican Party of Texas has been hostile to it. For example, the state party platform in the past has stated that the GOP "believes it is in the best interest of the citizens of the US that we immediately rescind our membership in, as well as all financial and military contributions to, the United Nations." . . . Mrs. Pirtle said . . . her nonprofit group provides information and education about the UN to the public . . . Ms. Miller's signed proclamation cited the need to support UN goals that promote equality for women in primary and secondary education around the world. (*DMN* 10-28-04)

The controversy attracted national attention, according to a report two days later:

> An international scandal of sorts has broken out in Texas, after Gov. Rick Perry rejected President Bush's request that the nation's governors sign a proclamation honoring the United Nations. Perry believes the UN has not shown enough support for the US's efforts to bring freedom and democracy to the world," said Kathy Walt, the Republican governor's press secretary. When asked whether she could offer specifics, she said: "I'm not going to. That is the extent of our statement."
> Suzanne DiMaggio, executive director of Global Policy Progress at the UNA in NY, said this is the first time a governor has rejected such a proclamation and called his decision 'profoundly misplaced and shortsighted."

> Dallas resident Beth Weems Pirtle, president of the Texas division of the UNA, . . . replied "But I am embarrassed that the state of Texas did not sign. The governor is just out of touch."

> Walt, the governor's press secretary, replied, "Governor Perry is a very principled and disciplined leader. I don't think it's an embarrassment to the state at all." (*DMN* 10-30-04)

New UN Secretary General Ban Ki-Moon Seeks Stronger US Partnership

UN Secretary-General Ban Ki Moon

Parade magazine, distributed in the *DMN*, commented on the new UN secretary general's ambitious goals in 2007:

Ban Ki-Moon became the UN's newest secretary-general in January 2007. He joked that his job is "Mission Impossible." . . . Ban, 63, has one chance to get it right. "Today, the UN is beset by scandal and in-fighting among its 192 member nations. Its ability to promote peace, prevent war, protect human rights and halt the spread of nuclear weapons—even its very relevance—will likely be decided on Ban's watch. And in the US, patience with the UN is running out . . ."

Kofi Annan, Ban's predecessor, was openly hostile to the US by the end of his term. When he left as UN chief, he delivered a stinging rebuke to the US on everything from human rights to its desire "to seek supremacy over all others." Anti-American sentiment currently runs high throughout the UN—if not the world. Even so, Americans are unwilling to give up on the

UN—yet. Some 75% still believe it should play a "major" or "leading" role in world affairs, the Gallup poll found . . .

He has chosen a risky course: to pursue a strong partnership with the United States." Ban has been pro-US since the Korean War. He taught himself English in part by watching American GIs. At 18 he won a Red Cross competition to visit the US where he met President John F. Kennedy in 1962. It changed his life. He says that JFK is his role model. "I saw how he contributed to world peace and security."

Ban's big challenges are nuclear threats, genocide, and peacekeeping. He has big dreams. He hopes to be "the secretary-general who restores trust and helps the UN commit to lifting millions out of abject poverty." (*DMN* 06-24-07)

"The World Affairs Council presented a well-attended program with Gillian Sorensen of the United Nations Foundation at 6 p.m. at the Rosewood Crescent Hotel" (*DMN* Community Calendar 11-27-11).

DUNA and Peacemakers, Inc. observed International Women's Day 2012, with women leaders from 18 countries, brought by the U.S. Department of State, speakers from UNF and UNA-USA

The Dallas Chapter of the United Nations Association partnered with Peacemakers Inc. to hold a luncheon to honor International Women's Day at the Tower Club, Dallas, with 110 persons present, including special international visitors.

1. The International Visitor Leadership Program of the US Department of State brought women leaders from eighteen countries. Visitors came from Botswana, Iraq, Latvia, Macedonia, Malawi, Malaysia, Nigeria, Pakistan, Philippines, Slovak Republic, Sri Lanka, St. Kitts and Nevis, Thailand, Turkey, and Vietnam.

2. Speakers included Sen. Timothy Wirth, CEO of the United Nations Foundation, and Patrick M. Madden, executive director of UNA-USA. Peacemakers Inc. named Wirth a "Peace Patron."

Tatiana Androsov presented DUNA's 2015 "Appreciation" to Shabnam Modgil

3. Award of International Woman of the Day was presented to Shabnam Modgil of the Dallas Chapter UNA by UNA-USA CEO Patrick Madden and president Nelda R. Reid.

4. Other cosponsors were the Thanks-Giving Foundation, Embrey Human Rights program at SMU, DFW International Community Alliance, and UNA-USA Oklahoma City Chapter (*DMN* 03-08-12).

Mr. Bill Bernstein, Mosaic Family Services, Dallas

In 2012, the "Dallas Chapter of the United Nations Association presented a UN Day dinner, reception and program from 6 to 9 p.m., with keynote speaker Mr. Bill Bernstein, Deputy Director of Mosaic Family Services, on 'Combating Human Trafficking: Global Problem: Local Solution,' at FunAsia Restaurant, Richardson. dallas-una.org" (*DMN* Community Calendar 10-20-12).

"The UN National Committee for UN Women launched its Dallas chapter at a luncheon at the Park City Club, 5956 Sherry Lane. The speaker was Teresa Fronsini of CBS-TV affiliate Channel 11, unwomen-usnc.org" (*DMN* Community Calendar 10-23-12).

New President of the US Institute of Peace Speaks in Dallas

USIP President Nancy Lindborg in Dallas with
Peacemakers, Inc. founder Vivian Castleberry

Nancy Lindborg spoke to the DUNA Chapter on April 1. *DMN* published a Q & A with her by editorial writer Tod Robberson, with several important observations, which were reflections from her work. The bipartisan (sic) institution conducts studies to help resolve violent conflicts around the world. She identified particularly with the issues in the Middle East and Africa. "If you don't become inclusive after a peace settlement, the likelihood of relapsing back into conflict is so much greater" (*DMN* 4-05-15).

She described the "warlike dynamic between Afghanistan and Pakistan," along with the fear in China about extremism affecting their territories, citing a "confluence of factors."

Recent conferences of sixty nations made it clear that these were not just US problems, but global in scope. "We have to understand that, at the end of the day, to finally get on the other side of this, we're not going to fight our way to that conclusion" (*DMN* 4-05-15).

The truly nonpartisan nature of the institute frees it to address "peace (is an) issue that's hard to be against . . . How do we deal with conflict so that we aren't only dependent on force?" The headline of the piece summed it up: "Giving Peace a Chance" (*DMN* 04-05-15).

Advocates for the UN engaged independently in the public discourse.

In a *DMN* Letters to Readers, Don Unger of Irving posted a positive observation:

With the support of the UN, we fought in Korea and the Persian Gulf War. Those actions are widely viewed as necessary and successful. Without the support of the UN, we fought in Vietnam and the Iraq war. Those actions are widely viewed as unnecessary and unsuccessful.

Two years ago many experts predicted that Iran could have a nuclear bomb in one year. With the support of the UN Security Council plus Germany, we have an agreement that will prevent Iran from developing a nuclear bomb for at least 15 years.

No service member death, in any war, is in vain if we honor their sacrifice by avoiding unnecessary future wars. (*DMN*/LTE 07-17-15)

DUNA Members Took Part in Community Events, Reported in Local Area Newspapers

DUNA members at Womens Equality Day: Ghada Muktad, Linda Evans, Dede Ramos, Bill Matthews, Shabnam Modgil, David Reid, Norma Matthews, and Ricky Cruz

Women's Equality Day has been celebrated annually for over 20 years with a program led by a local Dallas women's organization, Women's Issues Network (WIN). The group celebrated the 95th anniversary of the passage of the 19th amendment allowing women the right to vote with an event at Dallas City Hall on August 26.

Over 150 women attended, wearing white to represent the women suffragists who campaigned for women's voting rights. The Dallas Chapter UNA was one of the sponsors of the event. Several members attended, including President David Reid and his wife, Nelda Reid, South Central Regional Representative of UNA-USA. (WRLW 08-18-15)

Dr. Kathleen Kuehnast (center), USIP director of Gender &
Peace Building, with Vivian Castleberry and Jan Sanders

Peacemakers, Inc. celebrates the United Nations
International Day of Peace on Sept. 21. Each year the
Dallas Chapter United Nations Association is a co-
sponsor of the event. The speaker this year was Dr.
Kathleen Kuehnast, director of Gender & Peace Building
at the US Institute of Peace. She spoke on, 'Peace is
Action, and it starts with YOU.' Peacemakers Founder
Vivian Castleberry presented the Peace Patron Award to
Congresswoman Eddie Bernice Johnson. More than 160
guests attended the event. Several members of the Dallas
UNA attended the event at the Park Cities Hilton Hotel.
(WRLW 08-18-15)

Dr. Srgjan Kerim, Macedonia, 2015 UN Day keynote speaker

In the October 29 *DMN*, the Asian Culture and Community column edited by Deborah Fleck headlined an entry for

UN Day celebration. This year marks the UN's 70th anniversary. To celebrate this milestone, the Dallas Chapter of United Nations Association USA will present a program at 7:30 p.m. Tuesday (Nov. 2) at Dallas City Performance Hall . . . Dr. Srgjan Kerim, President of the 62nd session of the UN General Assembly, will deliver the keynote address. He will focus on human rights issues, including the refugee crisis in Europe. (*DMN* 10-29-15)

The Destination Imagineers children graphically
represented the U.N. SDGs, for 2015-2030

The music group the Obscure Dignitaries performed Margaret Barrett's "Universal Language," a multimedia, multilingual adaptation of the Universal Declaration of Human Rights with a libretto by Dr. David Silva.

Mr. Mike Beard from the United Nations Foundation introduced the newly adopted UN Sustainable Development Goals (DUNA Archives).

Mike Beard, UNF ED for Advocacy and Global Health

"The World Affairs Council presented a well-attended program with Gillian Sorensen of the United Nations Foundation at 6 p.m. at the Rosewood Crescent Hotel." Mrs. Sorensen has made several appearances in Dallas, very clearly and effectively advocating on behalf of the UN. (*DMN* Community Calendar 11-11-15).

News Breaking after 2015

UN Secretary-General Boutros Boutros-Ghali, 1991-1996

Boutros Boutros-Ghali, a veteran Egyptian diplomat who helped negotiate his country's landmark peace deal with Israel but then clashed with the United States as UN secretary-general, died Tuesday (02-16-16) at age 93.

Boutros-Ghali, the scion of a prominent Egyptian Christian political family, was the first UN Chief from the African continent. He stepped into the post in 1992, at a time of dramatic world changes with the collapse of the Soviet Union, the end of the Cold War, and the beginning of a unipolar era dominated by the United States . . . He worked to establish the UN's independence, particularly from the US, at a time when the world body was increasingly called on to step into crises with peacekeeping forces but with limited resources. . . . His renewal in the post in 1996 was blocked by the US, making him the "only UN secretary-general to serve a single term. He was replaced by Kofi Annan of Ghana." (*DMN* 02-17-16)

He called the Rwanda massacre "my worst failure at the United Nations." President Bill Clinton and other world leaders were opposed to taking strong action to beef up UN peacekeepers in the tiny Central African nation or intervening to stop the massacres. "The concept of peacekeeping was turned on its head and worsened by the serious gap between mandates and resources," he said (*DMN* 02-17-16).

"Boutros-Ghali helped spread thanksgiving through all the nations by reading the 1996 World Thanksgiving Proclamation in front of Norman Rockwell's Golden Rule Mosaic at the UN Headquarters Ceremony" (DUNA Archives—e-mail note from Dallas leader, Peter Stewart, founding member of the Thanks-Giving Foundation, Dallas, Texas).

Authors' note: further media notations are incorporated in chapter 5.

CHAPTER 5

DUNA Moves into the
Twenty-First Century

Section A
Dallas United Nations Association Time Capsules: 1980–1997

Marshall J. Doke, DUNA Board leader in the 1980s

Authors'Note: Capsules 1980–1997 were compiled from files "rediscovered" by Marshall J. Doke and whose name and related leadership activities appeared frequently in the records of DUNA. Although incomplete within these dates, they record significant developments for the Dallas Chapter, originals to be added to DUNA Archives. JWM[1]

1980

1980s DUNA logo for Dallas Chapter, UNA-USA

July 31. The DUNA Board met at the Faculty Club, SMU, 12:30 p.m., sponsored by Dr. Neill McFarland, George DeWald, chairman [*sic*].

- Present: Ambassador Bob Dean, Kenny French, Trini Garza, Jo Fay Godbey, Michael Lanham, Donald Lewis, Florence Lewis, Neill McFarland, Kenneth B. McIntosh, Mary Maura McNiel, Janet Pharr, Richard Rubottom, Jim Sands, Louis Saunders, Dick Sloos, and Gene Brownscombe, interim secretary.
- The president reported three items to be done: committee appointments for fall conference, deferred until spring; Patrick Cass research on UN regarding birth control, report forwarded to the president; Janet Pharr on committee to help refugees, contacted HEW for information, comments by Kenny French

---

[1]   Sourced from Marshall J. Doke Collection, DUNA Archives.

about churches, Dick Rubottom cautioned about local chapter involvement, Kenneth McIntosh cited other active organizations, decision to not take this on as a project.

- Minutes of May 28 meeting were summarized by the president, approved as submitted. Treasurer Neill McFarland reported $3,052.48 in transactions, expenses of $1,277.54, working balance of $1,736.93, to be reconciled, but "we are solvent."
- Prime business was planning and discussion for UN Day or Week in October. President DeWald will appoint Marshall Doke as chair (chair of the International Committee of Dallas Chamber of Commerce), with Bob Dean, Dick Rubottom, Ed Winn and two women. Further actions: President, Rubottom, and Dean to secure speaker, Treasurer to send $50 requested and approved from DUNA to Sue Sloos for Richardson League of Women Voters to hold a UN Day in Richardson.
- Louis Saunders advised that a talk be developed to give to clubs and other community groups to reach influential people.

October 1. *DUNA Newsletter* announcing UN Day on October 24 sent to the International Committee of the Dallas Chamber of Commerce by Chairman Marshall Doke.

- Theme: "The United Nations—Why Dallas Needs It," observing the thirty-fifth birthday of the UN, in the Grand Ballroom of the SMU Student Center; reservations through Mary Vogelson, price $8, with tables of eight at $64.
- Speaker: Ambassador H. Carl McCall, alternate representative for Special Political Affairs and ambassador with the United States Mission to the United Nations, appointed by President Carter in December 1979.
- Letter from Mrs. Clyde "Lorinne" Emery subscribed for a table at the luncheon. Also a letter from Marshall Doke, with regrets for missing the event, enclosing a check for a table to "use to invite persons to be guests."
- Notice of the next board meeting December 2, referred to "a recap of our successful UN Day celebration" (*DUNA Viewsletter*).[2]

---

[2]   *DUNA Viewsletter* Archives.

Fall 1980. *DUNA Newsletter* featured the announcement of the UN Day, with a detailed bio sketch of Ambassador McCall.

1981

May 11. President Ronald Reagan issued a presidential proclamation for UN Day: "The United Nations Association of the USA is an organization providing valuable information and discussion concerning the UN system . . . highlighting the world refugee crisis and UN efforts to meet this challenge . . . My administration is committed to improving the human condition and international well-being and will continue to play an important role in the United Nations to further these goals." Other points supported the Geneva Conference on African refugee aid and the 1981 International Year of Disabled Persons on "a humanitarian and non-political level" (*DUNA Archives*).

Winter 1981. *DUNA Newsletter* announced *Great Decisions '81*, based on a book series published by the Foreign Policy Association, with a series of meetings to be held at the home of Dr. Gladys Lett on Tuesday evenings, beginning February 10.

- Report of Dallas Committee for UNICEF special evening for children at Prestonwood Town Center on Hallowe'en, October 31, 1980. Area children and parents had picked up collection canisters at a booth in the Lord and Taylor Court the day before, which were returned with donations to the Children's Fund (*DUNA Viewsletter*).

DUNA Officers for 1980–81

- President—George DeWald
- VP Program—Pearl Wincorn (Mrs. Herbert)
- VP Membership—Mary Vogelson (Mrs. JM)
- VP Great Decisions—Gladys Leff (Mrs. Seymour)
- VP Speakers Bureau—Kenneth B. McIntosh
- Secretary—Eugene R. Brownscombe (until 1/1/81); Saralee Lamb (after 12/31/80)

- Treasurer—H. Neill McFarland
- Coordinators UNICEF—Saralee Lamb (Mrs. Herbert A. Jr.), Kenny French (Mrs. Edgar)
- Newsletter Editors—Janet Pharr (Mrs. William L.), Sharon Christen (Mrs. Fred)
- Nominating Committee Chair—Edward B. Winn

April 24. A Marshall Doke letter to President George DeWald expresses regrets for declining invitation to participate in the April 30 DUNA Annual Luncheon due to his trip to Europe. He commends two members to represent the Dallas Chamber of Commerce International Committee for recognition of support for DUNA.

- The program for the April 30 event on "The United Nations and the Third World" features the speaker, Dean Jeswald W. Salacuse of the SMU School of Law. His extensive academic and diplomatic experiences in Africa and the Middle East were cited in the program flyer.

April 28. The DUNA Annual Spring Luncheon, Grand Ballroom, SMU Student Center.

- Speaker: Mr. Robert M. Ratner, President of UNA-USA, "Why UNA-USA in Today's Changing World"

June 28. A special meeting of the DUNA Board at the home of Pearl Wincorn was led by Dick Sloos, chairman pro tem. Present were Pat Cass, Bernita Cogan, George DeWald, Marshall Doke, Jed Keith, Florence Lewis, Neill McFarland, David Ramsour, Steve Saunders, Pearl Wincorn, Ed Winn, and Gene Brownscombe, secretary pro tem.

- A letter from Pres. Ronald Reagan saluted UN programs for refugees and the destitute contributions to growth and stability. This was taken as a hopeful sign that the new administration would not be anti-UN, as had been feared.
- Treasurer's report showed a balance of $3,315.12 before deductions for the cost of the annual luncheon. Two savings accounts held

$1,225.10 and $1,838.18; motion to combine into a money market account was passed.

- George DeWald reported on UN Day plans, with Mr. Peter Stewart appointed as chair, Dr. Robert Muller from the United Nations directorate to be the speaker.
- Extensive discussions referred to community connections, meetings proposals, publicity, telephone and address options, Model UN, conference on world and local hunger awareness, perhaps to feature John Denver as an advocate.
- Action summary noted decisions to combine the savings accounts, combine telephone listing with UNICEF and DUNA, purchase of a UN display logo and podium banner, seeking a university person to organize a Model UN program and DUNA sponsor $100 seed money for a proposed UNICEF conference on hunger.

July 21. DUNA Board met at SMU Faculty Club, convened at 4:45 p.m. by Chairman George DeWald. Present were Robert Alther; Sue Anders; Bernita Cogan; Lorinne Emory; Trini Garza; N. Neill McFarland; Maura McNiel; Janet Pharr; Jim Sands; and Gene Branscombe, secretary.

- Officer changes in the board: Saralee Lamb asked to be relieved as secretary, Gene Brownscombe to continue. Newsletter editor would be Kathy Godby, nominating committee chair would be Lorinne (Mrs. Clyde) Emory.
- Discussion of meeting place and time favored 4:30 p.m., with SMU the preferred location at reasonable cost.
- Minutes of the June special meeting were reviewed, with reports on actions including mailing options, telephone decisions using UNICEF listing, DUNA share reimbursement. The money market investment of savings accounts was agreed to purchase of an eighty-nine-day CD paying 14.35 percent, redeemable without penalty at any time. The logo and Model UN questions had not been resolved. Hunger Conference plans were proceeding: $100 DUNA contribution would be sent. Bob Alther was to contact the Dallas Cowboys for possible sponsorship of publicity spots.
- Trini Garza reported on a September State Department–sponsored visit by international guests; DUNA set tentative plans to host a cookout and possible rodeo show visit on September 26.

- July 22 letter from Marshall Doke—discovered the membership renewal letters were not sent, so he sent two years' dues to Mary Vogelson for 1979–80 and 1980–91.

October 14. Pres. George DeWald letter to the board.

- Robert Muller could not come for UN Day luncheon "due to pressing situations at the United Nations." He asked Donald Keys of Planetary Citizens to speak instead.
- The new UNA-USA field coordinator Michael Seltzer met the board for lunch at the SMU Faculty Club, replies requested.

1982

January 8. Notice from Pres. George DeWald for noon DUNA Board meeting at the SMU Faculty Club.

- Dr. Gladys Leff was to present the series of *Great Decisions '82* to meet at her home, beginning February 2, booklets available at $6 each.
- Dick Sloos was to bring recommendations for the Annual Business Luncheon speaker for April 29, 1982.

April 5. Notice from President DeWald for noon DUNA Board meeting at the SMU Faculty Club.

- Final preparations for the Annual Business Luncheon, April 29 at the SMU Grand Ballroom. Speaker: Dr. Edwin Strong from Tulsa, Oklahoma, who was to critique the foreign policy of the present US administration.

DUNA Officers for 1982–83

- President—H. Neill McFarland
- VP Program—Dick Sloos
- VP Membership—George DeWald
- VP Great Decisions Program—R. Doak Bishop

- VP Model UN—Lucia Wyman
- VP Speakers Bureau—Kenneth B. McIntosh
- Secretary—Otto Mullinax
- Treasurer—Dr. Eugene Brownscombe
- UNICEF coordinator—Patrick Cass
- Newsletter editor—Katherine Godby
- Nominating committee chairpersons—Pearl Wincorn, George DeWald
- The board of directors membership was restructured on a two-year rotation, with twelve members to expire in 1983, twenty-one in 1984.
- Fifteen past presidents were named as honorary advisory board members.

August 6. DUNA Board met at luncheon at the SMU Faculty Club, convened by Pres. H. Neill McFarland. Present were Marvin Sadovsky; James W. Sands; Gloria Buller; John Luckadoo; Elizabeth Higginbotham; Robert Dean; Javier Escobar Jr.; Bernita Cogan; Dick Sloos; Otto B. Mullinax; Lucia Wyman; E. R. Brownscombe; Maura McNiel; Alexandra Mason; Yvonne Ewell; and James Harrell.

- After introductions, the chair pointed out that DUNA is a chapter of UNA-USA and, in turn, affiliated with WFUNA, the World Federation of United Nations Associations, with over sixty national associations. All are dedicated to furthering the goals of the United Nations, targeted to changing attitudes on international problems.
- Four objectives were outlined: increase the present 150 membership by each bringing five new members, establish regular meetings six or eight times during each year, join with like-minded organizations to sponsor public meetings on international issues, and reach more young people.
- Treasurer reported cash on hand $2,305; $1,946 in the youth account; $388 in Texas Federal Savings account; and $2,129 in a CD, making a total of $6,768.
- UN Day was announced for October 22 in the Grand Ballroom, SMU, with John Graham the possible speaker.
- Sands moved, seconded, and voted to cosponsor an event on September 15 on a theme of "Economics of World Security" with

town hall meeting, provided that the chair determined that it would be in keeping with aims and goals of DUNA.

- Sloos moved, seconded, and passed that the chair would secure appropriate stationery for the use of the chapter.

November 10. DUNA Board met for luncheon at the SMU Faculty Club, led by Pres. Neill McFarland; George DeWald; Otto Mullinax; Eugene Brownscombe; Pearl Wincorn Gloria Buller; John A. Luckadoo; Alexana Mason; Ken Smith; Marvin Sadovsky; and past president Donald Lewis and wife Florence.

- Minutes of September 29 were adopted without substantive change (though not in these files).
- Treasurer Brownscombe reported income of $1,045.79, including $806.65 for UN Day luncheon, with no expenditures; ending balance in bank $7,882.76, details filed with secretary.
- DeWald announced the next activity on December 10, on human rights, at the Martin Luther King Jr. Community Center, with speaker Dr. Ganji, former minister of education in Iran, who holds international law degrees from the University of Cambridge, operating "Crussiant Rial" in Dallas.
- President McFarland reported a very adequate turnout for the UN Day luncheon, gratified by the speaker John Graham, "seeking to set a new philosophical approach to the United Nations and its function." He was also gratified by a *Dallas Times Herald* article by Molly Ivins, supportive of the UN.
- DUNA cosponsored a speech by John Nesbitt, author of *Megatres*, with cassettes of the speech and Q&A available from Gloria Buller.
- Dick Sloos reported through the chair that two possible speakers might be available for the spring affair when new officers are installed. They are the president of UNA-USA Bob Ratner or the associate general secretary of the UN Mr. Akashi.
- The National Convention of UNA-USA was announced for May 28–31 at Marymount College, Tarrytown, New York. Two delegates and other observers could attend.

December 8. DUNA Board met for luncheon at the SMU Faculty Club, led by Pres. Neill McFarland, with Gloria Buller, Bernita Cogan, George

DeWald, Jim Harrell, Donald Lewis, Florence Lewis, Maura McNiel, Marvin Sadovsky, Marcia Stoez, Eugene Brownscombe, secretary pro tem.

- Dick Sloos was out of town, but had arranged for president of UNA-USA Bob Ratner to speak at the spring meeting on April 22.
- George reported that Human Rights Day would be observed at the Martin Luther King Center; Marcia would have a periodicals display table.
- Marcia reported an Amnesty International television program opposing the death penalty.
- Marvin reported on a Human Rights Day program on Channel 8, and the Transformation Institute had sent public service announcements that included UN information. DUNA program chair Dick Sloos had heavy work schedule with KLM airlines, thus unable to serve fully.
- Neill advised that the board hold a workshop, with extended time to discuss "knotty problems," such as membership development, diversity of meetings. Decision was taken to schedule the next board as a workshop on Saturday, January 15, from 1:00 to 5:00 p.m. at SMU.
- Neill led discussion of appropriate recognition for Judge Sarah T. Hughes, first DUNA president, highly acclaimed for many efforts for women, a "Texas hero." Plans were discussed.
- A cosponsorship with the Fisher Institute in October was a near disaster until John Mears took over and saved it; "right-wing drifters" had tried to take over. Future support by DUNA was deemed difficult.
- George reported that *Great Decisions* would continue this year at Bernita Cogan's home; Marshall Doke was also interested in a group.
- Gloria recommended a book by Robert Muller, *There Will Be No World War III*, as an excellent Christmas gift.

1983

January 15. The DUNA Board met in a workshop session at Kirby Hall, SMU at 1:25 p.m., led by Pres. Neill McFarland. Present were Gloria

Buller; George DeWald; Larry Egbert and guest Mrs. Marcel Egbert; Yvonne Ewell; Alexana Mason; Maura McNiel; Otto Mullinax, secretary; Marvin Sadovsky; Dick Sloos; and Eugene Brownscombe.

- Minutes from December 8 were approved with correction of Muller book *New Genesis.*
- Treasurer's report was filed with the secretary, with comment that some UN Day luncheon meals had not yet been paid, those in arrears to be contacted.
- Thanks and plans by Dick, especially for his alertness in securing Dr. Ganji as speaker for Human Rights Day.
- Program announced for March 25 at Wyatt's Cafeteria in Richardson, with Professor Rex Zedalias from University of Tulsa Law School speaking on the International Treaty on Law of the Sea and its surprise ending.
- Annual Spring Luncheon to be April 28, in the Grand Ballroom of the SMU Student Center with the speaker the Honorable Robert Ratner, president of UNA-USA; a meet-and-greet cocktail party for the board and the speaker was discussed. Another cafeteria dinner was being planned.
- George reported two *Great Decisions '83* series at Bernita Cogan's home and at Pearl Wincorn's home, each to continue for six weeks from early February.
- Membership reports from Maura who was searching for a UN movie and from Gloria on recruitment of new members.
- Members then enjoyed "the stimulus of forecasting the future, future purpose, roles, and program of the UN," adjourning at 5:10 p.m.

February 9. DUNA Board met for luncheon at the SMU Faculty Club, led by Pres. Neill McFarland, with George DeWald, Dick Sloos, Florence Lewis, Pearl Wincorn, John Luckadoo, Alexana Mason, Lucia Wyman, Otto Mullinax, secretary.

- Minutes for January 15 were approved. Treasurer's report was accepted and filed, showing assets of $7,145.08, as of January 31.
- VP DeWald reported on *Great Decisions* attendance and other matters.

- Twelve attended on February 7 at Bernita Cogan's home.
- Ten attended the first session on February 8 at Pearl Wincorn's home.
- DUNA display booth at Richland College International Student Day set for February 22.
- Gloria Buller had thirty people in her discussion group on foreign relations.
- DeWald believes the *Great Decisions* project should be "promoted further."
- Florence Lewis suggests "brown bag" groups at Dallas Public Library.
- Nominating committee canvassed candidates for the board, to be elected on April 28.
- Reminder of National Convention in May in Tarrytown, New York.
- Vice Chairman Sloos reminded the board of March 25 and April 28 meetings, previously announced.
- The discussion of an endowed chair in United Nations Functions and International
- Organizations progressed. Meeting adjourned at 2:00 p.m.

March 9. DUNA Board met for luncheon at the SMU Faculty Club, led by Pres. Neill McFarland, with George DeWald, Dick Sloos, Pearl Wincorn, Eugene Brownscombe, Gloria Buller, Benita Cogan, Maura McNiel, and Otto Mullinax, secretary.

- Minutes of February 9 and Treasurer's reports approved and filed.
- The chair was authorized by unanimous vote to cosponsor the World Population Day Conference at SMU on April 7, 1983. Sixty-eight similar programs were being held on as many campuses.
- Mr. Larry Newman, attorney with the City of Dallas, discussed the Sarah T. Hughes Law Fellowship, with its scholarship for worthy minority students who enter the SMU Law School.
- With reminder of the March 25 dinner and program, the meeting was adjourned at 2:00 p.m.

April 13. DUNA Board met for luncheon at the SMU Faculty Club, led by Pres. Neill McFarland, with James W. Sands; Ed Richards; Gloria Buller;

Marvin Sadovsky; Pearl L. Wincorn; Bernita Cogan; John H. Luckadoo; E. R. Brownscombe; and Otto Mullinax, secretary.

- Minutes of March 9 were corrected to record the presence of Yvonne A. Ewell; Marvin Sadovsky; and John Luckadoo—approved. Treasurer's report with balance of $7,605.16 was approved and filed.
- The scheduled World Population Day Conference did not occur due to a key speaker's emergency surgery. Chair was authorized to cosponsor at a later date.
- The March 25 cafeteria dinner was attended by only nine people although the speaker was well engaged and well informed on the law of the sea, in which the United States has refused to cooperate with UN agencies.
- A reception for our distinguished UN Day speaker, the Honorable Robert Ratner, was unanimously agreed to be hosted as invited to the home of Pearl Wincorn. "Board members and guests should avail themselves of this occasion."
- The general membership meeting was to be at SMU on April 28, with election of officers also scheduled.
- The proposed cafeteria dinner in May was cancelled.
- The chair was "offered to cosponsor" a meeting on June 2 with the Japan-America Society, with time and place to be determined later.
- The chair set a workshop on Saturday, June 11, for the incoming board on program, place to be announced.
- Marvin Sadovsky was to arrange publicity for the UN Day speaker on April 28 with the Channel 8 *Daybreak* show, on KAFM morning news, and a news conference at 11:00 a.m. in the SMU Banquet Room with four radio stations and two newspapers.
- Program flyer for April 28 is filed in the DUNA Archives.

May 11. DUNA Board met for luncheon at the SMU Faculty Club, led by Pres. Neill McFarland, Marvin C. Sadovsky; VP membership, Annemarie Brown, CPC; secretary, Gloria Buller; newsletter editor, George DeWald; James W. Sands; John H. Luckadoo; Yvonne Ewell; Christy McCarty; and Alexana Mason.

- Minutes of April meeting were discussed and accepted. Treasurer's report showed assets of $8,142.44, approved and filed with the secretary.
- Dr. McFarland reported success of the April 28 membership luncheon, with Mr. Ratner's talk well received. Thanks to Pearl Wincorn for hospitality and to Florence Lewis and Maura McNiel for assistance at the reception, with appreciation to James Sands and John Luckadoo for their help with the event.
- DUNA to cosponsor with the Japan-American Society a talk by Pres. David W. MacEachron on "US Japan Trade Frictions: How Bad Will They Get?" on June 16 at the Royal Tokyo Restaurant, $10, reservations urged for limited space; DUNA to mail invitations to membership.
- McFarland reported that he and Dick Sloos attended the Southwest Division of the national UNA, May 7, at DFW Airport, presided by division president Professor Willard Teace, to communicate and share ideas among the chapters.
- The National Convention of the CCD, Council on Chapter and Divisions, to meet on May 27, 28. President McFarland and program VP Dick Sloos to attend as official representatives, with Ed Wynn chairman of the National Council. Gloria Buller and James Sands moved, and it was approved to subsidize expenses of Dallas representatives, based on substantiated expenses with receipts over $10 submitted.
- Fall and spring luncheon meeting dates were considered and adopted.
- John Luckadoo asked for update on the Sarah T. Hughes issue; no new information was available.
- Annemarie suggested that the board look into obtaining a DUNA phone line; Marvin Sadovsky and James Sands volunteered to explore.
- A workshop meeting was announced for the next board meeting on June 11.

June 11. The DUNA Board met in a workshop session at Kirby Hall, SMU, 1:00 to 5:00 p.m., led by Pres. Neill McFarland, with Gene Brownescombe, treasurer; Annemarie Brown-Sadovsky, secretary; Dick Sloos, VP programming; Marvin C. Sadovsky, VP membership; Gloria

Buller, newsletter editor; Christy McCarty; Jim Sands; Ed Wynn; Barbara Materka; Guy Gooding; Henry Guy; Stephen Lerer; Pat Davidson; Genice Rabe; Edna Flaxman; Versia Lacy; Ernest Good; and Janet Pharr.

- Secretary's report included spelling correction for Prof. Willard Tice and meeting of the UNA, which was among chapter divisions. Treasurer's report showed assets of $7,000.45; reports approved and filed with the secretary.
- Marvin Sadovsky discussed survey of suggestions for DUNA activities. A talent and interest questionnaire was circulated to solicit the input from DUNA membership for program priorities, to be returned to him.
- Dates for the annual fall and spring luncheons were confirmed:

  - UN Day to be October 24 at the SMU Student Center Ballroom.
  - Spring membership and election meeting to be on April 24, 1984.

- Dr. McFarland suggested that the UN Day highlight the Metroplex area as an emerging international entity, suggesting Mr. Marshall J. Doke Jr., chairman of the International Committee of the Dallas Chamber of Commerce, as resource; it was moved and approved. A UN Day chair to be designated. Other suggestions were recorded from Dick Sloos, Marvin Sadovsky, Gloria Buller, Guy Gooding, and Jim Sands.
- McFarland reviewed the goals and purposes of DUNA, with discussion.
- McFarland as president, Dick Sloos as secretary of the national board, and Ed Wynn as chairman of the national committee reported on the recent national convention. Major issues are as follows:

  - US participation in the UN
  - Disarmament and peace
  - Law of the sea

- Gloria Buller gave the newsletter editor's report: format, mailing frequency, content. Dick Sloos suggested acknowledging new members. She was to check on bulk mailing rates.
- Christy McCarty volunteered for Model UN for Dallas as a former participant in high school and college. Guy Gooding, Ernest Good, and Janet Pharr also volunteered assistance. Plan, finances, and budget are to be submitted to the board in September. An adult Model UN Program was discussed, suggestion to purchase a kit for planning.
- Telephone survey committee appointed: Henry Guy, chairman; Gloria Buller; Marvin Sadovsky; Jim Sands; Dick Sloos; Steve Lerer; Barbara Materka; and Annemarie Brown-Sadovsky.
- Board meetings were set for first Wednesdays at the Faculty Club, SMU, with two board workshops in June and January each year—approved.
- McFarland reported a small increase in dues structure.
- Jim Sands to have the phone situation finished by September, contacting UNICEF about installing a UNA line.

September 14. DUNA Board met for luncheon at the SMU Faculty Club, led by Pres. Neill McFarland; Dick Sloos, VP programming; Bernita Cogan, VP Great Decisions; Marvin Sadovsky, VP membership; Annemarie Brown-Sadovsky, secretary; Gloria Buller, newsletter editor; Guy Gooding; George DeWald; Genice Rabe; Barbara Materka; Henry Guy; J.B. Walling.

- Secretary's report correction on national convention: Dick Sloos was a member of the national board and past secretary of the steering committee of the CCD presidents. Ed Wynn was past chairman of the steering committee and presided as chairman. Minutes of the June workshop were discussed and accepted.
- Treasurer's report showed assets of $7,318.94, filed, with note that $2,501.15 designated for the Youth Fund.
- Dick Sloos submitted a report by Christy McCarty, VP of Model UN Program. The Model UN Security Council had been received, given to Herbert Cochran at SMU, local educators had been contacted, estimated budget $1,500–2,000, McFarland suggested that we send young people to the national Model UN program.

- UN Day to be October 27; Mayor Taylor had appointed Marshall Doke Jr. as chairman. Guest speaker was to be Dr. Phyllis Daminsky, director of UN Information Center in Washington, DC. The luncheon was to be in the SMU Grand Ballroom, reservations $10, invitations to be sent. Marvin Sadovsky was to receive individual or group reservations.

- Human Rights Day was December 10, with speaker Dr. Willis Harman of Stanford Research Institute International, on "The Fundamental Human Right—A World of Peace," cosponsored with the Transformation Institute, no charge. The workshop was to be held at Northpark Inn beginning at 10:00 a.m., with the Helen Caldecott film from Canada, *For Those Who Love This Planet*. Panel with DUNA members and group discussion resumed at 2:00 p.m.

- Dick Sloos provided copies of the DUNA by-laws for review by the board members. Barbara Materka moved that Christy McCarty be officially appointed to VP of the Model UN, to replace Lucia Wyman, who had moved out of Dallas—approved. Dick suggested that the by-laws be retyped and revised, with structure sheets of the UN provided.

- Gloria Buller reported sending out 2,200 newsletters in the Dallas area. Marvin moved to approve mailing expenses, seconded by Dick Sloos, and it was approved. Gloria had designed a local membership application form. Dick moved that one thousand copies be printed; Marvin seconded and it was approved. Bernita Cogan suggested that the spring newsletter be published before the spring program.

- The board expressed appreciation to Florence Lewis for a dinner that honored guests, UN diplomats visiting Dallas from East Asia and the Pacific. Bernita suggested that an entertainment fund be provided to supplement special functions sponsored by volunteers for DUNA-related occasions.

- The Southern Region UNICEF director John Tsacrios had generously allowed DUNA to use a second line of the UNICEF telephone number.

President of the United States, Ronald Reagan, addressed the Second
Special Session on Disarmament on the morning of 17 June 1982

September 26. US president Ronald Reagan, statement before the UN
General Assembly: "Our goals are those that guide this very body. Our
ends are the same as those of the UN's founders. The UN has a proud
history of promoting conciliation and helping keep the peace . . . The UN
and its affiliates have made important contributions to the quality of life
on this planet, such as directly saving countless lives through its refugee
and emergency relief programs" (from Marshall Doke files).

October 5. DUNA Board met for luncheon at the SMU Faculty Club, led
by Pres. Neill McFarland, with Dick Sloos, VP programming; Marvin
Sadovsky, VP membership; Annemarie Brown-Sadovsky, secretary; Gloria
Buller, newsletter editor; Jim Sands; Henry Guy; Pearl L. Wincorn; Otto
B. Mullinax; John H. Luckadoo; Alix Mason; and Pat Davidson.

- Secretary reported on September minutes, corrected spelling of
  Herbert Corkran.
- Treasurer reported assets of $7,318.94, approved and filed.
- Plans for UN Day, October 27, speaker Dr. Phyllis Kaminsky, the
  first American appointed to direct the UN Information Center

at SMU. Reservation information shared; Jim Sands offered to transport the speaker from DFW Airport.

- Human Rights Day, December 10, was to have Dr. Willis Harmon of the Stanford Research Institute International as guest leader for a Saturday workshop.
- Model UN Security Council was scheduled for February 18, 1984, with February 11 to get together to write resolutions and get acquainted.
- General membership meeting, open to the public, set for Sunday, November 13, 7:30 to 10:00 p.m. at Selecman Hall, SMU. Briefing facilitated by Dick Sloos, with J.B. Walling explaining the workings of the Security Council, as orientation for the Model UN event next year.
- McFarland suggested having some board meetings in the evenings for some unable to attend luncheon times, to be further discussed.
- *Issues of the General Assembly* book available at $5 for members, $10 for nonmembers. Board members were urged to purchase, become acquainted with many issues and historical facts about the UN. Jim Sands moved that twenty copies be ordered by DUNA, available as stated, Gloria Buller to purchase books not sold. Sloos was to order.
- McFarland was to speak at the First Unitarian Church on October 23.
- Sloos suggested that UN issues of this decade, raised by Elliott Richardson and UNA leadership, be discussed at the next board meeting, to discuss the new UNA approaches.
- Annemarie raised the issue of appointing a DUNA officer in charge of public relations to be discussed at the next meeting.
- Sloos suggested that DUNA be listed in the Dallas Public Library computer. Jim Sands moved that Annemarie list DUNA, using her office telephone number for contact.

October 27. DUNA Annual UN Day Luncheon at 11:30 a.m. in the SMU Grand Ballroom, with speaker, the Honorable Phyllis Kaminsky, acting director of the United Nations Information Centre, Washington, DC, on "The United Nations: Images and Reality." At the head table were Secretary Annemarie Brown Sadovsky, VP membership Marvin Sadovsky, Arlette Douffiagues, assistant director of protocol, City of Dallas, Marshall Doke

Jr.; UN Day chairman, Neill McFarland, DUNA president; Kaminsky, the speaker; Dick Sloos, VP programming and UNA-USA national board member, with George McFarland, chargé d'affaires, Antigua, and J. B. Walling, national board member.

- Reservations were $10 for lunch, $80 for tables of eight.

November 2. DUNA Board met for luncheon at the SMU Faculty Club, led by Pres. Neill McFarland; Dick Sloos, VP programming; Bernita Cogan, VP Great Decisions; Eugene Brownscombe, treasurer; Marvin Sadovsky, VP membership; Annemarie Brown-Sadovsky, Secretary; George DeWald; Henry Guy; Alix Mason; Pat Davidson; Janet Pharr; Pearl L. Wincorn; and Edna Flaxman.

- Secretary presented minutes of October 5, approved. Treasurer's report showed assets of $8,536.11, approved and filed.
- The UN Day Luncheon success was reported; Kaminsky's speech available by request to the secretary. Dick Sloos thanked Keith Worrell for bringing teachers and students to the luncheon.
- Announcements and invitation to Model UN Security Council event on February 18, 1984, was to go out, all urged to attend and participate.
- Plans for Human Rights Day on December 10 brought Dr. Willis Harman from Stanford Research Institute for an extended workshop, as previously announced, cosponsored with the Transformation Institute.
- Plans for the annual spring membership meeting were to begin, as were further plans for the next several months. Annemarie suggested that board meet in late afternoons, to be followed with a dinner and program to which DUNA membership could be invited.
- Dick Sloos noted that some board members had not renewed UNA-USA membership dues, which were required to remain on the board.
- Also reported that Dallas mayor Starke Taylor Jr. would not sign the UN Day Proclamation "because he did not want to support the United Nations in any way" (Doke files).

179

1984

January 14. DUNA Board met at 3:00 p.m. at the SMU Faculty Club, led by Pres. Neill McFarland; Dick Sloos, VP programming; Bernita Cogan, VP Great Decisions; Eugene Brownscombe, treasurer; Marvin Sadovsky, VP membership; Annemarie Brown-Sadovsky, secretary; Otto Mullinax, nominations chair; Henry Guy; and Jim Sands.

- Minutes of November 2 were discussed and accepted. Treasurer reported assets of $6,799.74, approved and filed.
- Human Rights Day reported success, with over 100 people attending (see September entry for details of the program). Motion and approval voted for $800 honorarium to the leader, Dr. Willis Harmon.
- A special meeting was announced with Sharon Tennison on January 17, with honorarium of $400 approved and accepted by the board.
- Briefing for the February 11 Model UN Security Council, 1:00 to 4:00 p.m., mandatory for all delegates.
- SMU World Population Conference, on February 16, was led by speakers Dr. Nafis Sadik and Mr. Werner Fornos, from UN Fund for Population Activities and the Population Institute respectively. SMU sponsored a panel of professors in the afternoon: Dr. George Crawford; Dr. Maynard; and Dr. Bruce Pringle. A dinner in the ballroom culminated the daylong event—cost $12.50 per person, reservations to be made with President McFarland.
- Model UN Security Council on Saturday, February 18, 1:00 to 4:00 p.m., in Selecman Hall, SMU, for delegates and observers. Mr. Bob Ryan, retired assistant secretary general of the UN, attended, offering to speak to other groups about the UN.
- Annual spring membership meeting was scheduled for April 24 at the SMU Student Center.
- Discussion of ways to fund DUNA events recognized that our membership dues share was divided with UNA-USA. Otto Mullinax volunteered to contribute for each event; others were encouraged to do so. Discussion of bringing interested persons to be involved from Fort Worth.
- The Great Decisions program headed by Bernita Cogan was described in detail, with invitation to DUNA members to join groups.

January 17. DUNA special meeting with Sharon Tennison, RN, for her report on a trip to the Soviet Union on a "citizen diplomacy" trip at North Park Inn, 7:30 p.m.: "Who are the Russian people? 'The enemy?' Or can we make it a better world for all people?"

(Note by Bill Matthews: this started a series of "visits" to the Soviet Union that Ms. Tennison led, inspiring many to adopt the approach of being a citizen diplomat through the 1980s. Bill and Norma Matthews personally conducted five study and dialogue groups, 1986–1989.)

- Prior to the program, the board and advisory members were invited to a "dutch treat" dinner at 6:00 p.m.

February 2. DUNA Board met at 3:00 p.m. at the SMU Faculty Club, led by Pres. Neill McFarland; Dick Sloos, VP programming; Bernita Cogan, VP Great Decisions; Marvin Sadovsky, VP membership; Annemarie Brown-Sadovsky, secretary; with members Jim Sands, Guy Gooding, Alix Mason, and George DeWald.

- Minutes of January 14 discussed and accepted. No treasurer's report.
- Program plans confirmed for February.
- February 11, 1:00 to 4:00 p.m. Briefing for delegates to the Model UN Security Council at SMU.
- February 16—Guy Gooding arranged for Ambassador Bob Ryan to speak on global education at Community College District Conference at the Mountain View campus.
- February 17—Dick Sloos hosted a reception for Ambassador Ryan; also, a luncheon was to be scheduled.
- February 18—The Model UN Security Council met from 1:00 to 4:00 p.m. in Selecman Hall, SMU; delegates arrived at 10:00 a.m., brought their own lunch.
- Otto Mullinax was receiving nominations for the incoming board.
- Reactions to the presentation of Sharon Tennison were very positive.
- The board approved reproduction and distribution of UNESCO information to the DUNA membership.

March 7. DUNA Board met at 3:00 p.m. at the SMU Faculty Club, led by Pres. Neill McFarland; Dick Sloos, VP programming; Bernita Cogan, VP Great Decisions; Marvin Sadovsky, VP membership; Annemarie Brown-Sadovsky, secretary; Gloria Buller, newsletter editor; Jim Sands; Henry Guy; Alix Mason; Genice Rabe; and John H. Luckadoo.

- February board minutes were discussed and accepted. Treasurer reported assets of $5,485.24, approved and filed.
- Mr. J. B. Walling was recognized for $1,000 donation for the Model UN Security Council Program. The incredible success of the program was reported, with the participation of Ambassador Bob Ryan, who also spoke at the Dallas County Community College District Conference. Dick Sloos was thanked for hosting a reception for the Honorable Mr. Ryan.
- Resignation from the board of Ms. Edna Flaxman due to ill health was accepted with regret. The Jewish community was to be contacted to select a successor.
- The annual spring membership meeting of DUNA was scheduled for April 24 at noon at the SMU Student Center, for election of new officers of the board. Speaker was the Honorable Frank T. Jackman, consul general of Canada.
- Decision of meeting times and places was to be decided by new board members for the April meeting. There was a discussion of appointing a public relations person to the board.
- Letter on file from Otto Mullinax to Marshall J. Doke Jr. intending to nominate him to the board, with the answer from Mr. Doke requesting that he not be nominated, due to business and other schedule conflicts, expressing continued interest in the work of DUNA.

April 4. DUNA Board met at noon at the SMU Faculty Club, led by Pres. Neill McFarland; Dick Sloos, VP programming; Bernita Cogan, VP Great Decisions; Marvin Sadovsky, VP membership; Annemarie Brown-Sadovsky, secretary; Barbara Materka; Pearl Wincorn; Alix Mason; Gene Brownscombe; and John H. Luckadoo.

- Minutes of March 7 were discussed and accepted. Treasurer's report showed assets of $5,581.14, approved by the board and filed.

- Annual spring membership meeting and officer election to be held April 24 at noon in the SMU Student Center, with Ambassador Frank T. Jackman, consul general of Canada, to speak.

Mr. Dick Sloos, DUNA president 1984-1986

- Nominations for the 1984–1985 board were announced:
  - President—Dick Sloos
  - VP Programming—James Sands
  - VP Membership—Marvin Sadovsky
  - VP Great Decisions—Bernita Cogan
  - VP Speakers Bureau—Kenneth B. McIntosh
  - VP Model UN—to be filled by incoming board
  - Secretary—Annemarie Brown-Sadovsky
  - Treasurer—Eugene Brownscombe
  - Newsletter Editor—Gloria Buller
  - Nominations Chair—Edward Wynn
  - By-laws Chairperson—Pearl Wincorn
- Board Members carried forward: R. Doke Bishop, Pat Davidson, Lawrence Egbert, Yvonne Ewell, Guy Gooding, Ernest Good, Henry Guy, James Huffines, Gladys Leff, Nell Lewis, Eileen

Lynch, Alexana Mason, Barbara Materka, Roger Pagent, Janet Pharr, Genice Rabe, Keith Worrell, Pearl Wincorn, and John A. Luckadoo.
- Nominees for the 1984–1986 term: John Tsacrios; J.B. Walling; Helen Usitelo; Jack Cowley; Gayle Hudgens; David Notestein; Dwaine Kraegor; David Millheiser; and Claire Galbraith.
- The nomination report was accepted.
- The board voted to send and pay for Dick Sloos to represent DUNA at a luncheon with Jeane Kirkpatrick to speak.

April 24. A six-page report on the USA and UNESCO was sent to the DUNA membership, with notice of the Annual Membership Luncheon, April 24, inviting reservations for $11 individual, half tables of four for $44, and tables for eight for $88.

- The report from UNA-USA reported a US decision to be made by December 31, 1984, regarding its intention to withdraw from UNESCO. US ambassador to the UN Jeane Kirkpatrick and US ambassador to UNESCO Jean Gerard had recommended the action with assistant secretary of state Gregory J. Newell. The US decision was not supported in all quarters, however. More than a dozen other national organizations had filed unanimous support for UNESCO. (See December 20, 1984, report from *The Washington Report* in this timeline.)

September 10. Minutes not available.

October 8. DUNA Board met at 6:30 p.m. at the Unitarian Church, led by Pres. Dick Sloos. Present were Marvin Sadovsky, VP membership; Annemarie Brown-Sadovsky, secretary; Eugene Brownscombe, treasurer; Gloria Buller, newsletter editor; Barbara Materka, PR and publicity; Henry Guy; Duane Kraeger; Alexana Mason; Janet Pharr; Clare Galbraith; and Florence Lewis. Twenty-six officers and members were recorded as absent.

- Treasurer's report showed assets of $5,277.36, accepted and filed. Secretary's report on minutes of September 10, correction on arrival of Dr. Muller on Friday, not Thursday, accepted as corrected and filed.

- The October 13 UNA-USA briefing was postponed to November 17 at the Sadovskys' home.
- Dick urged the purchase of *The US, UN, We the People Shaping Our Future* by Carroll Cannon.
- Janet Pharr moved, seconded by Duane Kraeger, and approved that official UNA name tags and official dinner place tags be purchased.
- Barbara Materka reported for PR and publicity preparing and distributing press releases for twenty-nine newspapers and PSAs for ten TV stations and thirty radio stations. Marvin volunteered to take flyers to the central library, and Clare Galbraith reported that she and David Notestein were sending letters to two hundred businesses, announcing two upcoming programs.
- UN Peacekeeping Project chairperson Duane Kraeger reported that Dick had ordered 250 of the booklets *On the Front Line*. He was to mail out the book and a letter to ask members to form and join discussion groups to study the materials; opinions would be sent to national headquarters in February. Groups were limited to twenty people; also encouraged members who could not attend to read and send their opinions to this board. Annemarie moved and Barbara seconded, with approval to buy and send the books. Marvin was to check on nonprofit exemption for postage, with IRS report from New York.
- Annemarie moved and Marvin seconded to have a potluck dinner on December 9 from 6:00 to 9:00 p.m. Approved.
- Marvin reported sending invitations to UN Day to the DUNA membership.
- Gloria reported that the newsletter was ready to send. There will not be a reception after Dr. Muller's program but autographing of the books in the lobby. Annemarie suggested that UNICEF card sales be announced in the newsletter.
- Program reports on Dr. Muller's visit:

    1. November 2—Arrival at DFW Airport.
    2. November 3—Luncheon at Thanks-Giving Square with Mr. Peter Stewart.
    3. 1:00 p.m.—Visit Robert Muller School in Arlington.

4. 7:30 p.m.—Public speech at SMU McFarlin Auditorium "War Or Peace," followed by book signing.

5. November 4—He spoke at the Unity Church, Forest Lane, two services.

6. 12:30 p.m.—Luncheon at Ming Garden Restaurant: DUNA board and guests.

7. 2:00 p.m.—Speech on "New Genesis" at Unity Church.

8. 4:00 p.m.—Departure from DFW.

9. Clare and Janet reported that malls would not allow UNICEF card sales; Zales Corporation and Frito Lay allow sales in their buildings.

10. Board adjourned at 9:45 p.m.

December 20.

The United States formally ended 38 years of association with the United Nations Educational, Scientific and Cultural Organization (UNESCO) yesterday, announcing that it will withdraw at the end of the month because the agency has been politicized leftward and is financially irresponsible . . . Critics have charged that it was motivated more by the Reagan administration's conservative ideology than by UNESCO management problems . . . The move will deprive UNESCO of $47 million in US funds for fiscal 1985, or about 25 percent of its $200 million annual budget . . . Gregory J. Newell, assistant secretary of state for international organization affairs, said US membership could be renewed if the 116-nation institution makes certain changes in its operations.[3]

Newell has charged that UNESCO promotes "Soviet-inspired" world disarmament in some of its education programs, boosting the needs of states over the rights of individuals and demanding a 'new international

[3] Joanne Omang and Joanne Omang, "UNESCO Withdrawal Announced," *Washington Post*, December 20, 1984, https://www.washingtonpost.com/archive/politics/1984/12/20/unesco-withdrawal-announced/b9c6dc92-a31f-443a-977b-f3468faf44fe/?utm_term=.81f0bcf679a7.

economic order' critical of free-market capitalism. Poor, Third World nations have used UNESCO forums to vote sanctions against Israel, praise revolutionary organizations and to denounce and routinely outvote the United States.[4]

1985

November 18. DUNA Board met at 6:45 p.m., 3100 Monticello, Suite 450, led by Pres. Marvin Sadovsky. Present were Brown-Sadovsky; Brownscombe, treasurer; Materka, secretary; Buck, Cogan, Douffiagues, Hider, Mason, Rabe, and Walker for Reynolds. Absent were Sands, Mak, Sloos, Franke-Hill, Harris, Hunt, Lynch, Usitalo, Walling. Excused were Kraeger, Pharr, Gooding, Hennike, McIntosh, Price, and Wincorn.

- Secretary corrected October minutes on program "put on by DUNA," added "with the cooperation of" the Baha'i Faith. Approved for mailing.
- Treasurer reported balance on hand October 21: $7,738.11, income total $457.26, expense $597.63, with balance on hand $7,597.74, report approved and filed.
- Human Rights Day draft of program for December 10 by Brown-Sadovsky. Cosponsors: American Jewish Congress, Baha'i Faith, Greater Dallas Community of Churches, National Conference of Christians and Jews, and SMU. Five local issues were to be presented, focused on thinking globally and acting locally on human rights. Dallas City councilwoman Lori Palmer was to summarize and conduct a Q&A. SMU was to provide a hall and print the invitations, with each organization paying postage on its mailings; Baha'i was to provide PR. DUNA also was considering a women's conference centered on the Nairobi experience, either in January or February.
- *Great Decisions*—the president "stepped down" to recommend that this not be used as a fund-raiser, but rather as a consciousness raising and educational tool. Annemarie moved and Dean Buck seconded, with approval to order one hundred *Great Decisions* books.

---

[4]   Ibid.

- Communications announced several speaking engagements:
  - Marvin spoke at Thanks-Giving Square on International Day of Peace.
  - Marvin and Dick Sloos spoke at Spring Valley United Methodist Church on "The UN, UNA, and You."
  - Marvin was scheduled to speak on "Human Rights" on December 7 to the Bedford Baha'i's.
  - Judy Merino was doing press releases for Human Rights Day.
  - Arlette Douffiagues was giving DUNA a listing in the International Business Calendar, next deadline December 10.
- Model UN was discussed: Guy Gooding agreed to head up the program; Toni Hennike would help. Dean Buck, Judith Hider, and Annemarie Brown-Sadovsky were new volunteers for this committee.
- Dean Buck moved; it was seconded and passed that DUNA subscribe to the International Business Calendar at the cost of $90 per year.
- The meeting adjourned at 8:15 p.m.

1986

January 6. DUNA Board met at 6:45 p.m., 3100 Monticello, Suite 450, led by Pres. Marvin Sadovsky. Present were Brown-Sadovsky; Brownscombe, treasurer; Materka, secretary; Buck; Mak; Cogan; Gooding; Hennike; Hider; Mason; Price; Rabe; Walker; and Wincorn. Absent were Sands, Pharr, Douffiagues, Franke-Hill, Harris, Hunt, Lynch, McIntosh, Usitalo, and Walling. Excused were Kraeger and Sloos.

- Announcements: The UN Day Essay Contest had received no entries to be judged. No word had been received from national on proposed by-laws for DUNA, including suggestion to change our fiscal year to coincide with our program year. Marvin reported news that UNA-USA had received significant grants from the Rockefeller Foundation. UNICEF representative Kathryn Walker announced the release of their "State of the World's Children."
- Minutes of the November meeting were approved as mailed. Treasurer reported details for 1985, up to December 31, with

closing balance of $7,311.89, accepted for filing. Annemarie appealed to the board members to buy the *Thirty-Ninth General Assembly Issues* book, $8 a copy, and said we need to sell excess stock.

- High quality of the Human Rights Day event, cost to DUNA only $66 for postage, the president expressed regret that sessions were not recorded; committee planned to record in the future.
- Discussion of cosponsors for a February program on the Nairobi women's conference, plans for the April meeting, with Dallas World Salute to be involved.
- Model UN program: Buck moved; it was seconded and approved, to order kits for the high school and the college level for the committee meeting on January 25 planning meeting at the Sadovskys' home.
- The communications committee: Buck announced the desire to expand functions of the speakers committee, there having been no official appearances since early December.
- *Great Decisions* meeting schedules were listed for five times and locations; publicity for the program was needed.
- Newsletter next deadline is February 24, according to Mak; requested head-shot photos from each board member by February 15. She also requested interviews and for Letters to the Editor of public press, such as an article about Model UN for the next issue.
- Gratitude to Hans Mak for hosting a party for DUNA on January 18, with motion passed to reimburse their cost of beverages.
- Buck moved; it was seconded and passed, that DUNA support the Invitational International Leadership Congress, as requested by the Dallas Cultural Alliance, with our official letter of support and cosponsorship, including publicizing in our newsletter the event to be held over the Labor Day weekend at the Hilton Hotel in Grapevine, with over three hundred organizations to be involved.
- The meeting adjourned at 8:30 p.m.

September 8. The DUNA Board met at the offices of Pres. Annemarie Brown-Sadovsky at 6:45 p.m. Present were board members Brown; VP Dean Buck; Gina Cieri; Bonny Franke-Hill; VP Guy Gooding; Madan Goyal; Sunny Hider; Anna Lee; Eileen Lynch; Barbara Materka; Walter Palmer; Janet Pharr; Secretary Genice Rabe; past president Marvin

Sadovsky; Treasurer E. J. Tanner; and Pearl Wincorn. Three absences excused; twelve others absent.

- Commendations to the World and the Texas Cultural Alliances for the US-USSR Friendship Conference, cosponsored by DUNA.
- Programming assistance for Dean Buck was urged by the president.
- J. P. Muldoon was announced as speaker for UN Day; Dr. Jan LaCroy of Dallas Community College District is chair for the event.
- DUNA could volunteer to lease and staff a concession booth at Texas Stadium for a Cowboys game, receiving 10 percent of the proceeds; no action reported.
- President Brown was to speak about DUNA at the ZONTA service organization, October 9.
- Subscriptions to WFUNA were available for $4.35 each. The remaining fortieth Issues books was to be donated to the Dallas Public Library; forty-first Issues books would not be ordered, except on request by the board.
- The latest newsletter was commended, with suggestions for future editions from Franke-Hill and Goyal.
- Letter from UNA-USA president notified that House of Representatives had voted to cut funding to the UN by 45 percent; Secretary Cieri received an equivocal response from Sen. Lloyd Bentsen to her request for continued US support for the UN.
- Other announcements of plans for World Food Day, UN Day in October, Sunny Hider's trip to USSR to plan and organize 1988 Friendship Conference.
- Treasurer E.J. Tanner reported bank balance of $5,816.00.
- Program VP Dean Buck reported seventy-five participants at the US-USSR Friendship Conference, with speakers Joseph Montville, Jim Garrison, Willis Harmon, and David Ellzey.
- Details of plans for the International Day of Peace, September 16, at Thanks-Giving Square, with introduction by the DUNA president, invocation by Dick Suhm of the Baha'i community, children from the Robert Muller School for the program.
- The Peace and Justice workshop was to be held September 19–21, only cost $10 for Saturday evening program.

- Eight high-level Soviet economists visited Dallas, October 12–14, cosponsored by DUNA with the Dallas Council on World Affairs for a breakfast and forum panel on October 13. Eileen Lynch suggested contact with Dresser Industries for facilities.
- DUNA would hold its UN Day Dinner on October 20 at 7:00 p.m. at the Lincoln Hotel, with Dr. Hans Mak speaking. All cosponsoring organizations were requested to fill at least one table. The Baha'is were organizing a UN Day celebration at Thanks-Giving Square on October 24 with J.P. Muldoon to speak.
- Education VP Guy Gooding reported approval of a board of governors for the Model UN–MUNDO Dallas Organization. J.P. Muldoon was to speak at the introduction to Dallas educators on October 25 at the Fairmont Hotel.
- Newsletter: Gina Cieri reported that Virginia Harris was investigating a new publisher for a better price; deadline for next newsletter was October 15, materials to them; Guy Gooding and Dean Buck were asked for articles on MUNDO and UN Day.
- Marvin Sadovsky was acting VP for membership.
- Sunny Hider announced that she had T-shirts printed with "Coca Cola" in Russian. Over $20,000 had been donated in services and cash for the US-USSR Friendship Conference, but outstanding costs exceeded $10,000. She suggested that DUNA pay costs of mailings to membership, plus something extra. Dean Buck moved, seconded by Bonnie Franke-Hill, and passed, for DUNA to donate $500 to the Texas Cultural Alliance, to help defray conference expenses.
- The meeting adjourned at 8:20 p.m.

1989

HR Representative Eddie Bernice Johnson greets NBN
Kids from Dallas First United Methodist Church

October 24. DUNA Annual UN Day Luncheon at the Plaza of the Americas, 650 N. Pearl, noon. Honored speaker was Raymond Nasher, ambassador of cultural affairs for the City of Dallas, introduced by Beth Huddleston, VP of programming DUNA.

- Head table: Kwasi Ohene Bekoe, International Center director (invocation); Guy Gooding, DUNA president; Beth Huddleston; Raymond Nasher; Robert Rendell, Texas UN Day chairperson; Dr. Lawrence Tyree, chancellor of the Dallas County Community College District; Sheryl Slate, UNICEF; and Top Kemp, Multicultural Center of Dallas.
- Cosponsors: Dallas Council on World Affairs, Dallas County Community College District, the International Center, World Cultural Alliance, and Representative Eddie Bernice Johnson, Dallas UN Day chairperson.

1991

UN Secretary-General Boutros Boutros-Ghali, 1991-1996

October. Boutros Boutros-Ghali of Egypt was elected UN secretary general, served until failed reelection bid for a second term in 1996, opposed by the United States, due to conflict with his positions on the Bosnian War, the Rwandan genocide, and the 1996 subsequent US presidential election of Bill Clinton.

1994

September 1. Pres. Nadine Bell letter to Marshall Doke: Mr. Edward Winn was offering a working meeting of Dallas past presidents with the DUNA executive board to plan for hosting the National Council of Chapter and Division Presidents' Annual Meeting for November 11–13, to kick off UN50 activities. (No reply in the file.)

October 17. Memo from John C. Williams III to Mr. Edward Winn detailed requests to the past presidents to aid in commemorating the United Nations fiftieth anniversary—UN50. The six-page document comprised sponsorships, speaker, promotion, recommendations for speaking engagements and other events for 1995, and compilation of a DUNA history for publication.

November 11. Announcement: DUNA presented the Forty-Ninth United Nations Anniversary Dinner, "Can the United Nations Work?" featuring Sir Brian Urquhart, scholar in residence, the Ford Foundation, former head of UN Peacekeeping Forces, at the Stouffer Dallas Hotel, 6:00 p.m. reception, 7:00 dinner, 7:45 dinner.

1996

SG Boutros-Ghali Proclaims the Declaration of World
Thanksgiving at United Nations, 1996

November 4. The United Nations celebrated the 1996 Declaration of World Thanksgiving, marking the first time every country in the General Assembly unanimously voted in support of a spiritual idea. This proclamation was initiated by the Thanks-Giving Foundation (TGF) of Dallas, Texas, an NGO partner with DUNA in the Department of Information of the United Nations. TGF founding member, Mr. Peter Stewart, was among dignitaries who also brought greetings from their faith communities.

1997

December 16. Announcement of the 1997 holiday celebration, elections and installation of officers at Casa Rosa Restaurant, 6:30 p.m. social, 7:00 dinner and program, $15 suggested donation to UNA-USA Dallas, with a note to mail ballots to the DUNA mailbox address.

Section B
Dallas United Nations Association Time Capsules: 1998–2009

The entries in this section were assembled from reports filed in DUNA archives from varied sources, depending on available documents, also the Dallas Public Library online archives of the *Dallas Morning News* and the *DUNA Viewsletter* files. Each capsule summarizes significant historical developments during these times.

(Author's Note: Bill M.)[5]

1998

August. Pres. Beth Weems Pirtle sent a membership memo on "Upcoming 1998 Events":

- UNA-USA bake sale in the Bank One foyer, Preston Road at Northwest Highway.
- September 15, Third Quarter Public Forum: Disarmament
- October 1, Third Quarter Social Dinner, Russian cuisine
- October 24–25, Second United Nations Conference on Women, University of Texas at Dallas
- November 21, UNA-USA Dallas Chapter Presidents Banquet, Fairmont Hotel (Marshall J. Doke Collection, DUNA Archives)

August. Adopt-A-Minefield in Cambodia, planning dinner at Pirtle's with Kamyra Harding, director from UNA-USA, New York, and Dallas Chapter board members.

October 24–25. The Second North Texas Conference on Women, sponsored by the University of Texas at Dallas School of Social Services and DUNA, "Advancing Women through Global Policy," offered Saturday and Sunday lectures and breakout sessions (DUNA Archives).

---

[5]   Sourced from *Dallas Morning News* and DUNA Archives.

Raymond Nasher, chair, with DUNA president Beth Weems
Pirtle and Ambassador Djerejian, UN Day 1998

November 21. The DUNA Annual Banquet at the Fairmont Hotel featured Ambassador Edward P. Djerejian from the James Baker III Institute, Houston, on "United Nations and US Interests." The event was cosponsored by EDS, the Nasher Company, and Ambassador and Mrs. Richard Rubottom, with surprise entertainment from several nations, including Irish bagpipes, a Databuka Egyptian clay drum, an Irish dance group, songs by Cockney Pearly Queen, and music by President Beth and husband Rod Pirtle (*DUNA Viewsletter*).

December 12. The fiftieth anniversary of the adoption of the Universal Declaration of Human Rights was celebrated at Jaycee Park in Irving by dozens of Dallas and Fort Worth residents, cosponsored by DUNA and the Irving Baha'is, with speeches supporting victims of human rights abuses worldwide. (*DUNA Viewsletter*)

1999

January. Texas division president Nadine Bell announced the formation of a delegation from DUNA to attend the Second China-US Conference on Women's Issues in October in Beijing, China (*DUNA Viewsletter*).

Beth Weems Pirtle, DUNA, among delegates to
South Central Region, UNA USA, 1999

February. DUNA representatives met with South Central Region delegates from the eight-state area at the national conference of UNA-USA in New York City. Beth Weems Pirtle was elected member of the Steering Committee of the Council of Chapters and Divisions, with Katy Hansen of Iowa.

Bill and Norma Matthews sang "The Impossible Dream"

October 24. The 2009 DUNA UN Day converted the main ballroom of the Fairmont Hotel into a virtual village of Spain for a celebration of a spring fair, as La Feria de Sevilla, designed by Charlotte Karam. Keynote speaker was the Spanish ambassador to the UN Inocencio Arias Llamas. Honorary chair and emcee was Dr. Luis Martín of SMU. Colorful tents displayed cultural and informational features, with tasting booths from local Spanish restaurants. The program featured flamenco dancers and an outstanding guitarist, with songs from *Man of La Mancha*, by DUNA member Bill Matthews, accompanied by his wife, Norma. See chapter 6 for more complete reports.

2000

April 14. "Building a Culture of Peace" National High School Essay Contest deadline was announced, with prizes of $500, $250, and $100. Lesley Vann coordinated, local high school winners from Arlington, Plano, and Lancaster were honored in May by UNA president Kambiz Rafraf (*DUNA Archives*).

June 5. Committee on Refugees assisted prescreening of KERA special documentary, "Well-Founded Fear," looking inside the INS asylum system. Chair Linda Evans had received the 1999 Eckerd Salute to Women Award for the work of the committee (*DUNA Viewsletter*).

October 23. United Nations Day, "The United Nations Role in Peacekeeping and Promotion of World Peace": speakers were Ambassador Yves Doutriaux of France and Ambassador Ahmed Darwish of Egypt, held at Highland Park United Methodist Church, emceed by Mr. Kambiz Rafraf, DUNA president (*DUNA Viewsletter*).

November 10 and 11. Fourth North Texas UN Conference on Women, "The Power To Be Cool, Smart and Successful," cohosted by the University of Texas at Dallas School of Social Sciences and the United Nations Association Dallas Chapter and Texas Division. Planning and coordination was led by UNT Dean Rita Kelly.

November. Eight hundred fifty-two complimentary copies of the book *The United Nations, Come Along with Me*, written by Mrs. Nane (Kofi) Annan, were distributed by Dallas member Norma Matthews to area school libraries, cosponsored by Dallas County Schools and the DUNA Chapter (*DUNA Viewsletter*).

December 10. Human Rights Day, with DUNA leaders Mr. Kambiz Rafraf and Mrs. Regina Rafraf, Amnesty International president Rick Halperin, and hosted by the Spiritual Assembly of the Baha'i Faith Irving chairman Dr. Nasser Zonozy (*DUNA Archives*).

2001

Dean Rita M. Kelly, president Kambiz Rafraf, Kathleen Kelly,
Linda Evans, Evelyn Sheffield, Beth Weems Pirtle, Pam
Burns, David Griggs, Joseph Lake, and Mark Gilman

2001 Officers and Board United Nations Association Dallas Chapter

- President—Kambiz Rafraf
- Secretary—Mark Gilman
- Treasurer—Regina Rafraf
- Speaker's Bureau—Beth Weems Pirtle
- Advocacy VP/ Parliamentarian—David Griggs
- Programming VP—Pam Burns
- Membership VP—Margit Whitaker
- Refugee Committee—Linda Evans
- Foreign Affairs—Joseph E. Lake
- Education—Evelyn Sheffield, Kathleen McLaughlin
- Viewsletter editor—Bill Matthews
- Other resources—Charlotte M. Karam, Zia Shamsy
- Honorary directors—Robert Dean, Jeff Dumas
- President Texas Division—Beth Weems Pirtle

UNA-USA Staff Person in NY—Heather Reine
UNA-USA, Dallas Chapter, P.O. Box 797502, Dallas, TX 75379-7502
UNA-USA, Dallas Chapter Hot Line: 972/480-5236
UNA-USA, Dallas Chapter Web Page Address www.dallas-una.org
UNA-USA, Dallas Chapter Email Address unadallas@yahoo.com

May 14. Minutes of DUNA Board, President Kambiz Rafraf met with Pam Burns, Linda Evans, Mark Gilman, David Griggs, Beth Weems Pirtle, Kathleen McLaughlin, Evelyn Sheffield, and guest Margit Whitaker (later voted newest board member) present. Excused were Dean Rita Kelly (UTD), Regina Rafraf, Ambassador Joe Lake, and George Reasonover.

- Treasurer Regina Rafraf reported funds balance of $5,582.96. Beth reported attending Model UN at Mountain View College and a talk by Julian Bond at Temple Emanu-El on "Civic and Civil Rights Revisited: A Time to Speak, a Time to Act."
- Advocacy chair David Griggs shared controversy about the United States being voted off the Human Rights Commission and International Narcotics Board. Mark and Kathleen agreed to collaborate on an editorial about the US government's apparent disengagement from multilateral endeavors, such as ratification of treaties and conventions, including CEDAW, Landmine Convention, Treaty on Children, International Criminal Court, and nonpayment of dues for membership and peacekeeping.
- Reports were received from the Committee on Refugees by Linda, Adopt-A-Minefield by Mark, and plans for a new website by Mark. Plans were advanced to establish contact with the Asian-American Bar Association, Chamber of Commerce, professional associations, and student organizations (*DUNA Archives*).

August. Adopt-A-Minefield fund-raising campaign by DUNA with Dallas Peace Center and other agencies set a goal of $21,000 to remove landmines in Spean Youl village, Battambang province, Cambodia. Cambodian Dallas police officer Paul Thai joined DUNA president and Lon Burnam, director of DPC to launch the drive. (See 2002 report.) (*DUNA Viewsletter*)

November 1. The Fifth North Texas UN Conference on Women at University of Texas at Dallas heard keynote speakers on reproductive rights and women's health, drug policy and gender justice, and disarmament and landmines. Dean Rita M. Kelly was prime organizer with Beth Weems Pirtle, UNA-USA regional representative (*DUNA Viewsletter*).

2002

January 14. New president Bill (J.W.) Matthews met at Highland Park United Methodist Church with new treasurer Carol Bennett, Mark Gilman, David Griggs, Kambiz Rafraf, and Beth Weems Pirtle; excused were Pam Burns, Evelyn Sheffield, and Margit Whittaker.

- Treasurer reported balance of $4,503.66. Board invited Tina Patterson to join; withdrawing from the board were Joe Lake, Linda Evans, Regina Rafraf, and Kathleen McLaughlin. Carol Bennett and Bill Matthews were authorized as signatories for the Dallas Chapter account at Guaranty Bank.
- Kambiz and Mark were to work on programming ahead; next event to observe the fiftieth anniversary of the Dallas Chapter in February. Mark reported on Adopt-A-Minefield results (see later entry). Support voted for Dr. Lance Rasbridge project in Cambodia.
- Kambiz Rafraf from Dallas was elected central regional representative to the steering committee of the Council of Chapters and Divisions of UNA-USA (Texas Division archives).
- Chapter membership reported 210 members, plans to grow (DUNA Board Minutes).

February 22. Fiftieth birthday of DUNA, with speaker Dr. Lloyd Jeff Dumas, professor of political economy at UTD. Event at Maggiano's Little Italy restaurant, $25 per person tickets, attended by more than fifty persons.

April. The AAM (Adopt-A-Minefield) campaign raised $28,000, sent to UNA-USA for UNDP directed mine eradication in Cambodia. Several nights of 1,000 Dinners in November had boosted the total by $5,000 through the cooperation of DUNA, Dallas Peace Center, Cambodian Gardeners Club, state representative Harryette Ehrhardt, and other community sponsors and contributors (*DUNA Viewsletter*).
Note: See additional project reports of "Goal Success" in chapter 6.

August. Reports of the national UNA-USA Conference in June were given from DUNA president Bill Matthews and Texas division president Beth Weems Pirtle. Also reported were several Night of a Thousand Dinners for Adopt-A-Minefield fund-raisers, UNA displays at a Paul McCartney humanitarian event, meeting with Sierra Leone bishop (Lutheran) about the importance of peacekeeping, and human rights participation in a Dallas rally of the Muslim faith community for reconciliation, condemning terrorism (*DUNA Viewsletter*).

August 9. The AAM Landmine Removal Project Kickoff Luncheon was held at Wilshire Baptist Church to begin the campaign to clear a designated minefield in Cambodia. The goal of $27,250 was accepted by the steering committee of DUNA and the Dallas Peace Center, on recommendation of the national Adopt-A-Minefield program of UNA-USA.

- Several events began with Lunch in the Garden at the East Dallas Community Garden, where Cambodian gardeners raise many of their native vegetables, sponsored by the nonprofit Gardeners in Community Development.
- Plans were developing for a number of "Night of 1,000 Dinners" to be held on or about November 22.
- Two rummage sales were being organized, with sponsors providing promotion and administrative support so that 100 percent of proceeds would go to landmine removal. Greenland Hills United Methodist Church offered their venue for the sales (*Dallas Peace Times, DUNA Archives*).

October 26. Ambassador David J. Scheffer, UNA-USA vice president from New York, spoke at the UN Day event of DUNA, with 184 members and guests. He was the chief US negotiator in the UN talks to establish the International Criminal Court.
The event was cosponsored by the Dallas Peace Center at Maggiano's Restaurant.

- His address was on war crimes, crimes against humanity, human rights, international law, and other issues.
- He also attended the GEMUN (Global Elementary Model United Nations) conference with about one hundred children and their leaders, a luncheon at UTD, a reception with about thirty Dallas Peace Center members, a dinner at TCU, and a meeting with Texas Wesleyan Law School faculty and students in Fort Worth, Texas (*Dallas Peace Times, DUNA Archives*).

November 1–2. The Sixth North Texas UN Conference on Women was jointly sponsored with the University of Texas at Dallas on "Exercising Women's Voice in a Fearful World: Finding Freedom, Security and Peace."

- The planning committee was headed by UTD faculty members Dr. Bobby Alexander and Dr. Marie Chevriér and included UNA members Nadine Bell, Linda Evans, Beth Weems Pirtle, Kambiz Rafraf, and Margit Whitaker.
- In addition to UTD faculty members, distinguished national lecturers included Dr. Margaret Cawley; Guenet Guebre-Christos; Dr. Anne E. Brodsky; Dr. Nancy Felipe Russo; Dr. Joyce Marie Mushaben; and Dr. Susan M. Maloney (*DUNA Archives*).

2003

January 21. Local PBS panel and discussion about the UN; President Bill Matthews was interviewed on the McCuistion program.

January 31. Norma and Bill Matthews attended the CTAUN Conference (Committee on Teaching about the United Nations) in New York City on "Literacy Now: Building an Educated World," partnering DUNA with the local Eta Zeta Chapter of Delta Kappa Gamma Society International.

February 8. Night of a Thousand Dinners in Fort Worth to benefit Adopt-A-Minefield project was held with twenty-five persons present.

February 28. Adopt-A-Minefield interactive UNA display led participants through a simulated minefield, using inflated balloons. When stepped on, a balloon would burst, revealing a typical mine-blast injury. Pres. Bill Matthews organized and staffed the happening at the United Methodist National Deacon's Conference, Arlington, Texas, 400 registrants (*DUNA Archives*).

March 4. "UN Gets IT Done" President Bill Matthews presentation at Christian Women's Fellowship, East Dallas Christian Church, fifty persons present.

Elena Dodd portrays Eleanor Roosevelt

March 8, 10. DUNA hosted "Eleanor Roosevelt," portrayed by actress Elena Dodd from Boston, who came for a series of educational appearances in the Dallas area, celebrating the Universal Declaration of Human Rights, adopted in 1948 (*DUNA Viewsletter*).

April 10. Human Trafficking Panel at Center for Community Cooperation, sixty-five persons present.

April 12. UNA Display, Pres. Bill Matthews at Dallas Earth Fest, White Rock Lake Park.

April 21. "Dare to Compare: The Case for Interdependence" Assembly program for Greenhill School by Pres. Bill Matthews, with lively Q&A, with approximately one hundred students and faculty present.

April 24, 25. Jeff Laurenti from UNA-USA spoke at dinner and luncheon cosponsored with Dallas Democratic Forum and World Affairs Council.

May 15. UNA panel at Richland College, with Scott Branks, Peace Institute, and Pres. Bill Matthews; 25 students and faculty present.

May 18. UNA stakeholders four-hour Vision and Strategy Consultation led by Richard York.

June 25–30. UNA National Conference in Washington, DC; Bill and Norma Matthews received Landmine Removal recognition. Beth Weems Pirtle elected to National Steering Committee of Councils and Chapters.

August 13. DUNA partnered with Sweden UNA to complete the Cambodia Landmine Removal Project with a total of $36,000 forwarded to UNDP to restore the adopted community to usefulness. Twenty-five persons were present for report (*DUNA Viewsletter*).

August 19. DUNA Display at Alaska Wilderness Sierra Club event, Pres. Bill Matthews, approximately 150 persons present.

August 25. DUNA represented at International Institute for World Peace, approximately 100 persons present.

September 2. DUNA Display and Presentation at International Festival, Lovers Lane UMC, President Bill Matthews, approximately 100 persons present.

September 6. DUNA Display at Congressional Community Appreciation event, Pres. Bill Matthews, approximately 100 persons present.

September 11. DUNA represented at Church and Society Commission meeting, Pres. Bill Matthews, North Texas Conference UMC.

October 13. Frances Rizo interview on KNON Radio, on Literacy (advance for UN Day theme).

October 19. Mike Ghouse interview on KBIS radio, on Literacy (advance for UN Day theme).

Honorary Chair, Mrs. Chandler Roosevelt Lindsley

October 23. United Nations Day Program, "Literacy as Freedom: Local Realities, Global Possibilities," at Cityplace Conference Center, MC Bill Matthews, DUNA president; comments by honorary chairs: Chandler Roosevelt Lindsley and Beth Weems Pirtle, regional representative to UNA-USA CCR.

- Speakers: Mr. Larry Powell, *Dallas Morning News*; Dr. Gaye Lang, US Department of Education; Mr. George Peña, Dallas Reads; Mr. Andy Harris, Dallas Reads; Ms. Anne Bartlett, UNICEF Regional Manager; and Dr. Maman Sidikou, World Bank Senior Education Specialist.
- Cosponsored by Verizon Foundation, AAUW, Dallas Peace Center, Foundation for Pluralism, Highland Park UMC and Just Figs (*DUNA Archives*).

October 28. DUNA presentation at Tuesday Adventures Club, Highland Park UMC, Pres. Bill Matthews, 75 persons present.

November 2. DUNA presentation "UN Gets IT Done" for Wedding Ring Class, University Park UMC, Pres. Bill Matthews, 45 persons present.

November 8, 9. DUNA Display and "Peace Pathway" representation at DFW International Alliance Festival, Pres. Bill Matthews, Norma Matthews, others, est. 20,000 persons attended.

December 2. DUNA Business Compact Luncheon, "Corporate Sustainability" panel moderated by Bill Matthews.

December 9. Violence Against Women public panel, DUNA Board represented by member Nanette Thomas.

December 10. Human Rights Day program and annual meeting, "The Future of the United Nations and International Human Rights," at St. Martin's Restaurant. Speaker: International attorney Chip Pitts.

- Officers installed: President Tina Patterson, VP Advocacy Amanda Howe, Membership Henry Irving, Treasurer Joel Pugh, Board members Paul Belisch, Gae Hatton, Mary Ellen Irving, Harbans Lal, Charles Moss, Paul Pederson, Kambiz Rafraf, Maura Sheehan, Nanette Thomas, Margit Whitaker, Bill Matthews, past president (*DUNA Archives*).

2004

January 21. Membership Report for Dallas Chapter UNA-USA showed 115 active "units," 139 total members by National records, local total 154, with adjustments. Henry Irving was DUNA membership chair, responsible for recruitment.

February 24. Organizational records, dated 1995 to 2003, of DUNA, the Dallas Chapter of the United Nations Association, were donated for safekeeping to the Texas/Dallas History and Archives Division of the Dallas Public Library, with a file number MA 04.01.

March 4–8. Documents on file indicated reports to DUNA from Council of Chapters and Divisions Annual Meeting, which included Issues Sessions on Terrorism and UN Role, Iraq, Financing for Development, Collective Security, Role of Civil Society in UN and Decision-Making, status of Millennium Development Goals, the International Criminal Court, and UN High Level Panel on Global Security (*DUNA Archives*).

April 28. Board minutes: President Tina Patterson reported for Linda Evans at Women's Rights event March 24, including issues on AIDS, discrimination, refugee resettlement, and US roles. Paul Pederson announced Business Connections luncheon for June 9 with speakers attorney Chip Pitts and Oscar Gonzales. Dallas Reads affiliate agreement was to be ratified by e-vote (*DUNA Archives*).

May 12. 2004 Global Classrooms Model UN Conference program in Houston (on file) indicated participation by DUNA representatives (*DUNA Archives*).

June. Strategic Plan for UNA-USA with notes from Beth Weems Pirtle (on file). Priorities: Educate, Convene Policy Dialogue, Build Constituencies, Increase Membership, Mobilize Resources, and Strengthen UNA-USA, reported later to the DUNA at the June social (*DUNA Archives*).

June. *Response*, the mission magazine of United Methodist Women, devoted its June issue to "The United Nations in Our Daily Lives," which was used as a resource by DUNA leaders for several local educational programs. Eight specific articles indicated comprehensive coverage, with many photos that supported their themes:

1. "The United Nations: We the Peoples" by David Wildman. "Did you know a representative of each member state on the UN Security Council, whose role is to maintain international peace and security, is required to be present at UN headquarters in New York City at all times? Did you know the Security Council is the only body of the United Nations with authority to make decisions that member states are obligated under the UN Charter to carry out, rather than simply adopt as recommendations?"

2. "Church Center for the United Nations: Witness for Peace" by Mia Adjali. This 12-story building, located directly across the plaza from the United Nations Headquarters, was consecrated

on Sept. 23, 1963, to accommodate related meeting spaces, missional headquarters, and offices for Methodist and other NGO (nongovernmental organization) activities.

3. "United Methodists Impact United Nations" by Amy-Ellen Drake.
4. "Advocates Share UN Story, Push Governments" by Amy-Ellen Drake.
5. "Seminars: Transforming Global Insights" by Amy-Ellen Drake.
6. "Applying the Social Principles" by Amy-Ellen Drake.
7. "Women: Equality, Development, Peacemaking" by Vina Nadjibulla.
8. "No Women, No Peace" by Vina Nadjibulla. "In October 2000, the UN Security Council unanimously adopted the landmark Resolution 1325 on Women, Peace and Security, recognizing for the first time that wars affect women and men differently and that women's participation in peacemaking and peace building is essential to achieving sustainable peace."[6]

September. DUNA announced support for High School Model UN Programs. Austin College in Sherman, Texas, hosts a college Model UN and the Robert Muller School in Arlington organizes a Global Elementary Model UN (GEMUN) at a local community college campus.

- Refugee Services of Texas affiliated with DUNA to coordinate ten or more agencies serving the immigrant communities. The DUNA Committee on Refugees is headed by Linda Evans, volunteer (*DUNA Viewsletter*).

October 6. "The People Speak: America's Role in the World," forum at SMU, panel with Chris Bury, moderator from ABC News, Ambassador Robert Jordan and Ambassador Robert Oakley, cosponsors SMU Tower Center, DUNA, with World Affairs Council and Dallas Committee on Foreign Relations (*DUNA Viewsletter*).

October 13. Board minutes with notes by Beth Weems Pirtle; officer selection included Anoop Elath, secretary; Dick Sloos, Nirmal Nilvi, Dary Bowlin, members. Nominating committee: Nanette Thomas, Maura

---

6 Women's Division, General Board of Global Ministeries, United Methodist Church, "The United Nations in Our Daily Lives," *United Methodist Women Magazine*, June 2004.

Sheehan, Paul Durfee. Treasurer reported $5,000 bank balance. Amanda Howe agreed to judge essay contest.

October 24. Dallas United Nations Day, "Gender Equality and Empowerment in the New Millennium." Speaker Carolyn Hannon, Director of UN Division for the Advancement of Women; emcee Tina Patterson, DUNA president, at Highland Park UMC. Cosponsor with DUNA American Association of University Women and Crowne Plaza Hotel. Dallas mayor Laura Miller proclaimed UN Day. Chairs Kambiz Rafraf and Beth Weems Pirtle, honorary chairs Vivian Castleberry and Louise Raggio of Peacemakers Inc. (*DUNA Archives*).

November 10. Board agenda notes by Beth Weems Pirtle.

Annual Activities Report 2003 by President Tina Patterson:

1. Spoke to Rotary Clubs in Dallas, Frisco, Garland
2. Judge for International Ethics Debate at SMU
3. Spoke at Words of Women International Women's Day (March)
4. Cosponsored with Dallas Peace Center for Phyllis Bennis visit
5. Participated in World of Women for World Peace event by Congresswoman Eddie Bernice Johnson
6. Took part in Mother's Day program sponsored by Brahma Kumaris of Dallas (May)
7. Signed affiliation agreements with American Center for International Policy Studies and Dallas Reads
8. Hosted display at Global Elementary Model United Nations (May)
9. Hosted Business Connections program
10. Human Rights Day program with Donna Rohling, President of Project Chiapas
11. Provided student intern scholarship for UNA-USA office
12. Took part in UNA-USA High School Essay contest
13. Distributed Nane Annan, *Come Along With Me* to Russian orphanages through Park Cities Rotary Club and the International Rescue Committee
14. Cosponsored Bill of Rights Defense Committee Symposium
15. Supported Dallas Peace Center Peacemaker of the Year award to Chip Pitts, DUNA Advisory board member (*DUNA Archives*)

2005

January 1. National Membership Report Dallas Chapter 136 members.

January 27. "The United States and the United Nations: Can This Marriage Be Saved?" featuring Mrs. Gillian Sorensen, United Nations Foundation senior adviser, introduced by Mr. Raymond Nasher, former DUNA president.

- Sponsors: Dallas Committee on Foreign Relations, SMU Political Forum, Westin City Center Hotel, with thanks to Nadine Bell, Anoop Ellath, Emilia Lodish, Bill Matthews, Shabnam Modgil, Beth Weems Pirtle, Dick Sloos, Peter Stewart, and Lesley Vann.

March 2–6. "UN 60: A Time for Renewal"—the World Federation of United Nations Associations with UNA-USA, Marriott East Hotel, New York, NY. Attended from Dallas: Beth Weems Pirtle, a WFUNA director, with Bill and Norma Matthews, DUNA board.

April 22. DUNA president Tina Patterson presented the program on United Nations Sixtieth Year to the Rotary Club of Park Cities.

September 15. A Commemoration of the Opening of the United Nations at Thanks-Giving Square, Dallas, welcome by Elizabeth Esperson, greeting from Dr. Robert Muller, presentations by DUNA president Beth Huddleston and president elect Nadine Bell.

- *The New Genesis*, dramatization of Dr. Muller's book by students of the Robert Muller School and introductions to distinguished members of the Hemispheric Congress of the Spirit planning committee, here for a three-day planning meeting, cosponsored by The Center for World Thanksgiving and DUNA.

October 22. Dallas United Nations Day, "UN 60: A Legacy of Hope, Courage and Renewal for the World's Future—Our Children." Speaker: Dr. Maman Sidikou, senior education officer, UNICEF Iraq, introduced by Dr. Maura Sheehan, emcee Tina Patterson, at FunAsia, Richardson.

Proclamations by Dallas Mayor Laura Miller, Richardson Mayor Gary A. Slagel.

- Individual sponsors: Suzybelle Gosslee; Norma and Bill Matthews; Nirmal and Balbir Nilvi; Joel Pugh; Palmer Shepard; Maria Viera-Williams. Donors: Richard and Katherine Fleming; FunAsia; Dr. Ruth May, Mary M. Russell; Judge Barefoot and Jan Sanders; Evelyn Sheffield; and Mr. and Mrs. Edwin B. Winn.
- Special thanks for contributions to UNA Dallas Niger hunger relief project: Frank Barnes, Diane Bergander, Leslie Engelhart, Thomas Evans, Jeremy Halbreich, Dale Hinz, Ted and Susie Hoeller, Hadi Jawad, Deborah Kurtz, Bill Matthews, Lynne Novack, Beth Weems Pirtle, Lance Price, Joel Pugh, Andrew Rice, Carol Riffle, Reena Shellenberg, Amanda and David Schnetzer, Maura Sheehan, Sharlee Skaggs, Webb Spradley, Edward Thomas, Elizabeth Turichi, Debra Utech, Russell Wallace, Larry Washington, Margaret Werry, and Sheryl Wolfe.

November 5. Chiapas Project Black Tie Gala—"Millennium One" recognizing the UN Millennium Development Goal One—Eradiation of Poverty. Speakers: His Excellency Kofi Annan, secretary general of the United Nations, and Dr. Muhammad Yunus, founder, Grameen Bank, Bangladesh. Chair Kaki Hopkins, Chiapas Project founder Lucy Billngsley, and Chiapas Project president Donna Rohling.

November 15. Bill Matthews conducted a Peace-War Symposium for Bishop Lynch High School assembly, with historic references climaxing with Universal Declaration of Human Rights, with PowerPoint and hand-out copies (*DUNA Archives*).

2006

January 1. National membership report Dallas chapter: 139 members.

February 23. DUNA Board at Center for Non-Profit Management. Present: Beth Weems Pirtle presiding, Anoop Ellath, Paul Belish, Dick Sloos, Nirmal Nilvi, Maura Sheehan, Yussuf Kalib, Bill Matthews, Norma

Matthews, Dagmar Fleming, Mihir Mistry, and Maria Viera-Williams. Anoop highlighted recent meetings:

- January 10, board held a Holocaust ceremony at FunAsia.
- January 26, meeting at Pirtle's; Beth agreed to serve as interim president until new election, nomination committee headed by Dick Sloos.
- February 14, met at Pirtle's, new members to be nominated to board, Palmer Shepherd volunteered program for March/April with Chip Pitts.
- Anoop updated information about UN Undersecretary General Shashi Tharoor for a program to be cosponsored with World Affairs Council.
- New board members with Pirtle are Yussuf Kalib, Anita Titone, Kidane Alemayehu, Dagmar Fleming, and Maria Viera-Williams.
- Board voted $50 grants for Earl Eames Communication Award fund, $50 for UNA Grassroots Development Fund.

During this period, there was an intentional goal to expand and diversify board membership to include wider ethnic representation from the community (Author's notes Bill M.).

Ambassador Richard Rubottom, with Beth Weems Pirtle
and UNA USA CEO Sen. Timothy Wirth, 1999

March 23. DUNA Officers elected 2006:

- President Beth Weems Pirtle
- VP Programs Dagmar Fleming
- VP Membership Dick Sloos, Latha Nehru
- VP Education Norma Matthews, Maria Viera-Williams
- Treasurer Anoop Ellath
- Viewsletter Editor Bill Matthews
- Refugee Committee Linda Evans
- Directors Kapila Agrawal, Kidane Alemayehu, Yussuf Kalib, Harbans Lal, Shabnam Modgil, Melanie Neal, Nirmal Nilvi, Maura Sheehan, Anita Titone
- Honorary Director Lloyd Jeff Dumas
- Texas Division President Beth Weems Pirtle

April 25. "Human Rights: Inhuman Wrongs," speaker Mr. Cannon Flowers, CEO of Human Rights Initiative of North Texas, held at Richland College Crockett Hall, free admission.

Welcome by Beth Weems Pirtle, introduction by Linda Evans.

May 7. Night of 1,000 Dinners Fund-Raiser at home of Jim and Maria Viera-Williams for 25 persons, with Iranian food and music, contributions to Adopt-a-Minefield benefit.

June 6. Beth Weems Pirtle attended UNA-USA Mountain-Pacific Convention, Salt Lake City, made musical presentation.

July 27. DUNA Board reports from Program for August 26 announced, Membership. Dick Sloos reported on hotline calls: 77 unheard messages, 54 saved, follow-up by Roberta, Linda, Latha, and Beth. Education reported on Model UN by Anoop, Beth and Shabnam about Student Alliances, Global Classrooms at Richland College, and Essay Contest for grades 9–12. Maura Sheehan reported plans for UN Day October 24. Jane Nwoke proposed small group meetings on Micro credit and Water for the World.
Bank balance was $3,869.

Dallas area Muslim women offered public prayers
for peace at a solemn vigil in 2006

July 30. DUNA members joined to support a Muslim community Prayers for Peace Vigil in downtown Dallas, in the plaza behind the Old Red Courthouse, near the JFK Memorial.

Islamic families shared their deep concern for peace in a 2006 Dallas vigil

August 26. DUNA Social and Program on Darfur, highlighting humanitarian crisis, presented by Stanley Ukeni, with Q&A after DVD program. 37 persons attended at Cantina Laredo on Lovers Lane near Inwood.

October 24. DUNA United Nations Day, "Maternal Health and Well Being: A Cornerstone of the Millennium Development Goals," speaker Dr. Shershah Syed, general secretary, Pakistan Medical Association, at FunAsia Irving.

November 20. "Night of 1,000 Dinners" and board meeting, discussion and announcements. Present were Harbans and Amrit Lal, Bill and Norma Matthews, Felix Gakunga, Jane Nwoke, Ed Thomas, and Beth Weems Pirtle, with 12 absences, so no quorum present.

- Reports: Essay Contest notices sent in local area by Norma Matthews to 62 public and 42 private high schools. Maura Sheehan reported on UN Day Dinner, October 24 at FunAsia, good program on maternal health in Pakistan, $100 honorarium to speaker, 35 persons attended.

December 11. Officer election for 2007: President Latha Nehru (one year term), President Elect Dagmar Fleming, VP Membership Jennifer Whipple Griffin, Secretary Dennis Gakunga, and Treasurer Shabnam Modgil.

- Program on "Roots of Discord" Iran and the United States," speaker Mr. Ed Thomas, former diplomat and foreign service officer in Middle East area, DUNA member.

2007

January 1. National Membership Report Dallas Chapter—142 members.

January 20. UNA National High School Essay Contest: local winners were Thuy-Vy (Vivian) Ho, Marcus High School, Flower Mound; Ashley Easaw, Rockwall High School; and Kenan Andrew Ince, Plano West Senior High School.

February 2. Norma and Bill Matthews attended CTAUN, the Committee on Teaching about the United Nations, at United Nations Headquarters in New York City, with issues topics on Health/Nutrition, Literacy, Security, and Rights of the Child.

March 23. Bill Matthews—United Methodist publication reported his election as new President of Texas Division, UNA-USA (*North Texas ConferenceNews*).[7]

July 10–15. International Women's Peace Conference, Adams Mark Hotel, Dallas, organized by Peacemakers Inc., with DUNA and Texas Division among many cosponsors. Three Nobel Peace Laureates were featured,

---

[7]   *North Texas Conference News.*

from Northern Ireland, Betty Williams, 1976; Guatemala, Rigoberta Menchu Tum, 1992; and USA, Jody Williams, 1997, plus exceptional women leaders from Turkey, South Africa, Singapore, and Switzerland. More than a thousand registrants and community participants attended.

July series. Bill and Norma Matthews taught "Shalom, Salaam, Peace," a ten-hour course on interfaith understanding and cooperation among three major religions, emphasis on peacemaking, with frequent references to specific roles fulfilled by United Nations, 35 registrants. This was an approved course of Churchwide Missions Studies, distributed through the National Council of Churches, USA, and United Methodist Women.

- Abbreviated versions were also taught in four weekly sessions at University Park in April, and at Lovers Lane United Methodist Churches in May with approximately 85 participants.

Lucy Mashua, with Latha Nehru and Beth Weems Pirtle

August 28. DUNA board meeting at Central Market Community Room B. Present: President Latha Nehru with Dagmar Fleming, Jane Nwoke, Charu, Lucy Mashua, Ed Thomas, Beth Weems Pirtle, Yussuf Kalib, Dick Sloos, and Dennis Gakunga.

- Discussions were held on Texas Muslim Women's Foundation, the National High School Essay Contest, Dining for Darfur event at SMU, Model UN videos, Lucy Mashua with Refugee Choir at

SMU, Ambassador Chaudry at UTD in November, Elena Dodd as "Eleanor Roosevelt" in April, 2008, plans for UN Day for November 10, several upcoming events. Lucy Mashua, Nigeria, was an early advocate in Dallas of the campaign to stop FGM (female genital mutilation), later adopted by the UN.

September 13. Past president Noeli Biggs announced "Going Global with the UN" Video Series posting for access through LeCroy Center for Educational Television, Richland College cosponsored with DUNA. Viewable online through DFW cable channels, the topics included the UN Millennium Development Goals overview and eight individual programs.

November 10. DUNA United Nations Day Celebration at the Fairmont Hotel, president elect Dagmar Fleming presiding, message from President Latha Nehru, presentation by Dr. Doug Hardy, professor at UT Southwestern Medical Center and Helen Zimba, senior case manager of Bryan's House, Art reflections by Trevor Kobrin.

- Table sponsors: Dallas Peace Center, Highland Park United Methodist Church, Rev. and Mrs. Bill Matthews, and Richland College (*DUNA Archives*).

November 20. Guaranty Bank activity, including UN Day expense—10-19-07 beginning balance $2,587.97, deposits $2,270.00, checks paid $3,085.22, 11-20-07 ending balance $1,770.75.

December 7. Luncheon at the UN Headquarters in New York recognized the Thanksgiving relationships among nations, initiated by Thanks-Giving Foundation of Dallas, founding member Mr. Peter Stewart, a partner NGO which had arranged the mounting of The Golden Rule mosaic of Norman Rockwell's "Do Unto Others" painting in 1985 at UN Headquarters. Address was given by Ambassador Anwarul Chowdhury, former Under-Secretary General of the UN, and Permanent Representative from Bangladesh.

Comments followed by Ambassadors and representatives from Philippines, the Holy See, Bangladesh, Grenada, Burkina Faso, Chile, Ukraine, Zambia, and the U Thant Institute (*DUNA Archives*).

2008

January 12. UNA-USA National High School Essay Contest, "What can the US do to help combat HIV/AIDS, malaria and other diseases around the world?" Certificates of participation were signed by Norma Matthews, DUNA VP Education, and awarded (in lieu of cash prizes) to Paul Chung, Coppell Texas High School; Christina Leos, Coronado High School, El Paso, Texas; and Monique Renee-Molina Hawkins, Duncanville, Texas High School.

February 1. Norma and Bill Matthews attended the Tenth Annual CTAUN, the Committee on Teaching about the United Nations, at United Nations Headquarters in New York City with the theme of "Teaching and Learning in an Interdependent World."

March 9. DUNA president Tina Patterson spoke at the International Women's Day Dallas, "What You Should Know About Women," Emcee Linda Evans, DUNA Committee on Refugees.

June 10. "Day on the Hill," National UNA-USA Conference, Norma Matthews' notes on visits to congressional representatives.

- Representative Jeb Hensarling, Fifth District, Texas—excerpts from legislative correspondent Rachel Stewart interview: Foreign aid dollars don't get to people who need them; does not support abortion grants in family planning; no UNFP dollars to China; wants to prevent government waste for extras, earmarks.
- Senator Kay Bailey Hutchison met with Colby Miller, legislative assistant. Responses: KBH interested in peacekeeping efforts; seemed in favor of more off shore drilling for Texas, not much mention of alternative energy; no comment on our talking points for UN issues: climate change, paying dues, women's rights and CEDAW ratification, and human rights. He said KBH opposed the Law of the Sea treaty, didn't like control of passageways.
- Senator John Cornyn, met with foreign affairs and education assistant Brian Polley. Responses: JC knows about Defense Authorization Bill with UN Support, skeptical about Lieberman/Warner, wants more scientific study. Cornyn friends with Senator

Brownback who has two staffers on human rights, JC follows their information. JC is not anti-UN, but many rural Texas constituents want him to "Get the US out of the UN."

Noeli and Bill Biggs, with Jeanna Remington and Diana Urrutia from Richland College at UNA Goodman Awards Reception

- Richland College LeCroy Center and former Dallas Chapter President Noeli Biggs accepted the 2008 Earl Eames Award for distribution of United Nations videos through local cable TV channels and Worldwide Web distance learning services.

Noeli Biggs received the Goodman Award, 2008

July 18. Guaranty Bank statement showed ending balance $1,660.86.

August 8. "Compassion in Action: The UNA" Bill Matthews oped article reported attendance at the Conference of Chapters and Divisions of UNA-USA in Washington, DC. In addition to observance of sixtieth anniversary of the adoption of the Universal Declaration of Human Rights, emphases focused on Fair Share of US payments to the UN, Human Rights, Climate Change, International Law. Advocacy with Congressional representatives, the Millennium Development Goals (2000–2015) progress updates rounded out the program.

October 13. International Attorney Chip Pitts lectured to DUNA Group on the Persistence of International Law, from Norma Matthews notes on file: "Can't impose democracy . . . both sides abuse civil rights; basis of law is cooperation, not competition; the framework for global civilization comprised in the Universal Declaration of Human Rights. Iraq/Iran balance is difficult" (*DUNA Archives*).

October 26. DUNA United Nations Day Dinner "Environmental Sustainability," on the Millennium Development Goal #7, and other achievements, presented by Texas Division president Bill Matthews. Held at the Double Tree Hotel, LBJ at Midway, Dallas, sponsors were Church Women United, Peacemakers, Inc., Thanks-Giving Foundation, Highland Park United Methodist Church, and Rev. and Mrs. Bill Matthews.

- Welcome by past president Latha Nehru, special presentation by Jan Sanders, widow of the late Judge Barefoot Sanders, music by Mauricio Oliveros, and a message from President Noeli Biggs.

November 20. Coffee and Conversation with Gillian Sorensen, senior adviser, United Nations Foundation: "Barack Obama and the Future of US UN Relations" at the Farmers Branch Senior Center, apx. 65 persons present.

2009

March 10. DUNA Board Texas Division president Bill Matthews assumed interim chapter presidency (Latha Nehru unavailable due to work commitments), scheduled elections for June.

April 26. Peace House Dallas was dedicated at the Cathedral of Hope, 5910 Cedar Springs, Dallas, Texas, establishing "the coalition of six organizations under one roof . . . for peace and justice programming and advocacy." Office and conference room facilities were provided for The Dallas Peace Center, Dallas Chapter of United Nations Association of the USA, the office for Maryknoll Mission Education, the Peace Project, Hope for Peace and Justice, and Art for Peace, "creating an amazing synergy . . . for peace and justice in our world" (*DUNA Archives*).

May 12. DUNA Board and Membership, met at the North Texas Food Bank, for program, tour and business meeting, including election of officers to serve through 2010.

Sundiata and Preeti Patel Tellem, with Bill Matthews
and Beth Weems Pirtle, DUNA Leaders 2010

- President Sundiata Xián Tellem, Treasurer Preeti Patel-Tellem with Assistant Ngiyeh Chenyi, Secretary Norma Matthews, VP International Relations Noeli Biggs, VP Education Essay Contest Norma Matthews, Model UN Marilyn King, VP Communication Bill Matthews, Facebook Latha Nehru, Program Committee Shabnam Modgil, Marilyn King, and Linda Evans, YPIC Liaison Latha Nehru, Committee on Refugees Linda Evans,
- At large members Yussuf Kalib, Harbans Lal, Dick Sloos; Advisory Ed Thomas, ex officio Past Presidents Beth Weems Pirtle and Latha Nehru.
- Bill Matthews announced new DUNA and Texas Division office space at Peace House Dallas, in a wing dedicated April 26 at Cathedral of Hope, to accommodate six other, affinity-related agencies.
- Grants were voted to partially subsidize DUNA delegates to the National UNA-USA Conference in June. Beth Weems Pirtle

reported bank balance of $2,726.74, with $1,700.68 in savings account.

- Shabnam Modgil reminded the group of regular "UN Radio" broadcasts, features on FunAsia station 700 AM. Linda Evans announced plans for World Refugee Day on June 20.

June 9. DUNA Board detailed report of May activities from President Tellem included phone calls to members, "hotline" voice mail scheduling for monitors. Treasurer Preeti Patel-Tellem reported research on costs for Voicemail services, bank balance of $2,116.56.

- Communications issues were raised, to improve chapter connections by phone and surface mail. Shabnam has now identified her FunAsia Radio program as the UN news station.
- Efforts to secure a webmaster through Richland College continue; recommendation of fee to Argentine designer $500, plus $7 per hour for maintenance as invoiced.
- Staffing schedule for the UNA office at Peace House Dallas was organized. Other items were discussed without action.

June 20. World Refugee Day, "Return to the Kasbah," a cultural kaleidoscope was held at Lakeridge Village Shopping Center, cosponsored by DUNA with Catholic Charities. Program included crafts from Burma, Kenya, Zimbabwe, the Sudan, Ethiopia, Cameroon and the Middle East, performances by the Burundi Church Choir and a local Bhutanese youth group.

July 21. DUNA Board at Peace House Dallas; present were Sundiata Tellem, Marilyn King, Ed Thomas, Dick Sloos, Bill and Norma Matthews, Harbans Lal, and Shabnam Modgil, with guest Vidya Rajagopalan; quorum declared.

- President's report for July was filed. Treasurer's report filed by Preeti Patel-Tellem showed balance forward $2,775.46. Other officer reports were requested in advance, to be included in agenda. Discussion of PBS film on International Criminal Court and plans for October 24 UN Day were deferred. Centers for

Survival of Torture would still desire to co-sponsor, but has some organizational challenges.

- Beth Weems Pirtle moved that UNA pay $500 towards a table at the Mayors' Dinner of DFW International Community Alliance, undecided. Other items were discussed without action.

September 12–13. UNA-USA Steering Committee Report by Central Regional Representative Bill Matthews on file: Money and reputation issues for National UNA-USA, serious financial crisis; recruitment and funding important; small, systematic steps necessary; increase dues $25 to $30 recommended; appeal to integrate Model UN participants into membership drives while they are informed and enthusiastic; Student Alliance targets all students, urge local promotion; connect chapters to international issues through program presentation of Resolutions from June Conference in manageable formats.

September 15. DUNA Board at Peace House Dallas: President Sundiata Tellem, Preeti Patel-Tellem, Norma Matthews, Bill Matthews, Beth Weems Pirtle, Dick Sloos, Marilyn King, Harbans Lal, Shabnam Modgil, and guest Amitra Lal; quorum declared.

- August minutes not available, request from Peace House Dallas for $50 monthly rent, pay $500, save one month, approved. President's report filed; Treasurer reported balance of $3,002.46. VP Education—Norma Matthews reported 300 cards ordered for Essay Contest to be distributed to schools. VP Model UN—Marilyn King asked for schedules, DUNA will display on request. Membership—Beth will help, Bill maintains the database.
- Refugee Committee—Linda reported greetings from UNHCR, International Rescue Committee Open House September 24, Dallas Area Rescue Forum met September 11.
- Clarified status of several board members during leadership changes.

September 19–21. "Paths to Peace," Celebration of the International Day of Peace, a three-day series on a theme of "We Have a Dream," commemorating Dr. Martin Luther King Jr., with seven partner organizations (see April 26 entry), with the addition of the Progressive

Renewal Leadership Consultants. Events included presentations by Cindy Sheehan, Thom Hartmann, David Swanson, and David Rovics, Jim Burch. The first Peacemakers Inc. Luncheon featured Jean Houston keynote, Regina Montoya emcee, and a "Celebration, Education and Music" program, led by Jim Bunch and Mindy Audlin.

October 15. Peacemakers Inc. Forum with International Rescue Committee, DUNA. Norma Matthews facilitated, with PowerPoint of MDGs, the Millennium Development Goals, with DUNA panelists former United Nations international staff Tatiana Androsov and former foreign service officer to the Middle East Ed Thomas, with a Q&A and reception following.

October 24. United Nations Day, "Human Rights for the Vulnerable: US Protections," heard speaker: Mary Beth Garcia, immigration attorney for JFON (Justice for Our Neighbors), held at FunAsia Restaurant, Richardson. Welcome by President Sundiata Xián Tellem, UNA Essay Contest winners presented by Norma Matthews, and closing by UN Radio host, Shabnam Modgil (*DUNA Archives*).

November 17. DUNA Board at Peace House Dallas: President Sundiata Tellem, Preeti Patel-Tellem, Norma and Bill Matthews, Dick Sloos, Shabnam Modgil, no quorum.

- Discussion of GEMUN attendance at Brookhaven College, radio program about UN. Treasurer reported balance of $2,375.46 includes profit of $382 from UN Day event. Ongoing report of Essay Contest promotion cards and UN reports on FunAsia Radio. Advocacy reported that we will partner with local groups with missions similar to UNA. By consensus, voted $50 to 34 Million Friends program of UN Population Fund.
- Bill Matthews reported about maintaining website at no charge to the chapter.
- By-laws to be reviewed by committee chaired by Bill Matthews, with Sundiata, Dick, Harbans, and Beth Weems Pirtle, to serve for report in January.
- No meeting in December.

December 2009. UNA-USA Chapter and Division Report (filed online March 19, 2010).

- President Latha Nehru, eight Board meetings, reported events and programs in May, August, October.
- No meetings on International Criminal Court, UN Day featured local immigration attorney, MDG presentations at other times during the year, Texas governor declined to appoint UN Day chair.
- Office sharing in Peace House Dallas adds strength through common goals, expanded cooperation, with Dallas Peace Center, Hope 4 Peace and Justice program, Maryknoll Education, Peacemakers Inc., Peace Project.
- UNA-USA Advocacy Agenda highlighted at Board and Chapter meetings and online through website. Addition of local programs for hunger relief, homelessness.
- Strengths: tenacity in spite of adversity, core faithfulness, desire to be involved.
- Weakness: confusion on roles, leadership responsibilities, lack of initiative on duties, information exchanges.
- Successes: UN Day program, Peace House Dallas collaboration, partnerships with common interest groups.
- We had very painful internal leadership struggles, which had to be resolved in early 2010, optimistic for the future.[8]

Section C
Dallas United Nations Association Time Capsules: 2010–2015

2010

January 19. DUNA Board met at Peace House Dallas: President Sundiata Tellem, Preeti Patel-Tellem, Norma Matthews, Bill Matthews, Dick Sloos, Shabnam Modgil, Harbans Lal, Ed Thomas, Yussuf Kalib, quorum declared. Guests: Louise Chandler, Amrit Lal, Amyn Rajan.

---

[8] Notes submitted by Texas Division President Bill Matthews, who served as interim chapter president until March, 2009, continued on board through the following years.

- VP Norma Matthews reported on Essay Contest: 32 essays from Texas were selected, with judges recruited from Houston, Lloyd Jacobson, and Austin, Judy Sadegh; from Dallas, Norma, Bill, and Mary Beth Matthews with Marilyn King. Winners from each region were forwarded to National contest. Noted to NY the apparent difficulty of students who wrote for this year's topic MDG #8.
- Parliament of the World's Religions report by DUNA members who attended world conference in Melbourne, Australia, December 3-9; 5,100 participants, 220 religions, 80 nations, prominent world leaders, compatible with the UN NGO on Spirituality and Interreligious Concerns—Harbans and Amrit Lal, Bill and Norma Matthews, and Tatiana Androsov.
- Noeli Biggs reported that Richland College will host a Landmine Education Presentation on January 25, with Ambassador Bui the Giang, Vietnam, Kurt Chesko VP representing US Department of State, representative from Taiwan and Michael Blood, from Mine Action. She also reported that Dallas Mayor Tom Leppert would recognize the LeCroy Media Center at Richland for Model UN and Going Global with UN videos distributed online during the past four years (*DUNA Archives*).

February 16. DUNA Board met at Peace House Dallas: President Sundiata Tellem, Preeti Patel-Tellem, Yussuf Kalib, Marilyn King, Bill Matthews, Shabnam Modgil, and Dick Sloos; quorum declared.

- Tellem reported month's activities—no significant hotline activity. He and Preeti served in Cathedral of Hope feeding program, attended Peace House Dallas monthly meeting. Treasurer Preeti reported bank balance $2,806.70, change of former bank, now Compass Bank; she negotiated nonprofit status, no service charge.
- Reports from UNA Dallas Radio by Shabnam Radio included interview with Matthews and Beth Weems Pirtle from Dallas City Hall recognition by Mayor for Model UN. Dallas-UNA.org website updated, phone project in process. Several Dallas members will attend Regional UNA in Kansas City, with CCD President Ed Elmendorf speaking (*DUNA Archives*).

March 16. DUNA Board met at Peace House Dallas: President Sundiata Tellem, Norma and Bill Matthews, Shabnam Modgil, Beth Weems Pirtle, and Latha Nehru; no quorum present.

- Tellem reported month's activities—nothing significant on hotline, IRS Tax Form 990N due for nonprofit status, will be filed; he continues helping in CoH feeding program. Treasurer reported balance of $2,836.70, plan to review bank accounts.
- Pirtle reported mailbox contract ends March 31, agreed to use Peace House Dallas address. Also money-saving, telephone hotline will not be renewed, exploring alternatives.
- International Education—VP Biggs applying for Earl Eames Award, for combining radio and videos for UN information, committee to meet. Education VP Matthews reported order for 100 UNA Peace Calendars to use as incentive gifts, cost $70 approved by consensus.
- Refugee Committee, chair Linda Evans, announced special screening of *The Visitor*, a film about homeless immigrants, benefit for UNA partner IRC (International Refugee Committee).
- Report from National UNA on resignation of President Tom Miller, with request for special funding; decided rather to subsidize attendance by DUNA representatives.
- Issues about Peace House Dallas office sharing were raised, with questions of authority for decisions in negotiations with Cathedral of Hope.
- Mr. Tellem sent an e-mail letter notice of their resignations to the DUNA Board Members from him as President and Treasurer Preeti Patel-Tellem, for both of their offices, dated March 18 (*DUNA Archives*).

March 22, 23. DUNA Board was convened by teleconference; with quorum declared by the convener, Texas UNA Division president Bill Matthews. Joining in the call were Linda Evans, Yussuf Kalib, Marilyn King, Norma Matthews, Shabnam Modgil, and Beth Weems Pirtle. Votes by email were recorded from Bill and Norma Matthews, Noeli Biggs, Harbans Lal, and Dick Sloos. Ed Thomas was unavailable.

- The vote was unanimous to accept the resignations of President Sundiata Xián Tellem and Treasurer Preeti Patel-Tellem. A letter of thanks and acceptance of their resignations was sent upon request by former board leader Beth Weems Pirtle.
- Latha Nehru accepted election as president for the remainder of the 2010 term. Beth Pirtle agreed to serve as treasurer. Advocacy meetings will be scheduled on first Tuesdays and Board on fourth Tuesdays each month. Bill Matthews advised that a nominating committee should be named immediately, to prepare for December elections. Next meeting of the Board was set for April 27. Other future plans were discussed, and the teleconference meeting adjourned after 35 minutes (*DUNA Archives*).

April 24. Dallas UNA Chapter Board of Directors, as of March 23, 2010:

- President—Latha Nehru
- President Elect, Advocacy, and Program Chairs—vacant
- VP Education—Norma Matthews
- VP Membership/Communication—Bill Matthews
- Secretary—Norma Matthews
- Treasurer—Beth Weems Pirtle
- VP Resource Development, Parliamentarian—vacant
- Directors at Large
  - Linda Evans—Refugee Committee
  - Marilyn King—Model UN, Program
  - Shabnam Modgil—Program
  - Ngiyeh Chenyi—Student Alliance
  - Harbans Lal—Program
  - Dick Sloos—Communication
  - Edward Thomas—Advocacy
  - Yussuf Kalib—Communication
  - Bill Matthews—Ex officio president Texas Division
  - Beth Weems Pirtle—Ex officio past president
  - Noeli Biggs—Ex officio past president, International Education, Communication

Ex officio members participate fully, by local consensus (*DUNA Archives*).

April 27. DUNA Board met at Peace House Dallas Room 101. President Latha Nehru, Norma Matthews, Bill Matthews, Shabnam Modgil, Beth Weems Pirtle, Yussuf Kalib, Ed Thomas, Dick Sloos, Harbans Lal, Marilyn King, and Linda Evans; quorum declared.

- Minutes for previous two meetings were approved; available for review. Advocacy meetings will be scheduled on first Tuesdays and Board on fourth Tuesdays each month. DPH residents' meeting scheduled April 28, Latha and Bill will attend.
- Request from National CCD for funding was not approved, with an alternate proposal to support DUNA members to attend the June Conference.
- Bill reminded that he had taken five boxes of DUNA Archives to Dallas Public Library in 2004, members urged to preserve additional materials to be added.
- Beth reported that Dallas UNA had two accounts: checking balance $2,866.70 and savings with $1,770.90, recommended merging. Approved, with new signatories to be assigned, adding Latha with Beth. All mail will be directed to Dallas UNA Chapter, Peace House Dallas, 5910 Cedar Springs, Dallas, TX 75235, with mailbox provided near the office.
- Latha will secure a Google Voice Number for the future UNA hotline (*DUNA Archives*).

May 25. DUNA Board by teleconference, President Latha Nehru, Norma and Bill Matthews, Shabnam Modgil, Beth Weems Pirtle, Ed Thomas, Dick Sloos, Marilyn King; quorum declared.

- Nehru reported the National UNA had cancelled the Earl Eames award for this year. UN Secretary General Ban Ki Moon will speak at the June conference of CCD, with several DUNA members planning to attend.
- www.dallas-una.org website renewal due soon, approved.
- New Google Voice phone number for DUNA is (469) 248-7977 (*DUNA Archives*).

June 1. UNA-USA Advocacy monthly teleconference discussion on "Who's Afraid of the Big, Bad Nuke?" consideration of arms proliferation issues, with resources shared from internet, exchange of reactions among about 20 participants (*DUNA Archives*).

June 6–8. Bill and Norma Matthews attended National Conference of CCD and Steering Committee meetings, documents filed with archives, congressional visits to Representative Jeb Hensarling, met legislative assistant Kyle Jackson.

The Honorable Eddie Bernice Johnson, founder of the
World of Women for World Peace conferences

- Also called on Representative Eddie Bernice Johnson from Dallas, presented talking points on American engagement with United Nations. JH had expressed concern for transparency; EBJ expressed very enthusiastic support. About support for CEDAW, JH was cool, EBJ very warm.

Peter Yeo, President of the Better World Campaign and VP for
Public Policy and Advocacy at the United Nations Foundation.

Tuesday was devoted to "Day on the Hill," with contact interviews arranged
for annual advocacy visits by Conference delegates and participants to
individual Congressional Representatives, with talking points provided
from the Better World Campaign of the UNF - United Nations Foundation.
Inspiration and training was conducted by foreign policy experts arranged
by UNF for current US concerns about the United Nations.

UNA-USA officials present 2010 YPIC Award to DUNA's Latha Nehru

- Latha Nehru from DUNA received a 2010 YPIC (Young Professionals Award for service to young adults) presented by UNA-USA officers, including Ed Elmendorf and Alma Morrison (*DUNA Archives*).

June 22. DUNA Board meeting by teleconference. Called to order at 6:00 p.m. by President Latha Nehru, joined by Norma Matthews, Bill Matthews, Shabnam Modgil, Ed Thomas, Dick Sloos, Linda Evans, Yussuf Kalib, and Marilyn King; quorum declared.

- Bill reported a call from New York UNA about UN Day, offering to contact the Texas governor to sign on for the proclamation this year. Agreed, conference call scheduled July 21 about emphasis on MDGs for UN Day.
- Latha, Bill, Norma and Ed Thomas reported on the CCD Conference in Washington, June 6–8. Discussion of United Nations Foundation merger with UNA is in process, which would provide grass roots support for the UNF and allow UNA move forward. UN Secretary General Ban Ki Moon spoke to the Conference with a very warm, challenging, and inspiring talk.

UN Secretary-General Ban Ki Moon

- Latha Nehru received the Global Young Advocate Award for her work with Young Professionals in YPIC, in support of goals of the United Nations Charter.
- Plans to arrange for an intern to work with membership development for DUNA this summer were discussed. Arrangements for October UN Day will begin through Peace House Dallas with Cathedral of Hope. Beth invited the Chapter to their home for Summer Social on July 17.
- Next board meeting set for July 17 by teleconference. Advocacy discussion scheduled for August 3 at Preston Road La Madeleine.

September 9. Dallas UNA By-Laws, Revised edition adopted by DUNA Board. *DUNA Archives*

September 28. DUNA board regular meeting, Conference Room, Peace House Dallas. Present were Bill and Norma Matthews, Ed Thomas, Marilyn King, Beth Weems Pirtle, Shabnam Modgil, and Dick Sloos; Yussuf Kalib was absent. In absence of the president who had taken a job out of town, Texas Division president Bill Matthews convened the meeting; Shabnam moved that he continue until a nominating committee could convene for new officer election, Board agreed by consensus.

Bill presented copies of the agreement requested from each Chapter for the merger of the United Nations Association with the United Nations Foundation; Bill and Shabnam will serve as proxy participants in the October special conference in New York to formalize the new UNA-USA Better World Fund Inc.

Bill presented the revised by-laws for adoption, approved unanimously.

Upon their request, Linda Evans and Ed Thomas will serve as Advisory members of the Board. Beth reported a bank balance of $2,300.00; payments to Beth and Bill for chapter expenses were approved (*DUNA Archives*).

October 14. Notice from UNA-USA announced near-unanimous votes of the delegates to the Special National Convention of CCD, Council of Organizations, National Council and Board of Directors for two proposals:

1. Approval for the agreement between Better World Campaign (United Nations Foundation) and its subsidiary, the "New" UNA-USA, and the dissolution and distribution of assets of the "Old" UNA-USA
2. Approval to reduce the size of the Board of Directors of the "Old" UNA-USA to facilitate the Board's remaining formal work on the organization's dissolution
• Support letters and organizational guidelines were received later by mail to clarify and advance the Alliance between the former groups, which had been thoroughly presented at the May Conference of CCD in Washington, DC. (See June 22 entry.)

October 24. UN Day 2010 held a modest dinner in the Conference Room of Cathedral of Hope, where DUNA was officing in Peace House Dallas shared space.

DUNA Board member worked as a UN staff member for several years

- Tatiana Androsov was featured, reporting on her extensive work with the United Nations as a language interpreter and field worker in several locations. See a more complete report of her thoughtful history in chapter 8.

A "potluck dinner" was enjoyed by about 45 persons, with updates on United Nations Foundation priorities, including the Millennium Development Goals progress, NBN mosquito eradication campaign,

November 11. The World Affairs Council presented a well-attended program with Gillian Sorensen of the United Nations Foundation at 6:00 p.m. at the Rosewood Crescent Hotel (*Dallas Morning News* Community Calendar).

December 7. "What's Right about Human Rights!" a diverse local panel spoke to the priorities of food, shelter, and legal residence, in observance of UN Human Rights Day at the inauguration of the Interfaith Peace Chapel at the Cathedral of Hope (*DUNA Archives*).

2011

January 25. DUNA Board and Membership convened by Texas Division president Bill Matthews in a classroom of the Peace House Dallas, Cathedral of Hope. Norma Matthews was appointed interim Secretary. Fourteen persons attended.

Chapter reorganization was the stated purpose, as Bill recounted recent chapter history and the Texas Division status. Shabnam Modgil reported about "UN Radio," which she voluntarily carries on the FunAsia radio stations. Copies of the revised by-laws were available.

David and Nelda Reid served as Co-presidents of the DUNA Board, 2011-2012

The slate of new officers nominated were as follows:

- David and Nelda Reid—Co-presidents
- Shabnam Modgil and Marilyn King—Vice presidents for Program
- Beth Weems Pirtle—Treasurer
- Nelda Reid—Secretary
- Bill Matthews—Membership (Google Group administrator)
- Bill Kelly (to be confirmed)

Others volunteering to help were Noeli Biggs, Harbans Lal, and Dick Sloos.

Also attending: Jo Hoge, Barbara Gibson (Granbury), Patty Jantho, Madan Goyal, Riley Simmons, and Henny Hughes (*DUNA Archives*).

Norma and Bill Matthews at the UN in New York

February 11. DUNA was represented in New York at the 2011 Mid-Atlantic Regional Conference and UNA-USA Members Day at the UN by Norma Matthews and Bill Matthews, South Central Region Representative to the UNA-USA Council on Chapters and Divisions, who attended Steering Committee meetings later in the week-end.

- A wide range of speakers reported on leading issues for the United Nations, including topics on Upheaval in the Arab World, Energy and Climate Change, New Dimensions in Health, Gender, and Development, and Careers in International Affairs.
- The keynote speaker for the afternoon was Cheick Sidi Diarra, Under-Secretary General, Special Adviser on Africa and High Representative for the Least Developed Countries and Small Island Developing States.
- A panel on Africa's transformation in the 21st Century: "Capturing its Economic Dynamism, and another on Afghanistan, Is a Negotiated Settlement Possible?" completed the afternoon schedule.

February 22. DUNA Board, convened by Copresident David Reid; attending were Nelda Reid, Bill and Norma Matthews, Bill Kelly, Patty Jantho, and guests Yoana Ghimbasan and Deborah Mose.

Bill gave treasurer's report in Beth's absence: bank balance savings $1,830.39, checking apx. $2,000.00; request for Norma Matthews' attendance at national UNA-USA Conference part of expense $300 approved.

Nelda reported on Advocacy calls from national regarding priorities to meet with Congressional representatives to favor continuation of UN funding. Bill reported from national CCD Steering Committee meetings, realignment of regions with Texas in the "new" South Central. Yoana suggested that we partner with affinity agencies, which Council Of Organizations support.

Discussions included upcoming UN Day and need for membership promotion (*DUNA Archives*).

March 3. Bill Matthews' report on bank account arrangement for DUNA and Texas Division. To avoid bank charges for low balances, the two accounts were blended, with resulting balance of $4,571.12. Identified as Texas Division, $828.58; DUNA, $3,742.53. Future credits and debits are to be tracked accordingly.

June. Report by Norma Matthews to the newsletter of Delta Kappa Gamma, Eta Zeta Chapter, Dallas, NGO partner in UNDPI, about UNA-USA CCD Conference, June 12–14 (*DUNA Archives*).

September 27. DUNA Board at the Matthews' home, attending: David and Nelda Reid, Bill and Norma Matthews, Shabnam Modgil, Linda Evans, Patty Jantho, and Harbans Lal.

Treasurer's report bank balance: $3,933.14.

Program reports on August 28–September 3: hosted Nothing But Nets tour

- September 9, *Fragile State* film night at Fretz Library, display at SMU Human Rights Fair, September 21, hosted a table at Peacemakers Inc. luncheon for International Women's Day. Plans for future events were discussed.
- Inquiry about DUNA display at WorldFest in Arlington, October 22–23, volunteers to staff, include Nothing But Nets emphasis (*DUNA Archives*).

October 24. 2011 United Nations Day in Dallas, "Nothing But Nets" partnered with Peacemakers Inc., Interfaith Council of Thanks-Giving Square, the FunAsia Restaurant, and the Cameroonian Association of North Texas.

- More than 65 persons heard from local Cameroonian residents about the personal and family impact of malaria infection in a country that has suffered a 300% increase of incidence in the past 5 years. The United Nations Foundation set goals to deliver 225,000 "mednets" to kill mosquitoes and protect children and families in the West African nation at the cost of only $10 each. Several significant individual and group contributions moved us towards that goal to "Send a Net, Save a Child." The Ex-Saker Student's Association, alumni from their school in Cameroon, contributed $1,000 for NBN (*DUNA Archives*).

Shelly Lambé and wife with Matthews and Pirtles

November 11. The World Affairs Council presented a well-attended program with Gillian Sorensen of the United Nations Foundation at 6 p.m. at the Rosewood Crescent Hotel (*Dallas Morning News* Community Calendar).

December 10. DUNA Human Rights Day dinner heard Ms. Susan Armoni of Pax United National Mediation Center on the topic of bullying in schools, at La Madeleine Restaurant, Addison.

December 11. Financial report on file recorded beginning balance: $1,842.51; with December 15 closing balance: $7,183.14 (*DUNA Archives*).

2012

January 26. DUNA Board at Peace House Dallas, Copresident Nelda Reid, with Linda Evans, Patty Jantho, Harbans Lal, Norma and Bill Matthews, David Reid, Beth Weems Pirtle; absent Bill Kelly, Marilyn King, and Shabnam Modgil; Guests Philip Haigh and Tammie Smith-Long.

- Reports on recent events, plus nomination for South Central Regional Representatives—Bill Matthews and Philip Haigh (declared ineligible, one year membership required). Latha Nehru was nominated by YPIC representatives.
- Plans for March 8 with Senator Timothy Wirth, International Visitors guests, sponsorships, other arrangements.
- Discussed proposed $100/month fee for Internet and phone service at Cathedral of Hope office, to be further explored.
- Discussion of improved social media and website presence for DUNA (*DUNA Archives*).

2012 DUNA Board at International Women's Day

March 8. The Dallas Chapter of the United Nations Association and Peacemakers Inc. held a luncheon to honor International Women's Day at the Tower Club, Dallas, with 110 present.

- The International Visitor Leadership Program of the US Department of State brought women leaders from 18 countries. Visitors came from Botswana, Iraq, Latvia, Macedonia, Malawi, Malaysia, Nigeria, Pakistan, Philippines, Slovak Republic, Sri Lanka, St. Kitts and Nevis, Thailand, Turkey, and Vietnam.

Norma Matthews and Carol Donovan award "Peace Patron" to UNF CEO Timothy E. Wirth

- Speakers included Sen. Timothy Wirth, CEO of the United Nations Foundation, and Patrick M. Madden, executive director of UNA-USA. Peacemakers Inc. presented Wirth with a "Peace Patron" Award.

Shabnam receives International Woman Award from CEO
Patrick Madden UNA-USA, and Nelda Reid, DUNA

- The Award of International Woman of the Day was presented to Shabnam Modgil of DUNA by President Nelda R. Reid.
- Other cosponsors were Thanks-Giving Foundation, Embrey Human Rights program at SMU, DFW International Community Alliance, and UNA-USA Oklahoma City Chapter.
- Among other leaders were Bill Matthews, Peter Stewart, Timothy Wirth, Michael Ngiyeh, Chandler Roosevelt Lindsley, Patrick Madden, and Tatiana Androsov (*Dallas Morning News* Community Calendar, *DUNA Archives*).

DUNA Leaders with International Women's Day guests, March 8, 2012.

March 29. DUNA Board met at Peace House Dallas. President David Reid, with Nelda Reid, Norma and Bill Matthews, Beth Weems Pirtle, Linda Evans, Patty Jantho, Harbans Lal, Bill Kelly, Marilyn King, Shabnam Modgil, and Tammie Smith-Long.

- Treasurer's Report: BBVA Bank balance, $6,913.14; contribution check to NBN outstanding, $1,500.00 (included Cameroonian Ex-Saker contribution from UN Day), inquiry sent.
- Norma Matthews reported on the International Women's Day luncheon, which netted apx. $1,500.00 profit.
- Program plans include a film night April 7 for *The Girl in the Cafe* at the Fretz Library (*DUNA Archives*).

May 23. DUNA members attended and supported the *Women, Leadership, and Human Rights!* event at SMU, featuring 2011 Nobel Peace Prize Laureate Leymah Gbowee from Liberia. The community event was partnered at SMU by the Embrey Human Rights Program and the World Affairs Council of Dallas/Fort Worth, and sponsored by the Embrey Family Foundation, Donna Wilhelm, Trea Yip, and the Boone Family Foundation, with KERA, in cooperation with The Alliance for Human Dignity, TEDxSMU, and Empower African Children (*DUNA Archives*).

May 26. DUNA display and contact booth at DFW International World Festival, Dallas Arts District, staffed by Bill Matthews, Patty Jantho, Zia Shamsy, Linda Evans, Tatiana Androsov, and Nelda Reid. They signed up 73 interested persons during an eight hour presence (*DUNA Archives*).

June 1. Report on membership calls by Past President Dick Sloos, ten calls with follow-up recommendations (*DUNA Archives*).

June 10–12. Report by Norma Matthews on 2012 Annual Meeting of UNA-USA in Washington, DC. She attended, along with South Central Representatives Bill Matthews and Latha Nehru. Workshops were offered on Media Training, Membership Development, Model UN, Reproductive Health and Family Planning in the Global Arena, Human Rights, Peace and Security, Energy and Climate, and the latest campaign for immunization, called Shot@Life.

- Anti-polio campaigns have brought about 99% decrease, Measles has been reduced by 74%. The African proverb was cited: "If you want to go fast, go alone. If you want to go far, go with someone." UN Foundation is going with International Lions Club, Rotary Club, WHO, UNICEF, and others, to go far (*DUNA Archives*).

June 23. DUNA "Potluck" Social at home of Rod and Beth Weems Pirtle, 17 present included the Pirtles, Zia Shamsy, Linda Evans, Trudi and Joe Green-Bishop, Karen Giles, Philip Haigh, Yvonne Glass, Bill and Norma Matthews, Peggy and Alberto Bolzan and three daughters. Informal conversation about UN, UNA and related issues.

October 22. Mr. Peter Stewart, founder of Thanks-Giving Foundation of Dallas was awarded the first "Spirit of the United Nations" Award for Youth Outreach, by the NGO Committee on Spirituality, Values and Global Concerns in New York at the Church Center of the United Nations. Tatiana Androsov and Rev. Bill Matthews represented DUNA at the event (*DUNA Archives*).

Mr. Bill Bernstein, Mosaic Family Services, Dallas

October 20. The Dallas Chapter of the United Nations Association presented a UN Day dinner, reception and program from 6 to 9 p.m., with keynote speaker: Mr. Bill Bernstein, Deputy Director of Mosaic Family Services, on "Combating Human Trafficking: Global Problem: Local Solution," at FunAsia Restaurant, Richardson. dallas-una.org (*Dallas Morning News* Community Calendar, *DUNA Archives*).

October 23. The UN National Committee for UN Women launched its Dallas chapter at a luncheon at the Park City Club, 5956 Sherry Lane. The speaker was Teresa Fronsini of CBS-TV affiliate Channel 11, unwomen-usnc.org (*Dallas Morning News* Community Calendar).

President Norma Matthews welcomes Peacemakers, Inc. guests

December 12. Peacemakers Inc., frequent DUNA advocacy partner, at Christmas reception hosted by Carol Donovan, DUNA member and Peacemakers CEO.

2013

January 25. DUNA Board met at David and Nelda Reid's home, called to order by Nelda Reid. Present were David and Nelda, Bill and Norma Matthews, Beth Weems Pirtle, and Patty Jantho. Excused were Latha Nehru, Harbans Lal, Linda Evans, Marilyn King, and Shabnam Modgil, quorum not established.

- Treasurer's report: bank balance $7,671.87, approved.
- List of members presented for directors.
- Other reports: success of UN Day Dinner, with thanks to Patty Jantho, Marilyn King, and Shabnam at FunAsia for hosting. The December 2012 Human Rights Day was cancelled due to schedule conflict with SMU. Future program plans were discussed.

- International Women's Day partner with Peacemakers Inc. on March 8 was approved.
- Approved $400 toward expenses for Norma to attend February UN Members Day in NYC.
- Advocacy leader updates will be forwarded to all DUNA Board members for their action (*DUNA Archives*).

January 26. The Rotary District Peace Symposium included a presentation by UNA Texas Division president Bill Matthews, who spoke on "Peace Beyond Conflict: Freedom in Spirit," citing common roots for peace in the Declaration of Independence, the US Constitution, and the Bill of Rights, with reference to Martin Luther King Jr.'s writing, "The promise of democracy. . . a creative psalm of brotherhood" (*DUNA Archives*).

February 4. UNA Members Day, New York, keynote address by the Honorable Jan Eliasson from Norway, deputy secretary general of United Nations. Key issues: clean water and sanitation, violence against women, collective responsibility of nations to promote the principles of the UN.

- Other emphases: Patrick Madden, UNA-USA ED, on environmental policy and climate change; Kathy Calvin, president and CEO of UN Foundation, on continuing support for United Nations. Women and Girls issues are focused through UNWomen, Executive Director Michelle Bachelet, Chile (former president, reelected December 2013).
- Attended by Bill and Norma Matthews from DUNA (*DUNA Archives*).

February 16. DUNA Board met at home of Bill and Norma Matthews, called to order by Bill Matthews.

- Nomination of new officers for election at a general meeting, March 21, with explanation of previous nominations, confirmation to be at general meeting.
- Nominations for 2013–14 Board of Directors:
  - President—Norma Matthews
  - Secretary—Barbara Hood Roemer
  - Treasurer—David Reid

- Program chairs—Patty Jantho, Beth Weems Pirtle
- Education chairs—Trudi and Joe Green Bishop, with Linda Evans
- Resource Development chair—Anya Cooper, Jamal Gharbieh
- Communication/Membership chairs—Shabnam Modgil, Nelda Reid
- Parliamentarian—Anya Cooper
- Young Professionals—Dakota McCarty, Shay Gedam
- Council of Organizations—Tatiana Androsov, Nelda Reid, Almas Muscatwalla
- Refugee Coordinator—Linda Evans
- Directors at Large—Harbans Lal, Dick Sloos (past president 1964)
- Ex officio South Central Region representatives—Bill Matthews, Latha Nehru
- Plans announced for International Women's Day, March 8, at Thanksgiving Tower Club, with Peacemakers Inc. Tickets for a UNA table were bought by Norma Matthews, so members may reimburse her for $60 each (*DUNA Archives*).

March 21. DUNA Open Annual General Meeting, at FunAsia Restaurant, Bill Matthews, South Central Representative to CCR, presided.

- Confirmation of nominations (listed above in January meeting)
- Dallas Chapter Reports: minutes by Barbara Hood Roemer; treasurer's report by Norma Matthews; overview of past two years by copresidents Nelda and David Reid; advocacy report by a call-in by La Barron Boudreaux; program by Patty Jantho and Beth Weems Pirtle; education by Trudi, Joe Green-Bishop, and Linda Evans; membership and communication by Nelda Reid and Shabnam Modgil; parliamentarian, by-laws review, and resource development by Anya Cooper; Young Professionals unable to attend; Council of Organizations by Tatiana Androsov, Almas Muscatwalla, and Nelda Reid.
- Treasurer's Report—July 26, 2012, beginning balance $6,638.02; April 1, 2013, ending balance $7,194.78.

- Motion passed to represent DUNA at the Dallas International Festival, May 25, with display staffed by volunteers $150 fee, with $50 allowance for materials and supplies.
- Motion passed to provide up to four partial expense subsidies up to $400 each, for delegate/participants to the UNA-USA National Conference, June 1–3, in Washington, DC, reimbursement subject to vouchered costs for travel and accommodations (*DUNA Archives*).

Ms. Gillian Sorensen in 2010, valued Advocate for the
United Nations Foundation, spoke for DUNA and the Dallas
community at one of her several appearances over the years

March 26. Gillian Sorensen, Senior Advisor to the United Nations Foundation, spoke at SMU McCord Auditorium, co-sponsored by the Tower Center, Embrey Human Rights Program, Hunt Institute, with a table display by DUNA, staffed by President Norma Matthews, CCR South Central Region Representative Bill Matthews, and other DUNA members. *DUNA Archives*

April. With completion of 2-year terms as South Central Regional Representatives to the UNA-USA Steering Committee of CCR, nominations to replace Latha Nehru and Bill Matthews included Nelda

Reid from DUNA. She was elected by national voting, along with Teta Banks from Houston UNA for the 2014-16 term. *DUNA Archives*

April 25. DUNA Program and Board Meeting

- Shabnam Modgil introduced speaker Dr. Mona Kazim Shah, Producer/Host of program "Politics Today" on FunAsia (UN) Radio station, for "Terrorism and Its Effect on Pakistan."
- President Norma Matthews called the Board to order.
- Treasurer David Reid reported items approved for supplies and program expenses, including the Ronny Edry event and DFW International Festival.
- Elected members to attend national UNA-USA Conference in Washington, D.C. in June: Bill Matthews and Latha Nehru go as South Central Regional Representatives, Norma Matthews and Almas Muscatwalla elected delegates, Shabnam will represent YPIC, Jamal Gharbieh also wishes to attend. Tatiana Androsov will report on June meeting of Sports for Peace and Development in NYC.
- Other reports on partnership in 29 Pieces: Dallas Love Project, Anya Cooper on by-laws and UN Women (Barbara Hood Roemer, secretary, *DUNA Archives*).

May 2. DUNA presented a "Happy Hour" with Mr. Ronny Edry, peace activist from Tel Aviv, graphic artist who initiated a "We Love You" campaign to show mutual respect of the people of Israel for the people of Iran, to promote peace and understanding through social media and other efforts. About 30 people attended at Northaven United Methodist Church. *DUNA Archives*

May 4. DUNA helped sponsor the annual "A World of Women for World Peace" seminar organized by Congresswoman Eddie Bernice Johnson at McCord Auditorium, SMU, which also featured Mr. Ronny Edry (*DUNA Archives*).

DUNA Display at 2013 Fiesta Latinoamericana

May 25. DFW International Festival in Dallas Arts District, 10:00 a.m. to 7:00 p.m. DUNA sponsored a display booth in the Unity Garden. Over 20,000 guests visited extensive exhibits and took part in Children's Discovery, Get-Up-And Go games, Global Dance and Music stages, and Parade of Nations, led by the UN flag. Anne Marie Weiss Armush, CEO and President of DFW International Community Alliance, was organizer and coordinator of the annual event (*DUNA Archives*).

June 22. DUNA met at the home of Beth Weems and Rodney Pirtle for "annual" swim and potluck social, with nine members and two guests present. President Norma Matthews called the Board meeting to order at 8:10 p.m.

Dr. Mona Kazim Shah represents Pakistan views

- Norma and Bill Matthews and Mona Kazim Shah reported on the Annual Meeting of UNA-USA in Washington, D.C., June 1-4.
- Nelda Reid gave the treasurer's report in David Reid's absence, ending balance of $6,429.78.
- Norma reported the Dallas Love Project plans to train young artists for exhibitions from September 21 World Peace Day to November 22, in observance of the 50th Anniversary of the JFK Assassination. Tatiana Androsov moved, Harbans Lal seconded and it was voted to contribute $200, with check to go to Karen Blessen. James Duran offered to help coordinate for DUNA.
- Bill explained membership advantages of UNA-USA, stressing the importance of advocacy with Congressional representatives when they are in home offices, particularly to urge continued funding of the United Nations, and follow-up on the MDGs (Millennium Development Goals). Additional resources are UN Wire free service, United Nations Foundation emphasis on social media, and Tatiana gave the link for live streaming of the UN Webcast
- Norma announced the Girl Up campaign, with "Girl Rising" movie scheduled for showing at the Angelika Theater on July 25, with a commitment of $300 fund-raising.

- A new member, FaBrice Kabona, has had personal experience with UNHCR, with his family benefiting as refugees from the Republic of Congo. Marzuq Jaami recommended him to Shabnam Modgil, for radio interview on her "UN Radio" broadcast on FunAsia Radio. He also recommended KHVN for broadcast interview.
- Announcements included re-dedication of the Rockwell "Golden Rule" mosaic for February 4, 2014, at UN Headquarters in NYC, and a potluck for World Refugee Day on June 29 at Northway Christian Church (*DUNA Archives*).

June 30. DUNA contributed $200 as a seed grant partner in the Dallas LOVE Project, sponsored by the non-profit 29 Pieces organization. The MasterPEACE Young Artists Making A Kinder World program recruited 30 artists who worked with over 4,500 children in 16 schools, to exhibit 20,000 posters over the Dallas area in recognition of 50th Anniversary of JFK Assassination (*DUNA Archives*).

July 25. DUNA Board at FunAsia, Richardson.

- Present: Norma Matthews, presiding, Marzuq Jaami, Beth Weems Pirtle, Ed Thomas, Dakota McCarty, Tatiana Androsov, Shabnam Modgil, Almas Muscatwalla, Anya Cooper, Patty Jantho, Mona Kazim Shah, Linda Evans, Bill Matthews. Guests: Sonia Shukla, Madan Goyal, Joseph Glogowski, James Duran, Debra Shrader, Mary Beth Matthews.
- Proposed DUNA booth displays at DFW International Festival in Centennial Building at Fair Park on November 10, $100 fee, and Women's Equality Day at Dallas City Hall on August 21, $75 fee, both approved.
- Reports: Mona attended Mandela Day, July 18 at Fair Park, also the Washington UNA-USA Conference with Norma as delegates. Mona described her impressions, contacts, and her learning curve. Advocacy report from Bill, speaker at UN Foundation Dinner November 6, Steering Committee, importance of ongoing funding for UN, UN Women, advise visits to district offices during Congressional recess, Beth suggests planned schedule.
- Anya reported on marketing for "Girl Rising" campaign—150 tickets sold so far, she named organizations contacted: Dallas

International Girls Cup, Girls Rock Dallas, Foundation for the Education of Young Women, Girls Incorporated, Girls on Run at DFW, Boys and Girls Club Dallas, Peace Corps, Association of Former Peace Corps Volunteers, and UN Women.
- Plans announced for UN Day program, October 24 (details and results below).
- Invitation from Cameroonian Association for their Moghamo Project for July 26, Bill will speak for UNA (*DUNA Archives*).

August 1. Organized and presented a pubic showing of the documentary film, "Girl Rising" at the Angelika Film Center, for the campaign to "Educate Girls, Change the World." Using the public Eventbrite social media platform, 226 tickets were sold, to benefit the Gathr.us campaign, endorsed by UNA-USA (*DUNA Archives*).

August 3. Women's Equality Day at Dallas City Hall: DUNA contributed a sponsor donation of $100 to the Women's Interest Network organizers, about 12 DUNA members attended (*DUNA Archives*).

September 12. Letter to *DMN* Editor by DUNA member Bill Matthews, published to support UNA-USA advocacy for "compassionate conversation" by UN peacekeepers in pursuing peaceful solutions in the Syria conflict (*DUNA Archives*).

September 26. DUNA Program and Board Meeting

- Refugee Services of Texas, Inc., presented the program by Vice-President J. D. Newsom, with details of their policies, offerings, and profile of services, honorarium of $100 was given for speaking at the DUNA membership meeting.
- Connie Rensink reported on CTAUN, plans for Dallas Conference at SMU November 2., with emphases on UN Developments and planning post MDG development goals.
- Bill reported on Advocacy and the Syria crisis, estimates of four to five million displaced internal and external refugees. *DUNA Archives*

- Shot@Life world-wide immunization for children campaign by UN Foundation linked with Walgreens for flu shots, matched with donations of polio or other shots through UNICEF.
- Linda Evans sent an updated Volunteer Guide to Refugee Service Agencies in DFW.
- Next Board meeting November 21 (*DUNA Archives*).

October 3. Bill and Norma Matthews gave a UNA-USA presentation and seminar to the Staff Retreat for the Refugee Services of Texas organization, meeting at Clark Gardens, Weatherford, Texas (*DUNA Archives*).

October 2013. Mr. Edward Thomas, founder and past president of the Institute of Medieval and Post-Medieval Studies and a valued member and advocacy VP of DUNA, was honored with a parting tribute by the Institute in their monthly newsletter (*DUNA Archives*).

Mr. Bill Holston, ED of Human Rights Initiative

October 24. DUNA United Nations Day dinner at the FunAsia Restaurant, speaker: Mr. William (Bill) O. Holston, Jr., Executive Director of the Human Rights Initiative, "Shelter from the Storm: Immigrant Stories of Survival from Violence and Abuse," introduced by President Norma Matthews.

DUNA Readers Theater 60th Anniversary

- After the Proclamation by Beth Weems Pirtle, a readers theater drama "The Early Years," written by Patty Jantho on this 60th Anniversary of the Dallas Chapter founding in 1953. She, Anya Cooper, and Beth were the readers.
- The "Spirit of the UN" was awarded to Mr. Edward Thomas, former foreign officer in the Middle East and valued member of DUNA.
- Closing remarks were given by Bill Matthews, South Central Representative to the UNA-USA Council on Chapters and Regions.

Mrs. Chandler Roosevelt Lindsley and Vivian
Castleberry greeted by DUNA, UN Day 2014

- Attended by Mrs. Chandler Roosevelt Lindsley, granddaughter of Eleanor Roosevelt, and her daughter Ruth, who contributed ten "quotable" books from Eleanor and Franklin, for free future distribution as door prizes. "One's philosophy is not best expressed in words; it is expressed in the choices one makes . . . in the long run every single one of us must be responsible for himself and for his actions" (ER).
- Payment to FunAsia for dinners verified 70 guests at $25 per plate (*DUNA Archives*).

October 28. Norma and Bill Matthews gave a "United Nations 101" program on the MDG "Promote Gender Equality and Empower Women," in a PowerPoint show, "Girl Power." This was preceded with a history quiz "What's Your UN IQ," mailed to the membership of the local teachers' society, the Eta Zeta Chapter of The Delta Kappa Gamma International, and a brief history of the United Nations, in connection with their emphasis on Global Awareness (*DUNA Archives*).

DUNA advocacy display at SMU, president Norma Matthews

November 2. The first CTAUN Conference in Dallas was held at SMU on "Global Partnerships: Where do You Fit?" The Committee on Teaching about the UN cohosted by DUNA. Topics included Engaging Young Adults Here and Now, Connecting Your Classroom to the World through Social Networks, Finding Global Education Resources, Discovering World Travel Opportunities, and Understanding Sustainability from Vision to Action (*DUNA Archives*).

November 21. DUNA Board at FunAsia Restaurant (from Agenda, no minutes filed)

- Treasurer's Report: beginning balance $5,548.53; ending balance $7,371.68, with details from UN Day Banquet indicated net of $831, other transactions detailed.
- UNA Consultation on post-2015 Global Goals to be in Austin, Texas, December 4, at the Charles Johnson House. Three plan to attend.
- Nominating committee for vacancies on the Board and South Central Region: Chair Nelda Reid, Beth Weems Pirtle, Shabnam Modgil, Norma Matthews, retiring Regional Representatives, ex officio: Latha Nehru and Bill Matthews.
- Reports from successful Dallas Love Project, UN Day Program, other recent events (*DUNA Archives*).

December 5. Dallas Peace Center 27th Peacemaker Awards Dinner, cosponsored by Dallas United Nations Association, with other community partners; honored Awardees were Media Peacemaker Dianne Solis, Lifetime Achievement to Eva McMillan. Organization: Dallas Residents at Risk, headed by Dr. José Angel Gutiérrez, and Peacemaker of the Year Leslie Harris (*DUNA Archives*).

2014

GirlUp visit by American teens to Uganda

January 23. DUNA Board at FunAsia Restaurant, Norma Matthews presiding; present: Patti Jantho, Bill Matthews, Anya Cooper, Tatiana Androsov, Barbara Hood, Shabnam Modgil, Emily White, Sarosha and Raz Hansraj, M'Banna, Marzuq Jaami, Nuriddin Mustafaa, Mannem Sohhmoath, Soham Reedy, Dana and Brian Lankford, Margie Garcia, Andrew Tran, and Lola Awobokokum.

- Norma Matthews introduced a brief program: Girl Up Clubs in Richardson and Townview Magnet DISD—Emily White and Sarosha Hansraj spoke on their experiences, urged us to donate, spread the word, and advocate for girls.
- Advocacy report by Bill and Norma from teleconference of advocacy leads from other chapters and national staff.

Michelle Obama, 2015 GirlUp Hero for Passion

- The treasurer was absent, so no report, but a notation of Bill Kelly check received to fund a new banner. Board approval by email vote for $300 expense reimbursement for six members to attend UN Members' Day in NYC in February; and a specific grant approved for Rachel Sherman, new member and Americorps volunteer, based on her expense receipts to be submitted.
- Guest Marjorie Garcia requested self-nomination to the Board, referred to Nominating Committee (respectfully declined by NC).
- Observance of International Women's Day referred to Program Committee, with motion to invite Teta Banks from Houston

Chapter, with expenses and honorarium to be reimbursed, amended to refer and approved.

- Tatiana Androsov reported that the Rockwell Golden Rule mosaic "Do Unto Others" would be rededicated on February 4 at the United Nations Headquarters Building in NYC, members encouraged to attend if possible.
- President Elect position to be filled; Trudi Green-Bishop resigned from Board; Rachel Sherman will join the Board as Advocacy Chair; Board endorsed Nelda Reid's candidacy as South Central Representative to the CCR Steering Committee (*DUNA Archives*).

Rededication of the Rockwell "Golden Rule Mosaic" at
the United Nations Headquarters, New York City

February 4. DUNA cosponsored and several members attended to participate in the Rededication Ceremony of the Norman Rockwell "Golden Rule Mosaic: Do Unto Others," in the renovated United Nations Headquarters Building in New York City.

- The replica of the Dallas original mosaic of Rockwell's painting had been initiated and contributed in 1985 by the local World Center for Thanksgiving of the Thanks-Giving Foundation (TGF), through required, appropriate state and national channels, and then presented to the UN by the United States Mission to the United Nations.

- Dallas attendees included Interfaith Council of Thanks-Giving Square members, Beth Huddleston, City of Dallas representative, Nancy Marcus, emcee, Peter Stewart, Christopher Haley, UD graduate student, unidentified friends, Phillip Kingston, Dallas City Council member, Tricia Harris, John Whitehead, UNF Board member, Almas Muscatwalla, Chris Slaughter, CEO and President of Thanks-Giving Foundation, another friend, Rosie Stromberg, Marzuq Jaami, Sybil and Lyle Novinski, Bill and Norma Matthews, Suleiman Hemani, Interfaith Council of TGF, and Tatiana Androsov.

1997 Landmine Awareness Day, DUNA at Highland Park UMC, with Philip Winslow, Sandrine Tesner, Merrily Smith, Mary Wareham, Jerry White (landmine survivor), Rita Calvert, Beth Weems Pirtle, and Bob Dennis

- The very moving keynote speech was given by UN Deputy Secretary General Jan Eliasson from Sweden. "It reflects humanity—the wondrous mix of nationalities, creeds and colours," Mr. Eliasson said. "But it also reflects the very essence of our mission as set out in our Charter," he added. "At its core, the work is about narrowing the gap between the world as it is and the world as we want it to be," he said.

February 27. DUNA Board at FunAsia Restaurant, Norma Matthews presiding, present: Anya Cooper, Beth Weems Pirtle, Tatiana Androsov, David and Nelda Reid, Barbara Hood, Shabnam Modgil, Zia Shamsy, Marzuq Jaami, Nuriddin Mustafaa, Dana and Bryan Lankford, Margie Garcia, Jamal Gharbieh, and Bill Foster.

- Minutes, President's report on UN Members' Day in New York.
- Treasurer moved the budget for Women's Day—$531.65, approved. Bank balance: $5,750.18.
- Reports on Advocacy, program plans for International Women's Day, declined Margie Garcia for Board, recommended reconsideration next year. Tatiana reported on the February 4 rededication of the "Do Unto Others" mosaic at UN Headquarters (*DUNA Archives*).

March 1. International Women's Day, DUNA partnered with Words of Women international essay contest at the Bath House Cultural Center. Norma Matthews and Beth Pirtle staffed a resource table for UNA-USA with membership materials, UNF campaign promotions, and Girl Up banner. Representatives from about 30 affinity groups took part (*DUNA Archives*).

March 3. IRS verification of Dallas UNA-USA Chapter tax exemption status under the Better World Fund (BWF) Central Group EIN (*DUNA Archives*).

Linda Abrahamson Evans, Norma Matthews, and Tatiana Androsov represent DUNA at a 2012 SMU Women's Event.

March 5. DUNA provided a resource table of UNA-USA materials at the SMU 49th Annual Women's Symposium, staffed by Norma Matthews and Tatiana Androsov. About 300 people attended, the theme was "Women are Superheroes," with many students and young professionals attending (*DUNA Archives*).

The Hon. Teta V. Banks

March 7. Bill Matthews of the UNA-USA CCR Steering Committee arranged for the Honorable Teta V. Banks, President of the Houston Chapter, to speak at the Rotary Club of Park Cities for observance of International Women's Day, well received by the 150 members, with eleven DUNA members, some as members, others as guests.

- DUNA held an open Happy Hour with Teta Banks in the afternoon at the La Calle Doce Restaurant, with ample opportunity for personal sharing among members and guests (*DUNA Archives*).

Teta Banks at 2014 DUNA Reception, with Anya Cooper,
Nelda Reid, Norma and Bill Matthews, Tatiana Androsov

March 27. DUNA Board met at FunAsia Restaurant, President Norma Matthews called to order.

- Program: "Getting to Know our Board Members," David Reid and Anya Cooper.
- Expenses for International Women's Day: $531.66, Bath House IWD: $20, bank balance: $5,459.63.
- Membership report on board absences—two members removed, one desired continuation.
- Advocacy reported national teleconferences, Bill and Norma Matthews "online."
- Invitation to cosponsor with Pax Christi and Hope 4 Peace & Justice the "Campaign Nonviolence and the Nonviolent Life," speaker John Dear on May 17, no financial commitment—approved.
- President reported on International Women's Day events.
- Linda Evans filed a report on Refugee volunteer guide update, events at Center for Survivors of Torture, International Rescue Committee, and World Refugee Day plans in June.
- New project joint sponsorship of Dallas International Girls Cup Soccer tournament, benefit to Nothing But Nets and Girl Up, Anya Cooper coordinator, approved (*DUNA Archives*).

DUNA "Nothing But Nets" Display at 2014
International Girls' Soccer Tournament

April 19. "Nothing But Nets" Display for mosquito eradication was mounted by a DUNA team at the International Girls' Soccer Tournament, with many positive contacts by patrons. Norma and Bill Matthews, Patti Jantho, Michael Webster, Anya Cooper, and Beth Weems Pirtle staffed the display tent.

June 8–10. National Conference of CCR, UNA-USA, Washington, DC.

- Twelve DUNA members attended: Norma and Bill Matthews, Nelda and David Reid, Rachel Sherman, Tasriqui Islam, Madan Goyal, Zia Shamsy, Tatiana Androsov, Mona Kazim Shah, Connie and Steve Rensink.

DUNA delegation to 2014 UNA-USA Leadership Summit

- DUNA received an award from NBN, the Nothing But Nets campaign for malaria mosquito eradication, as "Top Fund-Raising Chapter" in 2013–2014.

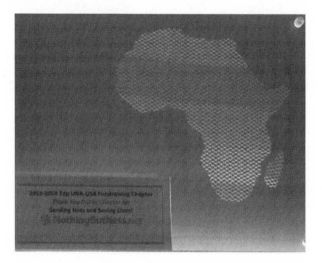

- Madan Goyal's report highlighted the "Advocacy Day on the Hill," with calls on Congressional representatives, his first attendance in over 20 years, dubbing it "very stimulating" (*DUNA Archives*).

June 22. "Annual" DUNA Potluck Social at Norma and Bill Matthews' home, 26 attended.

- Report on Dallas International Girls Soccer Cup, presentation of gift from the Club—Anya Cooper and Norma Matthews.
- Reports and discussion from Annual Conference in Washington from several who attended.
- Treasurer's Report included NBN pass through gift from Soccer Project to UN Foundation: $591.00, reimbursement for partial expenses to seven National delegates: $2,100, outstanding checks, ending balance: $3,292.27.
- Discussed plans for upcoming meetings (*DUNA Archives*).

August 20. Cosponsored Women's Equality Day at City Hall with Women's Issues Network, others, $75 contribution; several DUNA members attended, met affinity representatives (*DUNA Archives*).

FaBrice Kabona and Célestin Muzorewa listened to Hussein Elaydi

August 28. DUNA World Humanitarian Day at FunAsia Restaurant—featured a distinguished international panel of local persons, speaking from personal and leadership experiences. Moderated by Tatiana Androsov, former UN staff in overseas postings, with Dr. Célestin Musekura from Rwanda, founder of ALARM, Inc., African Leadership and Reconciliation

Ministries, now based in Dallas, and Dr. Mona Kazim Shah from Karachi, Pakistan, and Washington, D.C., now working as a freelance producer with Documentary Journalism and founder of Project Pakistan with Love.

- Also on the panel were Tasriqui (Tas) Islam from Bangladesh, now a student at UTA, University of Texas at Arlington, Youth Ambassador of Bangladesh to the U. N. on MDGs, FaBrice Kabona from the Democratic Republic of Congo, former refugee and at this time a student at UTA, volunteer with IRC, International Rescue Committee, and Assistant to the City Manager, Lancaster, TX. Guest panelist was Mr. Hussein Elaydi, formerly from Palestine.
- About 40 persons attended.
- Treasurer's Report—bank balance reconciled: $2,275.27 (*DUNA Archives*).

September 21. A World Peace Day Dallas festival was mounted by students at Southern Methodist University. DUNA members Madan Goyal and Bill Matthews added their handprints to a giant display poster to honor the day.

September 25. DUNA Board planning meeting for UN Day:

- Progress report on MDGs
- Nominations for persons for an Education Fair to represent each of post-2015, the 17 Sustainable Development Goals [later called "Global Goals"].
- Committee heads were designated for Reception, Set-up, Technical, Clean-up, Goals-Education, break-out leaders, etc. (*DUNA Archives*).

October 2. DUNA Board member Shabnam Modgil was director of the Mahatma Gandhi Memorial of North Texas, for dedication of an Honorary Gandhi Plaza in Irving, Texas. Norma and Bill Matthews attended representing DUNA (*DUNA Archives*).

October 4. Norma and Bill Matthews presented a program on "The UN Today" with emphasis on the accomplishments of the MDGs (Millennium Development Goals) and plans for future Global Goals to the AAUW (American Association of University Women) Dallas Chapter.

October 12. DUNA follow-up planning meeting for UN Day:

- Reception/check-in—Michael Webster and Beth Weems Pirtle
- SDG Representatives—stationery, need elevator speeches, possible breakouts
- Facilitators and Training—David Reid with Marty Jones, Brandon Morton, Connie Rensink, others
- Media/roving reporter—Deborah Fleck, *Dallas Morning News*
- All Things UN/USA—Tatiana Androsov and Tas Islam
- Awards to County Commissioner Judge Clay Jenkins, Shot@Life by Walgreens, Ahmed Ashmawy for Dallas International Girls Cup—NBN Award
- Program brochure (plan, design, printing)—David Reid, Bill Matthews
- Invitations to six elected officials, several universities (*DUNA Archives*).

October 24. UN Day for DUNA—"Building YOUth Futures for Global Citizenship"—at FunAsia Restaurant, Richardson: Educational Fair, Dinner and Awards, Consultation on UN Post-2015 Sustainable Development Goals.

- Straw vote ballots distributed, for priority selections by attendees.
- Awards:
    - Humanitarian Hero Award—the Honorable Judge Clay Lewis Jenkins
    - Commercial Partner in Health, Shot@Life by Walgreens—Ms. Kate Turner
    - Community Partner in Health, Nothing But Nets by Dallas International Girls Cup Soccer—Ahmed Ashmawy
- Sponsors included GROW North Texas, Sierra Club, AAUW (American Association of University Women), League of Women Voters, The Family Place, Mosaic Family Services, The Muslim Women's Foundation, and The Dallas Peace Center.

Mrs. Chandler Roosevelt Lindsley, DUNA friend, member,
and advisor, with daughter, Ruth Roosevelt Lindsley

- Greeting by DUNA member Mrs. Chandler Roosevelt Lindsley, granddaughter of Eleanor Roosevelt (*DUNA Archives*).

October 27. UN Day Financial summary showed total revenue: $4,350.00; total expense: $3,400.00; net $880.54 (with some adjustments noted).

October 28. Evaluation informal meeting on UN Day: Norma and Bill Matthews with Nelda and David Reid.

- Norma complimented the organization of the event, over 115 attended, energy and interest evident.
- Featured speakers ran long, affected schedule.
- Awards generated good publicity; having Mrs. Lindsley present was a plus.
- Intros of elected officials incomplete, recognition of exhibitors inadequate, due to time pressures.
- Interest expressed in reorganizing an Arlington Chapter; invitation to David to speak at a school in Fort Worth.

- Martin Huang expressed interest in presenting a Human Rights program on December 11 – Human Rights Day, follow-up by David.
- Michael Webster willing to become Treasurer for 2015, nominations to be solicited soon.
- Norma observed that no written history of Dallas Chapter exists, need to explore ways to research and write (*DUNA Archives*).

December 4. Dallas Peace Center 28th Peacemaker Awards Dinner, cosponsored by Dallas United Nations Association, with other community partners. Welcome by President John Fullinwider, emcee Mustafaa Carroll, invocation Rev. Diane Baker.

Awardees: Media Peacemaker of the Year, James Washington, *Dallas Weekly*; Lifetime Achievements, Norma Tevis Matthews, Peacemakers Inc. and DUNA, and Dr. José Angel Gutiérrez; Peacemaker Organization, Jobs with Justice, Rosemary Rieger; and Peacemaker of the Year, Colette Flanagan, Mothers Against Police Brutality. In memoriam: Mac Hall; Rev. Dr. William K. McElvaney; Curtis Castleberry. Valediction by Alia Salem.

Friends and family congratulated Norma, including Debra Matthews Shrader, California daughter, Harbans Lal, Tatiana Androsov, David and Nelda Reid, Shabnam Modgil, Mike and Patti Daves, Beth Weems Pirtle from DUNA, and Jade Hopkins, San Antonio great granddaughter.

Norma's family and DUNA friends honor her DPC
Lifetime Achievement Award, 2014

2015

January 1. DUNA President David Reid reported details on the year's activities. "The Dallas Chapter has always placed a heavy emphasis on education. Throughout our history, we have been fortunate that teachers were a critical element in our membership. Whether we were teaching in classrooms, volunteering for career days or attending Committee on Teaching about the United Nations (CTAUN) conferences, we endeavored to inform students and teachers in our region about the good work the United Nations does around the world."[9]

January 17. 2015–16 Planning Workshop at Norma and Bill Matthews' home, 9:00 a.m. to 3:00 p.m. Present: Tatiana Androsov, Linda Evans, Pauline Lai, Bill Matthews, Norma Matthews, President David Reid, Nelda Reid, Connie Rensink. Absent: Tas Islam, Marzuq Jaami, FaBrice Kabona, Harbans Lal, Shideh Lowary, Pierce Lowary, Shabnam Modgil.

- Bank balance forward from December 2014: $3,561.74. Ending balance at 1/16/2015: $4,110.74
- Committees on Program, Advocacy, Membership, and Communications went into breakout sessions, reviewed descriptions of duties, discussing priorities and plans. Additional committee areas discussed were Education, Fund-raising, GenUN, Outreach, Refugees and Human Rights, and Young Professionals.
- National UNA-USA reports 126 members verified for Dallas Chapter.
- A tentative calendar for 2015-2016 was reviewed, with comments (*DUNA Archives*).

January 2015. DUNA Board of Directors, with stated interests:

- President—David Reid, Fund-raising, Outreach
- Vice president—Connie Rensink, Programs, Membership
- Treasurer—Michael Webster, Programs, Young Professionals
- Secretary—FaBrice Kabona, Advocacy, YPs, Refugees/Human Rights
- Parliamentarian—Pauline Lai, GenUN, Young Professionals

---

[9] David and Nelda Reid reports on 2015 activities.

- Refugee Services Liaison—Linda Evans, Refugees/Human Rights
- Program and Events Chair—Connie Rensink
- Communications and Membership Chair—Nelda Reid
- Outreach Chair—Tatiana Androsov
- GenUN Chair—Tas Islam
- Young Professionals Chair—Pauline Lai, GenUN, Young Professionals
- Education Chairs—Shideh and Pierce Lowary, Education
- South Central Region Representative, Nelda Reid
- Advocacy Committee Lead, Bill Matthews, Texas Division President
- At-Large Members:
  - Jamal Gharbieh
  - Patty Jantho, Programs
  - Marzuq Jaami, Fund-raising
  - Harbans Lal, GenUN, Program, Outreach
  - Norma Matthews, DUNA History Project
  - Shabnam Modgil, Communications, Outreach
  - Almas Muscatwalla, Education, Outreach
  - Beth Weems Pirtle, Program, Fund-raising
- Other members interested or attending January Planning: Steve Raynor, Lena Ashwas, A. B. Ebrahim, Gabriella Castagno, Ghada Muktad, Mona Kazim Shah, Laura Moonan (*DUNA Archives*).

February 9. Death notice Mr. John Whitehead, longtime champion of UNA-USA, friend, and mentor of many in DUNA and of the Thanks-Giving Foundation of Dallas. He served on the cabinet of President Ronald Reagan, chaired the national UNA-USA, and chaired the Lower Manhattan Development Corporation for the rebuilding of the World Trade Center in New York.[10]

February 26. DUNA Board meeting at Center for Nonprofit Management, Dallas.

- President David Reid welcomed, with calendar review.
- Treasurer's report ending balance: $4,082.83.

---

[10]   Letter from UNA-USA CEO Chris Whatley, February 9, 2015.

- Dallas Chapter History Project—Norma Matthews updated; consultations with historians and writers included Darwin Payne, Andrew Graybill, Bill Simon, and Charles Hosch; advisory committee formed with Charlotte Karam, Beth Weems Pirtle, Nadine Bell, Harbans Lal, Patty Jantho, Bill Matthews, David and Nelda Reid, Linda Evans, and Latha Nehru.
- Bill Matthews distributed a human rights advocacy paper, listing nine core international treaties, with other information to energize and sustain advocacy efforts (*DUNA Archives*).

March 20. The Sierra Club Cross Timbers Group, which serves Denton and Collin counties, hosted a panel discussion on long-range water planning and conservation in Frisco, Texas. The panelists include Reggie James, interim director of the Sierra Club's Lone Star Chapter; Jennifer Walker, water resources coordinator of the Sierra Club's Lone Star Chapter; David Reid, president of the Dallas Chapter, United Nations Association; and Denise Hickey, public relations director for the North Texas Municipal Water District. The discussion went from 7:00 to 9:00 p.m. at the Depot in the Frisco Heritage Center (*DUNA Archives*).

March 26. DUNA board meeting at Center for Nonprofit Management, convened at 6:30 p.m. President David Reid, with Nelda Reid, Beth Weems Pirtle, Shabnam Modgil, Connie Rensink, Almas Muscatwalla, Linda Evans, Jamal Gharbieh, Marzuq Jaami, and Latha Nehru present.

- Secretary absent, notes by volunteer Jamal Gharbieh.
- Advocacy—Almas Muscatwalla volunteered.
- Communications—Nelda Reid urged wide use of all media resources to promote UN and its programs.
- Education—Shideh Lowary sent word urging outreach to new educational institutions.
- Fund-raising—David Reid and Almas Muscatwalla later signed up DUNA for North Texas Giving Day campaign.
- GenUN—Connie Rensink participated in national teleconference about Intergenerational Model UN.
- Membership—Nelda reported Dallas chapter report from national at 146 members.

- Program—Connie reported on Earth Day, April 22 at UNT; voted to support.
- UN Day will be observed November 3 by DUNA, with plans to organize program.
- Nelda reported that Nancy Lindborg, president of the US Institute of Peace, was coming to Dallas. A program was arranged for April 1 at the Center for Community Cooperation; Congresswoman Eddie Bernice Johnson and Judge Clay Jenkins, Dallas County Commissioner were invited.
- Refugee and Human Rights: Linda Evans noted that June 20 will be World Refugee Day, need to seek sponsors.
- Norma Matthews filed a progress report on the DUNA History Project.
- Nelda presented a plan to bring awareness on Anti-Agenda 21 Bill in the Texas Legislature.
- David raised question of Council of Organizations; Beth Weems Pirtle and Shabnam Modgil will move this forward.
- Adjourned at 8:45 p.m.

Nancy Lindborg with David and Nelda Reid

April 1. DUNA Chapter Board meeting with Nancy Lindborg, President of the US Institute of Peace, Washington, D.C., at the Center for Community Cooperation, at 5:30 pm for light dinner and program with Q & A. About

25 attended for a lively information and discussion meeting, including leaders from Peacemakers, Inc. and Dallas Peace & Justice Center.

Ms. Lindborg then presented a lecture and discussion in a nearby, larger room, with about 85 community leaders and interested parties participating. (Our chapter was recognized for leadership for this event at the June meeting of UNA-USA in Washington, DC.[11])

April 4. Information booth was set up and staffed by DUNA at the Dallas International Girl's Cup in Farmers Branch to benefit the Nothing But Nets campaign. See further report in Chapter 6.

April 23. DUNA Board meeting at Center for Nonprofit Management, 6:30 p.m.

- President David Reid welcomed, with a calendar review.
- Reports from Secretary and Treasurer not in files
- Michael Webster announced the Dallas International Girls Soccer Cup for Nothing But Nets sponsorship will be in May.
- Advocacy - Bill Matthews reported talking points in support of UN, and that Congress had voted to fully fund the UN for 2015, with thanks from UNA-USA for grass roots advocacy.
- Linda Evans announced plans for UN Day, November 3, at Dallas City Performance Hall, with Margaret Barrett's *Universal Language* program, libretto by Dr. David Silva, performance by The Obscure Dignitaries.
- Dallas UNA History Project—Norma Matthews has submitted grant proposals to two foundations without response so far. She and Bill will continue to research and begin compiling articles chronologically. Added to advisory committee were Vivian Castleberry, Karen Blessen, and past president Nadine Bell. Interviews with former Dallas mayor Adlene Harrison, and Jan Sanders, who has contributed the UN flag that belonged to Judge Sarah T. Hughes, willed to Judge Barefoot Sanders.
- UN Day Planning committee assignments were distributed by Connie Rensink. Budget projection totals for UN Day: $6,882, to be adjusted as plans progress (*DUNA Archives*).

---

[11]   Ibid., Reid.

The Honorable Eddie Bernice Johnson, founder of the
World of Women for World Peace conferences

April 25. A World of Women for World Peace, annual conference presented by Congresswoman Eddie Bernice Johnson, supported by DUNA with promotion and attendance. Panelists are Olivia Stokes Dreier, Karuna Center for Peacebuilding; Dr. Alma Abdul-Hadi Jadallah, Kommon Denominator Inc.; and Dr. Betty Gilmore, SMU Center for Dispute Resolution and Conflict Management; moderator LaToya Silmon, Fox 4 News.

Norma Matthews presented UN SDGs to the Altrusa Club, Richardson, TX.

May 5. Norma Matthews presented Sustainable Development Goals at the Altrusa Club, Richardson, TX.

2014 Anya Allen Cooper Farewell

June 6. DUNA Board bade farewell to its effective "Nothing But Nets" coordinator, Anya Allen Cooper, as she and her husband transferred to Atlanta.

June 8–10. National Leadership Summit, UNA-USA, Washington, DC.

DUNA reps at USIP, 2015

- Twelve DUNA members attended, including Jasmine Hunt, Norma Matthews, Dede Remo, Rachel Sakala, Bill Matthews, Nancy Lindborg, USIP, US Institute of Peace; David Reid, DUNA president; Nelda Reid, South Central Regional rep to CCR, Tatiana Androsov, who attended an informative workshop at the USIP.

Chris Whatley presented the Well Worn Advocate Award to DUNA's
David Reid for hosting USIP President Nancy Lindborg

- Also taking part on the "Day on the Hill" advocacy visits to Ted Cruz, John Cornyn, and other congressional representatives' offices were Shideh, Pierce, and Loy Lowary.

July 9. UN Day planning meeting for November 3. Connie Rensink convened and led the coordinating meeting.

- Tatiana Androsov recommended inviting Dr. Srgjan Kerim from Macedonia as keynote speaker. He was president of the 62nd General Assembly and a nominated candidate for election as Secretary General in 2016.
- Detailed plans for MC, staging and performance logistics, display area plans, tickets through EventBrite, box office on site, special guest invitations, student groups, publicity and advertising, printed program design ideas, reception before the "show," parking arrangements, sponsor solicitations, and possible t-shirt design and sales.
- Volunteers offered to help: Margaret Barrett with fund-raising, Brandon Gebo with tasks, Dede Remo with corporate sponsors (*DUNA Archives*).

A many year "tradition" was an informal Summer potluck and swim party, hosted at their home by Beth Weems and Rodney Pirtle

July 25. DUNA Summer Social and Board at the home of Rodney and Beth Weems Pirtle; nineteen members and guests attended for potluck dinner and informal meeting.

- Beth welcomed the group, explained how to join Dallas Chapter, UNA-USA; announced an invitation to a visit of a Pakistani photographer at the home of Mona Shah on August 1.
- Bill Matthews explained the UNA campaign of "Cities for CEDAW," to encourage cities to "ratify" the convention not yet ratified by Congress. Volunteers were Olia Bosovik, Jacqueline Bello, Dede Remo, Pauline Lai, and Brandon Gebo.
- Linda Evans announced plans for UN Day, November 3, at Dallas City Performance Hall.
- Norma Matthews reported progress on the DUNA History Project, including interviews with Mrs. Chandler Roosevelt Lindsley (granddaughter of Eleanor Roosevelt), and Guy Gooding, 1990 President of DUNA. An intern from UNT, Denton, is being sought to work with the project.
- Norma also showed pictures of the DUNA group visit to the US Institute of Peace in Washington, DC, during the national UNA-USA meeting, which eleven DUNA members attended (*DUNA Archives*).

August 21. President David Reid e-mailed a reminder letter, with advance details about the upcoming board meeting.

DUNA members at Womens Equality Day: Ghada Muktad, Linda Evans, Dede Ramos, Bill Matthews, Shabnam Modgil, David Reid, Norma Matthews, and Ricky Cruz

August 26. Women's Equality Day in Dallas: DUNA cosponsored the observance at Dallas City Hall with the Women's Issues Network and other community organizers. DUNA representatives were Ghada Muktad, Linda Evans, Dede Ramos, Bill Matthews, Shabnam Modgil, David Reid, Norma Matthews, and Ricky Cruz.

August 27. DUNA Board meeting at La Madeleine Restaurant, Mockingbird Lane.

- Present: David Reid presiding, Nelda Reid, Shideh Lowary, Linda Evans, Bill and Norma Matthews, Beth Weems Pirtle, Shabnam Modgil, Almas Muscatwalla, Harbans Lal, Tatiana Androsov, Pauline Lai, FaBrice Kabona, Marzuq Jaami, and Connie Rensink.
- David welcomed, presented calendar review, summarized financial report in absence of treasurer, noted a $1,000 service-match donation received from the Texas Instruments Foundation. This donation was in honor of David's volunteer work.
- David reported that about 300 persons attended the Women's Equality Day, August 26 event at Dallas City Hall, observing the 95th Anniversary of women's voting rights.
- DUNA will be a recipient of donations through North Texas Day of Giving campaign September 17th. Note: total of $150 reported on 10/16/2015.
- UN Day reports: Tatiana reported that Dr. Srgjan Kerim of Macedonia accepted invitation as keynote speaker. MC still open, sponsorship letter template was distributed, members urged to solicit, Latha will coordinate. Connie announced event tickets available soon, use online purchase—$70 reserved seats, $25 general admission, $10 for students.
- Plans for September 21 International Day of Peace: "Youth to Youth Refugee Panel," partner opportunities.
- Peace is Possible, second annual World Peace Day, September 18; FaBrice Kabona will be DUNA speaker.
- AKA Sorority: DUNA will help with event.
- Population Media Center: addresses worldwide population issues.
- Linking the World: an NGO working to break the cycle of poverty.
- Brahma Kumaris: evening of meditation on peace and nonviolence on September 21, International Day of Peace.

- Women's Summit at SMU, October 1: DUNA invited, help promote event (*DUNA Archives*).

September 1. Population Media Center, Happy Hour Meet and Greet, 6:00-8:00 at Restaurant Hibiscus, 2927 N. Henderson Avenue, Dallas 75206. RSVP by August 28.

- We have the opportunity to partner with **Population Media Center** in several ways. Bill and Norma have met with Yvette Hanshaw, the Exec. Dir. of the Texas Chapter of PMC.
- Nelda and I listened in on their statewide conference call on July 7. Their CEO, Robert Walker was interviewed August 12, on KERA's "Think with Krys Boyd." Population challenges are a significant part of the UN Sustainable Development Goals.

USIP Director Kathleen Kuehnast, with Nelda Reid,
Almas Muscatwalla, and Bill Matthews

September 15. Peacemakers Inc. hosted their seventh annual International Day of Peace luncheon at the Hilton Dallas Park Cities Hotel. DUNA had a long-term relationship with Peacemakers, Inc. The keynote speaker was Dr. Kathleen Kuehnast, Director of Gender & Peacebuilding at the US Institute of Peace, Washington, DC. Norma and Bill Matthews placed a DUNA ad in the program and set up an information booth.[12]

---

[12]   Ibid.

Nelda Reid and Connie Rensink represented DUNA at "Peace Is Possible," Dallas' International Peace Day 2015 in Klyde Warren Park

Peacemakers, Inc. Leaders, 2015 - Norma Matthews, Anita Marcos, Carol Donovan, and Vivian Castleberry.

September 18. "Peace is Possible," Second Annual World Peace Day Event, 6–9:00 p.m., Klyde Warren Park, Dallas. Amber Jackson, a student at SMU, is part of a grassroots organization called Peace is Possible. On their behalf, she invited DUNA to partner with the Embrey Human Rights Program, Human Rights Initiative, UNT Peace Studies Program, and Dallas Peace Center, to co-host their Peace is Possibleevent. They invited us to sponsor the event, to provide a speaker to share information about UNA-Dallas, and to have an information table. FaBrice Kabona was the DUNA speaker.

- The celebration was a music and arts festival, with guest speakers from local North Texas-based non-profits whose work is related to human rights and social justice. Their vision was for the festival to continue and to become a part of the fabric of Dallas culture on the International Day of Peace.[13]

Pierce Lowary presided for a public forum on Youth Refugees, 2015

September 19. "Youth to Youth Refugee Panel," observing International Day of Peace, at University Park United Methodist Church. Program for

---

13   Ibid.

DUNA organized by Shideh and Pierce Lowary, partnered with Linda Evans and International Rescue Committee.

- Pierce also organized an online web presence with http://www.unycdallas.org/. "The United Nations Youth Coalition (UNYC) was formed by Pierce Lowary, a student at Highland Park High School. Fueled by passion and great compassion toward social and economic issues affecting global youth, we set out to develop a voice for change, bridging a common cause across numerous cultures and languages."[14]
- Pierce also partnered for a Model UN sponsored by the AKA sorority and the YMCA.

Pierce Lowary represented the UNYC at the 2015 Alpha
Kappa Alpha ASCEND DFW Model UN Conference

September 26. "Make a Difference with the UN."
After we celebrated the International Day of Peace this week, world leaders representing 193 nations at the United Nations adopted a new plan for action for people and the world called the Sustainable Development Goals.

- Peter Yeo from the United Nations Foundation says, "People everywhere deserve societies free from fear and violence where

---

[14] "UNITED NATIONS YOUTH COALITION," accessed June 18, 2017, http://www.unycdallas.org/.

the rule of law, access to justice and transparency thrive. These priorities make the other global goals possible. There can be no sustainable development without peace, and no peace without sustainable development.

- "For example, people in states affected by conflict are three times more likely to suffer from hunger than their peers; in 2011, 28.5 million school-age children from conflict-affected countries had no access to education; and the average cost of civil war is equivalent to more than 30 years of GDP growth for a medium-size developing country.
- Together, we can make a difference by supporting the Dallas United Nations Association and advocating at UN Day on Nov.3."[15]

November 3. UN Day 2015, DUNA "70 Strong" theme observed the seventieth anniversary of the United Nations.

Mr. Peter Stewart, Thanks-Giving founder, with 2015 UN Day speaker Dr. Srgjian Kerim, Macedonia, and Tatiana Androsov, TGS and DUNA Board

- Keynote speaker: Dr. Srgjan Kerim of Macedonia, nominated for secretary general of the UN, president of the Sixty-Second General Assembly—2007–2008.

---

15   Bill Matthews, "Letters to the Editor," *Dallas Morning News*, September 26, 2015.

- Meet the Global Goals SDGs: Mr. Mike Beard, executive director for Advocacy and Global Health, UN Foundation, Washington, DC.

Mike Beard, UNF ED for Advocacy and Global Health

- Among other displays, an Islamic youth group presented a walk-through, interactive display of the Global Goals.

The Destination Imagineers children graphically
represented the U.N. SDGs, for 2015-2030

- *Universal Language* was a multimedia representation of the Universal Declaration of Human Rights, with musical setting by Margaret Barrett, libretto by Dr. David Silva, and performance by The Obscure Dignitaries, a local musical group.
- Emcee: Pierce Lowary, DUNA Education Co-chair, greeted in four languages.
- Recognitions: Connie Rensink, UN Day Program Chair
- Remarks: David Reid, President of the DUNA Board
- Sponsors: Ross Avenue Baptist Foundation, Carl Bell, chairman—memorial to Rev. Roy Harrell, for Interfaith, International support of youth leadership, also Jan Sanders, Bill Kelly, Loy, Shideh, and Pierce Lowary, Peacemakers, Inc., League of Women Voters of Collin County, Chandler Roosevelt Lindsley and Ruth R. Lindsley, Bill and Norma Matthews, the Embrey Human Rights Program at Southern Methodist University, the Population Media Center, Kelly Nash and Karen Blessen for 29 Pieces, and the Sikh Community.
- Supporting Sponsors: Vivian Castleberry, Beth Weems Pirtle, Masjid Hasan, Masjid Al Quran, Independent Plastic Recycling, DeSoto Islamic Center, Pax Christi Dallas, Sandra Noble, Robert and Shirley Cooper, 29 Pieces, Delta Omicron Chapter of The Delta Kappa Gamma Society International, Texas Muslim

Women's Foundation, Dallas Branch of The American Association of University Women, Best Fire Protection Service, Dallas Family Federation for World Peace, and David and Nelda Reid (*DUNA Archives*).

November 11. The World Affairs Council presented a well-attended program with Gillian Sorensen of the United Nations Foundation, Washington, DC., at 6 p.m. at the Rosewood Crescent Hotel (*Dallas Morning News* Community Calendar).

November 19. DUNA Board of Directors, at Center for Nonprofit Management, Dallas.

- Agenda on file, minutes not available.
- Finance report approved and filed
  - Opening balance 9/23/15: $1,907.36
  - Deposits recorded, UN Day and BWF Chapter Refund: $14,176.99
  - Disbursements, Honoraria and UN Day Expenses, ending balance: $10,607.99
  - Deposit in transit, checks outstanding, balance 9/23/15: $13,113.91
  - Other business discussed without action. *DUNA Archives*

December 12. DUNA Annual General Meeting, at Fretz Park Library, Dallas.

New Tech High School students presented Human
Rights Day program for DUNA, 2015

- Gathering, Welcome, Calendar Review—David Reid presiding
- "Human Rights Day" dramatic presentation by New Tech High School group was directed by Danae Boyd and student representatives.
- Nominations and election of officers for 2016:
- President—David Reid
- Vice president—Connie Rensink
- Secretary—Pauline Lai
- Treasurer—Almas Muscatwalla
- Advocacy Lead—Tatiana Androsov
- Refugees and Human Rights—Linda Evans
- GenUN—Tas Islam
- Membership—FaBrice Kabona
- Young Professionals—Pauline Lai
- Youth (Education)—Shideh Lowary/Pierce Lowary
- Texas Division/CEDAW—Bill Matthews
- History Project—Norma Matthews

- Outreach—Shabnam Modgil
- Fund-raising—David Reid
- Communication—Nelda Reid
- Programs—Connie Rensink
- Board members at large:
  - Jamal Gharbieh
  - Marzuq Jaami
  - Patty Jantho
  - Harbans Lal
  - Michael Webster
  - Past president Latha Nehru

December 15. DUNA Members reported from national UNA-USA: 162 "units," 170 individual members (*DUNA Archives*).

"For all those whose cares have been our concern, the work goes on, the cause endures, the hope still lives and the dream shall never die"—the words of Sen. Ted Kennedy ring true for the Dallas Chapter of the United Nations Association of the USA for ages to come, even as challenges continue to mount before our nation and our world.[1]

---

[1]   Matthew Moore, *The Telegraph*, online tribute on the death of Ted Kennedy, www.telegraph.co.uk/news, 26 Aug 2009.

Chapter 6

Dallas UNA Members Events, Activities, and Memoirs

1990–2015

Uncovering a treasure trove of memories, this chapter reports significant campaigns that supported the agenda priorities of the UN Foundation and of UNA-USA, plus program announcements and bulletins.

Personal recollections of their motivation and involvements by leaders and other members of the Dallas Chapter reflect the dedication and commitment that sustained the purposes of hope and peace.

Although sketched briefly in other media reports and the time capsules, these reports expand on individual activities to broaden the scope of individual and group efforts that furthered the goals and achievements of the organization.

1. Guy Gooding, DUNA president 1990–92
2. GEMUN (Global Elementary Model United Nations)
3. Nadine Bell, DUNA president 1993–95
4. Stanley Ukeni, DUNA president 1996
5. Beth Weems Pirtle, DUNA president 1998–1999, 2006
6. Dr. Harbans Lal, Sikh community Board member, 1993 continuous through 2015

7. Charlotte Karam, strong chapter volunteer, 1996, 1998
8. Noeli Biggs Reports, 2007, DUNA president 2008 (merge Earl Eames Jr.)
9. CTAUN Conferences in Austin 2012, Dallas 2013, and in Houston 2015
10. Connie Rensink's report from Houston CTAUN
11. DUNA Chapter Activities 2014 Norma Matthews' recap
12. Nothing But Nets, UN mosquito-eradication campaign cosponsored with Dallas International Girls Cup, Reports 2014, 2015
13. Marzuq Jaami, Muslim community Board member, 2014, 2015
14. Rockwell "Golden Rule Mosaic" Rededication at UN New York 2014
15. Adopt-A-Minefield Goal Success Report, 1998–2015
16. Partners for Peace, Karen Blessen, 29 Pieces
17. Linda Abramson Evans Report, 1998–16
18. Shabnam Modgil, UN Radio Voice 2015
19. Nelda and David Reid 2010–2017
20. Bill Matthews, Memory Garden of UNA Activities 2015

Guy Gooding, President, Dallas Chapter UNA 1990–1992[2]
My Experience with the Dallas United Nations Association

I joined the UNA as a board member in the mid-1980s anxious to connect the work of the UNA with ongoing efforts to increase exposure of international affairs to student life in the Dallas Community College System where I had been a student program director since the mid-'70s.

The UNA provided a platform addressing global diplomacy that I hoped could provide case study and cocurricular opportunities for our growing development of an international education curriculum. I served on the board with Annemarie Brown as president who was preceded by her husband, Marvin Sadovsky. Both were devoted to exposing the work of the UN and the concept of thinking globally and acting locally through the work of the Dallas UNA.

In 1990, I took the helm as UNA president with a commitment from past presidents Marvin Sadovsky and Anna Marie Brown that they would stay on the board and assist in establishing a Model United Nations

---

[2] Guy Gooding, "Letter from Guy Gooding, CEO, Goodelstet G4 Enterprises," July 29, 2015.

Conference for public and private high school students with councils headed by community college student leaders. We took a year to prepare and launch our first MUNDO, Model United Nations Dallas Organization. Southern Methodist University agreed to host the preparation workshops during the fall term followed by an early spring three-day Model UN conference.

Early in the preparations, we established an advisory board designed to lend a sense of legitimacy to this experiential study of international relations while a growing conservative view in Dallas was criticizing the UN for its suggested sympathy to countries that were not prone to supporting US interests.

There were, however, prestigious Dallas leaders who understood the benefit a model UN conference experience could do to sensitize young people to the complexities of living in a global community. Margaret McDermott agreed to serve along with Stanley Marcus; Richard Rubottom (former ambassador); Annette Strauss; Dr. Wright Lassiter; Rev. Zan W. Holmes, to name a few.

Letters of invitation were sent to all DISD and private high schools, including Hockaday, St. Mark's, Episcopal School of Dallas, Ursuline Academy, and Greenhill. In the fall of 1991, SMU and the Dallas UNA hosted the first workshop for the preparation by delegates to select a country to represent and begin the process of studying UN policy and current resolutions being deliberated by the UN council ambassadors.

Students gathered to discuss diverse and pressing international issues. Committees and topics included International Narcotics Trafficking, Loan Reform, and Debt Forgiveness for Developing Countries. A summit on women and conditions regarding women in government and policy was also held.

I believe the first year yielded eight schools, and by the third year, over fifteen schools represented over forty countries, with over 150 students participating. The majority of the UN Councils were chaired by student leaders in the DCCCD, Dallas County Community College District, who were members of the honors fraternity, Phi Theta Kappa. The majority of the UN roles, from council general to commissioners, were led by DCCCD student leaders and resulted in the DCCCD hosting its own districtwide annual conference for DCCCD students called Leadership as a World Citizen.

Another offshoot from MUNDO was the establishment of GEMUN, Global Elementary Model United Nations, an annual conference that is currently hosted by Brookhaven College and brings over 300 students together from throughout the Dallas metroplex. GEMUN has been active for over 15 years.[3]

Experiencing United Nations: Global Elementary Model United Nations (GEMUN)

The GEMUN name implies its meaning—elementary and middle school student role-playing the assemblies of the United Nations. This enriching, exciting opportunity was available in the Dallas/Fort Worth, Texas, area since 1990.

GEMUN provided an excellent hands-on approach to learning in a global context. By role-playing delegates to the United Nations, where they studied and confronted authentic issues, young people from varied backgrounds learned about other countries, cultures, and international relationships. Developing a global perspective about real issues that confront the world community today, they acquired many transferable skills.

During the school year, children and their sponsors received help through workshops and printed materials. Scheduled workshops were held during each year at Morningside Middle School in Fort Worth, Texas. Their preparation culminated in a two-day Model United Nations conference in Dallas.

Approximately 330 delegates attended the 2015 session of GEMUN, role-playing forty-five member nations of the United Nations. The participants included groups from Russia, Turkey, Florida, North Carolina, and Texas.

Students immensely enjoyed the collegiate setting while participating in GEMUN, held in recent years at Brookhaven College (DCCCD). Due to the authentic nature of the material and assignments, they saw direct application of the information to their daily lives, to the problems in the world and in their surrounding environment.[4]

---

[3] "Robert Muller," *Wikipedia*, December 17, 2016, https://en.wikipedia.org/w/index.php?title=Robert_Muller&oldid=755403177.

[4] "Global Elementary Model United Nations," *Global Elementary Model United Nations*, n.d., http://www.unol.org/gemun/.

The Honorable Robert Muller, UN Assistant Secretary General,
founder of Robert Muller schools in the Dallas area and elsewhere

Among prime sponsors of the program continued to be the Robert
Muller School, Arlington, Texas, started in 1979 to advance the World
Core Curriculum developed by the former assistant secretary general of
the United Nations, Dr. Robert Muller.

The valedictory speech by Angela Buller, the first graduate in 1989,
included these words:

> The Robert Muller School has specifically inspired me
> to work for peace. Last year I traveled to Switzerland for
> a week and met my peers in the world of children who
> also want peace. I have been asked to be one of the few
> young people who are to meet in Amsterdam and later in
> Costa Rica at the United Nations University for Peace at

the end of June, 1989, and participate in the drawing of the Charter for an official Children's United Nations. My work in the Robert Muller School with the Model United Nations has prepared me as fully as possible for such a job as we will be undertaking in Amsterdam.[5]

Nadine Bell, Dallas UNA President, 1993–1995 Recipient of UNA-USA 2000 Arnold Goodman Lifetime Achievement Award[6]

Nadine Bell reveled in the high honor of receiving the 2000 Arnold Goodman Award for Lifetime Achievement. She was presented the award on June 8, 2000, at the UNA-USA National Conference at the Doyle Hotel, Washington, DC.

Nadine Bell received the 2000 UNA-USA Goodman
Award for Lifetime Achievement

[5]   Ibid.

[6]   Information provided by Linda Evans, DUNA board member and chair of the DUNA Committee on Refugees in a letter dated February 14, 2000, when she nominated Nadine Bell for the 2000 Arnold Goodman Award. Nadine was the second member of the Dallas UNA Chapter to receive the Arnold Goodman Award. The first was Judge Sarah T. Hughes, the first president of the Dallas UNA Chapter, who received the award in 1981.

Linda Evans reported in her nomination letter for the award that "Nadine both follows and strengthens the example set by Arnold Goodman in service to UNA-USA." Linda described Nadine as "a remarkable woman" who has given unselfishly of her time and energy to both community, national, and international projects.

UNA-USA Plaque shows Nadine Bell Award 2000

During Nadine Bell's 1993–95 term as president, she revitalized the Dallas chapter, significantly increasing membership for which the organization was recognized, expanding and diversifying the board to reflect Dallas's diversity of cultures, conducting dynamic yearly board orientations, creating a committee structure for leadership training and new member involvement, and introducing quarterly program meetings.

With her direction, the chapter treasury grew from $200 to $5,000; the Model UN program was restored; and the Human Rights Expo program, which she conceived and chaired in 1991, was continued.

The DUNA chapter became well known in the community, networking with other NGOs including Soka Gakkai, the League of Women Voters, and Zonta International. She arranged and staffed booths for UNA information and recruitment at the Greater Dallas Chamber of

Commerce International Trade Fair, 1993–95, and the Dallas County Community College International Fairs in 1994 and 1995. DUNA past presidents were honored and involved in the 1994 UNA dinner.

Nadine became president of the Texas division, 1996–1998, working to maintain communications and cooperative efforts between Dallas, Houston, and Austin chapters. They met annually to share program ideas, speakers, and plans for membership recruitment and retention, to solve problems collaboratively. She was liaison with UNA-USA national office and the CCD (Council of Chapter and Division Presidents).

On the CCD executive board, 1994–1998, Nadine served on the resource development, nominating, and Arnold Goodman committees and hosted and chaired the 1993 annual meeting in Dallas. She facilitated the UNA-USA strategic planning meeting, chaired by Betty Sandford, and served as chair of the resolutions committee at the 1997 UNA-USA Convention. She was also on the technology committee of the Texas Division for three years.

From 1997 to 1999, Nadine was instrumental in the DUNA cosponsorship of the North Texas UN Conference on Women with the University of Texas at Dallas. She served on the planning committee—recruiting, orienting, and debriefing professional facilitators for each program topic. A professional facilitator, Nadine was past president of the International Association of Facilitators. She accomplished the creation and implementation of the IAF Facilitator Accreditation Program and the Community Outreach Task Force, to provide IAF members to train local organizations in community development and disaster recovery.

Nadine has been recognized for other professional and community endeavors:

1. The 1999 Molly Gerold Human Rights Award from the Texas Counseling Association
2. The Hillcrest Forest Neighborhood Coalition 1997 Community Leadership Award
3. The 1995 Models of Unity Award for Exemplary Achievement from the Spiritual Assembly of the Baha'is of Grapevine
4. The 1993 Excellence in Development Highest Honor Award from the North Central Texas Section of the American Planning Association
5. The 1983 Best Speaker Award from the Business and Professional Women's Club

In addition, Nadine Bell and Linda Evans worked together on many UNA-USA activities, including the Middle East Cousins Club, which Nadine cofounded to promote friendship among Arabs and Jews.

Thoughts on My DUNA Presidency—Stanley Ukeni[7]

Hi Bill, thank you for reaching out to me to share my thoughts on my experience during my presidency of DUNA. I am really honored by your gesture. Here are some of my thoughts of what transpired during my DUNA presidency for your book. I hope it's helpful. Please let me know if I can be of further assistance.

After a friend introduced me to the Dallas United Nations Association (DUNA), I became thoroughly fascinated with the organization. And like anyone who sought to make an informed decision on whether to get actively involved in an organization, I promptly began to research the history and past activities of the UNA-USA, and its Dallas chapter, since their organization's inception.

I quickly found that the more that I learnt of the organization's progressive activities, the more intrigued I became about being a part of DUNA's impressive legacy. I realized that my worldview and the stated goals and objectives of UNA-USA were aligned. After my research, I did not need any more convincing to get actively involved with DUNA.

After I got involved, and began to participate in the events, I began to talk to anyone and everyone who would listen to me about this incredible organization that I had recently gotten involved with. I talked to friends, acquaintances and even strangers about DUNA—urging them to get involved as well.

It did not take very long for me to realize that many in Dallas had this deeply held suspicion of multilateral organizations such as the United Nations, and any institutions that are intimately affiliated with it.

I was indeed surprisingly struck by people's apathy about, and at times outright hostility towards people whenever I would initiate a conversation about the organization. I figured that this deeply held aversion to DUNA was based, in part, on a lack of understanding about what UNA-USA is all about.

---

7   Stanley Ukeni, "Letter from Stanley Ukeni to Bill and Norma Matthews," January 21, 2016.

This apathy towards the United Nations and UNA-USA, I came to understand was most profound among the staunchly conservative-leaning elites of the Dallas society. I felt that it was vitally important to reach-out to this demographic group because they were, for the most part, the opinion shapers of the Dallas community—since they controlled virtually all the mass media platforms at the time.

Equally, as I got more actively involved with DUNA—as a member of its Board of Directors, it became clear to me how this misconception about what UNA-USA stood for was denying DUNA the much needed funding with which to most effectively advance the organization's objectives of community advocacy.

I wanted DUNA to receive the same level of financial patronage as organizations like the World Affairs Council of Dallas/Fort Worth.

Once I was chosen as the president of DUNA, I decided that elevating the organization to the same level as the World Affairs Council within the Dallas community was to be one of my main priorities.

I felt that it was important for the very affluent members of the Dallas society to be helped to appreciate the importance of the UN as a needful multilateral instrument for advancing United States' foreign policy objectives—and as a consequence the need for a robust community support of DUNA.

I realized that this ambitious goal that I was aiming to achieve was unusual, and as such would face resistance from within the DUNA board of directors and outside the organization. However, I felt it needed to be implemented, if DUNA was to effectively carry out its assigned mandate of community advocacy and legislative lobbying.

There were, of course, those who bought into the idea of my planned initiative, and then there were those who felt strongly that DUNA was better off remaining as a marginal organization within the Dallas community.

I must admit that I had a great deal of difficulty dealing with folks who would rather maintain the status quo. In fact, on a few occasions, I strongly contemplated resigning as president of DUNA before the end of my term.

We had limited finances, so we had to come up with innovative means of accomplishing our objective with little or no funding. I decided that one of the key means of implementing this objective was to have periodic social gatherings at the homes of affluent members of the community—where invited high profile speakers would educate our guests on the importance of the UN system in advancing the United States' efforts in maintaining global peace.

I appealed to Arend Koch for help in this regard. He graciously agreed to open up his beautiful home in University Park whenever needed. He also agreed to provide some of the refreshments that were served. DUNA hosted several successful events at the home of Arend Koch, which received notable attention for the organization.

One of the more profound of these social gatherings was when the Dallas entrepreneur, Raymond Nasher, hosted members of the Dallas community at his home in honor of the visiting United Nations Under-Secretary General, Gillian Sorenson. This event and others that were organized in honor of the Under-Secretary General were exceptionally successful.

Among many other high profile events that were organized during my tenure as DUNA president, was the hosting of the Chinese counsel general in Dallas, during a contentious period in US-China relationship, in 1996–1997—a period when the US media was rife with stories of a United States Department of Justice investigation into the possible involvement of agents of the Chinese government in a scheme to directly contribute money to the Democratic National Committee before the 1996 presidential campaign, in violation of US laws.

DUNA was the only organization that any Chinese official would agree to address during that period in their effort to set the record straight—even the Dallas World Affairs Council was unable to pull-off this feat, with all the resources at its disposal. This event provided the members of the Dallas community an opportunity to directly ask the Chinese official hard questions regarding this matter of grave concern to them at the time.

These events were extremely well attended, and helped elevate DUNA as an important institution in Dallas. Although we did not quite achieve the parity with the Dallas World Affairs Council that we aimed for by the end of my tenure as DUNA president, the organization did gain broader acceptance within the community.

We also organized a successful Model United Nations for Dallas high school students. It was held at Southern Methodist University campus.

I am sure that there are many details that I may have unwittingly omitted, but I hope that this summation provides clearer insight into the core vision that drove my leadership of DUNA from 1996 through 1998.

I will close by saying that, despite some challenges that I faced during my DUNA presidency, it was truly a rewarding experience. I learnt a lot of valuable lessons about effective leadership and about good stewardship. I continue to cherish my experience at DUNA with great fondness.

These are some of the events that I can recall at the moment. Please let me know if you have any questions. I wish you and Norma lots of luck with the new book. I'm confident that it will be well received in the UNA-USA community, and perhaps within the broader Dallas community.

Thanks, Stanley Ukeni.

Beth Weems Pirtle, DUNA President—1998–1999, 2006[8]

Beth Weems Pirtle retired in 1994 with twenty-six years of teaching special education. On the tennis court while subbing for her husband, she was asked if she had a fax machine and if she could help do some work for the United Nations Association Dallas Chapter. While doing that work at her house, she read the pages. "What wonderful work these people were doing!" she thought. In 1996, she joined them and began meeting some of these wonderful people. She became president a few years later!

Beth's background led her to this. Her mother took her to Mexico City for several summers while in high school. She audited classes at Mexico City College learning Spanish. Then she returned for her senior year there, where she graduated from the American High School. So she was ready for international work in 1996.

Her years 1998 and 1999 as president of UNA-Dallas were so exciting. UN Day was held at the Fairmont Hotel with over two hundred people attending. Past president Ray Nasher was honorary chairman of the day. Charlotte Karam was in charge of the event. What a marvelous day it was! Another project in 1999 was Adopt-a-Minefield, as the chapter raised about $30,000 to send to Cambodia to clear a minefield so children could go to school and play safely in their village.

---

[8]   Beth Weems Pirtle, "Letter from the Archives of Beth Weems Pirtle," n.d.

Beth Weems Pirtle, DUNA, among delegates to
South Central Region, UNA USA, 1999

She had the honor of being the Texas division representative on the national board during her early years with UNA-Dallas. She also served on the national board of UNA-USA as communication chairman, working with all the chapters in the United States.

The United Nations Association-USA Dallas Chapter (DUNA) is a local chapter of UNA-USA, a national nonpartisan not-for-profit organization.

The UNA-Dallas Chapter has a long and outstanding history. Eleanor Roosevelt came to Dallas and visited with Judge Sarah T. Hughes and lawyer Louise Raggio to give leadership for forming our new chapter in the early 1950s. Judge Hughes was our first president and the recipient of the first Arnold Goodman Leadership Award in 1981, given by UNA-USA for distinguished service.

Another outstanding leader in the Dallas chapter and recipient of that same award in 2000 is Nadine Bell. In addition to Judge Hughes and Nadine, our esteemed leadership has included Raymond Nasher, Ambassador Richard Rubottom, and former mayor Annette Strauss.

We were honored as the Dallas chapter received another award: The Earl Eames Communication Award in 2008. I am so proud of the recipient, Noeli Piccoli Biggs of Richland College. She has worked so hard to get the necessary people connected with the idea of the UN videos. Our community will be so much more educated about the world through this wonderful effort.

Rotary International and the United Nations

In 2000, UNA Dallas Chapter created a Speakers Bureau to take its message to the different communities and clubs. Beth Weems Pirtle decided to reach out to the Rotary Clubs in her husband's district, which had thirty-eight clubs at the time. She titled her speech "Rotary and the UN." She sent her request to all the clubs and received many invitations. Back in those days, many people were not in support of the UN; in fact, they spoke about not funding it and doing away with it. So the climate was not very welcoming, to say the least.

Beth Weems Pirtle, DUNA leader was crowned "Ms. Senior USA" in 2003

Undaunted, Beth set out. She had a great story, and when heard, the audience was with her. She knew about the Rotary Polio Plus program and their work to eradicate polio in the world. She asked her audience rhetorically how they went about doing that. They had no clue! So she pointed out that the money they raised—many millions of dollars—went to the World Health Organization (a UN agency) to buy the vaccine. Then she asked how they got the vaccine to the children and families all over the world. Again they had no clue, but they were catching on. Of course, it was delivered through UNICEF, the United Nations Children's Fund.

She reached a lot of people who needed to know this message. In addition to the Polio Plus program, Beth reminded them that Rotary International was present at San Francisco in 1945 to support the creation of the United Nations First Assembly. And she thanked them again!

Dr. Harbans Lal: As I Remember United Nations Association, Dallas Chapter[9]

Dr. Harbans Lal, DUNA Board volunteer, leader and representative of the Sikh faith community, an NGO of the DPI, UN

I am indebted to Norma Matthews for asking me to reminisce about my memory path in the DUNA. Actually I felt flattered to be asked to share my connection with UN and its advocacy group UNA. She also asked me to share with readers of her book how Sikhs have related to the UN and/or UNA. I am delighted to do so, that too particularly because UN and UNA are the invaluable organizations for minorities, and Sikhs are a significant minority. They are also vital for societies who wish to engage

---

9   Harbans Lal, "Letter from Harbans Lal, PhD; DLitt (Hons), (Emeritus Professor and Chairman, Department of Pharmacology & Neuroscience, Univeristy of North Texas Health Science Center, Fort Worth, Texas) to Bill and Norma Matthews," January 20, 2016.

with world communities and with civil societies for the betterment of whole human race. Sikhs are one of those communities.

Let me dwell a little longer on the issue of my community's involvement in these world organizations. I was born in the undivided Indian subcontinent where I became a refugee when I was just a high school student. I come from a community whose very existence was at stake less than a century ago, and whose near-demise came after the British occupants divided Indian subcontinent into India and Pakistan, forcing most Sikhs to become a Diaspora Nation.

British India was partitioned in 1947 and millions of non-Muslims had to leave their homes in Pakistan to migrate to the Indian side as millions of Muslims from Northern India had to migrate to Pakistan. Most of the Sikhs lived in the Pakistani part of India with the result that most of the Sikh community had to abandon their land where their ancestors flourished between the 15th and 21st centuries.

I rightfully address West Punjab, Khyber Pakhtunkhwa and Kashmir as our holy land on account of countless footprints of our Gurus widespread in those areas. There remain our historic monuments, forts, battlegrounds, commercial and residential establishments and our shrines. All of them became mute witness to the ineptness of Sikh leadership of the time who failed to gauge near fatal consequences of abandoning the Sikhs' National heritage. The same heritage had originally served as the foundational stone of Sikhs' existence.

Sikhs became a Diaspora community which spread everywhere in the world including North America. A significant number chose North Texas as their new home.

Thus our connection with UN and UNA becomes obvious. With this in mind I looked around for associations that connected us to other world communities. In that pursuit I was introduced to two significant institutions. In 1982 I joined the World Center for Thanks-Giving where all faith communities gathered and UNA where civil societies met to engage each other. I was introduced to Dallas UNA by Nadine Bell, who was soon to be elected President of DUNA in 1993.

I remained active with DUNA for that decade during which I became associated with the Millennium World Peace Summit of Religious and Spiritual Leaders, held 28–31 August 2000 at the UN Assembly and at the Waldorf-Astoria Hotel, New York. In that connection I came to know Bawa Jain, Secretary General of the Millennium Summit. He asked me to help identify the Heads of Sikh Religious institutions and to facilitate his invitations to the Sikh leaders for participation.

In that same series, Thank-Giving Square introduced me to Father Luis Dolan. Luis Dolan was one of the founding participants during the formative years of NAIN—North American Interfaith Network. When I met him, he was the representative of The Temple of Understanding to the United Nations. There, he was active in organizations such as the Values Caucus and the Association of Religious NGOs. He was also given responsibility to expand NGOs.

Father Dolan was representing NGOs to UN when I was introduced to him. He made me an ID for the UN campus so that I might attend various events there. There are two significant events that I will never forget.

Kofi Annan, Secretary-General of the United Nations at the time, motivated faith leaders to have their own summit at the UN campus with a view to organize themselves as well as to establish active relations with UN through organizing faith based NGOs. In that connection, I got in touch with Bawa Jain, Secretary General of the Millennium World Peace Summit of Religious and Spiritual Leaders to assist him in inviting Sikh religious leaders to that summit.

On August 28th through 31st of the year 2000, nearly two thousand of the world's preeminent religious and spiritual leaders representing the many faith traditions, gathered at the Millennium Summit. There they charted an ambitious program of action for the future of humanity. I had a unique opportunity to actively participate, as it was the first time in history that religious and spiritual leaders of the world's diverse faith traditions had come together to explore forging a partnership of peace with the United Nations.

My second unforgettable experience was again at the UNA in 2004. Here I would like to recognize Sister Joan Kirby who was admired for her activism with non-governmental organizations (NGOs) for a major part of her life. The Temple of Understanding honored her with the Interfaith Visionary Lifetime Achievement Award on October 19, 2010, during the Fiftieth Anniversary Gala and Juliet Hollister Awards Ceremony in New York City.

My own pleasant memories of meeting Joan first time was when she chaired 57th Annual DPI/NGO Conference at United Nations in New York. I made friendship with her that continued until her last breath in 2015. After I got well acquainted with her I remember her asking me why

Sikhs did not have a DPI/NGO of their own as I was there as a delegate of the World Center for Thanks-Giving. Further, she prodded me to take a day-long training course at UN towards helping Sikh organizations to qualify and submit applications. Since then we have three Sikh NGOs affiliated. Why not more is another story. On my part I worked with nearly half a dozen.

Sikh attendees of United Nations Organization NGOs meeting released the 2004 Declaration of Guiding Principles for Civil Society to nudge forward. These principles were taken from the universal wisdom of Sri Guru Granth Sahib compiled four centuries ago. They were signed by many national and international Sikh organizations and a few other faith leaders. Among them was included Tatiana Androsov, President and Executive Director of Thanks-Giving Square. Tatiana had a distinguished career in working at UN in many leadership capacities. She too is an uninterrupted friend and colleague in my association with DUNA and Thanks-Giving Square. In the past few years she became a friend of the Sikhs in Dallas Fort Worth Metroplex.

In conclusion, I would like to acknowledge with thanks for DUNA welcoming me with open arms. During my continuous tenure with this organization I have lived through exciting times with my friends and colleagues who similarly valued their association with this organization throughout these years.

Charlotte Karam, DUNA Volunteer Recollections of UNA 1996[10]

On May 22, 1996, when the UNA was called DUNA, we sponsored a program at Richland College with Dr. Kenneth L. Pike, a prominent international linguist who had 11 nominations for the Nobel Peace Prize. He demonstrated his Descriptive Linguistic Analytical Techniques with Prof. Charles Walton of the International Linguistic Center of Dallas, Texas (later called Summer Institute of Linguistics). The technique was

10   Charlotte Karam, "Letter to Authors by Charlotte Karam, Active in Dallas UNA Chapter during Beth Pirtle's presidency, 1996–1998 and following," July 6, 2015. Charlotte now lives in Jacksonville, Texas. She has been teaching ESL and Spanish, letter to the authors, July 6, 2015.

317

created to document unknown dialects throughout the world, thereby enhancing cross-cultural understanding among peoples of the world.

Program setting: Native speakers were chosen by DUNA, coordinated with Dr. Pike, to ensure that neither Dr. Pike nor Prof. Walton spoke the languages of the speakers. They had only brief familiarity of the areas of each language, based on the intonation and rhythm of the speakers. Two speakers from two different countries were invited to the stage separately, where one of the linguist experts was waiting with numerous blackboards and chalk.

One was an African who spoke English, but who was instructed to not respond in English, only in his native language. Dr. Pike or Prof. Walton spoke only in a dialect of the Philippines. The other was from the country of Goa, also in Africa.

Each expert began by bringing to the table a number of natural items, such as a large leaf and a small leaf, a large branch, a small branch, and a chair. Holding up a small leaf, the expert asked in the Filipino dialect what was the item called, and a speaker responded only in his own language. The expert wrote the word on the board phonetically. Then a larger leaf was shown and the word with its adjective was annotated. Later the expert sat down and a speaker stood up and wrote those words on the board. After about 30 minutes of exchanges, the expert then asked the speaker to explain in English what they had said so the audience could understand the relation between guesses and facts.

The demonstration and findings of the studies were fascinating and continue to be used by the Center today. Dr. Pike explained how this method has helped the Linguistic Center throughout their work in many countries of the world.

Dr. Kenneth Pike was the first President of the SIL Center (Summer Institute of Linguistics). His task was to train and equip hundreds of linguistic students to analyze and put into writing unwritten languages in the world. By "putting into writing" he, with the institute, created alphabets for each of the undocumented languages he studied. He expanded SIL's work to more than 50 countries and helped to establish SIL's academic integrity. An author of more than 20 books and 200 articles, Pike was an internationally recognized linguistic scholar and is missed by all with whom he had associated.

Dr. Kenneth Lee Pike (1912–2000) died in 2000; he is survived by his wife, Evelyn; three adult children, Judith Schram, Barbara Ibach, and

Stephen Pike; three grandchildren and two great-grandchildren; his sister, Eunice V. Pike (now deceased) and his wife, Evelyn, both traveled and worked side-by-side with him. They each have published numerous books about their work with him.

According to Dr. John Watters, the President of SIL today, many individuals continue to be trained at GIAL (Graduate Institute of Applied Linguistics) and are serving around the world. GIAL is an accredited institution that offers basic (upper level undergraduate) and advanced (graduate) linguistic training.

Twenty Nations Were Represented for the 1998 UNA Banquet[11]

On November 21, 1998, I took on the exciting feat of organizing the UNA Annual Banquet at the Fairmont Hotel in Dallas, Texas. As I am always so excited about anything international, I decided to go that route. I chose 20 nations that were members of the United Nations and decorated each table of eight guests with a flag from one of these nations. A program/menu was created for each country giving a description of the government, their leaders, their flag, and a brief history. Countries highlighted were:

United States, Russia, Vietnam, Spain, Chile, Mexico, Germany, China, El Salvador, Guatemala, Japan, Lebanon, Greece, Iran, Portugal, United Kingdom, Canada, France, India, and Armenia.

We prepared large baskets to represent each of the 20 countries and filled them with products imported from each nation. They were attractively decorated to show the outstanding items found in the Dallas area. Each basket measured approximately two feet tall and one and a half feet in diameter. The baskets were displayed on a table to be sold in a silent auction.

---

[11] Reports by Charlotte Karam, volunteer chair of the UN Day Banquet, 1998.

Raymond Nasher, chair, with DUNA president Beth Weems
Pirtle and Ambassador Djerejian, UN Day 1998

The program consisted of our speaker who was Ambassador Edward P. Djerejian, the founding director of the James A. Baker III Institute for Public Policy at Rice University, Houston, Texas, one of the United States' most distinguished diplomats, whose career has spanned the administrations of eight US presidents. Ambassador Djerejian is a leading expert on the complex political, security, economic, religious, and ethnic issues of the Middle East. He played key roles in the Arab-Israeli peace process, the US-led coalition against Saddam Hussein's invasion of Kuwait, successful efforts to end the civil war in Lebanon, the release of US hostages in Lebanon, and the establishment of collective and bilateral security arrangements in the Persian Gulf. He is the author of *"Danger and Opportunity*: *An American Ambassador's Journey through the Middle East"* (Simon & Schuster Threshold Editions, September 2008). Ambassador Djerejian speaks five languages.

Ms. Dorothy Reid, Dean of the Dallas–Ft.Worth Consular Corps introduced the speaker of the banquet, Ambassador Djerejian. An authentic Scottish Piper, Brad Madison, accompanied the ambassador from a special reception in his honor to the podium in the banquet hall where he delivered his speech.

Entertainment for the evening included the Shandon School of Irish Dance choreographed by Kay Legreca; Arabic Professor of Percussion Jamal Mohammed played the Egyptian Databuka Clay Drum adding to the international ambience; and Octavia, the Cockney Pearly Queen, sang cheerful songs from England. The final act put the finishing touch to the evening as Rodney and Beth Pirtle showed the guests what their music "looks" like. Rod sang as Beth eloquently signed the words to two songs.

The UNA Banquet in 1999 Celebrated the Feria de Sevilla (Spain)[12]

The following year, October 24, 1999, we converted the main ballroom of the Dallas Fairmont Hotel into a virtual village of Spain—the Feria de Sevilla (the Spring Fair of Seville, Spain). The guest speaker was the Spanish Ambassador to the UN, Ambassador Inocencio Arias Llamas. Our Honorary Chair, Master of Ceremonies, and expert tour guide was Dr. Luis Martín, retired Spanish professor from SMU.

Guests were elegantly met at the entrance to the ballroom by flamenco dancer Isabel Quintana, who presented guests with a red carnation, the flower of Spain. Upon entering, guests were invited to stroll down the "main street of Seville" lined with eight large tents decorated similar to those in that famous Andalusian city during their Spring "Feria." Each tent had a colorful curtain around each, while Spanish dangling globes and dimmed lights created a festive environment, experienced at the festival in Spain every year.

Three of the tents housed Spanish restaurants established in Dallas, who invited the UNA guests to sample their Sangria and Spanish Tapas. Other tents housed a Fortune Teller, sales of Spanish "abanicos" (fans), United Nations Association Literature, a picture-taking scene with a professional cameraman, and an art exhibit on loan from the well-known Dallas Museum of Art.

The program included Spanish Flamenco Dancers with the Daniel de Córdoba Company and flamenco guitarist David Quintana and his wife flamenco dancer, Isabel, and singer Bill Matthews dressed as Don Quixote who magnificently sang the lead song from *The Man of the Mancha*, "The Impossible Dream," accompanied by his wife, Norma.

A remarkable evening was experienced by all. To date, UNA-Dallas members ask when we will repeat that evening.

---

[12] Letter to the Authors, October 15, 2015.

Bill and Norma Matthews sang "The Impossible Dream"

Noeli Biggs 2007, DUNA Chair, International Education, Model UN, And *Going Global with UN* President Beth Pirtle[13]

In 2007, Noeli Biggs took initiative to organize a Model United Nations at Richland College, a Dallas County Community College, to promote opportunities for students and faculty members to understand the complexities of the issues facing the international community and to develop global viewpoints that would otherwise remain foreign to them.

The Richland College Model United Nations program offered the following initiatives to students:

1. *Going Global with UN*—the series contains 52 half-hour videos covering the work that the UN has been doing since 1945 in the following areas: millennium development goals, health and

---

[13]   Noeli Piccoli Biggs and Beth Weems Pirtle, "Letter to Authors Submitted By Noeli Piccoli Biggs and Beth Weems Pirtle," 2015.

environment, education, poverty and development, war and peace, gender and aging.

2. Richland College, in partnership with the LeCroy Center for Educational Telecommunications and United Nations Association of Dallas, implemented the *Going Global with United Nations* videos in the following formats:

3. Broadcast: the video series *Going Global with UN (GGUN)* was also made available in broadcast version on Dallas County Community College District educational cable to a half-million Dallas community residents. Richland College was the first higher education institution to broadcast the *GGUN* videos, making Dallas only the second city in the United States to have access to these videos through cable.

4. Streaming video: the *GGUN* videos were also available on the Web to the whole global community. Richland College is the first higher education institution to stream these videos worldwide.

5. Media center: The videos were available to DCCCD students, faculty, and employees (total of 67,107) through the campus media center.

Noeli Biggs, 2008: The Earl Eames Award[14]

Noeli and Bill Biggs, with Jeanna Remington and Diana Urrutia
from Richland College at UNA Goodman Awards Reception

---

[14] Ibid.

In 2008, Noeli Biggs, endorsed by DUNA, applied for the UNA Earl Eames Communications Award, which is a memorial to the late Earl W. Eames Jr. of Minnesota, the former chair of the Council of Chapters and Divisions (CCD) and president of the UNA of Minnesota from 1980–1986. The award, in the amount of $500, was presented during the 2008 UNA-USA Annual Meeting in New York City, to recognize the chapter or division that made the greatest progress in the use of electronic communications technology.

The criteria were as follows:

1. Media outreach for communication to the American public to show the relevance of the UN to their lives
2. The development of creative and effective use of media

Noeli Biggs received the Goodman Award, 2008

DUNA partnered with Richland College and LeCroy Center to stream the *Going Global with UN* video series, making them available online to the entire global community. The videos were also presented by broadcast on Dallas County Community College District educational cable channel, accessible to a half-million Dallas local community residents.

UNA-USA Dallas Chapter, Richland College, and LeCroy Center received the Earl Eames Award 2008 for

1. being the first to locally broadcast the *GGUN* videos, making Dallas only the second city to offer access through cable to these videos, and
2. for being the first to make the videos available on the web to the whole global community through unlimited internet connections.

President Noeli Biggs, 2008

In 2008, Noeli Biggs worked with the Dallas City Protocol office to attain a Special Recognition Award from the Dallas city mayor Tom Leppert. The DUNA Chapter, with Richland College and LeCroy Center representatives, received their certificates in a ceremony at Dallas City Hall, where Mayor Leppert on behalf of Dallas City Council announced the award and congratulated the team in achieving the high recognition and for promoting opportunities for Dallas citizens to understand the United Nations, within the complexities of issues facing the international community and to expand their global viewpoints.

CTAUN Conferences: Three Reports

The Committee on Teaching about the United Nations (CTAUN) provides educators worldwide with opportunities to learn about the work of the United Nations and to incorporate this global awareness into curricula and school activities at all levels.

1. They organize conferences to bring educators together with international experts at the United Nations and around the country.
2. They facilitate curriculum development on international issues.
3. Through best practices awards, they recognize teachers' hard work, dedication, creativity, and resourcefulness.
4. They believe with Nelson Mandela that "education is the most powerful weapon which you can use to change the world."

In Austin, Saturday, Sept. 22, 2012: "Promoting Tolerance: Solutions for Change"

DUNA at 2012 CTAUN with Teta Banks, Anne-Marie Carlson

With keynote address by Mr. Maher Nasser, acting director of the Department of Information at the United Nations, workshops relating to the theme included the role of information, global technology, internet issues, and panels on keeping your kids safe in their digital world, diplomacy, and solutions for change. The closing keynote featured Dr. Patricia Alvey from Southern Methodist University, author and publisher of World Citizens Guide. Mrs. Anne Marie Carlson, national chair of CTAUN, was introduced by Dr. Rosemary Morrow, local chair of the meeting, held at the Joe B. Thompson Center, UT Austin, Texas.

DUNA members attending included Norma and Bill Matthews, Teta Banks (Houston), Meredith, Nelda, Stephanie, and David Reid, shown with Mrs. Carlson.[15]

---

[15] "2012 Austin," accessed June 12, 2017, http://www.ctaun.org/conferences/austin-conference-2012/.

In Dallas, Saturday, Nov. 2, 2013: "Global Partnerships: Where Do You Fit In?"

Connie Rensink, DUNA Board Program Chair, CTAUN Coordinator

Connie Rensink, Dallas chair of the Conference Committee, welcomed everyone to the first CTAUN Conference held in Dallas, Hughes-Trigg Student Center, Southern Methodist University.

Anne-Marie Carlson, National CTAUN Chair

She thanked the committee and the sponsoring organizations. Then she introduced Anne-Marie Carlson, the national chairperson of CTAUN (Committee on Teaching about the United Nations). Anne-Marie was pleased to announce that this is the twenty-fifth CTAUN conference nationally and the third to be held in Texas. She then introduced Ramu Damodaran, the deputy director for Partnership and Public Engagement in the United Nations Department of Public Information (DPI).[16]

In Houston, Saturday, April 11, 2015: "Cultural Awareness; A Pathway to Peace"

Dr. Barbara Bathe, conference chair, Anne-Marie Carlson, chair of CTAUN, and Dr.Regen Pecen, university president welcomed 145 attendees gathered at North American University in Houston for a day of interactive global learning.

Keynote speaker was Emily Garin, Division of Data, Research and Policy, UNICEF. Ms. Garin introduced her topic: UNICEF—what it is and what it does. Founded after World War II to provide food for Europe's starving children, it is a part of the United Nations that works today in remote villages in 167 countries. It won the Nobel Peace Prize in 1965.

The closing afternoon panel was a "Coming to America" discussion. Adult immigrants and college students from Peru, Panama, Turkmenistan, Kazakhstan, Nigeria, and Bosnia told of their experiences trying to assimilate into Texas American society.

Many of them talked about the focus of learning English, with the emphasis on smiling and friendliness. One student talked about the discord that happened when she wanted to hang out with her American friends instead of her international friends.[17]

Connie Rensink, Dallas UNA, CTAUN, Houston, April 11, 2015

Connie Rensink was the only Dallas UNA member who attended the CTAUN in Houston. She provided additional information from the

---

[16] "2013 Dallas," accessed June 12, 2017, http://www.ctaun.org/confer ences/2013-dallas/.
[17] "2015 Houston," accessed June 12, 2017, http://www.ctaun.org/confer ences/2015-houston/.

conference. The morning panel discussion was focused on local organizations that foster intercultural connections in the Houston community. Speakers were from the Japan-American Society, World Affairs Council of Houston, Harmony Public Schools, and Asian Chamber of Commerce.

One takeaway here was that people need to know what to expect of communication norms in countries they are visiting or where they are working. There is a need for more integration. The Harmony Schools used Science, Technology, Engineering, and Math (STEM) academics to build this integration.

Connie also attended the Global Classrooms workshop, presented by Dr. Teta Banks, UNA Houston. Dr. Banks demonstrated the newly developed UNA Model UN app. The app provides complete lesson plans that can be implemented as a forty-five-minute lesson or a weeklong unit. It includes background information on countries, UN committee process frameworks, and six different issues that can be deliberated.

Connie described the hand model Dr. Banks shared at the end of her program. One fist represents a closed person. Two fists, one on top of the other, shows awareness. Two open palms facing upward signify two different ways. And finally, two hands intertwined symbolize creating a new culture.

The committee provided a wonderful fiesta lunch. International students presented their native countries with a display board and in native dress. After lunch, Connie attended a breakout session by a teacher from Carnegie Vanguard HS in Houston called Fostering Global Awareness and Connectivity in the Classroom. It was designed for the middle school or high school world history, literacy, or philosophy classes. Many of the lessons are designed to give students the opportunity to make difficult choices in classroom assignments created around real world conflict resolution.

Connie described a very successful CTAUN conference. She was program committee chair in Dallas UNA during 2015.[18]

---

[18]   Report from Connie Rensink, filed in DUNA Archives.

Norma Matthews, Recap of 2014 DUNA Chapter Activities, President 2013–2014[19]

Jan 23   UNA board meeting, Girl UP representatives

Jan 26–28   Texas Impact Legislative Event; Norma and Bill Matthews represented UNA, Austin

Feb 4–8   Thanks-Giving Golden Rule Mosaic Rededication at UN, UNA Members Day, Steering Committee NYC

DUNA Strategic Planning Meeting, June, 2014 - Mark Hernandez, Marzuq Jaami, FaBrice Kabona, Harbans Lal, and Tatiana Androsov

Feb 27   UNA board meeting

---

[19]   Submitted to UNA Board Members attending 2015 Planning Workshop, January 17, 2015, by Norma Matthews, Past President, Dallas Chapter UNA-USA.

DUNA Planners Zia Shamsy, Guest, Tasriqui Islam, and Mark Hernandez

Mar 1	Booth at Bath House Cultural Center, International Women's Day, Beth and Norma
Mar 5	Booth at SMU Women's Symposium event, SMU luncheon, Norma and Tatiana
Mar 7	UNA at Park Cities Rotary Club lunch, Hon. Teta Banks, speaker
	UNA Happy Hour with Hon. Teta Banks, president Houston chapter, celebrating
	International Women's Day; 13 attended
Mar 27	UNA board meeting, getting to know board members, David Reid and Anya Cooper
Apr 1	Membership committee meeting, Shabnam, Norma, David, and Nelda
Apr 14	Dinner with Chris Whatley, executive director UNA, at Reids' home, 22 attended

Apr 15	Opening night ceremonies International Girls Soccer Tournament, SMU, Norma and Bill attended and Anya Cooper interviewed on stage re: Nothing But Nets work.
Apr 16	Banquet Event International Girls Soccer Tournament, at hotel, Norma and Bill attended
Apr 19	UNA booth at Soccer Tournament, soccer fields, Carrollton—all day, staff: David and Nelda Reid, Mike Webster, Tatiana Androsov, Patti Jantho, Beth Weems Pirtle, Anya Cooper, Norma and Bill Matthews
May 17	UNA cosponsored John Dear, speaker, Campaign NonViolence and the Nonviolent Life at Cathedral of Hope, along with Pax Christi and Hope for Peace and Justice
June 6-10	UNA-USA annual meeting, Washington, DC, NEA Headquarters, 12 members attended, UNA-USA Advocacy Day on Congressional Hill
June 21	Letters to the Editor, *Dallas Morning News* Bill Matthews: UN Peacekeeping, as advocacy chair.
	Ebola funds, WHO, Aug. 9, 2014
	Immigration, Nov. 11, 2014
June 22	Chapter Social Event at Matthews', potluck, 34 attended
Aug 20	Dallas UNA cosponsored Women's Equality Day, at city hall, several members attended
Aug 28	UNA board meeting, panel, Fun Asia, celebrating World Humanitarian Day, 37 attended
Sep 18	Peacemakers Luncheon, had booth and purchased a table
Sep 21	Bill M. and Madan Goyal put handprints on mural at SMU for World Peace Day festival, picture in *DMN*, representing UNA
Sep 25	2014 UN Day Consultation and Education Fair Planning Meeting, 20 attended
Oct 2	Dedication of Mahatma Gandhi Memorial in Irving, Shabnam Modgil, UNA board member; Bill and Norma tried to attend in the midst of terrible storm.

	Later in day, Bill set up AV for Mona Shah at La Madeleine, SMU, Pakistan event.
Oct 4	Bill and Norma spoke to Dallas Chapter AAUW, information on UN and UNA, 11 people
Oct 12	David and Nelda spoke at Arlington Unitarian Universalist Church on UN and UNA.
Oct 12	Planning meeting for UN Day dinner and consultation, La Madeleine, David and Nelda
Oct 24	UN Day Consultation and Education Fair on Sustainable Development Goals Post 2015

Fun Asia, 3 awards given: Humanitarian Hero Award Ebola; Clay Jenkins, Commercial Partner in Health-Walgreens Shot at Life and Community Partner in Health; Dallas International Girls Cup, Dallas Texans Nothing But Nets

Chandler Lindsley honored for her gift of Roosevelt Quotation books

115 plus present; David and Nelda Reid, producers of event

Oct 28	Evaluation meeting re: UN Day event at Henks Deli—David and Nelda, Bill and Norma

Notes on file in president's binder

Nov 20	David and Nelda attend Houston Chapter event on Post 2015 Goals
Dec 4	Norma Matthews, president of UNA Dallas, received the Dallas Peace Center Lifetime Achievement Award, Doubletree Hotel
Dec 11	Observance of UN Human Rights Day, Fun Asia, 5 speakers; Peace Corps, Bangladesh, Rwanda, and Syria good attendance; David and Nelda, producers, outgoing president recognized.
Jan 14, 2015	National UNA office reported Dallas Chapter has 126 members

Nothing But Nets for Mosquito Eradication Supported by Partners[20]

Community groups worked in 2010 on the "Imagine No Malaria" campaign through the United Methodist Church. Congresswoman Eddie Bernice Johnson included an information booth at her Appreciation Rally in September.

HR Representative Eddie Bernice Johnson greets NBN
Kids from Dallas First United Methodist Church

The Dallas International Girls Cup, along with its organizers, Premier International Tours and the Dallas Texans, partnered with the Dallas chapter of United Nations Association (DUNA) to support the Nothing But Nets campaign in 2014 and 2015. This campaign raised money to send mosquito nets for $10 each to Africa, protecting families from malaria.

---

20   Compiled from DUNA Archives.

2014 Dallas International Girls Cup Banner

Malaria is spread by a single mosquito bite. These nets can be used to save lives. In many cases, several family members share a net to benefit them all. Cameroonian families told moving stories of their experience of malaria at UN Day 2011.

In 2014, local businesses pledged money gifts for every goal scored, which was matched by Premier International Tours, the Dallas Texans, and UNA Dallas members, and further bolstered by other local supporters. As a result, the event raised enough money to deliver 185 nets to families in need!

DUNA "Nothing But Nets" Display at 2014
International Girls' Soccer Tournament

The 2015 Dallas International Girls Cup raised more money to send more mosquito nets to Africa to help save even more lives. The Nothing But Nets campaign had a tent display at the Ross Stewart Soccer Complex during the tournament playing days. Players and families stopped by to donate or just simply get more information on this campaign and about the United Nations Association.

DUNA Members attended an NBN Awards
Reception, at the Bush Library, 2015

DUNA board and members met other NBN staff leaders and advocates at anawards reception in April 2015 at the George W. Bush Library near SMU.

What Made Me Join the UNA—Marzuq Jaami[21]

Marzuq Jaami, active DUNA Board Member and community Advocate

I grew up in a family that was religious and a community that was caring. If people didn't have clothes or food, my parents would cook some food or gather some clothing to send to them. Even if it was two miles up the road, they would still take it to them. They believed it was better to give than to receive, even though we didn't have much ourselves.

Looking at the hurt and the needs of people locally and globally, one of my late leaders, Imam W. D. Mohammad asked us a question, "What are you all doing as Muslims to help eliminate problems in America and around the world?"

One day I heard Norma Matthews talking to Dr. Harbans Lal about the UNA, and I said to Dr. Lal, "I would like to make a contribution to

---

21   Dr. Marzuq Jaami, "Recollections from Dr. Marzuq Jaami, Masjid-Al-Islam, Director of Public Relations, DeSoto Islamic Center, Member, DUNA Board and Interfaith Council, Thanksgiving Square," April 30, 2015.

become a member of the UNA." I have been a member of the UNA for two years now, thanks to Dr. Lal and Bill and Norma Matthews for helping me understand the work and the role of the UNA.

May G-d forever bless them for the leadership they displayed at the local branch of the UNA because it allows me to make a continued contribution to the work they are doing.

Rededication of the Norman Rockwell "Golden Rule" Mosaic February 4, 2014, 4:00 p.m., at the United Nations Headquarters by the Thanks-Giving Foundation, Dallas, the United States Mission, and the United Nations[22]

Events of February 4, 2014 in New York City placed Dallas at the forefront of cities promoting the major global value of thanksgiving, and the hope that future generations may truly be spared the "scourge of war."

Following major renovation of the UN Secretariat building in New York City, the occasion provided by the restoration of the Golden Rule Mosaic celebrates the powerful world symbol of diversity, inclusion and understanding through its realistic depiction of humanity together. Rededication of the historic mosaic was sponsored on February 4, 2014, by the Permanent Mission of the United States to the UN. A reception and program at the nearby Church Center for the UN followed the ceremony.

---

[22] Bill Matthews, "OpEd Submitted to Local Press by Rev. Bill Matthews, Interfaith Council Chair, Thanks-Giving Square Foundation. Not Published. Expanded for This Book from Personal Files," January 14, 2014.

Rededication of the Rockwell "Golden Rule Mosaic" at
the United Nations Headquarters, New York City

Inspiration for the Golden Rule Mosaic to express thanksgiving to
the Almighty began with a small group of Dallas businessmen, who
spearheaded a movement to create the Thanks-Giving Foundation (TGF)
in 1964. They remembered a 1907 Dallas event, when a priest, a pastor
and a rabbi had organized a joint community thanksgiving, beginning a
tradition that continued for over 50 years. When tragic events in Dallas
took on wider significance, the largely lay group initiated a new series
of thanksgiving observances that would emphasize the spiritual healing
power of gratitude and compassion.

This year's rededication coincided with the Thanks-Giving
Foundation's 50th anniversary year and also the beginning of the UN Week
of Interfaith Harmony. This special annual occasion included not only
US and other top diplomats and UN officials, but also the Alliance of
Civilizations, civil society leaders, the National Arts Club, American Field
Service students and international leaders in New York, other sponsors,
along with a loyal group of leaders from Dallas.

The Thanks-Giving Foundation (TGF) was established in Dallas to promote the universal value of thanksgiving. Research into the backgrounds of many traditions found that they honored a mutual human value inherent and observed in all religions and cultures. Even before Thanks-Giving Square opened in 1977 as the physical center of the Foundation, the nascent institution had attracted both national and international interest. For many years, international faith leaders endorsed an annual Proclamation of Thanksgiving initiated by the TGF. Members of the United Nations staff also expressed their desire to join and celebrate their own thanksgiving.

By the 1980's, a deep friendship had developed between Peter Stewart, then the President and one of the original Founders of TGF, and the late Robert Muller, then an Assistant Secretary General of the UN. The two came up with the brilliant idea of a gift to the UN on its 40th anniversary—a mosaic version of Norman Rockwell's painting, "Do Unto Others—The Golden Rule." Stewart and Muller worked very hard to have the mosaic accepted: they had to diplomatically convince the proper authorities of the United States to offer the gift and the proper authorities in the United Nations to accept it. This was very complicated since only nations can properly give gifts to the United Nations.

Members of the 2015 DUNA Board at the TGS
"Golden Rule" Mosaic in Dallas

The Golden Rule Mosaic was accomplished in 1985 by an artisan group in Venice, Italy, supported by primary funding through TGF with Dallas and Texas citizens, which further included donations from businesses and individuals from about a dozen states. The symbolic memento was then transferred to the US government. "The gift of the People of the United States to the People of the World," as TGF labeled it, was dedicated and mounted in the prominent place by the entrance to the Economic and Social Council Chamber (ECOSOC) by First Lady Nancy Reagan and Secretary General Javier de Cuellar, where it has been displayed ever since in United Nations Headquarters until the recent renovation project began several years ago.

In Norman Rockwell's own words, the painting was born out of the desire to "say something serious to help with the world situation" to be "spared the scourge of war." It was based on a "ten-foot-long charcoal drawing" of his "UN picture," in which he "had tried to depict all of the peoples of the world gathered together."

The Mosaic, with its touching overlay of people of all races, ages, cultures and religions, joined together in prayerful, thankful mode, has attained iconic international status. In 1993 it was chosen by the Parliament of World Religions as its exemplary symbol as that body met for the second time after 100 years in Chicago. It has been used on the fronts and backs of books. Depictions of the Mosaic have appeared in various forms including posters to key chains and have been among the best-selling articles in the UN bookstore. In February 2013 it was utilized by the United Nations for its announcement of the Week of Interfaith Harmony. Rockwell's accomplishment has thusly become even greater than his goal.

The Rev. Bill Matthews, 1997–2014 chair of the Interfaith Council, and Board member of the Thanks-Giving Foundation, volunteered after retirement in the North Texas Annual Conference, United Methodist Church. He was elected to the Steering Committee of the United Nations Association of the USA. Council of Chapters and Regions in 2007, representing the South Central Region until 2014.

Landmine Removal Campaign Success: Adopt-a-Minefield[23][24]

In humanitarian response to the immensity of the worldwide landmine crisis, DUNA partnered with the Dallas Peace Center, the Cambodia

---

[23] Compiled from the Dallas United Nations Association Archives.
[24] Compiled from Dallas United Nations Association Archives.

Outreach Program, and other community organizations, to develop strategies for education and fund-raising support in 1999 and 2000, which campaign was then extended through 2005.

When Cambodia was identified as a priority area, we connected locally with Dr. Lance Rasbridge, a medical anthropologist, who helped found in 1992 and continues to coordinate the Refugee Outreach Program for Dallas' Parkland Hospital. In 1998, he began the Cambodia Outreach Program to provide health and development programs to refugees and the poor inside Cambodia. His consultations helped guide us with introductions to the local area Cambodian community.

UNA-USA Coordinated an International Campaign

AAM Launch: Paul Thai-DPD, Chanda Sovan-
Cambodian American Association, Kambiz Rafraf-DUNA,
Lon Burnam-Dallas Peace Center, Aug 2001

Adopt-A-Minefield (AAM) was initiated in response to the 1997 Mine Ban Treaty (MBT). In the late 1980s and early 1990s, the landmine crisis reached critical levels, with each new year yielding an additional 20–25,000 new casualties. After the treaty entered into force in 1999, Adopt-A-Minefield (AAM) was created by UNA-USA to engage American civil society in mine action. UNA-USA successfully concluded the AAM campaign in December of 2009. At the conclusion of the campaign, the national AAM had raised over $25 million for mine action, cleared over 1,000 minefields, and assisted thousands of survivors.

The Dallas Landmine Removal Project was launched on August 10, 2001, with a community lunch at Wilshire Baptist Church, with about 150 persons attending. A Cambodian priest led a Buddhist blessing, followed by Paul Thai, the Dallas police officer liaison with the Cambodian community, telling his life story as a refugee. Chanda Sovan, president of the Dallas Cambodian American Association, spoke of the immigrant issues. An outline of the needs and challenges was led by Bill Matthews for DUNA and Lon Burnam for Dallas Peace Center.

2001 UN Day speaker Nahela Hadi, Adopt-A-Minefield head for UNA-USA, with DUNA leaders Bill Matthews, Kambiz Rafraf, and Beth Weems Pirtle

Nahela Hadi, director of Adopt-A-Minefield for UNA-USA, inspired us at the 2001 UN Day in Dallas: "The campaign for landmine removal is 'not just raising funds, but it's also raising awareness. Landmines prevent life from happening . . . removal helps give life back to a community. We are all a part of one planet earth, responsible for improving life in this world.'"

One notable strategy recommendation was the "Night of a Thousand Dinners," in which home hosts invited groups to dinner, with suggested contributions collected and forwarded to the AAM campaign. Reports noted that during one year, over $5,000 had been added to the benefit total, gathered from more than fifty dinners held in this area.

The campaign announced "Goal Reached" on Human Rights Day, December 10, 2001, with $24,400 received at this time. Dallas attorney

Chip Pitts addressed "Why the US Needs the UN," refuting the top ten reasons for objections. The UN is "not only the best, but it's the only forum dealing with international conflicts today," he concluded.

Dallas Partners Reported Successes

In 2002, the partners presented an update event to celebrate the good news that $25,387.91 had been raised and forwarded to AAM in New York. Cambodian poet U Sam Oeur spoke, from his self-published book, *Sacred Vows*: "'Villages were ablaze, schools, pagodas, turned to battlefields . . . Providence, History, Culture perished. Debauchery paralyzed the entire society."[25]

2002 Adopt-A-Minefield Rummage Sale Volunteers Beth Weems Pirtle, Michael Li, Stephen Brown, with Cherry Haymes and friends (seated)

Bill Matthews, DUNA president, wrote in a 2004 letter to the community: "The Dallas Peace Center, in partnership with the Cambodia Outreach Program and the United Nations Association-Dallas, is pleased to announce the 2004 Landmine Removal Campaign. With your generous support, we have raised $42,000 in our previous campaigns, and we partnered with UNA Sweden to contribute a total of $62,000. Those

---

[25]   Bill Matthews Archive, Posters and online images represented the AAM Campaign through DUNA, used by permission.

lands are now clear, allowing for the development of roads, schools, and markets for the people of Battambang Province."

The two projects in Battambang, Cambodia, were focused on the villages of Spean Youl and O Chrey, which freed their children to attend a dormant school and access for farmers to work their land. Lance Rasbridge and Stephen Brown delivered a final contribution of $8,250 directly to the landmine removal authority in O Chrey village.

Through joint efforts of several volunteer agencies, many individuals, and the UNA-USA, a total of $70,250 was made available to the dedicated persons in Cambodia, who carried out the perilous task of removing threatening mines from their lands to make them habitable again.

Additional images augment the story of the work of the campaign:

1997 Landmine Awareness Day, DUNA at Highland Park UMC, with Philip Winslow, Sandrine Tesner, Merrily Smith, Mary Wareham, Jerry White (landmine survivor), Rita Calvert, Beth Weems Pirtle, and Bob Dennis

Cambodian Temple Dancers help launch AAM campaign, 2001

Dr. Lance Rasbridge delivered Dallas' AAM landmine removal check
to O Chrey leaders, Battambang Province, Cambodia, 2002

O Chrey villagers thank Friends of Dallas, Texas, USA, 2000

Partnered AAM with Sweden 2003

Cambodian Minefield detectors for removal, 2008

Karen Blessen, 29 Pieces: Teaching Peace through Art[26]

Karen Blessen, co-founder of 29 Pieces, teaching peace through art

Our Mission

The 29 Pieces program uses art to awaken, uplift and give voice to the creative human spirit to make genuine, positive social change. While not directly involved with DUNA, the educational goals and purposes prompted several members to partner with their program.

Our Story

The vision for 29 Pieces was born of tragedy. In August 2000, a young man was murdered in front of Karen's home. She processed the profound psychic toll of this event by writing and creating art. The result was "One Bullet," a deeply personal story published in the *Dallas Morning News* in 2003.

Following "One Bullet," Karen was compelled to do something to uplift children and adults, something to give them the courage and strength to stand against the violence that permeates our culture. In what

---

[26] "29 Pieces Education," *29 Pieces*, accessed June 12, 2017, http://29pieces. org/29-pieces-education/.

Karen calls her creative "big bang," a vision emerged: monumental change through monumental art. 29 Pieces was established as a 501(c)3 nonprofit organization in 2005 to develop and deliver arts programs to the Dallas-area community.

Cofounder of 29 Pieces, Dr. Barbara Miller serves as the executive director of Recruitment and Admissions for Texas A&M Baylor College of Dentistry in Dallas, Texas. Dr. Miller received her BS degree from Texas A&M University, her DDS degree from Baylor College of Dentistry, and her MS degree in oral biology from Baylor University.

For eight summers, she studied cultural issues, human rights, ethics, and world religions at Oxford University in England. She has further training in nonviolent communication, cultural competency, and diversity issues.

Karen teaches "hands on" with eager students

29 Pieces Education: Artists Making a Kinder World is one of our core programs. It is an innovative art-based hands-on curriculum that fosters social and emotional learning and essential values like kindness and compassion, and important life skills such as conflict resolution and

analytical thinking. This curriculum can be applied to teaching social studies, science, and other STEM skills.[27]

The creative, innovative approaches of 29 Pieces clearly qualify them as worthy partners to further the principles and practices of the human rights goals of the United Nations for children and the whole of society. In particular, the Sustainable Development Goal 4 recommends "Ensure inclusive and equitable quality education and promote life-long learning opportunities for all."[28](See listing in the appendix.)

Linda Abramson Evans: Tireless DUNA Volunteer/Advocate for Refugees and Immigrants

Linda Abramson Evans, DUNA Board, Refugee Committee Head

Linda Abramson Evans joined the Dallas chapter in 1988, and with an affinity for collaborative networking, she spent her first ten years building bridges between DUNA and other community organizations. In 1998, she focused her attention on refugee issues while preparing this topic for a session of the North Texas UN Conference on Women. The Committee on Refugees and "Volunteer Guide to Refugee Service Agencies in Dallas/

---

[27]   Ibid.

[28]   Florencia Soto Nino, "Sustainable Development Goals - United Nations," *United Nations Sustainable Development*, accessed June 18, 2017, http://www. un.org/sustainabledevelopment/sustainable-development-goals/.

Fort Worth," which Linda originally created for the conference, became an independent project that she has maintained to the present time as a board member of UNA-USA Dallas Chapter.

The Volunteer Guide enables community members to support agencies including International Rescue Committee, Refugee Services of Texas, Catholic Charities Refugee Services, Human Rights Initiative of North Texas, Center for Survivors of Torture, Mosaic Family Services, and other service providers in the Dallas/Fort Worth Metroplex—assisting newly arrived refugees and asylum seekers on their path to self-sufficiency. She emphasizes that refugees soon become contributing members of society, adding value to our local communities.

For this effort, and other issues such as human trafficking and violence against refugee and immigrant women, Linda was among 100 national recipients of the 1999 Eckerd "Salute to Women" Award for significant volunteer initiatives. Over the years, she has also been honored by the refugee agencies she serves. More recently, receiving the 2016 Peace Legacy Lifetime Achievement Award from the Dallas Peace and Justice Center, the citation read, "It is most appropriate that Linda Evans be recognized for her impact as a 'community builder, volunteer facilitator, and advocate for refugees,' and for others in adverse situations, both locally and globally."

Linda Abramson Evans, DUNA Refugee coordinator, presented at 2015 International Women's Day public event, Whiterock Bathhouse Center

Her wider community service includes the Thanks-Giving Square Interfaith Council as a representative of Congregation Beth El Binah and assistant to Faith Forward Dallas, and participation in organizations such as Peacemakers Inc., Texas Business Women, TexTESOL, AAUW Dallas Branch, NCJW Greater Dallas Section, Daughters of Abraham, and others.

Linda Abramson Evans, Norma Matthews, and Tatiana Androsov represent DUNA at a 2012 SMU Women's Event

Both she and her husband, Gary, are advocates for organ donation in gratitude for the liver transplant that saved his life—and together they perform with Resounding Harmony, a philanthropy chorus whose concerts benefit local charities.

In her professional life, Linda teaches advanced English as a Second Language at Southern Methodist University, where she was hired in 1999 to develop the training program for International Teaching Assistants and additional courses for international graduate students. She received the 2017 Faculty/Staff Volunteer Award for her refugee advocacy and other community service beyond academia, and she conducts several voluntary projects on campus that benefit her students and the SMU community. In private practice she works with business and professional clients on American English communication skills.

The United Nations Association of the United States of America, in tandem with the UN Refugee Agency (UNHCR) and its fund-raising arm USA for UNHCR, works through such programs as the recently launched "Adopt-a-Future" initiative, to prevent losing a generation by giving to refugee children the education they need to build a better future. In our day, more than 65 million people have fled their homes and risked their lives in search of refuge. Most are children, less than half of whom have access to education.

As the world faces its largest refugee crisis since World War II, Linda's long-term refugee advocacy is ongoing and has served as a model for other communities beginning to develop similar volunteer programs.[29]

Shabnam Modgil, UN Radio Voice for DUNA

Shabnam Modgil received the International Woman of the Year Award, with Patrick Madden and Nelda Reid, 2012.

Longtime dedicated volunteer for the Dallas Chapter of UNA, Shabnam Modgil often featured an official UN radio news segment, mixed in with news and other reports during her hosting of the regular weekday "Morning Show" on FunAsia Radio, through both its AM and FM broadcast frequencies.

Keeping the community informed about all activities of DUNA, she also interviewed visiting dignitaries on the air, as well as local UNA-USA leaders. FunAsia Theaters in Richardson, Texas, has also periodically shown movies related to UN goals and activities.

[29] Compiled by Bill Matthews, edited by Linda Abramson Evans, 2017.

As the CMO of FunAsia, she arranged for the restaurant to serve as the venue for many UN Day events and other activities, at a reduced cost or often with no charge. It was also the favored location for many routine DUNA chapter board and other high-profile program meetings.

Tatiana Androsov presented DUNA's 2015 "Appreciation" to Shabnam Modgil

Shabnam served on the board of DUNA for many years, among her many civic responsibilities in the Southeast Asian community. She received the Woman of the Day award during the special 2012 International Women's Day in Dallas, and DUNA recognized her with a Special Appreciation award in 2015 for her years of faithful service.

Authors' note: Shabnam was elected president of the DUNA Chapter in 2017.[30]

---

[30] Compiled by Bill Matthews.

Nelda and David Reid, 2010–2017

Nelda was raised in the United Methodist Church and was active in United Methodist Women, which sparked an interest in social justice, global issues, and human rights. Nelda first became involved in the Dallas chapter of the UNA as a result of her activities in the Dallas Peace Center. Through the DPC, she met Jan Sanders and Norma and Bill Matthews. Responding to their invitation, she and David attended UN Day dinners and other special events, and they began to identify with the UNA Mission. Soon after September 11, 2001, Nelda joined a dialogue group of Christian and Muslim women to explore common ground and support each other in life's journeys.

In 2002, she was part of a thirteen-member delegation of United Methodist Church Peace with Justice coordinators. The delegation visited Israel and Palestine to better understand both sides of that issue. She was a speaker for church and university groups over the next two years. Her involvement in global issues had definitely begun. During this time, she began her teaching career as an ESL teacher, again relating to the plight of international students, many of whom had struggled in their home countries due to poverty, war, and violence.

During this time, David was working at Texas Instruments, serving for twelve years as a TI vice president and ethics director. As a global business executive, David traveled extensively. With numerous business trips to Asia and Europe, David was experienced working with TI employees, corporate partners, and government officials at various TI locations worldwide. Throughout his travels, David became interested in the various cultures, governments, and perspectives of the local populations.

DUNA Board members Shabnam Modgil, David Reid, Nelda
Reid, Norma Matthews, Linda Evans, Harbans Lal, Beth
Weems Pirtle, and Bill Matthews, at 2015 Dallas UN Day

At the end of 2010, Nelda and David responded to the call to serve
on the DUNA board and served as DUNA Chapter copresidents and
secretary in 2011–2012. From 2013–2017, David was treasurer of the
chapter, and Nelda served as communications chair from 2013–2016. He
was elected president for the 2014–2016 term, giving stellar leadership, and
literally bearing the load of representative responsibilities, providing their
home apartment address and space for the chapter office. To encourage
volunteering by TI employees and retirees, the TI Foundation supports the
organizations where the TI employee or retiree volunteers. David applied
his volunteer hours and received two grants through this program, which
he applied to augment DUNA funds.

Nelda was elected to the National Council of UNA-USA in 2014
and will serve through 2018 as regional representative for the South
Central Region. On the National Council, she served as a member of the
nominating committee and the communications committee. She chaired
the nominating committee and cochaired the communications committee
for the 2016–2018 term.[31]

---

[31] Memoir of service by Nelda and David Reid.

Bill Matthews: My UN Memory Garden
Early Inklings[32]

Bill & Norma Matthews, at UNA-USA 2014

Even from growing up in the remote regions of rural West Texas, my interest in world affairs following the horrors of World War II, prompted my personal fascination with the budding possibilities of cooperative efforts focused on the United Nations. With little sophistication about the process, I became at least vaguely aware of inauguration events in San Francisco and Geneva and then the establishment of headquarters in New York.

Though it would be years before my learning details of the 1948 Universal Declaration of Human Rights, adopted during my sophomore year in high school, experiences with Anglo-Mexican tensions and resolutions in Marfa, Texas, prepared me about the need for growing understanding of interracial, intercultural issues.

My innate "nose for news" grew from writing and editing news in high school, then a radio speech major in college, during which international news included frequent references to United Nations activities. Focusing later on practical ministries emphasis in seminary studies and church gravitated toward "Church and Society," with human rights issues attracting my particular attention.

---

[32] Personal memoir of Rev. Bill (J.W.) Matthews.

First Direct Exposure to the UN

Developing an interest in social structures through college and seminary years included our first visit to New York in 1963, as my wife Norma and I included a tour of the UN headquarters in a family trip. The next year, 1964, we were more substantively exposed to United Nations operations during training for overseas missionary service, which also included studies and experiences to develop broader cross-cultural understanding. A six-week broadcasting internship with Riverside Radio WRVR in New York City during the "long, hot summer" took a strong civil rights turn through their extensive coverage of civil rights challenges.

International Connections

Our assignment to Manila, Philippines, for work with broadcasting, 1965–69, encompassed development concerns in a third-world context that accelerated my appreciation for the expert resources of United Nations agents and agencies such as UNESCO, WHO, and UNDP. Within our limited news resources for the nonprofit National Council of Churches Broadcasting Network based in Manila, the staff soon discovered compatible and informative friends in these UN agencies who would feed freely into our concerns so we could broadcast reliable analysis and education about social and economic issues being faced by the so-called "common tao," the local people living at the most basic levels of their needs.

Applying so-called "appropriate technology" in the situations faced by our associates became a guideline for the types of work we adapted and applied, to best serve the needs we met. Learning to listen to indigenous informants as prime sources for planning and programming was invaluable to the successes we may have achieved.

Our second assignment to serve in over twenty South Pacific islands while based in Fiji afforded even wider exposure to the importance of working toward practical solutions, such as the multiple use of limited agricultural land. For example, in the isolated island of Niue, three crops were cultivated on single plots of plantation—with pineapples near the ground, papaya trees at middle height, and tall coconut palms producing their adaptable fruit on the top level. Nutritious vegetables were planted interspersed on the ground level.

Through the auspices of United Nations educational opportunities, village women received training in various South Pacific Commission programs for learning simple animal husbandry with chickens and eggs, about raising pigs, and vegetable crops that could sustain family nutrition and health. Oil barrels salvaged and cleaned after a diversity of WWII uses were split and filled with dirt to preserve soil that could grow a variety of edible vegetables, saving the dirt from washing away in frequent rains.

Finding UNA Back in the United States

Soon after our 1973 rotation from missionary service back to the US to Dallas, Texas, our overseas experiences with UN agencies prompted me to search in order to remain engaged. Learning about the United Nations Association of the USA, I discovered the Dallas Chapter, first joining in 1974.

Although we attended several board meetings, other job responsibilities precluded my active involvement at that time. Moving out of town, we lost touch until our return to Dallas in 1979 when I resumed occasional contact with the Dallas chapter board.

Interactions with persons of like mind in peaceful pursuits, health promotion, human rights advocacy, gender equality, and education inspired me to greater involvement. Volunteering for programs and attending multi-cultural events provided further stimuli.

After 1997 retirement as communications director of a large church, the then president of the Dallas chapter, Beth Weems Pirtle, approached me about serving as editor of a newsletter for UNA Dallas. Agreeing somewhat reluctantly, nevertheless we generated the UNA Dallas "Viewsletter" for the next ten years on a quarterly basis, with occasional time lapses.[33]

Volunteer Leadership Opportunities Grew

Meeting regularly for information purposes with the board as editor, I was then elected president in 2002 for a two-year term. Motivated to become more familiar with the overall organization, my wife Norma and

---

[33] Some issue covers may be seen in the appendix of this history.

I first attended the national UNA-USA conference in June 2003, which we have continued through 2015.

As Ms. Pirtle rotated from positions as Texas division president and Central Region representative to the Council on Chapters and Divisions (CCD) of the UNA-USA, I was elected to fill those places in 2006, 2008, and 2010, continuing through 2015.

Present from DUNA at 2014 National UNA-USA Advocacy "Day on the Hill" were Tas Islam, Tatiana Androsov, Norma and Bill Matthews, Rachel Sherman, and Teta Banks (Houston)

Affiliation of the UNA with the United Nations Foundation in 2012 led to realignment into the four-state South Central Region and my election as one of two representative positions, along with Ms. Latha Nehru, for a two-year term. During this period, three chapters were active in Texas, two in Oklahoma and one new chapter in New Orleans.

Several efforts to connect with a previously active chapter in San Antonio were unsuccessful. We had brief interest from a student association at West Texas State University in Canyon, Texas, which did not apparently continue after a year.

Visits to the chapters in Austin, Houston, and Oklahoma City seemed productive for greater understanding of our roles in advocacy and organization.

As titular head of the Texas division during these years, I sought to maintain e-mail and telephone contact with the twelve to twenty-three members who were geographically widely separated. There seemed to be low interest in their possible affiliation with other chapters or for attending joint meetings with other members.

Although it was recommended, we did not organize a board for the division, only designating Norma Matthews as treasurer. Due to low financial activity, bank charges became untenable for our small nonprofit account purposes, so we petitioned and agreed with the Dallas chapter to merge funds into one account, tracking the small deposits to Texas division, with a spreadsheet line item for identification purposes.

From the national perspective, both local and division funds are identified within one EIN by the Better World Fund, which precluded our distinct filing with IRS after 2012. This eventuated in subsequent revocation of nonprofit exemption for the Texas division. Funds received since then are endorsed and deposited into Dallas UNA-USA account to validate their gift intention as nonprofit donations.

DUNA members Matthews and Reid families at 2011
CTAUN with Teta Banks, Anne-Marie Carlson

We personally shared in conferences of CTAUN—the Council on Teaching about United Nations in New York, Austin, and Dallas, particularly since Norma retired from public school teaching but has continued to volunteer to represent United Nations information and education concerns in the Dallas Chapter and in her church commitments.

Connections Continued Commitment

With national officer elections of 2014, Bill rotated off the UNA-USA Steering Committee, as Nelda Reid and Teta Banks were elected as South

Central Region representatives. He was invited to observe without vote in the 2015 meetings as continuing president of the Texas Division.

Conferencing by phone, the three are exploring options for further organization and programming in Texas and the region as of this writing, summer 2015.

Bill and Norma Matthews Lifetime Achievement
Award from UNA-USA, 2016

To our great surprise, we were encouraged to attend the 2016 Leadership Summit of UNA-USA, when we were notified that we would jointly be accorded the Lifetime Achievement Award for this year. As a longtime team together, we were greatly honored to receive such signal affirmation for our ongoing commitment to the causes of human rights, justice, and peace.

The latest joint venture by the Matthews has been to research, compile, and write this book, *Hope Over Fear*—a history of the Dallas chapter of UNA-USA, after discovering that no such documentation of its more than sixty years of existence had been published. We have been inspired by the dedication of those who went before, sustained by our colleagues in the causes with their counsel and advice, and deeply gratified by the interest generated to illuminate the ongoing saga of "Hope over Fear."

CHAPTER 7

Texas Division, United Nations Association

Purpose

The Texas Division was established as an educational organization about the United Nations, formed to develop an understanding of the UN and to support the position of the US Government as related to the international organization. (Statement reported in a *Dallas Morning News* article, 3-1-65.)

Section 8: Divisions [definition from Standard Operating Procedures, CCR of the UNA-USA 2013]

- UNA-USA Divisions support the activities of UNA-USA Chapters within a designated state, section of a state, or chapters in contiguous states. A Division is expected to help strengthen Chapters in its designated area but does not have authority over those Chapters. Divisions may organize or coordinate programs, projects, advocacy activities and events to promote the mission of UNA-USA and work with Chapters to build their membership. A Division board of directors shall include representatives from the Chapters in its designated area and is responsible for fostering communication among these Chapters. Divisions may elect officers, adopt bylaws, and have a treasury. Divisions must have at least three Chapters in good standing (DUNA Archives).

Reports from Texas Division Records

DMN—3-9-63, 5-2-63, 8-18-66. Three articles: Raymond Nasher, president Texas (division) of the United Nations Association, comprising 13 chapters in cities of Texas. Some details are in timeline capsules, chapter 5 (*DMN Archives*).

1963, March 9. Mrs. John T. Sutcliffe, Southwest Regional field director of the American Association for the United Nations, served a 4-state area including Texas, Oklahoma, Louisiana, and Arkansas, the sixth region in the nation. Office will be at 3526 Cedar Springs, Dallas (*DMN Archives*). (NB: No reports or records have been found *DUNA Archives*.)

1965. First Texas Division Conference, Holiday Inn Central, Dallas. Delegates came from eight Texas cities.

1965, February 24. Joseph J. Sisco, deputy assistant secretary of state for International Organization Affairs, will be the main speaker during a one-day conference of the Texas Division of the United Nations Association.

- Morning and afternoon workshops will be conducted by Ms. Estelle Linzer, executive assistant to the executive vice president of the UNA. She will present discussions of the model chapter in the UNA-USA (*DMN* and *DUNA Archives*).

1965, March 1. Officers of Texas Division are Nasher as chairman of the Texas Division Board from Dallas, with other officers from Fort Worth, Tyler, and Houston.

- 70 delegates attended from 12 cities that have chapters (13 reported in 1966), including Austin, El Paso, Lubbock, and San Antonio among others.
- Judge Sarah T. Hughes was chosen as honorary chairman of the board. Jack Goren succeeds Raymond Nasher of Dallas as division president (*DUNA Archives*).

- (NB: Further research in Dallas Public Library Archives may yield additional reports and notes for the intervening years.)

1991, March 16. Minutes of Texas division board meeting, Houston, Texas.
President Shirley Quisenberry, Houston; Beth Huddleston, Richard Sloos, Dallas; G. Doyle, Vincent Maggio, and Phineas Washer, Houston.

- Reported 162 UNA members at large (not related to a chapter) in Texas. Treasurer transferred from Dick Sloos to Vincent Maggio balance $1,499, later reported $1,723 on 3-22-92, nominating committee named (*DUNA Archives*).

1992, March 28. Minutes of Texas division board:

- Treasurer's report showed balances for 1992, $1,974; 1994, $2,429; income from UNA USA for grants and dues shares, $1,866, included UNA Grant to Houston, $750; interest, $125; total $2,741; enthusiasm for HAMUN, statewide mock UN Assembly.
- With sixty members in Austin area, advisory proposals to activate chapter, likewise questions about similar situation in San Antonio. Beth Huddleston elected president beginning October; she also agreed to review by-laws of division.
- To celebrate UN fiftieth anniversary in 1993, president noted grants available to local chapters from UNA USA up to $1,000, applications due by May 15 (*DUNA Archives*).

1993. Undated memo from Huddleston reported a request from Dallas chapter president Nadine Bell for two projects, $250 each for third annual human rights expo and a newsletter, depending on Division funds available (*DUNA Archives*).

1994, April 6. Agenda for the annual Texas division meeting with chapter reports from Houston, Austin, Dallas, Huntsville update and San Antonio plans. Program ideas, Global Policy project funding from MacArthur Foundation for speakers, UN50—Texas Event listed items (*DUNA Archives*).

1994, June 6. Minutes of Texas division board meeting, Austin, Texas:

- Elected Beth Huddleston president; C. Reed vice president; A. L. Bruner recording secretary; V. Maggio treasurer (*DUNA Archives*).

1995, March 3. Minutes of Texas division meeting, Dallas, Texas:

- Pres. Beth Huddleston, with Cynthia Reed, Vince Maggio, Nadine Bell, and Anna Louise Bruner.
- Treasurer Maggio reported $2,086 balance, $750 expended from UNA-USA grant for Phineas Washer's letter-writing project (San Antonio), approved $100 for chapter-forming effort.
- Additional action approved $100 to each chapter for membership promotion during fiftieth year of UN Efforts reported for "circuit" visit of Ambassador Madeleine Albright to Texas chapters in the fall.
- Other items: letters to legislators on SB5 funding for UN peacekeeping, San Francisco conference, reports on Texas state conference with adult Model UN in September in Dallas, request from National UNA to develop local chapters in relation to community college systems, announced Houston event in May with UN SG Boutros-Boutros Ghali to speak, travel reimbursement 29¢ a mile or flight tickets available on invoiced request to treasurer Maggio (*DUNA Archives*).

1996, February 24. Texas division board meeting:

- Treasurer's report, Vince Maggio, income UNA-USA $881, total $951; expenditures $1,451. Balance '96, $2,316; '97, $1,816 (no other papers in file).
- Dallas chapter "Priority Objectives for 1996" with topic heads for education (Model UN, speaking, advocacy with teachers, Global Policy participation by public); citizen involvement/advocacy (community liaison committee, government relations committee); resource development (membership drives with chambers of commerce, religious institutions) (*DUNA Archives*).

1997, April 7. Minutes of Texas division meeting, Houston, Texas:

- President Nadine Bell recapped previous activities, minutes not available. Chapters reported highlights included in annual reports to UNA. Other items: Impact of Common Core—resource development (outreach to possible markets, upcoming funds campaign by national for $10 millions, local prospects); advocacy (letters to legislators, business connections); education (UN materials into curriculums, cable TV).
- UNA-USA Strategic Directions—seeking greater representation on board of governors, perhaps regional offices, chapters encouraged to send delegates to national conference.
- Chapter activities 1997: seeking national speaker for Houston, Austin, Dallas—Kofi Annan (?). Chapter developments in San Antonio and El Paso, coordination for national fund-raising, buddy system for responsibility support (*DUNA Archives*).

1998. Report in viewsletter of Dallas UNA-USA:

- Mr. Donald Djerejian, founding director of the Baker Institute, Houston, former US ambassador to Syria and Israel, spoke at the Annual Chapter Banquet in Dallas on "United Nations and U.S. Interests" (*DUNA Archives*).

1999, June 11. Manuscript report:
President Anna Louise Brown, vice president Beth Weems Pirtle, secretary Charlotte Karam, treasurer Vince Maggio.

- Reported two viable chapters, Houston and Dallas, hopes to revive Austin and San Antonio; Brown wrote invitation to leaders for Houston staff retreat in January, informational letter to statewide members urging advocacy for HR 1355—UN arrearage legislation.
- Annual report to UNA attached: Finances '98: balance $1,204; income $1,055; expenses $1,119; year-end balance $1,140. Expenses included conference call in lieu of division meeting, travel for president to national UNA-USA, grant to UTD for women's conference *(DUNA Archives)*.

2000, February 19. Minutes of Texas division meeting, San Antonio, Texas:

President Anna Louise Bruner (Houston), vice president Beth Weems Pirtle (Dallas), treasurer Vincent Maggio (Houston), secretary Anita Landenberger (Dallas), in home of Rev. Phineas Washer, San Antonio, with other local guests. Officers agreed to serve another year.

- Bruner reported seventy at-large members in Texas; Houston chapter has 170 members, 20 board members. Efforts to activate San Antonio chapter were discussed, with funding offered; they currently have 18 members.
- Treasurer reported December balance of $1,108, with expenses last year $666 for administration and $200 grant to United Nations Conference on Women at UTD, Dallas, approved $600 travel for president and vice president to attend the UNA-USA conference in June. End-of-year balance: $704. Analysis by treasurer showed reductions of income from national shares, anticipated budget forward of $700 per year (*DUNA Archives*).

2002, April 14. Annual report filed.

- Board president Beth Weems Pirtle, vice president David Griggs, treasurer Anita Landenberger, Dallas, secretary Elaine Talarski, San Antonio.
- Pirtle noted Austin, Dallas, Houston chapters strong, Arlington and San Antonio struggling. Vince Maggio resigned as treasurer, bank account transferred to Guaranty Bank, Addison, Texas. Reported communications with regional representatives, campaigns on elimination of landmines, electronic communications, cooperation with Council on Organizations.
- Financial report: opening balance $458.00; UNA-USA receipts $498.99; expenditures on administration $509.77; closing balance $447.22.
- Kambiz Rafraf from Dallas was central regional representative to the Steering Committee of the Council of Chapters and Divisions of UNA USA (*DUNA Archives*).

2003, March 3. Annual report filed.
Officers continued from 2002. Pirtle noted meeting with Houston board, communications with Austin, Arlington, and San Antonio chapters not viable. Continued contacts with chapters and national UNA-USA.

- Financial report: opening balance $208.25; checkbook balance $447.22; UNA-USA receipts $643; expenditures on administration $613.50; closing balance $684.97.

2004, January. National Membership Report Texas Division: 32 members.

2005, January. National Membership Report Texas Division: 25 members.

   April 4. Annual report filed.
   Officers continued from 2003.

- Bank accounts merged with Dallas Chapter (*DUNA Archives*).

2006, June 10. Texas division received Award for Membership Growth at National Conference UNA-USA.
National Membership Report Texas Division: 34 members (*DUNA Archives*).

2007, January. National Membership Report Texas Division: 22 members.

   March 23. Bill Matthews elected president of Texas division, March 23, 2007 (*North Texas Conference News*).

2010, April 27. UNA USA Central Region Conference, Truman Library, Independence, Missouri, hosted by KC chapter, president Jay Sjerven. Speaker: Edward Elmendorf, UNA-USA president.

- YPIC public meeting "The World Acts to Aid Haiti Earthquake Victims," with panel: Jon North, Heart to Heart Int'l., James Walley, Fort Leavenworth Center for Army Lessons Learned, others.
- Afternoon best practices workshops, caravan to UN Peace Plaza, memorial to deceased UN Peacekeepers (*DUNA Archives*).

2011, 2012. Texas division held no meetings during these years. The positions of president and treasurer were maintained. The president sent occasional e-mails and tried phone contacts with some of the UNA-USA members within the state who were not otherwise related to a local chapter, with few responses.

- Due to widely separated locations, little or no interest was shown in attending the nearest chapter activities. Such "at large" members seemed content only to associate with the organization. Attrition rates were very high, year to year (Texas division president Bill Matthews).

2013, March. Membership report from UNA-USA: 6 members/3 lapsed.

2013, notice from IRS. "Your organization's tax-exempt status was automatically revoked." Due to anomaly of EIN confusion in the relationship with the Better World Fund, the requirement to file annual information report was unclear, thus no filing was accomplished. Funds transfers continued to be managed through the EIN assigned to the Dallas chapter, with local accounting crediting the proper recipient by agreement between the respective treasurers of the Dallas chapter and the Texas division (Texas division president Bill Matthews).

2014, March. Membership report, UNA-USA: 22 members/7 lapsed.

      April. 10 members, all active.
      June. 26 members/5 lapsed.
      December. 17 members/2 lapsed.

2015, May. Membership report, UNA-USA: 25 members/5 lapsed.

      December. Membership report, UNA-USA: 34 members/22 active, 12 lapsed.

2014, 2015. The status of the Texas Division was continued as a placeholder. Due to inactivity within the division as such, the president attempted contacts with leaders in the existing Texas chapters. No compelling desire for joint meetings or conferences was expressed, therefore none were held.

- Consultations continued with the South Central representatives of the UNA-USA CCR, exploring possibilities of reorganization and reactivation of a viable organization. No decision was reached by the end of 2015 (Texas division president Bill Matthews).

CHAPTER 8

Tatiana Androsov, United Nations Staff and UNA Volunteer

A Narrative of Recollections in Her Own Words

Tatiana Androsov, former UN staff, dedicated
advocate and volunteer with DUNA

First Steps toward an Unusual Journey

They say that the journey is important. However, what led to the journey is perhaps even more important. I have started this with the background that led to my journey with the United Nations, as well as parts of that journey, especially because it was not the usual path to the United Nations, nor was the journey itself the usual journey.

The Beginning

There was once a girl who was born in Belgium, just ten days after her parents had crossed the border as refugees with United Nations Relief Organization papers. Her mother, who had been deported to the deep north by Stalin as an enemy of people since her parents were landowners, had subsequently been taken by the Germans when they overran parts of the Soviet Union.

Later, as she was luckily assigned to take care of two children in a German doctor's home, she went through the Allied bombings of Dresden. She took that opportunity to run away and walked all the way to Bavaria where a wonderful farming family took her in and fed her back to life. As my mother always said, there are wonderful people in the worst of places as there are horrible people in the best of places.

Her father had been a Soviet soldier, taken prisoner by the Germans in what she much later learned had been the greatest tank battle of World War II. He, too, had seen the best of the worst, as the Soviet soldiers were deprived of food and drink in the camp they were taken to by the Germans.

After seven days, a group of German mothers came with food and told the head of the camp that if that was the way their sons, now prisoners in Russia, were treated, they would never be able to come back. They, as mothers, could not put up with that. The food was distributed and the camp head started treating the prisoners much more properly. In fact, my father became a driver for them and once in France, as they were stealing salads from local farmers in the night, he ran away and right into the arms of the 3rd American Army. Yes, and being a mechanical engineer he wound up taking care of our U.S. tanks.

Of course, after the war, as the result of the Yalta agreement, he was supposed to be repatriated. He was so happy to go home but, then, on the way discovered from a friend, whom he saw from the truck in which he was driven, that he would be sent to Siberia, as he had dared not to commit suicide when the Germans were coming upon him in that tank battle. You see, every Soviet soldier had signed an oath that he would never let himself be taken prisoner, that if he did, it would be considered treason.

So, my father who did not consider it treason to work with the American Allies, leapt from the truck and from then on went through incredible interrogations, declaring himself a Pole. He signed on to work in the Belgian coal mines so as not to be subject to Siberia.

Hearing about the United Nations

Interestingly enough, the first time I ever heard anything about the United Nations—not the relief agency which had made it possible for my parents to go to Belgium after WWII—was in Ms. Davis's fifth-grade class in Passaic, New Jersey. We had a weekly newsletter, *My Weekly Reader*, and the United Nations was often the first article on the first page.

Well, Passaic, after all, is only fifteen miles from Manhattan so that was perhaps just normal. Then I saw a debate on television on Channel 13, then a new public television station. They used to broadcast the General Assembly gatherings. I saw Henry Cabot Lodge, our ambassador to the UN. I saw all the other countries and the Russians when Kruschev was banging his shoe!

What struck me was that they were talking—irrespective of their differences. They were not killing each other. That made so much sense to me, as I, at the dinner table, especially on Sundays, heard all the horrors of WWII, the horrors of the Stalin era. As an only child, I was not spared any tragic adult reminiscences.

So by the time we all hunkered down in an exercise to avoid the worst of a nuclear weapons strike during the Cuban missile crisis, I knew exactly what I wanted to do—I wanted to be part of those "enemies" who dared to talk with each other in order to live with their differences without resorting to force. I wanted to be part of the United Nations. That was my goal when I went to Mount Holyoke College.

Although I could not major in international relations, I studied as much of world history, politics, and languages (including Chinese) as I could, amassing so many credits in all that in the end, I was forced to stop concentrating on those subjects and later took an introduction to astrophysics as an elective.

After a year in Europe, I came back to the New York area to get a summer position with the United Nations Scientific Committee on the Effects of Atomic Radiation. For six weeks, I substituted for their librarian and learned things that I have since always carried with me, including the knowledge that their skin was checkered, for people who had been wearing checkered clothes, as radiation penetrates different colors to different degrees.

Yet that same somber experience had its wonderful parts, especially because, though I was on the thirty-second floor, we were part of the secretary general's office—the thirty-eighth floor. My administrative officer was Secretary General U Thant's administrative officer, and the thirty-eighth floor was open to us. One of our great Americans was there, too—Ralph Bunche.

This, and a chance meeting and acquaintance with Ambassador Williams, then the head of the Asia Society, led me to become the first student to be accepted into a brand-new international relations program at Fairleigh Dickinson University. That program was headed by Nasrollah Fatemi, an Iranian who had been his country's ambassador to UNESCO during Mossadegh's takeover. Fatemi's brother was the foreign minister, the only person who was killed when the shah came back to power.

Dr. Fatemi, a profound Sufi, had incredible contacts at the United Nations. Thus, many of our courses were actually taught by UN ambassadors and international civil servants. In fact, one of these was Ambassador Rossides of Cyprus, who was so impressed by what I did that he asked me to write some of his speeches for the Sixth Committee of the United Nations, the International Law Committee. Thus, at the age of twenty-three, my words were spoken in that august assembly by the dean of the United Nations Diplomatic Corps—for that was who Ambassador Rossides was.

Almost, but not Quite, "In at the UN"

Yet in spite of this background, when it came to getting a permanent UN position upon receiving my master's degree, I was not among those who were selected. I was a finalist (one of three) for a public relations position at UNESCO, but—and this was explained to me by our US permanent representative to that body, was not chosen because I was a single young woman, one on whom they would "waste" time and money, only to have me leave when I married and had children.

Oh yes, they could be very blunt in those days and do things that they would not even dream of today. This was 1973. The same happened with a position at UNIDO in Vienna.

There was only one way out, and that was to become a simultaneous interpreter. With Russian, French, and English as native tongues, something that had its pros and cons, I went to a very small school in England run by Pat Longley, who had been the first chief interpreter at UNESCO.

When the UN examiners came to test us at the end of seven months in stiff six-day-a-week training, they stopped me in the middle of an interpretation in which California played a role. The reason? I had suddenly switched from a completely British accent to an American one. I still made it to Geneva and acquired a "mid-Atlantic" way of speaking.

Interpreting Years: 1974–79

Being a simultaneous interpreter was quite an experience. My colleagues came from different places—Latin America, Europe, Asia, even Africa. There were two groups—the original simultaneous interpreters, the ones nearing their retirement, and the new bunch.

The chief interpreter, Basil Yakovlev, was among those who had started simultaneous interpretation. A Frenchman of Russian aristocratic lineage, he had been in the group that had used new technology at the Nuremberg trials to try this new technique, one that avoided the loss of time inherent in consecutive interpretation. Pat Arztrouni was another. His father had fled to France with twenty cars from the communist takeover in Russia.

No, I did not fit in. I was not an aristocrat—worse, I came from the second immigration, the one after World War II.

Interpretation had brought a state of well-being to these people, and they were thankful for that. They prided themselves on their knowledge of words, their ability to interpret subjects they knew very little about and actually cared very little about. They had their own little world. They gathered together for parties.

Of course, that was not my interest. I was interested in the subjects that I interpreted—well, some of them. I must say that the types of potatoes that were planted in the Economic Commission for Europe did not exactly excite me. I liked mines—my poor father had worked in one for nine years and I loved the one on cars—the heights of fenders will always remain in my memory. The Italian delegate, Poggi, whose language was colorful, would say in a version of French (Italian was not an official language), "How can you expect a Ferrari to have the same fenders as a truck?"

In fact, as my wonderful chief, Basil, used to say, I was great at some subjects and absolutely lousy at others. Whenever he wanted people to cry for some horrible event that had occurred or some commemorative celebration, he would send me, as I rose to the occasion and made the interpretation as moving as the original.

The younger interpreters were wordsmiths and hung around together. I ran and played tennis but played tennis at the Reserve, an exclusive hotel, and not the UN tennis club. I skied but not on weekends with UN groups. I went away for at least a week at a time and did it with people outside of the United Nations.

In my first year, we had an incredible conference in Bucharest, the first world population conference. It was the time that the world's population had reached the four billion mark and scientists were warning about the effects of overpopulation and resource depletion. This was the time right after the issuance of the Club of Rome's book *Limits to Growth*. The delegates from Latin America objected, saying, "How can we rely on people in their fifties and sixties? We need young people in their twenties and thirties."

Romania was incredibly poor, and a group of us—this time I was with other young interpreters—decided to take a train to go to the countryside. We were happily installed in a compartment in first class but for some reason had to go through the corridor. As I did, a young man with walking sticks lunged at me and bit me in the arm. That was my first encounter with what real anger and frustration can do. On the other side of the scale, there was a grand reception with Ceausescu when the tiny dictator came up to me and kissed my hand. I was dressed like a Roman in my own creation of a toga.

And then there was Jaap von Arendung, the number two of the newly created United Nations Population Fund team. As always, interested in the subject, I wound up with those—including the lady Pakistani head—who dealt with the issues. This would be the first of many times that I would wind up with what for interpreters was the wrong side—that is, those actually dealing with the world's challenges.

The same happened when I went to Nairobi for a world UNCTAD (United Nations Conference on Trade and Development) conference in 1976. That was a memorable gathering with more government ministers per square meter than any previous conference in the world. I wound up being asked by the Zorin, the Soviet representative, to take part in a special closed session meeting between what were then Group B (the Soviet Union and Eastern Europe) and the Group of 77 (the developing countries). This was to work on a document and not to be an interpreter. The head interpreter from Geneva for that conference had to agree and did so most reluctantly.

There was also another minor clash. My dear friend by now, Lisa, and I had pooled our per diem together and gotten a great room at the renowned Stanley Hotel. Well, Secretary General Waldheim was also there, and he objected to the fact that mere interpreters were on the same floor as he—giving us horrible looks as we accidentally got into the same elevator.

Yet the most memorable event during that mission was a side trip to Ethiopia. Six of us went—young and no interpreters, but three UN and three International Red Cross workers. We had been told not to do it because it was dangerous, but we went.

This was 1976. A plane took us from Addis Ababa to Lalibela, the place of rock-hewn churches in the north. It was in a retrofitted B-52 bomber, a leftover from WWII. Our host was a burly but smiling man, who barely fitted in the aisle. We flew in the middle of the day, very low over desert with pockets of different air temperatures slightly bouncing us up and down in wavelike fashion.

Suddenly we heard a scream, and all turned back. The rear door had opened. We were terrified. Our hefty host simply walked up the aisle and ordered the fear-paralyzed passenger in the row closest to the door to hold him, the host, by the waist. He then stretched and brought the door back in. In the meantime, more than a couple of airsickness bags had been opened and filled. No, not mine.

We landed some time later in the "airfield," a kind of very large flat piece of land with some grass and chickens. We were led to our hotel—kind of concrete minimalist bungalows, but at least a roof over our head.

We went to visit "a school"—a teacher with a stick tracing letters in the ground while children sat on the dirt watching. I looked into a pair of eyes. Flies were swarming around. A belly was protruding—kwashiorkor (severe protein-energy malnutrition). I wished I had something to give. Why hadn't I thought of bringing pencils, pens, and paper? I gave some things I had, but this sight and all the steps we took in town just deepened the ache in my belly.

We went to one of the churches, the cathedral, hewn into the depth of the land, descending into rock and coolness. A priest was officiating at the altar, a man in rags, just like everyone else there. "That is the bishop," our guide told us. The bishop? And I am staring at him—I am well dressed, well fed. How does he know that I am a fellow human being?

Slowly I started walking toward him in the aisle. The service was finishing, and he was holding the cross. "He is my brother," my mind said. Slowly I went up, crossed myself, and kissed the cross—our common cross, the suffering of humanity, the suffering we needlessly impose upon each other. He looked at me and reached out.

Except for holidays and visits in other religious places, I had not been to church in years, hurt by cultural attitudes that had nothing to do with the Almighty. That day made it clear. A bridge had been built, and the bishop became our guide, leading us to places where the official guide could not have gone.

But before that, as we walked out, we were faced with a vision from thousands of years ago—yes, another man in rags, but this one a leper with a leprous cat beside him. Time had been frozen here. We had gone to the moon, but here in Lalibela, we were back in the Bible era.

There was a war going on, one that was at this point not really being talked about. The people in Asmara, Muslims, wanted their independence. Even we were caught in it, first because there was literally almost nothing to eat. We had strong dark coffee and greasy, sweet donut-like bread—that was it, but so much better than what anybody else had. We went to bed in dirty sheets on what really could not be called a mattress, and I fell deeply asleep, just as I still do.

I was woken up by shouting and banging on the door. My next-door neighbor, one of the Red Cross group, was trying to come in. I opened the door. "Can't you hear it? Bombing!"

We were caught in crossfires with nothing we could do. She came in and could not believe I had been sleeping. She wanted at least to stay together. She hunkered down on the floor. I don't think she even covered herself. I fell asleep again. When in the morning, with everything quiet, she asked how I could do that, my answer was "What can we do, we don't even know where it is safe. At least sleeping, we can think better if and when we get up." I learned that night that I could take this.

But the whole experience was not over. Back in Addis, a lanky, tall Algerian was waiting for me. A government minister who was at the UNCTAD meeting in Nairobi, one of the FNL that had fought for independence against the French, had said that before I left, that he would take me to the slums of Addis when I came back. I thought it was just talk. It was not.

We actually had tea with a large group in the middle of human efforts to make the best of detritus. And if you wonder why I was so treated, well, there was a famous Tanya in those days—Che Guevara's love—and the fact that I bore her name opened many doors.

Coming back to Nairobi, the luxury of the Stanley, and the high-level government officials, I made my decision. I would do everything I could to go into some real UN work. From that day on, I considered that I could not remain a very well-paid parakeet—for interpreters hear but cannot do.

Noteworthy Things before I Left Interpretation

One was a memorable five-year six-week annual summer stint as a preferred interpreter with the International Law Commission. These were men who highly respected each other in spite of great differences in approach and goals. Of course, they included great international lawyers from the United States, USSR, Great Britain, and France, but also outstanding, incredibly qualified individuals from other countries, including New Zealand, Peru, and Afghanistan. One of the consistent topics that were discussed from year to year was what international obligations were carried forward by countries irrespective of government changes. This was where even a comma had to be interpreted.

And of course, I wound up having coffee with them, discussing particular meanings, being part of some of their wonderful social gatherings, for these men and their wives were friends. One day, I inadvertently called from the interpreter's booth Tabibi, the Afghan delegate, "Habibi." In the hall during coffee break, the guys laughed and I added, "But I am not his 'habibiti'" and that shocked all of them, for I had pointed out in Arabic that I was not his "beloved."

One of the members of the group was Casteñada of Mexico, whose son, my age, was a friend of all the girls in what was then the "new section" of the Palais des Nations in Geneva. It was funny seeing Jorge (the son) years later on television when he had become the foreign minister of Mexico and then for some time an expert on all matters relating to Mexico.

But the most striking event was a lovely flirt—no, not with me. One summer, my mother visited and wound up coming with me to our evening social gatherings. One of these great minds, a widower, a very handsome man, just could not get enough of my mama's company. I literally had to watch over her for the benefit of my father.

Yet it was how I finally made the giant step to leave that stands out. One day, Hikmat Nabulsi, the first head of the then newly formed United Nations volunteers and a close neighbor, asked if a friend of his could stay in my apartment while I was on mission in Africa. I was very particular—my one bedroom was an oasis.

Tatiana Androsov with the first Executive Director of UN Volunteers, Hikmat Nabulsi, in Geneva, 1977; she in white dress, he's identified with mustache

"Hikmat," I said, "you know me. If I find anything out of place, I will be upset." "This friend is as bad as you," he answered, laughing.

"All right," I agreed. Hikmat had asked me to talk to women volunteers and advise them how to dress, as too often they did not understand cultural and religious differences. He had pointed out one day, "The bus driver almost drove us down a deep gulley as he could not take his eyes off the knees of our new recruits! What am I to do?"

When I came back, the apartment was as perfect as I had left it and a present had been set precisely on my modern Italian glass-topped dining room table. "Eugene said that you should not be an interpreter. With the books you have, you should be with us." Eugene was Eugene Youkel, the director of personnel of the United Nations Development Program.

At Fletcher: 1979–1981

Just a bit over a year later, in September of 1979, I was at the Fletcher School of Law and Diplomacy.

Oh yes, one of my last missions was in Hamburg, Germany, where the Law of the Sea was adopted. Should I have become an international law specialist??

Off to school again! Think that it would really be nice at my age now, at sixty-seven, but I was thirty-one with a career behind me and a 1924 red Porsche to show for it—my very own, with the color I had ordered from the VW/Porsche people themselves, my guys at the Safety of Vehicles office in the Economic Commission for Europe, complete with the tan interior that no one else had!

But I was going back to a dorm—yes, the full experience.

I felt very old compared to most of the students, though only five or six years separated me from the majority. Actually, a good 10 percent were older. What none had was the world behind them, knowledge of things spoken and unspoken, things that are not even here in this short overview. And that knowledge weighed upon me, as it does to this very day.

It was also obvious to many of my professors, a few who went as far as saying to my roommate (actually apartment mate) that they were happy I was not taking their classes. Of course, there were some with whom, with a blink of an eye, a look—unshared words sped like waves from face to face.

The unspoken was shared with tokens—in one case a box of wonderful cigars.

One thing I was sure of, and carried out—that I would not choose development or security as one of the "fields." I actually chose public diplomacy. In those days, that was something to literally laugh about. We were in the Cold War, and playing out nuclear strikes and their effects was one of the favorite "war games" on the Fletcher campus. Edward R. Murrow's School of Public Diplomacy only had three pupils from my class of over a hundred. But that was my choice—one I will never regret!

Yes, "secret diplomacy" has always had, and will always have, a place; but knowing how to reach people openly, how to get people to understand the challenges that the world faces is far more important, for the power of the weak should not be underestimated. It rises and falls like waves in the ocean, and like waves in the ocean, when the weak have had enough, those waves gather strength and momentum and sweep all illusions of power away.

One of my professors, Rosemary Rogers, understood me so well that she used me literally as a coteacher in her class, one on communications between different peoples and cultures. Unfortunately, Rosemary did not live for many years afterward, as she was carried away by cancer.

A most interesting thing that happened at Fletcher was that I got to sit beside or close to Henry Cabot Lodge a couple of times—yes, the very Lodge whose presence on television as our ambassador to the United Nations first caught my imagination. Although much older, his bearing was still that of a real diplomat and brought to mind the old New England saying, "The Lodges only speak to the Cabots and the Cabots only speak to God."

An interesting thing happened my second year—the United Nations Development Program sent a recruiter to Fletcher. I was not even told about it, but the recruiter asked specifically for me. Eugene Youkel, the director of personnel, wanted me back in the system.

I actually thought about Citibank and went as far as having an interview. However, here they sent me to a woman vice president (a rarity at that time) who told me that I would have to cut my hair and wear less-defining suits. My suits were simply well-cut European suits, most of them actually made by my mother and me. For me, the request went much too far.

In September of 1981, I was back in the United Nations system in the second "class" of the newly devised management training program.

Management Training, United Nations Development Program: 1981–1982

It was actually known as the administrative training program at the time. Among others, I kept pointing out that it would be better to call it a "management training program." However, they did not listen, at least during our "class year."

There were twenty-five of us, from countries ranging from Canada to Turkey, with rather different backgrounds from those with some previous in-house experience, to those with national service to unusual cases, like a lady lawyer from France. The program was not only thorough, but it really taught those coming in the workings of the United Nations system as a whole. It lasted from September to September, with the last three months being practice in the field. We literally learned from ninethirty in the morning until five thirty at night with, of course, an hour's break at lunch. Besides that, we had specially prepared "socials" and were encouraged to attend many others.

What was really unusual in the program, and here I compare it to the Citibank program that my best friend from Fletcher was undergoing at the same time, was that we really started in the basement and went up all levels of the system. Yes, we were sent to the basement of the United Nations where the diplomatic bags came in and hauled them, unsealed them, and went through them personally. We also swept the floor. The people who actually did the job, at the very "lowly" general service levels of the organization, judged us. We were in the garages, the cubicles where cleaning materials were held.

Down the line expecting to become "resident representatives" in any one of the more than a hundred countries with UNDP offices, we were shown the enormous bottom part of the iceberg that kept the top officials in their suits in their spacious quarters. Though destined for the top, we would know every part that supported it, from knowing how to personally fill every paper form and thus to properly judge the contributions made by each of those working with us. At least that was the hope.

Of course, we had real classes where we not only learned the history, the financial system, the administration, the changes, and the hopes of the organization, but also the reasons behind them. And we worked next to the big offices, with the regional directors smiling at us, getting reports from their assistants, as they the directors would be "vying" for the best among us for our first assignments.

I loved it, all except the socials. This was a very special time, the waning years (they did not know it) of the hedonistic life of the '70s in so many places. I must admit that I was shocked by the alcohol and the drugs. After barely hauling the French lawyer to a sofa in my studio, I stopped going to anything but the most restrained gatherings.

Do not think that had a positive effect. Although I was told by both Eugene and the head of the program that I was the best, and though they discussed having me and another person skip the first administrative post and become an assistant resident representative, they finally decided to treat everyone the same way. But there was more, as they decided to send the famous lady lawyer along with me to Madagascar, the place I so coveted for the three months of onsite training. They said, "You can take care of her." I refused! I was sent to Senegal. She went to Madagascar.

Interestingly, almost the minute I arrived in Senegal, the then administrative officer announced that he was going on a two months' vacation. Thus, instead of getting more training, I was doing the job. No problem.

I had my first experience of death. One of our experts, a young Belgian, had gotten drunk, taken his motorcycle, and fallen on a curve on the way back. It rained that night. He was taken by hypothermia. I had to go to the morgue and then to witness his body being sealed in a steel coffin.

A couple of years before as an interpreter, I was sent to a hospital in New Delhi for an additional vaccination. I had run away. Now, duty bound me to the sights and the smells of something we would have not even dared call a hospital in any Western land. I stood and, then at home, had an extra glass of wine with my fish.

For there were marvelous things in Senegal, including the seafront road on which I jogged, the market that I loved, and Mamadou, my manservant, who prepared the best of food. There were trips to towns in the north, dirt roads that I had missed while at Fletcher and New York, the caravan of camels as we crossed into Mauritania, the desert. As I write, I miss it. I miss the air, the time past, the still half-colonial atmosphere, and most of all the smiles as I walked into the office, the wonderful people trying their best in their own way.

Another Watershed Time: Women Had Tough Choices: 1982–1983

Since this is a UN biography, I have not delved much into my very personal life. Actually, I wrote a novel instead, *Choices*, one which I hope I will be able to publish as I think today's women need to understand not only what those of their mothers and previous generations often went through, but because they should see what so many women still face today.

I was posted to Cameroon as the UNDP's administrative officer. It started in a very funny way. When I arrived in Douala, the seaside city which at that time had the international flights, I was not let through in spite of my UN diplomatic passport. Why? Well, at that time, a certain Andropov headed the then Soviet Union and my last name, Androsov, made them make a mistake. They thought I was a relative!

After two hours in a booth, where they were most polite and made more than one phone call, they realized that I was just this weird person born in Belgium of mixed Eastern European heritage and an American to boot! They welcomed me and sent me on my way to Yaounde, the capital.

For me, it was a beautiful city, with red earth and green hills in the background. I got a wonderful apartment with a giant living room—I mean giant—overlooking those hills. Besides, it was on the fourth and top floor of the building, high enough for the overwhelming majority of mosquitoes and cockroaches not to make it—they were just too lazy!

That was not true office in the office building. Except for the downstairs offices housing the resident representative (UN coordinator), the deputy and the national officer, it was a mess! On top of that, the man I was replacing, an Alexandrian Greek recruited during the Congo mission that saw the death of Hammerjhold, was still there and refused to leave. He had his wife chauffeured in a UN car by one of the drivers. He was doing exactly what we had been trained to stop and not to do! And the accounts and stuff in the closets was another mess! You opened a door and there was a tire—yes, a tire—that was crawling with cockroaches! The downstairs closet, the one no one opened, was a paper dining room for the same beasties.

The resident representative, Blanch-Soler, an intelligent, cultivated man with great understanding of the problems facing developing nations, never went upstairs and certainly did not open the closet. His words were, "Well, let him do something until he retires in about nine months."

The Greek, grumbling, was moved to the other side of the second floor while I moved to what had been his office. Of course, it started with clearing and cleaning, but very slowly, as one never knew what kind of important piece of paper was to be found among the garbage. Luckily, I had a wonderful secretary whose office next to mine was very tidy and well organized. I also had a great accountant, an American from Delaware who had married a local man. She was a treasure—tall, imposing, dressed in local garb, with a big smile and absolutely impeccable skills with figures. She was actually the opposite of the secretary who chose French-type clothes and spent her summer vacation in France.

But the best was my sweeper with a twinkle in his eye, seemingly just as old as the Greek, but with a different take on life, happy to have someone who actually appreciated his work and really needed his help. To this day, I have his lucky charm, a local wooden "elf."

Even today, so many years later, as I write, I know that I disappointed these very special people. Had I stayed longer, I truly could have changed more things.

To try to compensate for my great disappointment, Blanche-Soler let me be the program officer for a television project. Cameroon was going to start having television, but instead of limiting it to its capital and perhaps having another broadcast point in the port city of Douala, it was going to have enough repeaters to cover the whole country immediately. The project team consisted of a special bag of Italians, Yugoslavs and a Belgian, the first two basically because not only did they have the experience with repeaters, but also they did so in countries full of hills and mountains, just like Cameroon.

Even our office had its famous two floors because it was built into a hill. The second floor led out to the back entrance directly onto a road. The mango tree on the side of the building sprung at the level of the first floor, and from our piece of grass outside our second floor door, we could reach out to pick the fruit.

But having one project could not compensate for my disappointment at having too little to do. When I complained to headquarters, they told me "have a good time," but that was not my character. Yes, I signed up for the American tennis club, where I spent most of my lunchtimes between tennis, Jane Fonda workouts (that was the era), and reading a novel a day.

On Saturday mornings, when he was there, Blanche-Soler and I would go through the diplomatic pouch and read the newspapers and talk about the world situation. Once in a while, I would go for a day or two outside into the country to see the work being done on the repeater stations. Once, out of curiosity, I went to see a local healing plants project.

Another time, having noted that one project had been going on for years without any actual progress, I went into the jungle and actually descended down into the mine that was part of it. Doing that, I nicked my knee pretty badly and had to rush back to Yaounde to have it treated at the Seventh Day Adventist's clinic. I actually discovered the reason for the unending project. It required diamond bits for boring through the rocky soil, and those were being replaced much too often.

Of course, again, I just could not "have a good time," being completely uninterested in the local expatriate social life, with its intrigues and its romances. One of my television team wound up with a divorce as a result of his involvements. A colleague from school was one of the first waves of those with the "slim" disease—yes, the horrible very first years of AIDS. I saw him and could not believe it was he. He died shortly after.

One of my rare evenings out turned out to be very special. Our local national program officer and her husband took me along to see a local play, *Mr. Newrich*. Yes, it was about a newly rich Cameroonian. I was the only one with white skin in an auditorium of over a thousand people and, yes, was stared at from every side. The play was hysterically funny, and in spite of being rather uncomfortable, I started laughing, literally roaring along with the rest. My neighbors as they roared turned to me and their neighbors to them. All of a sudden we were all one, as together, we realized that human foibles tend to be the same throughout our little globe. I was adopted—I was one of "them."

When Personal and Professional Create an Impasse: 1982–83

It may seem from what I have written so far that I might not have had a rich private life. To the contrary, it was too rich.

First, I had wonderful very special parents. Immigrants to Belgium and then the United States, they had never really adapted to an independent life in this country. They were dependent upon me, their only child. They never really learned the language, the culture, or the customs. They gave me everything they could as far as an education was concerned, but it was understood from the very beginning that I would take care of them in turn.

My father had just turned seventy when I was in Cameroon and faced cancerous polyps in his intestines. My mother was six years younger. I had thought that they would come to visit me, but there was no possibility of that. My mother was demanding that I return home to help her take care of my father. When I said that I had just been posted and could not do that, she insisted with long letters and crying on the phone. "Get a transfer!" she demanded. And she wanted a posting close to them, that is, New York or somewhere in a "normal" country, that is, Europe. This was before computers, before great connections. The best I could do was a phone call a week from the central Yaounde post office or a phone call I would pay for from the office. I wrote long letters, too.

And then there was my fiancé, a young man I had met at Fletcher. By the time I had left for Cameroon, we had known each other for over two years. He had always insisted that he would be more than glad to follow me, as my career had more potential, and he, due to past experience, could find something in any place I went to. But all of a sudden, he changed and said that the woman follows the man. The world has changed since then, and more and more men are following their wives without shame. That was not the case in 1983.

I caved in, basically to my parents because I knew that they would literally fall apart. Do I regret it? No, but I still feel guilty about leaving that office and not sticking it out, in spite of all the challenges.

Besides, through a miracle, I was not going back to nothing. I had gotten an interview at the UN's Food and Agriculture Organization's headquarters in Rome.

On the way there, I stopped for two weeks to be with my fiancé, now stationed in Istanbul. I realized that what was perfect when we were students just did not mesh in the world beyond, that his tastes and style of living had nothing to do with mine. In Rome, a new world literally opened itself up to me. My parents would certainly love to come there, I mused. Happily, I boarded the plane to New York.

Years passed and Rome and FAO will have to wait for another time and another space, as the opening of a special period years later comes on.

The Cat Was Taking on Another Life

In the spring of 1989, Ambassador Paul Marc Henry, who was Paul Hoffman's (the Marshall Plan) closest collaborator and with him the cofounder of the United Nations Development Program, chose me to be his "teammate" for a giant preliminary study mission to Africa, one requested at the highest levels.

Tatiana Androsov with Paul Marc Henry on
UNDUGU Mission in Uganda, 1989

The mission was based on the river, road, and railroad systems that then tied together the central part of Africa as well as they could (badly) remember, leaving out South Africa at the time. Our mission was to improve those systems so that there could be real linkage and development through the heart of the continent. We traveled from Egypt down through Uganda and Rwanda and across through Zaire. The study was also to see if we could use the one great natural inexhaustible potential in Africa—the Inge Dam at the end of the Zaire River. If properly managed with grids, it could not only supply great parts of the continent with "green" energy, but also with a tie-in to provide green electricity to Europe.

I still have that report, UNDUGU (in Swahili means "brotherhood" or "fraternity"), even now on my computer because it was acclaimed but accomplished only one thing—the report's significance influenced the election of Boutros Boutros-Ghali as UN secretary general. It could have changed development in Africa—but now that can only be part of a book on what could have been. Yes, I am the coauthor, Paul Marc having insisted on that although I was his junior. I was for him what he had been for Paul Hoffman.

Tatiana Androsov reviewing the UN Peacekeeping troops
in Nampula Province, Mozambique, summer, 1993

Continuing . . . for the United Nations

Cats do have nine lives and, so what am I doing now in Dallas as the Dallas UNA advocacy chair?

Yes, years and stories fill the time between 1989 and now. My stories continue—of France, the breakup of Yugoslavia, Cambodia, South Africa, Mozambique, the Global Forum of Spiritual and Parliamentary Leaders on Human Survival, and the Thanksgiving Foundation. Each one could be a book, and yet it is UNDUGU and the great unfulfilled promise of a continent and the great unfulfilled promise of a world that could be, if we all worked together for it, that keeps me striving at age sixty-eight for the United Nations.

A population of seven and a half billion people, with diminishing resources, and ever- growing aspirations, the only possible road is cooperation between people and nations. We may fight it and actually do so in conflicts that continue to increase, our refugee rolls exacerbate our unwillingness to accept the other as their ways rub against our own, but we will all have to accept each other if we are to survive and perhaps even prosper.

Henri Laugier, French Under Secretary General, with Eleanor Roosevelt, at Human Rights Commission first session, 1947

I advocate because I, just one little person, stand on the shoulders of giants, the people I have talked about, and others like Henri Laugier, the first French undersecretary general, and the one who, with First Lady Eleanor Roosevelt, opened the first session of the Human Rights Commission, a man who wrote a book on being a citizen of the world, as well as one's country. He was my Pierre's godfather. Oh yes, another story. For you see, the girl who came into Belgium as a refugee in her mother's womb wound up with those who had been instrumental in starting the UN, and to her last breath will be dedicated to continuing their work.

2015 DUNA Summer Seminar and Social in Tatiana Androsov's Garden

When the Dedication Intersects with the Personal

Just a bit of that story, one that deserves a whole book. Paul Marc wound up in the hospital having to have his old hip replacement, full of infection, replaced with a new one. There was fear for his life, and through the Washington bureau chief of one of the French television channels, I learned that he wanted to see me. Air France let me fly to Orly Airport as a member of his family. When I got there, a man holding a Le Monde, was waiting for me. Not tall, not handsome, with a moustache, and a deep profound, soothing voice—Pierre Ganem.

My appointment at the hospital was in the afternoon, and it was French lunchtime, breakfast time in New York. I was very hungry and indicated that to Pierre, whom I had been told was very close to Paul Marc, a professor working on a book on the effects of transnational project agreements on international law. We went to a *bistrot* and I ordered "steak et frites." "Ca se voit que vous etes quand meme restee un peu belge," said Pierre, smiling. (One can see you're still a bit Belgian.) I smiled back as I chewed. When coffee came, Pierre asked if he could smoke a cigar. Oh yes, those were the days when one could still do so in a restaurant in France. "Why not, if I can have one, too!"

Pierre is on the left, Paul Marc's Danielle on the right. It is the fall of 1992. I am visiting from Cambodia and Vaison la Romaine with Seguret, and have just gone through the worst floods in more than a half a century

He told me months later that he had been struck by what I wore when he saw me coming through—a safari suit. His father, Andre Ganem, "eminence grise" (the brains) of the French ministry of foreign affairs, had always worn one when traveling. The French delegate to the UN's Fifth Committee until almost the end of his life, he was the one who had brought Paul Marc to that ministry. And when I asked for that cigar, Pierre fell in love. Of course, I did not for a long time and only started to look at him as more than a friend when coming back to visit Paul Marc around Christmastime. I fell sick with the flu, and Pierre brought homemade soup and a soft, warm sweater as I lay, looking horrible, in the guest room sofabed.

The little refugee girl, brought to Belgium in her mother's womb then as a child to New Jersey, wound up with the son of one of those who had helped create and build the United Nations system, in a world where Picasso was a poor painter in the 1910s who depended upon what people like Henri Laugier would buy from him, a world where reality still created books, and potentially world-changing ideas came from those around the dinner table.

As I sit here, Pierre's book, *Securisation contractuelle des investissements internationaux*, graces the shelf of my study. Unfortunately, he is no longer there to make me laugh or our cat Diva to make me crumple paper into a ball to toss as we sit, each in front of our respective computers in our living room overlooking "le parc Montsouris." Pierre passed away from an aneurism just several weeks after Paul Marc's burial in Seguret in March of 1998.

Ambassador and Alice Pickering hosted Tatiana Androsov in New York, 1990

I carry on the UN and family tradition with Laika, my part-time dog, on the other side of my desk in Dallas, Texas.

Tatiana Androsov, May 10, 2016
Advocacy Chair, DUNA

Tatiana makes her point as Advocacy Chair of DUNA, 2015

CHAPTER 9

Teaching about the United Nations in Texas

The United Nations and Textbooks

In this chapter, the authors present some of the issues in the United States dealing with the United Nations and American social studies textbooks at the junior/senior high school level, basically grades seven to twelve. After the horrific attacks of September 11, 2001, public interest in "American foreign policy and the international system, the world beyond the United States, and the role of the UN as prime mover in the global community" rose significantly.[1]

Even though there was strong support for the United States and the UN, knowledge of what the UN actually does and how it works was woefully lacking among Americans. Textbooks are part of the problem, says William H. Luers, president and CEO, UNA-USA, in the 2002 book *Textbooks and the United Nations* by Gilbert T. Sewall, American Textbook Council.

When "essential information on how the international system works gets left out of textbooks, Americans are brought up with little awareness of the role of multilateral institutions in the advancement of democratic ideals and economic stability worldwide."[2]

---

[1] Gilbert T. Sewall and William H. Luers, "Textbooks and the United Nations: An Education Report of the United Nations Association of the USA, The International System and What American Students Learn About It" (United Nations Association, 2002), foreword & 5.

[2] Ibid., foreword & 6.

To correct these omissions, the American Textbook Council, a private research center in New York City, was commissioned by the United Nations Association to do a study and report on the findings of the inclusion of goals teaching about the UN in American high school social studies textbooks. President Luers stated that Americans need to know how the world works and about the broad reach of the UN system, the UN role in keeping peace, fighting poverty, protecting the environment, helping to save lives and societies following national calamities, human rights, health, education, and building democracy. With this knowledge, our educational institutions would produce citizens better equipped to function in "an increasingly interdependent world."[3]

Why the United Nations Is an Important Topic

The U.N. is important because the work of its decision-making and implementing institutions is everywhere, often invisible, working behind the scenes, vitally important as an agent of order, protection, and (sometimes) human improvement. The U.N. and its related agencies have become nerve centers of international politics, organizing responses to political and economic crises, and holding states accountable for serious violations of such law. In a major transformation of international relations since 1945, the U.N. has been at the center of the growing field of international agreements and law, trying to govern everything from information transfer, trade access, and prescription drugs to nuclear terrorism and the conduct of war itself.

The notion of "international community"—a term now widely accepted as normal usage among foreign policy specialists, academics, and the media—represents a dramatic development of the past several decades. It implies that a political system capable of debating and voting on expressions of the will of this international community is possible and to be desired.[4]

---

[3]   Ibid.
[4]   Ibid., 22–23.

The authors have not done an in-depth study of UN teaching goals in American social studies textbooks, and this is beyond the purview of this book. However, we are acutely aware of the need for reform on this topic. Because of our involvement in the local Dallas Chapter UNA-USA, we are aware of the lack of accurate knowledge about the UN among the ordinary citizens.

Norma Matthews taught school in the Dallas Independent School District for several years and after retirement worked part-time with the Dallas County Schools from 1998–2014, working with the TEKS, the Texas Essential Knowledge and Skills. These published goals were the essential knowledge and skills that every student is required to master in Texas before graduation.

There was a serious deficiency of information about the workings of the UN in the TEKS during this period. In fact, there was opposition even to teach about the UN coming out of the Texas State Board of Education. Furthermore, much of the information disseminated from the State Board of Education was erroneous, as can be seen from the following sample entries in this chapter.

Experiential Learning Applied in Model UNs

By contrast, many teachers have discovered and used experiential Model United Nations programs, where students assume positions of responsibility to role-play actual United Nations functions in meetings of mock assemblies, with leaders and national representatives studying and debating actual issues, reflective of the UN in action.

These activities often extended through much of an academic year, culminating in a several-day conference involving several schools together. The MUNDO (Model United Nations Dallas Organization and GEMUN) Global Elementary Model United Nations programs have been carried on in the Dallas area and nationally for many years, from the 1990s through the present. Volunteer support from school teachers and administrators enables students to experience the challenges and problem-solving approaches employed by functionaries in the UN.

Global Classrooms Offer Deeper Study

UNA-USA offers a more structured pattern through *Global Classrooms*, an innovative educational program that engages middle school and high school students in an exploration of current world issues through interactive simulations and curricular materials. *Global Classrooms* cultivates literacy, life skills, and the attitudes necessary for active citizenship.

At the core of *Global Classrooms* is Model United Nations, wherein students step into shoes of UN Ambassadors and debate a range of issues on the UN agenda. For over 60 years, Model UN has thrived in highly selective high schools and colleges—institutions with the resources to match a strong student interest in world affairs. Prior to 2000, when *Global Classrooms* was created, students in economically disadvantaged public schools rarely had the opportunity to participate.

Even though the Model UN, GEMUN, and Global Classrooms programs have been successful in many schools, not all schools in Texas offer these opportunities. If there were strong requirements in the TEKS and basic social studies curriculum about the UN, that would mean that all students would have the opportunity to learn about the workings of the UN rather than just the schools that offer the Model UN, GEMUN, and Global Classrooms events.[5]

---

[5] "Global Elementary Model United Nations," *Global Elementary Model United Nations*, n.d., http://www.unol.org/gemun/.

United Nations Education Issues: Samples from Texas Sources
Sampling of online searches, March 31, 2015

"Rewriting history? Texas tackles textbook debate," CBS/AP News report, September 16, 2014[6]

In 2010, while approving the history curriculum standards that this year's round of new books are supposed to follow, conservatives on the board required that students evaluate whether the United Nations undermines U.S. sovereignty and study the Congressional GOP's 1994 Contract with America. (http://www.cbsnews.com/news/rewriting-history-texas-tackles-textbook-debate/)

Texas Freedom Network: Religious Right Watch review of the 2014 Texas GOP Platform, various textbook proposals

"The party also opposes U.N. Agenda 21, which has been cited by far-right activists as a ploy to hand over U.S. sovereignty to foreign entities. (P-34)"

"And in one of the most absurd platform planks on the United Nations, the party makes reference to a discredited rumor on ownership of the Alamo. In October 2013, an email circulated by the president of the San Antonio Tea Party implied that management of the Alamo would be handed over to the United Nations.

The claim was quickly debunked by the Texas Land Office and by Land Commissioner Jerry Patterson, then a Republican candidate for lieutenant governor. In reality, all the United Nations did was name the Alamo a World Heritage Site that should be protected and preserved. Still, the baseless claim of a U.N. takeover of the Alamo made its way into the Texas GOP platform. (P. 35)" (http://www.tfn.org/site/PageServer?pagename=issues_religious_right_watch_2014_TXGOP_briefing_paper)

---

[6] "Rewriting History? Texas Tackles Textbook Debate," *CBS News*, September 16, 2014, http://www.cbsnews.com/news/rewriting-history-texas-tackles-textbook-debate/.

"Conservative Texas Lawmakers Target United Nations," *Texas Tribune*, February 26, 2015[7]

In the latest effort by conservatives to fight what they see as overreach by the United Nations, two Texas Republican lawmakers have filed legislation aimed at a nonbinding plan for sustainable development that the United States and more than 100 other countries SIGNED in 1992. The plan is KNOWN as Agenda 21, and it seeks to encourage governments to promote ENVIRONMENTALLY FRIENDLY development such as preserving open spaces and discouraging urban sprawl.

The identical bills proposed last week by state Rep. Molly White of Belton and state Sen. Bob Hall of Edgewood would choke off state and municipal funding—including money from public universities—to organizations "accredited by the United Nations to implement a policy that originated in the Agenda 21 plan." The anti-Agenda 21 proposals come on the heels of a national conservative outcry, with similar legislation being considered in statehouses across the country. (Only Alabama has successfully passed it so far.)

Critics say Agenda 21's basic tenets—especially those promoting PUBLIC TRANSPORTATION for denser communities—are a threat to private property rights and states' sovereignty. White said her bill would protect Texas from a "global agenda" propagated by "a handful of unelected, unaccountable people." (http://www.keyetv.com/news/features/top-stories/stories/conservative-texas-lawmakers-target-united-nations-24414.shtml)

On another front,[8]"Defending the Alamo—from a UN takeover," March 6, 2015, Jim Hightower Lowdown website

Wait . . . didn't the Battle of the Alamo take place in 1836? And didn't the Alamo fall to Santa Anna's army—with Davy Crockett, Jim Bowie, John Wayne, and nearly every other defender being killed?

---

[7]   Neena Satija and Ryan McCrimmon, "Conservative Lawmakers Target United Nations," *The Texas Tribune*, February 26, 2015, https://www.texastribune.org/2015/02/26/conservative-lawmakers-continue-assault-un/.

[8]   Jim Hightower, "Defending the Alamo—From a UN Takeover," *The Hightower Lowdown*, March 6, 2015, https://hightowerlowdown.org/podcast/defending-the-alamo-from-a-un-takeover/.

Yes. But you history buffs, preservationists, and aficionados of the absurd will be glad to know that the battle continues in Texas today. One lone state senator has risen to re-defend the Alamo—not from the Mexican government this time, but from the ferocious invading forces of the United Nations. Sen. Donna Campbell, a tea party Republican from Pluto, startled even her far-right Republican colleagues by introducing a bill to ban any foreign ownership of the Alamo, warning darkly that it is in danger of falling to the UN.

What spurred Sen. Campbell to rush to the barricades was a news item that United Nations Educational, Scientific, and Cultural Organization (UNESCO), is considering including the Alamo as a World Heritage Site. That would place it on a small and very prestigious list that includes the Statue of Liberty and the Grand Canyon. It's an honor, noted her colleagues, who also pointed out that the state owns the iconic structure and that the heritage designation doesn't alter that ownership at all.

Moreover, they added, being a heritage site has proven to give a big boost to tourism and jobs.

Another fellow Republican observed that no Texas politico would even think of selling such a chunk of state history. "I'm trying to figure out what problem we're trying to solve here," he said gently to her. But the learned senator had an answer for that: "Anything that starts with 'the UN' gives me cause for concern." (http://www.jimhightower.com/node/8565)

For more "insights" on political attitudes—this from a generally sympathetic source[9]

"It's time to knock the Trans-Pacific Partnership off the 'Fast Track.'
"New trade pacts create secret, pro-corporate tribunals that use their powers to eviscerate our democratic laws.

"When I was just a tyke, my momma warned me not to eat anything unless I knew where it came from. Sensible advice—so good that even Congress has acted on it.

"In 2002, responding to public demand, lawmakers decided that you and I have a need and a right to know where the meat sold in supermarkets

---

[9] Jim Hightower, "New Trade Pacts Create Secret, pro-Corporate Tribunals That Use Their Powers to Eviscerate Our Democratic Laws," *Hightower Lowdown*, January 5, 2015, https://hightowerlowdown.org/article/tpp/.

comes from. Thus, Congress enacted a simple and straightforward law called COOL (Country Of Origin Labeling), requiring meat marketers to tell us right on their packages whether the enclosed steak, pork chops, lamb shanks, chicken wings, etc., are products of the USA, Mexico, China, or Whereintheworldistan. There's more, about the WTO and administration complicity in the moves." (*Hightower Lowdown online January, 2015 edition* (http://www.hightowerlowdown.org/tpp)

And from Hightower's post of 2/15/2015 "Wither the tea party?"[10]

Foremost on today's tea party agenda is a full bore assault on something that isn't even there: A United Nations' plot to destroy American life and establish a UN dictatorship. Yes, the same international debating society that the right wing used to mock as meek and weak is presently being recast as a fearsome totalitarian behemoth stealing our sovereignty.

The UN's weapon is a piece of paper titled Agenda 21. This is a series of non-binding UN recommendations to encourage sustainable economic growth in developing nations through voluntary actions. It's an innocuous document with zero force behind it, passed way back in 1992 with the support of Republican President George H. W. Bush. Some threat.

But in recent months, Agenda 21 was lifted from obscurity and turned into a foaming-at-the-mouth cause by the far-out right's nattering nabob of nuttiness, Glenn Beck. So Beckian flakes are rushing to the barricades waving the tattered tea party banner to, by God, defend America from this . . . well, from this piece of paper." (http://www.hightowerlowdown. org/node/3242)

And from the NEA, about Texas textbooks: Controversial changes may be in store for your textbooks, courtesy of the Texas state school board[11]

History, Winston Churchill famously said, is written by the victors. Don McLeroy no doubt agrees.

---

[10] Jim Hightower, "Wither the Tea Party?," *Hightower Lowdown*, January 22, 2013, https://hightowerlowdown.org/podcast/wither-the-tea-party/.

[11] Tim Walker, "Will Texas Decide What's In Your Textbook?," *NEA: National Education Association*, accessed June 18, 2017, http://www.nea.org// home/39060.htm.

McLeroy is a dentist from Bryan, Texas, a self-described Christian fundamentalist, and an outgoing member of state school board of education (SBOE). Over the past year, McLeroy and his allies formed a powerful bloc on the 15-member elected board and pushed through controversial revisions to the statewide social studies curriculum.

"Sometimes it boggles my mind the kind of power we have," McLeroy recently boasted.

"To many Texans, however, what's more mind-boggling are some of the revisions. Critics charge that they promote Christian fundamentalism, boost conservative political figures, and force-feed American "exceptionalism," while downplaying the historical contribution of minorities.

Rita Haecker, president of the Texas State Teachers Association, believes the year-long review process deteriorated into a political and divisive spectacle.

"The circus-like efforts of right-wing board members," Haecker said, "to impose their own religious and political beliefs on the public school curriculum have been and still are a national embarrassment.

"The standards will guide textbook purchases and classroom instruction over the next decade—and maybe not just in Texas. National publishers usually cater to its demands because the school board is probably the most influential in the country. Texas buys 48 million textbooks every year. No other state, except California, wields that sort of market clout."

(http://www.nea.org/home/39060.htm)

Perhaps no further comment is necessary, save to say that the educational impact of Texas standards carry influence far beyond the decisions of the Texas State Board, often restricting historical integrity that seriously affect the balances of equanimity in public education.

CHAPTER 10

Afterword, Soles in the Sand: How the UN Applies Spiritual Principles to Benefit Humanity

MDG Momentum poster, UNA-USA 2015

What are the ways that spirituality applies to daily living? Although boundary lines often blur between the traditional separation of church and state, of faith applied to life, our thinking remains confused. Full disclosure: my career has been committed to service as a practical theologian, not as a statesman or politician. Yet I have increasingly experienced a strong sense of desire to apply my convictions to actions, from the heart to the head to public advocacy.

> He who attempts to act and do things for others or for the world without deepening his own self-understanding, freedom, integrity, and capacity to love, will not have anything to give others.[1]

Richard Rohr follows with, "Too many reformers (social activists) self-destruct from within. For that very reason, I believe, Jesus and great spiritual teachers first emphasize transformation of consciousness and soul."[2]

One proof of living out religious tenets translates spiritual convictions into direct actions that apply universal human rights to world situations. This is best embodied in the comprehensive works of the United Nations. More than just "Boots on the Ground," the United Nations performs principles practically parallel to the beliefs of all major religions. "Soles in the Sand" embody benefits for the whole of humanity by addressing the primary needs of God's people in all the world.

Symbolic hymn words apply the challenge. "God send us people (men *sic*) whose aim 'twill be, not to defend some ancient creed, but to live out the laws of Christ (faith – sic) in every thought, and word, and deed."[3]

Our choir anthem recently was "As I went down in the river to pray, studyin' about that good ol' way and who shall wear the robe and crown; good Lord, show me the way!"[4]

---

[1]   Thomas Merton and Lawrence Cunningham, eds., *Thomas Merton: Spiritual Master: Essential Writings* (Mahwah, NJ: Paulist Press, 1992), 375.

[2]   Richard Rohr, *Everything Belongs: The Gift of Contemplative Prayer* (The Crossroad Publishing Company, 1999), 73–75.

[3]   Frederick J. Gillman, *The Methodist Hymnal* (Nashville, TV: Board of Publications of The Methodist Church, Inc., 1964), 191.

[4]   *Down in the River to Pray* (Morningstar Music Publishers, Birnamwood Publications, 2009).

Soles in the Sand or Souls in the Sand! Despite the amazing maze of its organizational complexity, the UN manages to apply a soul model of Matthew 25:35–36 to the so-called "sandy" beach fronts of the world, as they work together in so many ways to literally feed the hungry (nutritional advances, emergency food); to slake the thirst of the thirsty (develop healthy water resources); to welcome the stranger (refugee shelters); to clothe (and protect) the naked; to heal the sick (immunization, eradication of polio, malaria, HIV/AIDS); and to "visit" prisoners of injustice (human rights, rule of law).

While the Universal Human Rights, so well advocated by the work of Eleanor Roosevelt, defined mandates for societal and cultural fulfillment in practical humanistic terms, the innate spirituality of all sentient beings provides a wholistic, gestalt foundation for all reality.

Spiritually related principles personify prime tenets that pertain to virtually every major religion in every culture, as reflected particularly within the Hebrew Bible, the New Testament, and the Qu'ran: "So in everything, do to others what you would them do to you."[5]

Souls in the Sand represents the myriad manifestations of caring, compassionate commitment to the well-being of people for the whole of humanity throughout the entire world of nations.

Robust and respectful exchanges of ideas at UN conference tables effectively avoid the destructive horrors of war, where conflicts among

---

[5]   *Holy Bible*, New International Version NIV (http://biblica.com/, 1973), v. Matthew 7:12.

so-called winners and losers have inevitably resulted in unconscionable collateral casualties. Ballots beat bullets in the interchange of mutual desires and concerns among the family of nations, as they extend with nonviolent passion to affect the lives of real, respected, and vitally valued human beings.

Primary, basic values are established in the Preamble to the Universal Declaration of Human Rights:

> Whereas the peoples of the United Nations have in the Charter reaffirmed their faith in fundamental human rights, in the dignity and worth of the human person and in the equal rights of men and women and have determined to promote social progress and better standards of life in larger freedom.[6]

Mothers and children awaiting medical care through UNICEF, one Millennium Development Goal addressed in the 2000-2015 program

The MDGs (Millennium Development Goals) adopted by the UN in 2000 set eight targets for fulfillment by the year 2015. Significant successes were attained in every area although much more remains to be done. And

---

6   "Universal Declaration of Human Rights," *Wikipedia: The Free Encyclopedia*, November 27, 2016, https://en.wikipedia.org/wiki/Universal_Declaration_ of_Human_Rights.

now a much greater multilateral process supports a new set of Global Goals or SDGs (Sustainable Development Goals), which were determined after worldwide participation, through open polling and voting. These have now been refined and applied for the next period between 2016 until the year 2030 and beyond.

Proposals from millions of inputs from around the world were solicited, submitted, and compiled into seventeen areas that then were consolidated and proposed for Global Goal solutions. As the world's largest democratic assembly, the UN thrives on participation by the smallest alongside the greatest nations to accomplish common objectives, working through to peaceful consensus that was previously nearly unimaginable except by violent, irreconcilable conflict.

> People across the world are looking to the United Nations to rise to the challenge with a truly transformative, peaceful agenda that is both universal and adaptable to the conditions of each country, and that places people and planet at the center. Their voices have underscored the need for democracy, rule of law, civic space, and more effective governance with capable institutions; for new and innovative partnerships, including responsible business and effective local authorities; and for a data revolution, rigorous accountability mechanisms, and renewed global partnerships.[7]

The dynamic possibility that humanity can indeed work together to meet the greatest needs of people in all the world stimulates our minds, bodies, and spirits, to cooperate with the decisions and join efforts through the United Nations to fulfill global goals for the ultimate benefit of us all.

Rev. Bill (J. W.) Matthews
May 2017

---

[7]   www.post2015hp.org/the-report/.

Appendix

Adoption of the Universal Declaration of Human Rights
Eleanor Roosevelt, Drafting Committee Chair

The Universal Declaration of Human Rights (UDHR) is a declaration adopted by the United Nations General Assembly on 10 December 1948 at the Palais de Chaillot, Paris. The Declaration arose directly from the experience of the Second World War and represents the first global expression of rights to which all human beings are inherently entitled. The full text is published by the United Nations on its website.

The Declaration consists of thirty articles, which have been elaborated in subsequent international treaties, regional human rights instruments, national constitutions, and other laws. The International Bill of Human Rights consists of the Universal Declaration of Human Rights, the International Covenant on Economic, Social and Cultural Rights, and the International Covenant on Civil and Political Rights and its two Optional Protocols. In 1966, the General Assembly adopted the two detailed Covenants, which complete the International Bill of Human Rights. In 1976, after the Covenants had been ratified by a sufficient number of individual nations, the Bill took on the force of international law.

Precursors to UNDHR

During World War II, the Allies adopted the Four Freedoms—freedom of speech, freedom of religion, freedom from fear, and freedom from want—as their basic war aims. The United Nations Charter "reaffirmed faith in fundamental human rights, and dignity and worth of the human person" and committed all member states to promote "universal respect for, and observance of, human rights and fundamental freedoms for all without distinction as to race, sex, language, or religion."

When the atrocities committed by Nazi Germany became apparent after the war, the consensus within the world community was that the United Nations Charter did not sufficiently define the rights to which it referred. A universal declaration that specified the rights of individuals was necessary to give effect to the Charter's provisions on human rights.

Creation and Drafting

The Declaration was commissioned in 1946 and was drafted over two years by the Commission on Human Rights. The Commission consisted of 18 members from various nationalities and political backgrounds. The Universal Declaration of Human Rights Drafting Committee was chaired by Eleanor Roosevelt, who was known for her human rights advocacy.

Canadian John Peters Humphrey was called upon by the United Nations Secretary-General to work on the project and became the Declaration's principal drafter. At the time, Humphrey was newly appointed as Director of the Division of Human Rights within the United Nations Secretariat. The Commission on Human Rights, a standing body of the United Nations, was constituted to undertake the work of preparing what was initially conceived as an International Bill of Rights.

British representatives were extremely frustrated that the proposal had moral but no legal obligation. (It was not until 1976 that the International Covenant on Civil and Political Rights came into force, giving a legal status to most of the Declaration.)

Broad Representation

The membership of the Commission was designed to be broadly representative of the global community, served by representatives from the following countries: Australia, Belgium, Byelorussian Soviet Socialist Republic, Chile, Republic of China, Egypt, France, India, Iran, Lebanon, Panama, Philippines, United Kingdom, United States, Union of Soviet

Socialist Republics, Uruguay, and Yugoslavia. Well-known members of the Commission included Eleanor Roosevelt of the United States (who was the Chairperson), René Cassin of France, Charles Malik of Lebanon, P. C. Chang of the Republic of China, and Hansa Mehta of India. Humphrey provided the initial draft which became the working text of the Commission.

Despite the central role played by the Canadian John Peters Humphrey, the Canadian Government at first abstained from voting on the Declaration's draft, but later voted in favor of the final draft in the General Assembly.

The draft was further discussed by the Commission on human rights, the Economic and Social Council, the Third Committee of the General Assembly before being put to vote. During these discussions many amendments and propositions were made by UN Member States. According to Allan Carlson in Globalizing Family Values, the Declaration's pro-family phrases were the result of the Christian Democratic movement's influence on Cassin and Malik.

Adoption

On 10 December 1948, the Universal Declaration was adopted by the General Assembly by a vote of 48 in favor, none against, and eight abstentions (the Soviet Union, Ukrainian SSR, Byelorussian SSR, People's Federal Republic of Yugoslavia, People's Republic of Poland, Union of South Africa, Czechoslovakia, and the Kingdom of Saudi Arabia). Honduras and Yemen—both members of UN at the time—failed to vote or abstain.

South Africa's position can be seen as an attempt to protect its system of apartheid, which clearly violated any number of articles in the Declaration. The Saudi Arabian delegation's abstention was prompted primarily by two of the Declaration's articles: Article 18, which states that everyone has the right "to change his religion or belief"; and Article 16, on equal marriage rights. The six communist nations abstentions centered around the view that the Declaration did not go far enough in condemning fascism and Nazism. Eleanor Roosevelt attributed the abstention of the Soviet bloc nations to Article 13, which provided the right of citizens to leave their countries.

Universal Declaration of Human Rights
Official Document

Preamble

Whereas recognition of the inherent dignity and of the equal and inalienable rights of all members of the human family is the foundation of freedom, justice and peace in the world,

Whereas disregard and contempt for human rights have resulted in barbarous acts which have outraged the conscience of mankind, and the advent of a world in which human beings shall enjoy freedom of speech and belief and freedom from fear and want has been proclaimed as the highest aspiration of the common people,

Whereas it is essential, if man is not to be compelled to have recourse, as a last resort, to rebellion against tyranny and oppression, that human rights should be protected by the rule of law,

Whereas it is essential to promote the development of friendly relations between nations,

Whereas the peoples of the United Nations have in the Charter reaffirmed their faith in fundamental human rights, in the dignity and worth of the human person and in the equal rights of men and women and have determined to promote social progress and better standards of life in larger freedom,

Whereas Member States have pledged themselves to achieve, in cooperation with the United Nations, the promotion of universal respect for and observance of human rights and fundamental freedoms,

Whereas a common understanding of these rights and freedoms is of the greatest importance for the full realization of this pledge,

Now, therefore,

The General Assembly,

Proclaims this Universal Declaration of Human Rights as a common standard of achievement for all peoples and all nations, to the end that every individual and every organ of society, keeping this Declaration constantly in mind, shall strive by teaching and education to promote respect for these rights and freedoms and by progressive measures, national and international, to secure their universal and effective recognition and observance, both among the peoples of Member States themselves and among the peoples of territories under their jurisdiction.[1]

United Nations
Universal Declaration of Human Rights

Simplified Version

This simplified version of the 30 Articles of the Universal Declaration of Human Rights has been created especially for young people.

1. We Are All Born Free and Equal. We are all born free. We all have our own thoughts and ideas. We should all be treated in the same way.
2. Don't Discriminate. These rights belong to everybody, whatever our differences.
3. The Right to Life. We all have the right to life and to live in freedom and safety.
4. No Slavery. Nobody has any right to make us a slave. We cannot make anyone our slave.
5. No Torture. Nobody has any right to hurt us or to torture us.
6. You Have Rights No Matter Where You Go. I am a person just like you!
7. We're All Equal before the Law. The law is the same for everyone. It must treat us all fairly.

---

[1] "Universal Declaration of Human Rights," *Wikipedia: The Free Encyclopedia*, November 27, 2016, https://en.wikipedia.org/wiki/Universal_Declaration_of_Human_Rights.

8. Your Human Rights Are Protected by Law. We can all ask for the law to help us when we are not treated fairly.

9. No Unfair Detainment. Nobody has the right to put us in prison without good reason and keep us there or to send us away from our country.

10. The Right to Trial. If we are put on trial, this should be in public. The people who try us should not let anyone tell them what to do.

11. We're Always Innocent Till Proven Guilty. Nobody should be blamed for doing something until it is proven. When people say we did a bad thing, we have the right to show it is not true.

12. The Right to Privacy. Nobody should try to harm our good name. Nobody has the right to come into our home, open our letters, or bother us or our family without a good reason.

13. Freedom to Move. We all have the right to go where we want in our own country and to travel as we wish.

14. The Right to Seek a Safe Place to Live. If we are frightened of being badly treated in our own country, we all have the right to run away to another country to be safe.

15. Right to a Nationality. We all have the right to belong to a country.

16. Marriage and Family. Every grown-up has the right to marry and have a family if they want to. Men and women have the same rights when they are married and when they are separated.

17. The Right to Your Own Things. Everyone has the right to own things or share them. Nobody should take our things from us without a good reason.

18. Freedom of Thought. We all have the right to believe in what we want to believe, to have a religion, or to change it if we want.

19. Freedom of Expression. We all have the right to make up our own minds, to think what we like, to say what we think, and to share our ideas with other people.

20. The Right to Public Assembly. We all have the right to meet our friends and to work together in peace to defend our rights. Nobody can make us join a group if we don't want to.

21. The Right to Democracy. We all have the right to take part in the government of our country. Every grown-up should be allowed to choose their own leaders.

22. Social Security. We all have the right to affordable housing, medicine, education, and childcare, enough money to live on and medical help if we are ill or old.
23. Workers' Rights. Every grown-up has the right to do a job, to a fair wage for their work, and to join a trade union.
24. The Right to Play. We all have the right to rest from work and to relax.
25. Food and Shelter for All. We all have the right to a good life. Mothers and children, people who are old, unemployed or disabled, and all people have the right to be cared for.
26. The Right to Education. Education is a right. Primary school should be free. We should learn about the United Nations and how to get on with others. Our parents can choose what we learn.
27. Copyright. Copyright is a special law that protects one's own artistic creations and writings; others cannot make copies without permission. We all have the right to our own way of life and to enjoy the good things that art, science, and learning bring.
28. A Fair and Free World. There must be proper order so we can all enjoy rights and freedoms in our own country and all over the world.
29. Responsibility. We have a duty to other people, and we should protect their rights and freedoms.
30. No One Can Take Away Your Human Rights.[2]

Dallas United Nations Association
By-Laws (Revisions adopted 09/28/2010)[3]

Article 1: Name & Affiliation

The name of this organization shall be the United Nations Association of the United States of America, Incorporated, Dallas Chapter, also known as UNA-USA, Dallas Chapter.

---

[2] "United Nations Universal Declaration of Human Rights Summary: Youth for Human Rights Video," accessed June 18, 2017, http://www.youthforhumanrights.org/what-are-human-rights/universal-declaration-of-human-rights/articles-1-15.html.
[3] DUNA Archives, Dallas United Nations Association.

Article 2: Purpose & Function

The United Nations Association of the United States of America (UNA-USA) is a nonprofit membership organization dedicated to building understanding of and support for the ideals and work of the UN among the American people. Its education, policy and advocacy programs emphasize the importance of cooperation among nations and the need for American leadership at the UN. UNA-USA is affiliated with the World Federation of United Nations Associations, which began in 1946 as a public movement for the UN.

The purpose of the Association, as expressed in its national charter is:

To heighten U.S. public awareness and increase public knowledge of global issues and their relation to the United Nations system

To encourage, where appropriate, multilateral approaches in dealing with these issues

To build public support for constructive U.S. Policies on matters of global concern

To enhance the effectiveness of the United Nations and other international institutions

To actively solicit funds and membership to achieve these goals.

We are dedicated to educating, inspiring and mobilizing Americans to support the principles and vital work of the United Nations, strengthening the United Nations system, promoting constructive United States leadership in that system and achieving the goals of the United Nations Charter.

Article 3: Membership

Categories

Individual or Family membership is open to any United States resident. Membership in the National U.N. Association links to the local, and to the state or regional division, if any.

Member Organizations

Open to local units of national organizations in the Council of Organizations and to other local groups supporting the purposes of UNA-USA.

Service fees and voting rights of an organization carries one vote within the chapter, determined by the chapter board of directors.

Sponsors and Patrons

Honorary—positions awarded in recognition of community service or other acts of merit.
Financial—recognition of companies and philanthropists who support UNA-USA, Dallas Chapter.

Meetings and Events

There shall be at least one Annual Meeting of the chapter membership for election of officers and directors of the board. The meeting shall take place within each calendar year, prior to the beginning of the next calendar year, to allow sufficient time to install elected officers and directors and to complete orientation in performance of duties.

There shall be a minimum of three events or activities during the year in addition to the Annual Meeting, to carry out the education programs of the chapter.

A notice stating the purpose of all meetings and events shall be circulated to members required in attendance at least one week before the event.

A quorum for voting purposes shall consist of 25 percent of Board membership for Board Meetings; or ten percent (10%) of the chapter membership for voting at a general meeting.

Article 4: Officers

Any person who is a paid member of the chapter qualifies to be nominated as an officer.

Nominations for officers of the organization shall be made by the Nominating Committee. The Nominating Committee shall consist of five (5) persons: The Chairman, appointed by the President, two (2) members of the Board of Directors appointed by the President, and two (2) other members elected by the Board of Directors.

The officers of the organization shall consist of:

1. President
2. Secretary
3. Treasurer
4. President-Elect
5. Advocacy Chair
6. Program Chair
7. Education Chair
8. Resource Development Chair
9. Membership-Communication Chair
10. Parliamentarian

The Executive Committee of the Board shall be the President, President-Elect, Secretary, and Treasurer, and shall meet on call for purposes of interim decisions, subject to ratification by the Board as a whole, by email or at a regular meeting of the Board.

The election of officers of the organization shall be held at the Annual Meeting of the membership. All officers shall be elected for a term of one (1) year, with the privilege of re-election for one additional one (1)-year term. The term "Chair" implies that the Chair will form a committee to set and carry out the objectives of the particular responsibilities, consistent with the purposes of the Organization.

Officers shall take office immediately following the Annual Meeting of the membership or upon the first day of the following calendar year, whichever occurs last.

In the case of the vacancy of the office of President, the President-Elect or Program Chair shall assume the duties as acting President until the Board elects a new President, term effective upon election until the next Annual Meeting. In the case of the vacancy of any other office, the Board of Directors shall elect a successor to serve until the next annual election.

Vacant officer positions may be nominated at any regular Board Meeting with quorum present and voting, with election at the next Board Meeting with quorum present and voting by simple majority.

Article 5: Board of Directors

The Board of Directors shall conduct the affairs of the chapter.

The Board of Directors shall consist of not less than nine (9) nor more than nineteen (19) in number who shall be elected for a two-year term. Elected officers, as identified in ARTICLE 4 above, shall serve as members of the Board. The President shall preside over Board meetings. Another Board Officer may conduct business with a quorum of the Board present for a regular meeting, in case of absence of the President.

The Board members shall be nominated through the Nominating Committee, or upon the advice of the President, with the consent of the existing Board.

Election of directors shall occur at the Annual Meeting as further described in ARTICLE 3.II.

Any current member of the chapter may serve on the Board of Directors for a term of two (2) years. The Board shall be divided into two (2) equal groups with overlapping terms of two (2) years each. The term of one-half (1/2) of the directors shall expire each year at the Annual Meeting.

Meetings of the Board of Directors shall be conducted monthly, or otherwise, as agreed by Board action.

Written or verbal notice of any meeting of the Board of Directors shall be given at least seven (7) days in advance. Notice shall set out the date, time and place of the meeting, and shall provide an agenda.

A quorum of not less than twenty-five (25%) of the members of the Board shall suffice for decision, but a simple majority vote of those present shall be required for decision.

Any vacancy occurring on the Board of Directors may be filled by a majority vote of the Board of Directors at any regular or special meeting of the Board, upon nomination by the President or the Nominating Committee. The interim board member shall serve the remainder of the unexpired term until the next Annual Meeting.

Attendance is required for service on the Board. A board member can be placed upon probationary status upon recommendation of the President, subject to approval of the Board, after three (3) unexcused absences from Board meetings during one calendar year. Prior to removal, the delinquent board member shall be given written notice and an opportunity to recommit attendance and service to the chapter and shall be placed on probationary status. If on probationary status, removal is automatic upon an unexcused failure of attendance at the subsequent Board of Directors meeting.

Excused absences are defined as follows:

1. Prior to meeting or event—the board member shall notify the President or any other executive office of the anticipated absence and shall appoint a substitute to submit reports or make recommendations on his or her behalf if same is part of the scheduled agenda for the forthcoming meeting.
2. After meeting or event—the board member shall submit reasonable excuse or explanation for non-attendance, unless the board member has unexcused absences allowed under the prior section describing the attendance requirements. However, courtesy dictates reasonable explanation and substitution of duties to an appointee.

3. Activity—Each board member will accept appointment or election only upon committing to give full support and active assistance required under the duties as a board member, to participate and encourage attendance of others at chapter activities, and to provide support of his or her resources in furtherance of the goals and programs of the chapter through employment of the director's individual creative talents, administrative abilities, financial support, attendance, and physical assistance in chapter projects.

4. No board member is ever expected to contribute time, money, interest or labor to his or her detriment. Your support is solicited, not exploited. [See insert below for "model" from the UNA National Chapter in Washington, DC.]

5. As one of my top priority charitable organizations, I will make what for me is a substantial financial donation every year. I recognize that as a member of the UNA Board, I am required to contribute a minimum $200 tax-deductible contribution each calendar year.

6. My personal "give" pledge is $▨▨▨▨. This will be:

7. ▨ a one-time donation on or before ▨▨▨▨.

8. ▨ several times a year. Please list dates: ▨▨▨▨.

9. In addition, I pledge to "get" an additional contribution of $ ▨▨▨▨ from friends and colleagues.

10. Fund-Raising—Each board member will engage his or her best talents or abilities to solicit, promote, and encourage individuals and companies to provide financial assistance or services.

11. Membership—Each board member will cooperate and provide active assistance to all membership-promoting activities. The board member should submit a list of not less than ten (10) persons, including names and addresses, of prospective members or supporters.

12. Public Awareness—Board members will continuously search for and recognize opportunities to promote the chapter and its programs to the community. Active work as a speaker at community events or solicitation of media and business contacts is requested.

Article 6: Ratification & Amendment

By-laws shall be adopted by a two-thirds (2/3) vote of those present at the Annual Membership Meeting of the chapter, provided that the proposal does not violate any policy or procedure of the national office of UNA-USA. Ten (10) days written notice of the date, time, and place of the meeting, and the full text of the proposal shall be provided to the members, by mail or posted by email or social media.

By-laws may be amended by a two-thirds (2/3) vote of those present at the Annual Membership Meeting of the chapter, under the same provisions described herein.

By-laws may be amended or adopted by a three-quarters (3/4) vote or not less than a majority of the members of the Board of Directors if:

The proposed by-law or amendment is set out fully in writing and delivered to each member of the Board of Directors not less than one (1) week before the next scheduled meeting of the Board of Directors; each board member shall be served with written notice of the date, time, place, and agenda for said meeting.

Written proposals for changes or discussions thereof shall be submitted to the President or Secretary not less than three (3) days prior to the scheduled Board meeting, said proposals or changes to be docketed as part of the prior agenda.

Article 7: Standing Committees

The standing committees shall organize projects and activities in specified areas of the organization's program for the membership and for the community. The standing committees and their reporting structure are identified in the appended organizational chart.
(The description of committee duties are not included at present time.)

Article 8: The Office of the Chapter

Site, address and the facility of the Office of UNAD shall be determined from time to time and maintained by the President after obtaining a consensus from the Executive Board.

Article 9: Financial Administration

The fiscal year shall coincide with that established by the National Board of Directors, which presently operates on a calendar year basis.

Committee chairmen shall submit proposed projects and budget requests to the President or Secretary for review by the Finance/Budget Committee no later than the December meeting of the Board of Directors, and prior to the subsequent year. The Finance/Budget Committee and Treasurer shall submit their recommendations to the Board of Directors. A tentative budget based upon proposed program scheduling for the coming year shall be reviewed and approved by the Board not later than the February Board meeting. A copy of the adopted budget, together with the report concerning the prior year's activities shall be forwarded to the national office of the association.

A financial audit report shall be submitted to the national office within sixty (60) days after the close of the fiscal year or as instructed to comply with legal requirements.

The amount and distribution of annual membership dues shall be established by the National Convention of the UNA USA or by the national Board of Directors. Local dues may also be determined upon approval by the UNA USA Dallas Chapter Board of Directors.

Article 10: Parliamentary Authority

Robert's Rules of Order Newly Revised shall govern this association wherever it is applicable and is not inconsistent with these by-laws, and shall be administered under the direction of the officers and the Parliamentarian.

United Nations Stamps: First Day of Issue[4]

A series of commemorative stamps were issued annually, 1953 to 1959 and 1970, to honor programs and agencies of the United Nations, collected and contributed to DUNA by Jo and John Wharton of Dallas, active members of Peacemakers, Inc. and the DUNA Chapter.

---

4   DUNA Archives, Jo and John Wharton Collection, Dallas United Nations Association.

DUNA "Viewsletter" Samples[5]

Two issues of the occasional periodical *DUNA Newsletter* reported on people and activities of the Dallas United Nations Association Chapter. These samples included reports on the 1998 and 1999 United Nations Day events.

---

[5]   DUNA Archives, Dallas United Nations Association.

ViewsLetter

Volume 16, Issue 1   January 1999

United Nations Association U.S.A. — Dallas Chapter

UNA
USA

DAL
LAS

UNA-USA Dallas Chapter Calendar of Events

Jan 23 UNA Board Orientation—9:30 a.m.-1:00 p.m.

Jan 25 UNA GENERAL MEMBERSHIP MEETING— 6:30 pm social—7:00 dinner ($15.00) and Election of Officers for 1999—Casa Rosa Restaurant, 165 Inwood Village—mail check to UNA for reservation by Jan 17

Feb 9 UNA Board Meeting
Feb 25 UNA Social— restaurant celebration $15, mail to UNA by Feb 17.
Feb 28 UNA workshop with New York personnel

Mar 6-9 UNA National Convention in New York City
Mar 9 UNA Board Meeting
Mar 12-16 International Year of Thanksgiving, World Assembly—ThanksGiving Square
Mar 16 Global Issues Lecture Series—7:00 p.m.-8:30 p.m.— UTD Student Union
Mar 22 UNA General Membership Meeting— 6:30-7:30 «Dutch Treat» dinner—7:30 program— Casa Rosa Restaurant—165 Inwood Village

Apr 13 UNA Board Meeting
Apr 22 UNA Social—TBA
Apr 27 Global Outreach —TBA

Editor: Bill Matthews,
call: 214-827-1047
fax: 214-827-0686
or email:
bilmat@ibm.net

ViewsLetter deadline: Mar 20, June 20

Annual Banquet presents fine program for enthusiastic crowd

Ray Nasher, Beth Pirtle, and Edward Djerejian

Cosponsors EDS, The Nasher Company and Ambassador and Mrs. R. Rubottom helped make the 1998 Annual Banquet a success in every respect. Held at the Fairmont Hotel on November 21, the UNA-USA, Dallas Chapter was honored by the presence of Keynote Speaker, Ambassador Edward P. Djerejian, founding Director of the James Baker III Institute, Houston, who spoke on the "United Nations and U.S. Interests," a hot topic in daily headlines.

President Beth Weems Pirtle introduced Honorary Chair, Mr. Raymond D. Nasher. The highly respected and well-known Dallasite, former UNA-USA chapter president, explained why he felt that the United Nations is of utmost importance. Ms. Dorothy Reid, Dean of the Dallas-Ft. Worth Consular Corps, noted the number of offices in the Dallas-Ft. Worth area that represent many countries providing services to citizens, businesses and travelers. Ms. Reid introduced Ambassador Djerejian.

Surprises for the evening included professional entertainment from several nations. Excitement began when Scottish Piper Brad Madison piped the honored guests into the International Ball Room. After dinner, Dr. Jamal Mohamed, Professor of Percussion-SMU, played the Databuka (an Egyptian clay drum), The Shandon School of Irish Dance, choreographed by Kay Legreca, danced a set, and Octavia, the Cockney Pearly Queen, sang cheerful songs from England. The final act put the finishing touch to the evening as Rodney and Beth Pirtle showed the guests what their music "looks" like. Rod sang as Beth eloquently signed the words to two songs. A Silent Auction offered baskets of products from 20 different nations.

More, see "Dinner," page 2

General Meeting & Officer Election: Jan 25, '99 at Casa Rosa

To start off the new year on the right foot we are hoping all members and prospective members will attend our first general meeting, which will be on January 25, 1999, 6:30 to 9:30 PM, at Casa Rosa, in Inwood Village Shopping Center (5550 W. Lovers Lane). A wonderful Mexican buffet will be served - cost $15 per person.

Each board member will highlight the projects held during 1998 and will discuss new plans for 1999. This is a good time to

voice your opinions about activities and to sign up where you would like to volunteer.

Reservations and checks must be sent in no later than January 17, 1999. Checks must be made out to UNA-USA, Dallas Chapter. Dinner tickets will be picked up at the door on the evening of the event. Door prizes will be given. Members are urged to attend to elect new Board Officers.

Viewing the U.N. through Spanish Eye[s]

Ambassador Inocencio Arias Llamas

The 1999 Annual banquet of the UNA-USA Dallas Chapter is being planned for Sunday, October 24, 1999, to coincide with the 54th birthday of the United Nations.

With future plans to tour the many member-nations in this annual gala, the first stop will be the country of Spain. Full of surprises, the banquet room at the Fairmont Hotel will be converted into a virtual village of Spain in festivity. Come experience Spain through the eyes of the UN and the UN through the eyes of Spain.

* * *

We will be honored to receiv[e] our Keynote Speaker, the Spani[sh] Ambassador to the UN, Amb. Inocencio Félix Arias Llamas. [A] permanent ambassador working [at] the UN on a daily basis, he will [be] able to discuss with us his view[s on] the UN and U.S. and European participation.

Our Honorary Chair and Mas[ter of] Ceremonies will be Dr. Luis M[a..] professor of history at SMU. W[ell] known to many in Dallas, Dr. L[uis] Martin will be our expert tour g[uide].

Reservations for the gala ma[y be] made by calling the UNA-USA Dallas Chapter Hotline 972-480[-] 5236. Tickets will go on sale at [the] end of August. Individual ticket[s are] $65 per person, which will inclu[de] dinner and entertainment.

Inquire about tables of eight, [also] available to organizations wishi[ng to] be a sponsor of this exciting eve[nt.] There are various levels of spon[sor]ship.

This "tour of Spain" will beg[in at] 6:00 PM sharp! Don't miss you[r] virtual flight!

* * *

...embers honored Miss Crystal Williams of Elsie Robertson
...ool, Lancaster, Texas, winner of the annual essay contest.
... Dallas president, essay chair Lesley Vann, Williams,
... Kelly, and Dr. Rita Kelly, stood with the array of flags,
...ng the member nations.

Proclamation 3533—United Nations Day, 1963
April 20, 1963
By the President of the United States of America
A Proclamation[6]

JOHN F. KENNEDY
XXXV *President of the United States: 1961-1963*

Whereas the United Nations symbolizes man's eternal quest for enduring peace with justice, and provides us with our most promising means for achieving that high purpose; and

Whereas the United Nations has, on numerous occasions during its brief life, clearly and forcefully demonstrated its value as a vital diplomatic forum in times of international crises; and

Whereas the United Nations, through its participation in programs for social and economic development, has provided significant material assistance and leadership throughout the world in efforts to raise standards of life; and

Whereas the United Nations actively sponsors and advances the cause of human rights; and

Whereas the United Nations serves the interests of this Nation by promoting humanitarian principles which we share; and

---

[6] John F. Kennedy, "John F. Kennedy: Proclamation 3533—United Nations Day, 1963," *The American Presidency Project*, April 20, 1963, http://www.presidency.ucsb.edu/ws/index.php?pid=24095.

Whereas citizens of the United States should recognize the aims and accomplishments of the United Nations; and

Whereas the General Assembly of the United Nations has resolved that October twenty-fourth, the anniversary of the coming into force of the United Nations Charter, should be dedicated each year to making known the purposes, principles, and accomplishments of the United Nations

Now, Therefore, I, John F. Kennedy, President of the United States of America, do hereby urge the citizens of this Nation to observe Thursday, October 24, 1963, as United Nations Day by means of community programs which will demonstrate their faith in the United Nations and contribute to a better understanding of its aims, problems, and accomplishments.

I also call upon the officials of the Federal and State Governments and upon local officials to encourage citizen groups and agencies of the press, radio, television, and motion pictures, to engage in appropriate observance of United Nations Day throughout the land in cooperation with the United States Committee for the United Nations and other organizations.

In Witness Whereof, I have hereunto set my hand and caused the Seal of the United States of America to be affixed.

DONE at the City of Washington this twentieth day of April in the year of our Lord Nineteen hundred and sixty-three, and of the Independence of the United States of America the one hundred and eighty-seventh.

JOHN F. KENNEDY
By the President:
DEAN RUSK,
Secretary of State

Sustainable Development Goals—2016 to 2030[7]

These seventeen goals are targets which were adopted by the United Nations for the period ensuing 2016–2030. Implementation through UN agencies depends on cooperative actions by individuals, governments, and compliant societies. Together they acknowledged, for example, that the United Nations Framework Convention on Climate Change is the primary international, intergovernmental forum for negotiating the global response to climate change.

On September 25th 2015, countries adopted a set of goals to end poverty, protect the planet, and ensure prosperity for all as part of a new sustainable development agenda. Each goal has specific targets to be achieved over the next 15 years.

Goal 1: End poverty in all its forms everywhere.

Goal 2: End hunger, achieve food security and improved nutrition, and promote sustainable agriculture.

Goal 3: Ensure healthy lives and promote well-being for all at all ages.

Goal 4: Ensure inclusive and equitable quality education and promote life-long learning opportunities for all.

Goal 5: Achieve gender equality and empower all women and girls.

---

7   Florencia Soto Nino, "Sustainable Development Goals—United Nations," *United Nations Sustainable Development*, accessed June 18, 2017, http://www. un.org/sustainabledevelopment/sustainable-development-goals/.

Goal 6: Ensure availability and sustainable management of water and sanitation for all.

Goal 7: Ensure access to affordable, reliable, sustainable, and modern energy for all.

Goal 8: Promote sustained, inclusive and sustainable economic growth, full and productive employment and decent work for all.

Goal 9: Build resilient infrastructure, promote inclusive and sustainable industrialization and foster innovation.

Goal 10: Reduce inequality within and among countries.

Goal 11: Make cities and human settlements inclusive, safe, resilient and sustainable.

Goal 12: Ensure sustainable consumption and production patterns.

Goal 13: Take urgent action to combat climate change and its impacts.

Goal 14: Conserve and sustainably use the oceans, seas and marine resources for sustainable development.

Goal 15: Protect, restore and promote sustainable use of terrestrial ecosystems, sustainably manage forests, combat desertification, and halt and reverse land degradation and halt biodiversity loss.

Goal 16: Promote peaceful and inclusive societies for sustainable development, provide access to justice for all and build effective, accountable and inclusive institutions at all levels.

Goal 17: Strengthen the means of implementation and revitalize the global partnership for sustainable development.

BIBLIOGRAPHY

"1975 World Conference on Women, Mexico City, June 19-July 2, 1975."*5th Women's World Conference*, 2006. http://www.5wwc.org/conference_background/1975_WCW.html.

"29 Pieces Education."*29 Pieces*. Accessed June 12, 2017. http://29pieces.org/29-pieces-education/.

"2012 Austin." Accessed June 12, 2017. http://www.ctaun.org/conferences/austin-conference-2012/.

"2013 Dallas." Accessed June 12, 2017. http://www.ctaun.org/conferences/2013-dallas/.

"2015 Houston." Accessed June 12, 2017. http://www.ctaun.org/conferences/2015-houston/.

"Barack Obama." *Biography*. Accessed March 13, 2017. http://www.biography.com/people/barack-obama-12782369.

"Barefoot Sanders." *Wikipedia*, November 14, 2016. https://en.wikipedia.org/w/index.php?title=Barefoot_Sanders&oldid=749559950.

Basic Facts About the United Nations. New York: News and Media Division, United Nations Department of Public Information, 2003.

Black, Allida M. *Casting Her Own Shadow*. New York: Columbia University Press, 1996.

Castleberry, Vivian. *Daughters of Dallas*. Dallas: Odenwald Press, 1994.

Dallas Morning News, n.d. Dallas Morning News Historical Archives.

Down in the River to Pray. Morningstar Music Publishers, Birnamwood Publications, 2009.

"Edward Winn Obituary - Dallas, TX | Dallas Morning News." Accessed June 18, 2017. http://www.legacy.com/obituaries/dallasmorningnews/obituary.aspx?pid=86788108.

Feldman, Ross. "About Us." *United Nations Association of the USA*. Accessed January 22, 2017. http://unausa.org/about-us.

"First World Conference on Women (1975)." *United Nations System: Chief Executives Board for Coordination*, 2016. http://www.unsceb.org/content/first-world-conference-women-1975-0.

Gillman, Frederick J. *The Methodist Hymnal*. Nashville, TV: Board of Publications of The Methodist Church, Inc., 1964.

"Global Elementary Model United Nations." *Global Elementary Model United Nations*, n.d. http://www.unol.org/gemun/.

Gooding, Guy. "Letter from Guy Gooding, CEO, Goodelstet G4 Enterprises," July 29, 2015.

Goren, John. Oral Interview with John Goren, Dallas, Texas, May 8, 2015.

Hall, Cordye. "What Can One Person Do?" Dallas, TX: Ken Gjemre, 1988.

Hightower, Jim. "Defending the Alamo--From a UN Takeover." *The Hightower Lowdown*, March 6, 2015. https://hightowerlowdown.org/podcast/defending-the-alamo-from-a-un-takeover/.

———. "New Trade Pacts Create Secret, pro-Corporate Tribunals That Use Their Powers to Eviscerate Our Democratic Laws." *The Hightower*

Lowdown, January 5, 2015. https://hightowerlowdown.org/article/tpp/.

———. "Wither the Tea Party?" *The Hightower Lowdown*, January 22, 2013. https://hightowerlowdown.org/podcast/wither-the-tea-party/.

Holy Bible. New International Version NIV. http://biblica.com/, 1973.

"Human Rights Day, 10 December 2008." Accessed February 15, 2017. http://www.un.org/en/events/humanrightsday/2008/.

Hyfler/Rosner. "The Rev. Luther Holcomb; Met JFK at Dallas Airport." Google Groups. *Alt.obituaries*, November 20, 2003. https://groups.google.com/forum/#!topic/alt.obituaries/pTlVMDuVAFM.

Jaami, Dr. Marzuq. "Recollections from Dr. Marzuq Jaami, Masjid-Al-Islam, Director of Public Relations, DeSoto Islamic Center, Member, DUNA Board and Interfaith Council, Thanks-Giving Square" April 30, 2015.

Karam, Charlotte. "Letter to Authors by Charlotte Karam, Active in Dallas UNA Chapter During Beth Pirtle's Presidency, 1996-1998 and Following," July 6, 2015.

Ki-moon, Ban. "At General Assembly Debate, Secretary-General Says Regional Organizations Critical to Shaping Post-2015 Agenda, Reaching Sustainable Development Goals | Meetings Coverage and Press Releases." *United Nations Meeting Coverages and Press Releases*, May 4, 2015. http://www.un.org/press/en/2015/sgsm16729.doc.htm.

Lal, Harbans. "Letter from Harbans Lal, PhD; D.Litt (Hons), (Emeritus Professor and Chairman, Department of Pharmacology & Neuroscience, Univeristy of North Texas Health Science Center, Fort Worth, Texas) to Bill and Norma Matthews," January 20, 2016.

Matthews, Bill. "Letters to the Editor." *Dallas Morning News*, September 26, 2015.

Matthews, Bill. "OpEd Submitted to Local Press by Rev. Bill Matthews, Interfaith Council Chair, Thanks-Giving Square Foundation. Not Published. Expanded for This Book from Personal Files," January 14, 2014.

Matthews, Norma. Oral Interview Maura McNiel at the Tea and Conversations with Icons Reception, March 13, 2016.

Melvin, Ann Adams. "Headliner Portrait: Jack Goren." *Dallas Morning News*, March 24, 1963. Dallas Morning News Archives.

Merton, Thomas, and Lawrence Cunningham, eds. *Thomas Merton: Spiritual Master: Essential Writings*. Mahwah, NJ: Paulist Press, 1992.

Miller, Edward H. *Nut Country: Right Wing Dallas and the Birth of the Southern Strategy*. Chicago, IL: The University of Chicago Press, 2015.

Minutaglio, Bill, and Steven L. Davis. *Dallas 1963*. New York: Twelve Hachette Book Group, 2013.

"Nasher Sculpture Center." *Wikipedia*, February 27, 2017. https://en.wikipedia.org/w/index.php?title=Nasher_Sculpture_Center&oldid=767703319.

Nino, Florencia Soto. "Sustainable Development Goals - United Nations." *United Nations Sustainable Development*. Accessed June 18, 2017. http://www.un.org/sustainabledevelopment/sustainable-development-goals/.

n***@webtv.net. "My Interview W/Rev. Baxton Bryant & Family." *NARKIVE: Newsgroup Archive*, January 6, 2004. http://alt.assassination.jfk.narkive.com/cMGKabE0/my-interview-w-rev-baxton-bryant-family#post1.

Obama, Barack. *The Audacity of Hope*. Vintage Books, Random House, Inc., 2006.

"Obituary." *Dallas Morning News*. March 14, 2007.

Omang, Joanne, and Joanne Omang. "UNESCO Withdrawal An
nounced." *The Washington Post*, December 20, 1984. https://www.
washingtonpost.com/archive/politics/1984/12/20/unesco-withdraw
al-announced/b9c6dc92-a31f-443a-977b-f3468faf44fe/?utm_ter
m=.81f0bcf679a7.

Payne, Darwin. *Big D*. Dallas, TX: Three Forks Press, 1994.

———. *Indomitable Sarah: The Life of Judge Sarah T. Hughes*. Dallas, TX:
Southern Methodist University Press, 2004.

"Pearl Lichtenberg Wincorn's Obituary," *Dallas Morning News*. Accessed
March 13, 2017. http://www.legacy.com/obituaries/dallasmorning
news/obituary.aspx?n=pearl-lichtenberg-wincorn&pid=425875.

Piccoli Biggs, Noeli, and Beth Weems Pirtle. "Letter to Authors Submitted
by Noeli Piccoli Biggs and Beth Weems Pirtle," 2015.

Pirtle, Beth Weems. "Letter from the Archives of Beth Weems Pirtle," n.d.

Raggio, Louise Ballerstedt, and Vivian Castleberry. *Texas Tornado*. New
York: Citadel Press, 2003.

"Raymond Nasher." *Wikipedia*, September 12, 2016. https://en.wikipedia.
org/w/index.php?title=Raymond_Nasher&oldid=739067610.

"Rewriting History? Texas Tackles Textbook Debate." *CBS News*, Septem
ber 16, 2014. http://www.cbsnews.com/news/rewriting-history-tex
as-tackles-textbook-debate/.

"Robert Muller." *Wikipedia*, December 17, 2016. https://en.wikipedia.
org/w/index.php?title=Robert_Muller&oldid=755403177.

Rohr, Richard. *Everything Belongs: The Gift of Contemplative Prayer*. The
Crossroad Publishing Company, 1999.

Roosevelt, Eleanor. "Statement to the United Nations General Assembly
on the Universal Declaration of Human Rights, 9 December 1948."

Accessed February 15, 2017. http://www2.gwu.edu/~erpapers/docu
ments/displaydoc.cfm?_t=speeches&_docid=spc057137.

———. *Tomorrow Is Now*. New York: Harper & Row, 1963.

Sanders, Jan. Conversation with Jan Sanders, Widow of Judge Barefoot
Sanders. Northaven United Methodist Church, Dallas, Texas, Spring
2015.

Satija, Neena, and Ryan McCrimmon. "Conservative Lawmakers Target
United Nations." *The Texas Tribune*, February 26, 2015. https://www.
texastribune.org/2015/02/26/conservative-lawmakers-continue-as
sault-un/.

Seeligson, Molly Fulton. Conversation with Molly Fulton Seeligson,
Daughter of Bernard Fulton, Second President of the Dallas United
Nations Association, 1954, Unknown.

Sewall, Gilbert T., and William H. Luers. "Textbooks and the United
Nations: An Education Report of the United Nations Association of
the USA, The International System and What American Students
Learn About It." United Nations Association, 2002.

Schlein, Lisa. "WHO: Progress in Millennium Development Goals
Still Not Sufficient." *VOA*, May 13, 2015. http://www.voanews.
com/a/progress-in-millennium-development-goals-still-not-suffi
cient/2765936.html.

"Stanley Marcus." *Wikipedia*, February 18, 2017. https://en.wikipedia.
org/w/index.php?title=Stanley_Marcus&oldid=766135689.

"The Annette Strauss Legacy." *Moody College of Communication*. Accessed
March 12, 2017. http://moody.utexas.edu/strauss/annette-strauss-leg
acy.

The Associated Press. "Annette Strauss, 74, Former Mayor of Dallas."
The New York Times, December 21, 1998. http://www.nytimes.
com/1998/12/21/us/annette-strauss-74-former-mayor-of-dallas.html.

Ukeni, Stanley. "Letter from Stanley Ukeni to Bill and Norma Matthews," January 21, 2016.

"UNITED NATIONS YOUTH COALITION." Accessed June 18, 2017. http://www.unycdallas.org/.

"United Nations Universal Declaration of Human Rights Summary: Youth For Human Rights Video." Accessed June 18, 2017. http://www.youthforhumanrights.org/what-are-human-rights/universal-declaration-of-human-rights/articles-1-15.html.

"The Universal Declaration of Human Rights." United Nations General Assembly (General Assembly Resolution 217A), December 10, 1948. http://www.un.org/en/universal-declaration-human-rights/index.html.

"Universal Declaration of Human Rights." *Wikipedia: The Free Encyclopedia*, November 27, 2016. https://en.wikipedia.org/wiki/Universal_Declaration_of_Human_Rights.

Walker, Tim. "Will Texas Decide What's In Your Textbook?" *NEA: National Education Association.* Accessed June 18, 2017. http://www.nea.org//home/39060.htm.

Weinberg, Melvin H. "Rabbi Levi A. Olan (An Untired Liberal)." Spertus Institute for Jewish Learning and Leadership, 2015.

Women's Division, General Board of Global Ministeries, United Methodist Church. "The United Nations in Our Daily Lives." *United Methodist Women Magazine*, June 2004.

Wurst, James. *The UN Association-USA: A Little Known History of Advocacy and Action.* Boulder, CO: Lynne Rienner Publishers, Inc., 2016.

INDEX

Bernstein, Bill, 151, 250
Bhutanese, 226
Bible, 55, 78, 102, 380, 409, 439
Biesele, Mrs. Rudy, 15
Biggs, Noeli Piccoli, xii, 220, 222, 224–25, 230–32, 241, 301, 312, 322–25, 441
Billingsley, Lucy, 213
biodiversity, 435
bi-partisan, 63, 115
birth control, 161
Bishop, R. Doak, 166
Bishop College, 113
Bishop Lynch High School, 213
Black Chamber of Commerce, 44
Blanch-Soler, 387
Blessen, Karen, xi, 257, 283, 296, 301, 349
Block Partnership, 44
Blood, Michael, 230
board of directors, 6, 110, 135, 421, 423
Board of Governors, 142
Bohlen, Charles E., 113
Bolzan, Alberto, 249
Bolzan, Peggy, 249
Bond, Julian, 201
Bonham, 68
Boone Family Foundation, 248
Boots on the Ground, 408
Bosnian War, 193
Boston University, 51
Botswana, 150, 245
Boudreaux, La Barron, 253
Boutros-Ghali, Boutros, 158–59, 193, 367, 392
Bowlin, Dary, 210
Boyd, Danae, 298
Boys and Girls Club Dallas, 259
Boy Scouts of America, 30, 84
Brachman, Malcolm J., 67
Brahma Kumaris of Dallas, 211

Branks, Scott, 205
Brannin, Carl, 15
Brannin, Laura, 15
Bridwell Library, 56
Brite Divinity School, 124
British, 127–28, 315, 377
Brodsky, Anne E., 204
Brookhaven College, 228, 303
Brown, Annemarie, 172–73, 175, 177–82, 184–85, 187–89, 301
Brown, Stephen, 344–45
Brown-Sadovsky, Annemarie, 173, 175, 177, 179–82, 184, 187–89
Brownscombs, Mrs. E. R., 104
Bruner, Anna Louise, 367, 369
Bryan Place, 43
Bryant, Baxton, 20, 66–70, 440
Bryant, Lacrisha, 69
Bryant, Phala, 69
Bryant, Zoe, 69–70
Bucharest, 378
Buck, Dean, 187–91
Buck, Raymond, 121
Buckley, William F., 81, 130
Buffum, William, 142
Buller, Angela, 304
Bulletins (viewsletters), 163, 196–97, 199, 201–3, 205–6, 210, 215, 360, 429
Bunche, Ralph, 376
Bundy, Edgar, 91
Burch, Jim, 228
Burnam, Lon, 201, 343
Burundi Church Choir, 226
Bury, Chris, 210
Bush, George H. W., 134, 405
Bush, George W., 146–47, 337
Business and Professional Women of Dallas, 26, 132
Business Connection, 145
bylaws, 365

Delta Omicron, 296

Democrat, 29, 48, 69–70, 88, 126

Denver, John, 165

deputy assistant, 120, 128, 131, 365

DeSoto Islamic Center, 296, 337, 439

developing countries, 10, 142, 294, 302, 379

DFW International Community Alliance, 151, 227, 247

Diarra, Cheick Sidi, 242

diaspora, 315

dignity, 4, 35, 248, 410, 416

DiMaggio, Suzanne, 147

disarmament, 89, 93, 107, 174, 177, 186, 195, 201

discriminate, 417

discrimination, 33, 46–47, 209

disillusion, 136

Djerejian, Donald, 368

Djerejian, Edward P., 196, 320

Dodd, Elena, 145, 205, 220

Doke, Marshall J., xi, xvii–xviii, 160–62, 164, 166, 169, 174, 176–79, 182–83, 193, 195

Dolan, Luis, 316

Domestic Violence Intervention Association, 44

Donosky, Lea, 134

Douala, 387–88

Douffiagues, Arlette, 178, 187–88

Do Unto Others, 220, 267, 269, 340

Doutriaux, Yves, 199

Doyle, G., 366

Doyle Hotel, 305

Drake, Amy-Ellen, 210

Dreier, Olivia Stokes, 284

Dresden, 374

Dresser Industries, 191

Dr. Neill McFarland, xvii

Duke University, 51

Dumas, Jeff, 144, 200

Dumas, Lloyd Jeff, 202, 215

Dunham, Donald C., 122

Duran, James, 257–58

Durfee, Paul, 211

E

Earl Eames Award, 222, 231, 323, 325

Earl Eames Communications Award, 214, 233, 312, 324–25

earth and planetary sciences laboratory, 122

Easaw, Ashley, 218

East Berlin, 113

Ebrahim, A. B., 280

Ecologist, 133

Ecology Center of Louisiana, 133

Ecuador, 109

Edry, Ronny, 255

EDS, 196

education, 8–10, 30–31, 49–50, 75, 146, 207, 215, 221, 224–25, 227–32, 279–81, 322–23, 398–400, 405–6, 419–21

Edwards, Walter V., 136

Egbert, Larry, 170, 183

Egbert, Marcel, 170

Egypt, 193, 199, 391

Egyptian, 158, 196, 321

Ehrhardt, Harryette, 46, 202

80 Women from Dallas, 93

Eisenhower, 84, 90, 100, 111, 120

Eisenhower, Dwight D., 90, 120

Elaydi, Hussein, 275

El Chico, 136

Eleanor Roosevelt Man of Vision Award, 75

Eliasson, Jan, 252, 268

Ellzey, David, 190

Elmendorf, Ed, 8, 230, 236, 370

Elmwood Methodist Church, 68

Embrey Human Rights, 151

Emery, Lorinne, xv, 141, 162, 165
Emery, Mrs. Clyde, xv, 141, 162, 165
Emmanuel Chapel United Methodist
    Church, 132
Emory University, 56
Empower African Children, 248
Engelhart, Leslie, 213
English-Speaking Unions, 128
Episcopal School of Dallas, 302
Equal Employment Commission, 55
equality, 3, 9–10, 46–47, 57, 146, 154,
    210–11, 258–59, 263, 274, 289,
    332, 360
Equal Rights Amendment, 48
era, 48
erroneous information, 400
Escobar, Javier, Jr., 167
Esperson, Elizabeth, 212
Essay Contest, 188, 199, 211, 215,
    218–19, 221, 225, 227–28, 230
Eta Zeta, xii
ethics, 146, 211, 350, 356
ethics director, 356
Europe, Central, 112
Europe, Southern, 112
Evans, Linda, xi, 154, 199–202, 209–
    10, 215, 225–26, 231–33, 243–
    44, 248–49, 253, 271, 279–83,
    288–89, 305–6, 351–52
Evans, Linda Abramson, 301, 351–54
Evans, Luther, 105–6
Evans, Thomas, 213
Evers, Medgar, 80
Ewell, Yvonne, 167, 170, 172, 183
Exchange Club, 104
executive vice president, 121, 365
Explore, 44
export and customs compliance, 146
expression, 413, 418
extremists, 78–81, 120

F

Facts Forum, 41
Faculty/Staff Volunteer Award, 353
Fairleigh Dickinson University, 376
Faith Forward Dallas, 353
Family Place, 45, 276
fascism, 415
Faso, Burkina, 220
Fatemi, Nasrollah, 376
FBI, 29, 79, 84
female genital mutilation, 220
Ferguson, Canon, 15
Ferguson, Edward B., 104
Feria de Sevilla, 321
FGM, 220
Fiji, 359
financial obligations, 113
Finland, 142
First Methodist Church, 105
First Presbyterian Church, xv, 134
First Unitarian Church, 74, 112, 178
Fisher Institute, 169
Flanagan, Colette, 278
Flaxman, Edna, 174, 179, 182
Fleck, Deborah, 156, 276
Fleming, Dagmar, 214–15, 218–20
Fleming, Katherine, 213
Fleming, Richard, 213
Fletcher School of Law and
    Diplomacy, 383
Flowers, Cannon, 215
Foreign Corrupt Practices Act, 146
foreign policy, 56, 113, 166
Foreign Policy Association, 163
Fornos, Werner, 180
Fortnight, 58
Fort Worth, viii, 56, 95, 180, 203, 277,
    314, 352, 365, 439
Fort Worth Chamber of Commerce, 121
Fort Worth Chapter of the UNA, 124

Huang, Martin, 278

Huddleston, Beth, xvii, 192, 268, 366–67

Hudgens, Gayle, 184

Huffines, James, 183

Hughes, George, 16–17

Hughes, Henny, 241

Hughes, Sarah, 16–18, 24, 35–36, 41, 48–49

Hughes, Sarah T., viii, xii, xiv–xv, xx, 15, 18–22, 24–25, 30, 35–36, 46, 49–50, 52–53, 66, 78, 173

Hughes, Sarah Tilghman, 13, 15, 25

human environment, 133–34

human rights, 4, 31, 33–35, 45, 73, 100, 142–43, 145, 148, 187–88, 221–23, 248–49, 409–10, 416–19, 443

Human Rights Initiative of North Texas, 215, 352

human trafficking, 145, 151, 205, 250, 352

Humphrey, John Peters, 414–15

Hungary, 127

hunger, 9–10, 165, 213, 229, 294

Hunt, H. L., viii, 36, 58, 79, 93

Hunt, Jasmine, 286

Hurst, 143

Hutchison, Kay Bailey, 221

I

immoral, 134

impact of youth, 132

Ince, Kenan Andrew, 218

India, 109–10, 126, 134–35, 315, 319

Indiana State University, 128

indifference, 120

Indomitable Sarah, xviii, 17–18, 20–21, 36, 49–50, 52–53, 66, 78, 441

Indonesia, 101

infrastructure, 435

Inge Dam, 391

Institute of Human Relations, 62

integration, 37, 47, 54, 56, 90, 329

Interfaith Council, 337–38, 341, 352, 439–40

interfaith dialogue, 121

Interfaith Harmony, Week of, 339, 341

International Bill of Human Rights, 413

International Covenant on Civil and Political Rights, 413–14

International Covenant on Economic, Social and Cultural Rights, 413

International Federation of Business & Professional Women, 19

International Girls Cup, 259, 301

international law, xvii, 4, 39, 41, 66, 203, 223, 394

International Law Commission, 381

International Narcotics Trafficking, 302

International Refugee Commission, 112

International Rescue Committee, 211, 228, 271, 275, 293, 352

International Security Subcommittee, 92

International Trade Association, 141

International Treaty on Law of the Sea, 7, 170, 221, 383

International Women's Peace Conference, 42, 218

International Women's Year, 46, 142

International Year of Disabled Persons, 163

interpreter, 239, 377, 379, 381, 383, 386

Inwood Village, 136, 217

Iran, 109, 153, 168, 218, 223, 255, 319

Iraq, 150, 153, 209, 212, 223, 245

Irving, Henry, 208

Irving, Mary Ellen, 208

Irwin, Wallace, 133

Islam, Tasriqui, 272, 275, 331

Israel, 128, 135–36, 138, 158, 187, 255, 356, 368
Ivins, Molly, 168

J

Jaami, Marzuq, xii, 258, 265, 268–69, 279–81, 289, 299, 301, 330, 337, 439
Jackman, Frank T., 182–83
Jackson, Amber, 291
Jackson, Douglas, 55, 112
Jackson, Kyle, 234
Jacobson, Lloyd, 230
Jadallah, Alma Abdul-Hadi, 284
Jain, Bawa, 315–16
James, Reggie, 281
James Baker III Institute, 196
Jan Sanders, xii, 66, 442
Jantho, Patty, xi, 24, 29, 241–44, 248–49, 251, 253, 258, 262, 265, 272, 280–81, 299, 332
Japan, 132, 141, 172–73, 319, 329
Japan-American Society, 172–73, 329
Jawad, Hadi, 213
Jenkins, Clay Lewis, 276, 282, 333
Jenkins, William A., Jr., 67
J. Erik Jonsson Central Library, 145
John Birch members, 63
John Birch Society, viii, 17, 79–81, 90–91, 117, 127, 129, 131
John Goren, xii, 438
Johnson, Eddie Bernice, 155, 192, 211, 234, 255, 282, 284, 334
Johnson, Francis S., 122
Johnson, Lady Bird, 82
Johnson, Lyndon B., 19, 26, 53, 55, 65, 70, 87
Jones, Penn, 68
Jordan, Robert, 210
Judd, Walter, 130
Judy, Robert Dale, 128

Just Figs, 207
Justice for Our Neighbors, 228
Juvenile Delinquency Department, 48

K

Kabona, FaBrice, 258, 275, 279, 289, 292, 298, 330
KAFM, 172
Kalib, Yussuf, 213–15, 219, 229–33, 236–37
Kambiz Rafraf, xii, 199–200, 202, 204, 208, 343, 369
Karcher Auditorium, 144
Kasbah, 226
Kashmir, 315
Kaur, Rajkumari Amrit, 110
Kazemzadeh, Monirch, 144
Keith, Jed, 164
Kelly, Bill, xiii, 241–42, 244, 248, 266, 296
Kelly, Rita, 199, 201
Kemp, Top, 192
Kennedy, John F., 19, 55, 58, 63, 79–80, 82, 93, 117
KERA, 44, 199, 248, 290
KERA-TV, 44
Kerim, Srgjan, 156, 287, 289
Kestenberg, Louis, 128
keynote speaker, 111, 114, 120, 127, 151, 198, 201, 242, 250, 287, 289–90, 294, 328
Keys, Donald, 166
Khrushchev, 89
Khyber Pakhtunkhwa, 315
Kilgore, Mrs. John, 14
King, Marilyn, 225–27, 230–33, 236–37, 241, 244, 248, 251
King, Martin Luther, 37, 168–69, 227, 252
Kingston, Phillip, 268
Kirby, Joan, 316

Lodge, Henry Cabot, 127–28, 130, 134, 375, 384
Lodish, Emilia, 212
London, 56, 106
Longley, Pat, 377
Louchheim, Katie, 128, 131
Love Field, 58–59, 67–70
Lowary, Pierce, 279–80, 287, 292–93, 296, 298
Lowary, Shideh, 279–81, 287, 289, 293, 296, 298
Lowe, Jack, Sr., 44
Lower Mekong Basin Development, 132
Loyal Liberal Labor Minority, 69
Luckadoo, John, 167, 170, 172–73
Luers, William H., 398, 442
Lynch, Eileen, 183–84, 187–89, 191, 213

M

MacDonald, Mrs. Colin T., 67
MacEachron, David W., 173
Macedonia, 150, 156, 245, 287, 289, 294
Madden, Patrick M., 150, 246
Madison, Brad, 320
Maggiano's Little Italy restaurant, 144, 202
Maggio, Vincent, 366, 369
Magnet School System, 44
Mahatma Gandhi Memorial, 275, 332
mainstream, 88, 109, 130–31
Malawi, 150, 245
Malaysia, 150, 245
Maloney, Susan M., 204
Mamadou, 386
Management Seminar for Women Executives, 139
Mann, Gerald C., 20, 66
manuscript, xx–xxi, 15, 368
March of Dimes, 128

Marcus, Nancy, 268
Marcus, Stanley, viii, 52, 57–60, 66, 81, 85, 87, 125, 302, 442
marine resources, 435
Marks, Edward B., 112
Marshall J. Doke, xvii
Martín, Luis, 198, 321
Marxist, 79
Mashua, Lucy, 219–20
Mason, Alexana, 168, 170, 172, 184
Mason, Alix, 177, 179, 181–82
Matthews, Bill, 180–82, 202, 204–8, 212–14, 220–34, 236–38, 240–42, 244–58, 262–66, 270–72, 274–84, 288–90, 340–44, 354–58, 370–72
Matthews, J. W. "Bill," 202, 411
Matthews, Mary Beth, 230, 258
Matthews, Norma, 198–99, 212–13, 217–19, 221, 225–34, 236–37, 240–44, 248–49, 251–58, 263–66, 268–72, 274–75, 277–83, 288–91, 330–33
Mature Woman Award, 127
Maura Award, 45
Mauritania, 386
May, Ruth, 213
Maynard (doctor), 180
M'Banna, 265
McCall, H. Carl, 162–63
McCarran, Pat, 92
McCarthy, Joseph, 14, 40
McCarthyism, 56
McCartney, Paul, 202
McCarty, Christy, 172, 174–76, 253, 258
McCarty, Dakota, 253, 258
McDermott, Margaret, 302
McElvaney, William K., 278
McFarland, Neill, xvii, 161–62, 164–73, 175, 177, 179–82

McFarlin Auditorium, 109, 130, 186

McGarr, Janie, 73

McGee, Ann, 133

McGee, Gale, 138

McGehee, Frank, 60, 79, 83, 86

McIntosh, Kenneth B., 161, 163, 167, 183

McKeever, Porter, 136

McLaughlin, Kathleen, 200–202

McLeroy, Don, 405

McMillan, Eva, 265

McNiel, Mary Maura, 161

McNiel, Maura, viii, 44–46, 165, 167, 169–71, 173, 440

MDG, 229–30, 259, 263

Mears, John, 169

mednets, 243

Mehta, Hansa, 415

Melvin, Ann Adams, 64, 115, 440, 443

Menchu Tum, Rigoberta, 219

Mercer, Lucy, 32

Merino, Judy, 188

Merrimon Cuninggim, xiv, 105, 110

Merrow, Chester E., 109

Merton, Thomas, 408, 440

Messer, Sarita, 56

Metropolitan Dallas, 128

Mexico City, 46–47, 311

Meyerson Symphony Center, Morton H., 72

Middle East, 107, 152, 164, 218, 226, 228, 262, 308, 320

Midway Hills Christian, 44

milestone, 11, 144, 156

Millennium Summit, 315–16

Millennium World Peace Summit of Religious and Spiritual Leaders, 315–16

Miller, Barbara, 350

Miller, Colby, 221

Miller, Giles, 88

Miller, Laura, 146, 211, 213

Miller, Robert, 144–45

Miller, Tom, 231

Millheiser, David, 184

mines, 30, 345, 375, 378

Minneapolis, 127

Minutaglio, Bill, 58, 77

Minutemen, 83

Minute Women, 90

mirror of the world, 120

Miss United Nations, 109

Mistry, Mihir, 214

mock assemblies, 400

Model UN, 165, 176, 188–89, 201, 215, 230, 232, 249, 293, 322, 367, 401

Model United Nations Conference, 301, 303

Model United Nations Dallas Organization, 302, 400

Modgil, Shabnam, 151, 212, 215, 218, 225–33, 236–37, 240–41, 243–44, 247–48, 253, 258, 264–65, 278–82, 288–89, 354

Moghamo Project, 259

Mohammad, W. D., 337

Mohammed, Jamal, 321

Molly Gerold Human Rights Award, 307

Montoya, Regina, 23, 228

Montville, Joseph, 190

Moonan, Laura, 280

Morningside Middle School, 303

Morris, Robert B., 79

Morrison, Alma, 236

Morrow, Rosemary, 326

Morton, Brandon, 276

Mosaic Family Services, 151, 250, 276, 352

Mose, Deborah, 242

mosquito eradication, 272, 334

Whitehead, John C., 7
Whittaker, Margit, 202
WHO, 12, 85–86, 142, 249, 332, 359, 442
Wildman, David, 209
Wilhelm, Donna, 248
William H. Luers, 398, 442
Williams (ambassador), 376
Williams, Betty, 219
Williams, Jody, 219
Williams, John C., III, 193
Williamson, David, 128
Wincorn, Mrs. Herbert, 66, 163
Wincorn, Pearl, 73, 163–64, 167–68, 170–73, 177, 179, 182–84, 190, 192, 441
Winston School, 31
Wirth, Timothy, 150, 214, 246–47
Wise, Wes, 43
Wolfe, Sheryl, 213
women's role, viii, 302
Women for Change, 45–46
Women Helping Women Award, 44–45
Women's Alliance of the Unitarian Church, 47
Women's Center of Dallas, 17, 45
Women's Equality Day, 289
Women's History Month, 46
women's issues, 45–46, 128
Women's Issues Network, 45, 154
women's liberation, 16, 45
women's liberation movement, 16, 45
World Affairs Council of Houston, 329
World Anti-Communist League, 130
World Citizens Guide, 326
World Core Curriculum, 75, 304
World Court jurisdiction, 112
WorldFest, 243
World Health Organization, 12, 138, 142, 313
World of Revolution, 124, 126

world peace and security, 107, 149
World Peace Sunday, 108
world politics, 110, 127
World Population Day, 171–72
World Thanksgiving Proclamation, 159
World Trade Club, 141
world war II, 1, 6, 13–14, 40–41, 53, 59, 64, 74, 328, 354, 358, 374, 377
Worrell, Keith, 179, 184
Wright, Jerauld, 109
WRVR, 359
Wyman, Lucia, 167, 170, 176

Y

Yakovlev, Basil, 377
Yale University, 65
Yalta agreement, 374
Yaounde, 387, 389–90
Yarborough, 19, 69
Yeo, Peter, 235, 293
Yip, Trea, 248
YMCA, 84, 293
York, Richard, 206
Youkel, Eugene, 383–84
Young Americans for Freedom, 83
Young Democrats club, 48
Young Professionals Award, 236
Youth Foundation, 132
Yugoslavia, 113, 392
Yunus, Muhammad, 213
Yvonne A. Ewell Townview Center, 54
YWCA, 26, 50, 127

Z

Zaire, 391
Zedalias, Rex, 170
Zimba, Helen, 220
Zonozy, Nasser, 199
Zonta Award, 44, 141
Zonta Club, 17
Zorin, 379

Made in the USA
Lexington, KY
11 May 2018